Punishment

Punishment is a topic of increasing importance for citizens and policy-makers. Why should we punish criminals? Which theory of punishment is most compelling? Is the death penalty ever justified? These questions and many others are addressed in this highly engaging guide.

Punishment is a critical introduction to the philosophy of punishment, offering a new and refreshing approach that will benefit readers of all backgrounds and interests. The first critical guide to examine all leading contemporary theories of punishment, this book explores – among others – the communicative theory of punishment, restorative justice, and the unified theory of punishment. Thom Brooks examines several case studies in detail, including capital punishment, juvenile offending, and domestic abuse. *Punishment* highlights the problems and prospects of different approaches in order to argue for a more pluralistic and compelling perspective that is novel and groundbreaking.

Punishment is a textbook designed to introduce both undergraduate and postgraduate students to the topic of punishment. It will be essential for undergraduate students in philosophy, criminal justice, criminology, justice studies, law, politics, and sociology.

Thom Brooks is Reader in Law at Durham University. He is the editor and founder of the *Journal of Moral Philosophy*.

Lucid, fair minded, and well informed, Thom Brooks' *Punishment* offers a superb introduction to a complex and contentious subject. Many a perplexed student will find illumination in his patient discussion of each of the leading theories. The way Brooks shows their interconnectedness and application in practice – to capital punishment, juvenile offenders, domestic violence, and the like – will interest not only students but scholars as well.

—*Stuart P. Green, Distinguished Professor of Law and Nathan L. Jacobs Scholar, Rutgers School of Law*

As a topic in moral and political philosophy, punishment has been jolted back to life. In the last quarter century, retribution has returned with a vengeance, both in the theoretical literature and (with a very different emphasis) in public policy. The rise of the victim as a player in the criminal justice system has also fuelled a counter-trend, placing an emphasis on redress. Human rights, privatization, globalization, the rise of the therapist, the lobbyist, the terrorist: all have affected our ways of punishing and of thinking about punishment. A new survey of the terrain is overdue. And who better to conduct it than Thom Brooks, whose grasp of the literature and feel for the issues is second to none? From the noble ideals of 'communicative' theory to the grim realities of children in prison: in *Punishment* Brooks covers it all with insight, rigour, and energy.

—*John Gardner, Professor of Jurisprudence, University of Oxford*

Thom Brooks has produced a valuable introduction to, and critical survey of, current theoretical approaches to punishment together with an analysis of their implications for practice. In addition, he has provided a spirited defence of a new, unified theory inspired by the British Idealists and encompassing retributive, consequentialist, and restorative elements. Written in a lucid and engaging style, the book will interest a wide range of readers – students, theorists of punishment, as well as those engaged in criminal justice policy.

—*Alan Brudner, Albert Abel Professor Emeritus, Faculty of Law, University of Toronto*

Punishment

Thom Brooks

 Routledge
Taylor & Francis Group

LONDON AND NEW YORK

First published 2012
by Routledge
2 Park Square, Milton Park, Abingdon, Oxon OX14 4RN

Simultaneously published in the USA and Canada
by Routledge
711 Third Avenue, New York, NY 10017

Routledge is an imprint of the Taylor & Francis Group, an informa business

British Library Cataloguing in Publication Data
A catalogue record for this book is available from the British Library

Library of Congress Cataloging in Publication Data
Brooks, Thom.
Punishment / Thom Brooks.
  p. cm.
Includes bibliographical references and index.
ISBN 978-0-415-43181-1 (hbk.) – ISBN 978-0-415-43182-8 (pbk.) –
ISBN 978-0-203-92942-1 (ebook) 1. Punishment – Philosophy.
2. Restorative justice. 3. Capital punishment. 4. Juvenile delinquents.
5. Family violence. 6. Sex crimes. I. Title.
K5103.B76 2013
364.6 – dc23   2012017736

ISBN: 978-0-415-43181-1 (hbk)
ISBN: 978-0-415-43182-8 (pbk)
ISBN: 978-0-203-92942-1 (ebk)

Typeset in Times New Roman
by Taylor & Francis Books

Printed and bound in Great Britain by the MPG Books Group

For my parents, Alan and Kathy

Contents

Preface

The literature on punishment has exploded in recent years. One of the main reasons is the increasing popularity of retributivist theories. A further significant reason is the rising popularity of several important alternative approaches, including the communicative theory of punishment, the restorative justice model, and new work on the unified theory of punishment. One aim of this book is to present a critical guide to the latest research on the leading theories of punishment and the most important alternative approaches. While there have been several excellent previous guides, these have become somewhat dated given the rapidly expanding literature in this field. It is my hope that this book will help readers become more familiar with the prospects and problems facing each approach to punishment.

The book is arranged to introduce readers to competing approaches to punishment and then to consider their application in particular contexts, such as the use of capital punishment, juvenile offending, and the punishment of domestic violence, rape, and child sex offences. Punishment is more than theory; it is about practices. It is my hope that the book's arrangement by theory and then practice will help improve the understanding of both abstract philosophical issues and how theories of punishment may fare as a practice – an aspect that has often been absent in previous commentaries but which is illuminating and thought-provoking.

This book is designed to attract a wide audience. Examples are drawn that are meant to have relevance for readers from different backgrounds, and this book is neither aimed primarily at a North American nor British audience, but rather both and much more. While I am an American by birth, I am a dual national with both American and British citizenship: I have adopted the spelling and grammar of my newly adopted home, but this book's arguments and research address punishment from a wide perspective. Examples will be drawn from the US, UK, and beyond to illustrate arguments throughout.

One further important aim of this book is to speak to politicians, legal practitioners, and policymakers. Chapters will include various recommendations on criminal justice policy, and these are summarized in the conclusion. These recommendations flow from my defence of a unified theory of punishment that is both pragmatic and pluralistic, bringing together compelling elements of other views on punishment within a single, coherent, and comprehensive theory of punitive restoration. This theory has been the subject of much of my research over the years and was recently recognized as one of the top 100 'Big Ideas for the Future' in British universities.[1] This book presents the most thorough explanation and defence of the unified theory of punishment to date.

I have incurred any number of substantial debts to several friends and colleagues, as well as highly supportive institutions. If I were to thank them for all the help that they have given me over the years, then the list would run to far more pages than this book. I must record my sincere thanks for their continued support and encouragement on this and many other projects.

First of all, I must begin by thanking Brian O'Connor for supervising the initial research that has developed into this book. Few can claim to have had a better supervisor, and he always encouraged me to follow the arguments wherever they led. I owe further thanks to Bob Stern and Leif Wenar for supervising further initial work for this book.

Furthermore, I must warmly thank my former colleagues at Newcastle University and, most especially, Peter Jones and Richard Mullender for their many helpful discussions on crime and punishment, which have led to several amendments in this book. I should also thank the Newcastle Ethics, Legal, and Political Philosophy Group and colleagues more generally for the luxury of providing me with such a highly stimulating place to work.

My research has benefited tremendously from the financial support of several institutional bodies. I must first thank Newcastle's School of Geography, Politics, and Sociology for their generous assistance. I am also very grateful to Newcastle's Arts and Humanities Research Fund Awards and a Research Leave Grant from the Arts and Humanities Research Council, which together helped make writing this book possible. I have also benefited from a Visiting Fellowship in the Department of Moral Philosophy at the University of St Andrews through their Centre for Ethics, Philosophy, and Public Affairs. The research undertaken during this fellowship was fundamental in the drafting of several chapters. I further benefited from my time as an Academic Visitor in the Faculty of Philosophy at the University of Oxford and as a Visiting Fellow at the Department of Government at the University of Uppsala.

Different versions of several chapters have been presented at a variety of conferences and departmental seminar series over the years. I must thank audiences at the American Philosophical Association – Eastern Division conference in Baltimore; the Centre for the Study of Mind in Nature at the University of Oslo; the European Congress of Analytic Philosophy at Lund University; the Institute for Public Policy Research North; the Joint Session of the Aristotelian Society and Mind Association at the University of Kent, Canterbury; the Newcastle Ethics, Legal, and Political

Philosophy Group workshop; the Political Studies Association annual conferences at the universities of Bath, Leeds, and Swansea; the Scottish Postgraduate Philosophy Association conference at the University of Stirling; the annual Society for Applied Philosophy conference at St Anne's College, Oxford; the Senior Postgraduate Philosophy Seminar at the University of Sheffield; and the law, philosophy, and politics departments of the universities of Cardiff, Edinburgh, Glasgow, Lancaster, Lincoln, Newcastle, Oxford (and the Oxford Jurisprudence Group), St Andrews, Sheffield, University College Dublin, Uppsala, and York. I am very grateful to the audiences at these events for their helpful feedback.

I have benefited greatly from comments and discussions with a number of friends and colleagues over the last several years, including John Alder, Dave Archard, Liz Ashford, Clara Ramirez Barat, Hilary Benn, Chris Bennett, Mark Bevir, Brian Bix, David Boonin, John Broome, Gary Browning, Kim Brownlee, Elaine Campbell, Simon Caney, Alan Carter, Jenny Chapman, Willie Charlton, Jerry Cohen, James Connolly, Angelo Corlett, Ed Cox, Rowan Cruft, Michael Davis, Michelle Madden Dempsey, Maria Dimova-Cookson, Lynn Dobson, Antony Duff, Maureen Eckert, Sam Fleischacker, Christel Fricke, Miranda Fricker, John Gardner, Brian Garvey, Gordon Graham, Les Green, John Haldane, Nicole Hassoun, Tim Hayward, Clare Heyward, Ken Himma, Jules Holroyd, Chris Hookway, Gerry Hough, Stephen Houlgate, Sue James, Duncan Kelly, Tim Kelsall, Sadiq Khan, Dudley Knowles, Matthew Kramer, Jim Kreines, Matthew Liao, Matthew Lister, Margreet Luth, Liz McKinnell, Ali Madanipour, Raino Malnes, Bill Mander, Dan Markel, Sandra Marshall, Matt Matravers, Mary Midgley, David Miller, Tim Mooney, Dean Moyar, Rick Muir, Richard Mullender, Peter Nicholson, Brian O'Connor, Patrick O'Donnell, Ian O'Flynn, Diarmuid O'Scanlain, Jim O'Shea, Mike Otsuka, Gerhard Øverland, Thomas Pogge, Jon Quong, Tracey Robson, Doug Ryan, Geoffrey Scarre, Fred Schauer, Guy Sela, Russ Shafer-Landau, Stephen R. Shalom, John Skorupski, Saul Smilansky, Richard Stalley, Bob Stern, James Sweeney, Will Sweet, Bob Talisse, John Tasioulas, Helen Thompson, Jens Timmermann, Mark Tunick, Colin Tyler, John Vail, Helga Varden, Andrew Vincent, Vaughan Walker, Jeremy Watkins, David Weinstein, Mark White, Jo Wolff, and Leo Zaibert. While the usual qualifications apply, I am certain that this book has benefited substantially from their help and good advice, no matter how close or far the book settles their queries.

I must also record my special thanks to several more colleagues. Fabian Freyenhagen discussed the full contents of this book with me at length many times over the last few years and provided rich feedback. His advice remains invaluable and everything that follows has improved as a result. I owe a great debt to discussions with David Boucher, Peter Jones, Rick Lippke, Jeff McMahan, Martha Nussbaum, and Leif Wenar over the years, which have helped clarify several earlier confusions. In particular, I must also note my very special debt to the work and constructive discussions I have had with Martha Nussbaum. While I may never fully answer her many probing questions, I am much the better for them.

I have also learned much from Bhikhu Parekh. His inspiration guides much of my work here and much more; Lord Parekh's influence on my thinking is profound in these pages and beyond. My work has benefited enormously from his intense intellectual rigour.

I owe warm thanks to my friends at Routledge, including Gerhard Boomgaarden, Emily Briggs, Ann Carter, Jenny Dodd, and Miranda Thirkettle, for their support of this project from its very beginning. My particular thanks for their being so supportive despite many delays. It has been a genuine pleasure to work with such a great—and very patient!—team. I am especially grateful to three anonymous readers for their useful suggestions on improvements as well. This book has benefited enormously from their constructive advice and helpful criticisms.

Special thanks must also go to my wife, Claire, whose excellent advice, patience, and warm support were never in short supply. My work and much more are all better because of her. This is not least because she regularly reminds me that there is much more to life than scholarly pursuits and meetings with politicians.

I warmly dedicate this book to my parents, Alan and Kathy Brooks. I will never forget trying to explain to them why I thought entering academic philosophy a more promising career path than continuing with my pursuit of a career in music as they listened bemused. However much they may never understand my attraction to philosophy and topics such as punishment, I would never be in the position I am in today without their love and support. I will never be able to thank them enough, but I suppose a book dedication is at least a small step in the right direction.

Mom and dad, this is for you.

T.A.K.B.
Newcastle upon Tyne

Introduction

Introduction

Crime and punishment grip the public imagination. The media regularly bombards us with the latest news on crime statistics while our airwaves are saturated by pundits debating how crimes should be punished. Moreover, crime and punishment affects us. Today, approximately seven million Americans are either in prison or on probation or parole.[1] Nearly 60 million Americans have a criminal record. This is almost 30 per cent of the US adult population.[2] The associated costs have increased 660 per cent from $9 billion in 1982 to $69 billion in 2006.[3] It is, then, easy to understand the increasing importance of crime and punishment to citizens and politicians alike. Some have even suggested that 'the penal system is in a state of crisis'.[4]

The central question of this book is 'how should we punish crimes?' This question will be addressed in the following way. We will examine the leading theories of punishment individually in order to understand the diversity, strengths, and weaknesses of each.[5] Some theories centre on a particular goal of punishment while others are hybrid theories and more pluralistic. They will each be considered individually before moving to specific case studies where we will examine how different theories of punishment may be applied. My approach throughout will be to assume that the reader may have come to this topic for the first time although there will be much of interest to those already deeply engaged with the field. We will learn that while different theories of punishment may often address attractive intuitions about punishment, these theories run into problems requiring a fresh perspective and new approach.

What is 'punishment'?

Punishment may be defined in the following way:

(1) Punishment must be for breaking the law.
(2) Punishment must be of a person for breaking the law.

(3)   Punishment must be administered and imposed intentionally by an authority with a legal system.
(4)   Punishment must involve a loss.

Any punishment must satisfy all four parts of this definition to count as 'punishment'. Therefore, if someone was 'punished' for breaking a law and the penalty was not imposed by a legal authority, then no punishment has taken place. I will examine each part to show more clearly why this is the case.[6]

Punishment must be for breaking the law

We use the term 'punishment' in any number of different ways. Consider the following examples:

(1)   Alan *punished* his dog for soiling the carpet.
(2)   Betsy *punished* her son by grounding him because he had failed to perform promised chores.
(3)   Chris was *punished* with extra work for coming into work late.
(4)   Danielle was *punished* by the state for a crime.

While we might speak of someone being *punished* in each of these cases in our casual everyday talk, we should be more precise about what we are specifically referring to. This is because what passes for being *punished* varies widely from one context to the next and it could lead to much unnecessary confusion.

The first three examples have at least one thing in common: they involve arbitrary executive decisions made by private individuals outside of a legal system.[7] Now consider the fourth example. When we say that Danielle was punished for her crime, our use of 'punish' takes on a very different character from the other three uses of 'punishment'. Danielle was not punished simply because someone else disagreed with her. Instead, she was punished because of a particular act that she performed. This particular act is her committing a crime.[8] Crime has a different character because it is enshrined in the criminal law.

When we speak of someone being *punished* in this book, we refer to someone who has committed a crime. This may appear controversial to some readers. We might believe that, in fact, there is no essential difference between a parent 'punishing' her child and the state 'punishing' a citizen. Indeed, some philosophers would argue this is correct although I believe this is a mistake.[9] Of course, there are limits on how a parent and the state may act in these cases. However, there is also a crucial distinction. When the parent 'punishes', she acts for whatever reason she finds most appropriate: it is largely an issue between parent and child alone. These reasons may be largely arbitrary. Contrast this case with state punishment: the only reason why the state may punish is because a person has performed a crime.[10] So the definition of punishment as a response to crime is more than merely terminological. Punishment is a matter of public justice and of a very different character than the disciplining of children by private individuals.

If punishment must only be for breaking the law, then it need not follow that every violation of law entails punishment. Instead, we should accept that punishment can only be justified on account of someone performing a crime whether or not we do impose a punishment for that crime.[11] Where there is no crime, there is no punishment. The justification of punishment may rest upon the justification of law.[12] This is because it is difficult to conceive of a case where punishment is justified for unjustified crimes: any discussion of justified punishments must presuppose on some level that the crimes they correspond to are themselves justified. There can be no just punishment of an unjust law. For example, John Mabbott says that 'The justification of punishment is that a law has been broken; the justification of law is quite another matter'.[13] We will be more interested in the former than the latter. We will ask which theory of punishment is best if, and only if, a relevant law is justified. The possibility of justified laws reveals the horizon of just punishments.

Punishment as response

What then counts as a punishment for crime? One well-known distinction is offered by Joel Feinberg.[14] Feinberg separates 'penalties' from 'punishments'. Penalties are sanctions, such as fines and warnings. Punishments are understood as 'hard treatment', or 'imprisonment'. The difference between penalties and punishments is not simply in severity, but in character. For Feinberg, punishment as imprisonment is not only a more severe sanction than imposing a fine, but imprisonment alone 'expresses' public censure to the criminal.[15]

There are several problems with this distinction. For example, why should we not also call fines 'punishment'?[16] Any sanction, including fines, might be said to 'express' public censure to the criminal. Of course, a small fine cannot be said to convey the same message as a substantial prison sentence. However, the difference here is simply that one sanction is more severe or punitive than the other: it is not the case that the two are entirely different in kind. Both may arise in relation to crimes, and penal sanctions are often embodied in fines and imprisonment. The view that penalties and 'punishments' (understood as imprisonment) are different in character is then a distinction drawn too sharply that we should reject.

Only about 5 per cent of all convicted offenders receive a custodial sentence. A theory of punishment that is unable or unwilling to account for the punishment of most, if not all, convicted offenders is incomplete at best.[17] This book will consider punishment broadly conceived as a response to crimes and how it may be justified as a response. Punishment understood here is pluralistic in form where punishment may take the shape of a penalty, imprisonment, or some other alternative. It is worth noting that one important merit of my approach is that it coheres best with current practice and policy-making on punishment.

Our study of *punishment* is a study of the best *response* to crime. We might call this the *punishment as a response to crime approach*.[18] This response to crime may take the form of a fine, imprisonment, a written warning, or other alternatives.[19] Whatever our response, punishment must only be for breaking the law.

Punishment must be of a person for breaking the law

We have now seen that punishment must only be for breaking the law. A further necessary part of punishment's definition is that punishment must be of a person for breaking the law. This is an important consideration. Suppose that a murder has taken place on your street. If punishment need only be a response to someone's breaking the law, then it might follow that we can punish whomever we like so long as a crime has taken place. It would not be necessary to punish the person who actually did break the law. However, this would be deeply unacceptable. When we punish in response to a crime, we must only punish the person(s) who broke the law(s). We do not punish groups where not all broke the law nor other innocent persons.

Indeed, this part of the definition is often understood as *the punishment of the innocent objection*. The objection is that it is always unjustified to punish those who have not broken the law. There must be a connection between the person punished and crime committed. Where a person is innocent, this person has not acted in such a way that would warrant punishment and, thus, he should be unpunished.

Punishment must be administered and imposed intentionally by an authority with a legal system

Our definition of punishment remains incomplete. Suppose that a person has stolen goods from a local store and we arrest the person for this crime. Punishment demands not only that it must be for breaking the law and of a person for breaking the law. It is important that punishment is also distributed in a particular way. For example, the local thief may deserve punishment, but it would be wrong if we simply attacked him in the street. It is the legal system that determines the relevant crimes and the means for dealing with criminal transgressions. Punishment is not distributed arbitrarily: it is intentionally inflicted on a criminal for his crime. Therefore, punishment cannot be something that happens to criminals by accident or unexpectedly. Instead, the punishment of criminals for their crimes must be intended.

Moreover, the punishment of criminals must be intended by an authority with a legal system.[20] This makes sense because punishment must only be of criminals for their crimes: it is necessary to have a legal system so we can identify the crimes to be punished. It would be unacceptable for any individual to act in a private capacity in carrying out punishments. Instead, the administration and imposition of punishment must only be managed by an authority with a legal system.[21]

Punishment must involve a loss

Finally, punishment must also involve a loss. If punishment did not involve a loss, then it might be a reward instead. The loss in terms of punishment may be understood in a variety of ways, including a loss of liberty, a loss of money through a fine, or some degree of suffering. The fact that punishment must involve a loss does not reduce punishment to a form of sadism. First, a loss is not to be imposed for public amusement, but instead as a response to criminal activity. Second, torture and six weeks imprisonment may both entail a loss, but this does not mean that all losses are justifiable: this will largely depend upon the overall theory of punishment that we defend. Instead, the loss of punishment is often temporary, such as the suspension of movement or a one-off fine.[22]

Many argue that punishment must include some idea of pain: the loss that punishment involves must be painful. Some abolitionists who oppose punishment claim there cannot be any satisfactory explanation for why punishment must include suffering. It may be the case that the imposition of punishment will involve a loss that is painful. For example, imprisonment is the loss of a criminal's freedom of movement. This may be painful because these persons are unable to meet with family and friends at will. The mistake these understandings of punishment have involving pain or suffering is that punishment's loss need not always be painful or include suffering. Punishment may take many forms, such as the payment of a fine or a suspended sentence. It is difficult to see precisely how all impositions of a suspended sentence, for example, are inflictions of 'suffering'. Such cases would be instances of a loss, namely, a loss of full freedom of movement, as future offending might necessitate time in prison. Punishment must involve a loss, but this loss need not always include pain and suffering, understood as some physical discomfort or ordeal. Perhaps the loss of punishment should aspire to be a *painless loss* if possible, and punishment should be more goal-oriented rather than pain-oriented.

The aim and distribution of punishment

Now our definition of punishment is complete. Punishment must be for a crime: punishment is a response to crime. We must only punish the person(s) who broke the law and not innocent persons. The punishment must also be administered and imposed intentionally by an authority with a legal system, such as the state. Finally, the punishment imposed must involve a loss. Together, these four parts must be present for there to be punishment in the sense we will understand 'punishment' in this book.

There are two further considerations that we should note before proceeding. Herbert Hart set out a system that we can use to classify any theory of punishment:

(1)   The definition of punishment
(2)   The general justifying aim of punishment
(3)   The distribution of punishment.[23]

Our discussion above has addressed the *definition* of punishment. However, this is only one aspect of our understanding of punishment. A further consideration is 'the general justifying aim'. This refers to the general justification of punishment. Any leading theory of punishment will adhere to our definition of punishment above and, yet, each theory will differ often significantly from each other with respect to their general justifying aims. Such an aim may be to deter potential offenders. Or an aim might be to rehabilitate offenders. These aims will differ from one theory to the next and principally characterize and distinguish it from others.

A further consideration is the distribution of punishment. Let us suppose we have any plausible theory of punishment before us. This theory satisfies our definition, and its justifying aim is to deter potential offenders, for example. We must now understand how this justifying aim is to be applied in dealing with offenders. If punishment aims at deterrence, then how do we distribute punishments so that this aim is achieved?

To conclude this part of the discussion, any theory of punishment must first satisfy the definition of punishment. We must then identify the general justifying aim of punishment and how this aim may be achieved through the distribution of punishment. We best grasp a theory of punishment when we understand how it satisfies the definition of punishment, we can identify its general justifying aim, and we have a view to how the punishment should be distributed. The following chapters in Parts 1 and 2 offer different ideas about what the general justifying aim of punishment should be and how punishment should be distributed.

Legal moralism and the harm principle

Before concluding this introduction, we should become aware of a highly relevant and important debate. We have seen that punishment is intrinsically linked with crime: where there is no crime, there cannot be punishment. One broader implication of this fact is that our views on criminalization – our theories of what distinguishes crimes from non-crimes – may affect our views on punishment. I will limit my discussion to the two main rival criminalization principles of legal moralism and the harm principle.[24]

Legal moralism

Any number of things may serve as laws, and odd examples may be readily identified.[25] Many philosophers argue for not only what should serve as our theory of punishment, but also what should be our theory of criminalization. One leading view is called *legal moralism*. Legal moralists link the criminalization of certain acts with their immorality.[26] This perspective has broad intuitive plausibility. For example, it is not difficult to understand the criminal law as primarily focused upon criminalizing immorality. For example, consider the crimes of assault, murder, rape, and theft. These crimes are forbidden by all major religions and all modern societies. One important reason why this might be universally the case may not simply be because believers or citizens are simply happier living in a community where murder is condemned, but rather because murder is viewed as a grave wrong. It is then easy to see the initial attractiveness of legal moralism. Why not consider crimes as moral wrongs when we understand most, if not all, crimes in this way? This view of law is captured well by Antony Duff: 'The criminal law does not create wrongs: it does not make wrong what was not already wrong by criminalizing it. Rather, it declares certain kinds of pre-existing wrong to be public wrongs – wrongs that concern the whole polity'.[27] Crimes are public wrongs because they are moral wrongs of certain kinds.

Legal moralism has many attractions, but it has also attracted several criticisms. One objection is that suppose we only wish to criminalize immorality. This need not entail that we criminalize all immorality. An illustrative example is lying. Many acts of lying may be immoral. Someone might lie to win an interview for a new job. Or a witness may lie about a defendant's whereabouts in order to settle an unrelated personal vendetta. In these cases, we might support the right of employers to immediately terminate the contracts of employees who knowingly misrepresented themselves in being hired. We might also support sanctions against witnesses who knowingly offer false testimony. While many lies are immoral, this is not clearly true for all lies. Would it be immoral to deceive a friend about a surprise party for her that evening? I doubt many of us would find this immoral. Surely, no one would believe it criminal. If so, then there is good reason to believe that not all immorality should be criminalized. The objection then is that if some, but not all, immorality should be criminalized, we must have some threshold: it is not enough to say that because some act is immoral then it should be criminalized. The 'good' citizen need not be morally good to avoid punishment: she need only avoid what is criminalized.

A second problem concerns what we mean by 'immoral'. If we claim that some act is immoral, then we find this immoral in relation to a moral standard. This is because we require a standard to distinguish between the moral and immoral. The problem is that these standards may differ and we must choose between them.[28] There is often no moral consensus to be found.[29] Take abortion. Some people believe abortion is immoral. Legal moralists might argue that abortion should be criminalized because it is immoral or that it should not be if they argued abortion was not immoral.[30] The way we understand what should be criminal will depend largely on which moral standard we endorse. Therefore, a problem for legal moralism is not merely the fact that we may fundamentally disagree about what we find immoral, but also about what we find sufficiently immoral to justify its being criminal.

There is a final problem. We might argue that any plausible theory about criminalization should be able to account for widely recognized crimes. Thus, for example, a theory about criminalization that could not justify criminalizing murder or theft would be highly objectionable. A problem for legal moralism is that not all crimes are immoral, or at least not immoral in any straightforward sense. For example, Douglas Husak notes various crimes in the United States such as 'the transportation of alligator grass across a state line, using the slogan "Give a hoot, don't pollute" without authorization, pretending to be a 4-H Club member with intent to defraud, and including a member of the armed forces in a voter preference poll'.[31] Perhaps these examples are unproblematic. These may be laws now, but a useful theory of criminalization need only capture crimes we must account for. We might argue that crimes about transporting alligator grass fail this test.

There are other crimes that clearly pass this test and pose a real challenge for legal moralism. One important part of modern criminal law is traffic law violations. These violations include illegal parking and speeding.[32] Such crimes have widespread acceptance – and are the crimes that most of us have performed: it has been said that 'the typical criminal of today is the motorist'.[33] Furthermore, traffic law violations are often victimless crimes. For example, my speeding along a quiet country road is no less criminal where my crime does not directly affect others. There are other victimless crimes, such as drug offences, that are also not clearly immoral in any straightforward sense. The problem for legal moralism is that many of the things we would want to criminalize are not clearly immoral. Legal moralism might only be applicable to considerations about how we might punish some crimes, but not all crimes we might want to punish.

This question of whether crimes are criminal because they are immoral or because they have been criminalized is often discussed in terms of the distinction of *mala in se* crimes and *mala prohibita* crimes. *Mala in se* crimes are those crimes that we might find wrong independently of law. Common examples include crimes such as murder, rape, and theft. *Mala in se* crimes often involve harm to another. The idea is that we would find murder wrong even if it was not criminalized: it is a moral wrong.

Mala prohibita crimes are those crimes that are wrong because they are crimes. They are public, not moral, wrongs. Possible examples often include drug and traffic offences. For example, speed limits have been often justified on the grounds of reducing fuel consumption rather than public safety.[34] Moreover, we might accept that 'there is little intrinsic moral difference ... between driving at 70 miles per hour on the highway and driving at 75; but the latter is an offence'.[35] Thus, crimes are illegal, but not always immoral. The possible existence of *mala prohibita* crimes is a potential threat to legal moralism. This is because such crimes are not criminalized on account of immorality. Therefore, the fact of *mala prohibita* crimes may render legal moralism impractical or even obsolete.

A common reply by legal moralists is to argue that, if our legal system is morally justified, our laws are also morally justified on account of their being enmeshed within the legal system. It then does not matter whether some may view a particular crime as holding a sin-like status for the legal moralist. One example of this position is offered by David Boonin: 'the problem of punishment is not the problem of figuring out how legal punishment can be legal. It is the problem of figuring out how legal punishment can be moral'.[36] Legal punishment can be moral if it can be morally justified. If we can morally justify a legal system that includes a traffic code, then legal moralists believe they can accommodate so-called *mala prohibita* crimes and overcome this concern. All crimes would be morally justified in the sense that they are chosen within a morally justified legal system. It is a weaker claim than arguing that all crimes are crimes because they are immoral. This is because what is morally justified is merely the context within which we determine crimes.

This reply is unconvincing. There may be many strong reasons for defending the moral justifiability of a legal system. However, the question is whether the moral justification of the whole entails the moral justification of the parts. For some legal moralists, the one flows from the other. The problem is that there is a crucial distinction overlooked. Suppose a legal system enjoys satisfactory moral justification. Does this entail an absence of *mala prohibita* crimes? No, it does not. This is because the moral justification of the wider context does not extend to the moral justification of individual laws. So a law may be agreed in a process that is morally justified. However, the moral justification of the process may not always entail the moral justification of *the product* of this process. The legal moralist's assumption is that the morality of the process will ensure the morality of its products, but the morality of one may be distinct and different from the other.[37] An illustration is the market. Suppose that we enjoy a morally justified economic system. The moral justification of the system does not entail that all market choices arising within this system will share equal moral justification. Likewise, a legal system entailing a particular view about constitutional law may enjoy moral justification on the whole, but this does not mean that all laws adopted will only select certain kinds of pre-legal wrongs as public wrongs ripe for criminalization. The lesson here is that our analysis of crime and punishment should be careful to avoid *the naturalist fallacy*: there is no necessary connection between crime and immorality, even if there is often this connection.[38]

The harm principle

There is a second widely popular view on criminalization in addition to legal moralism. This view is the harm principle. John Stuart Mill says:

> That principle is that the sole end for which mankind are warranted, individually or collectively, in interfering with the liberty of action of any of their number is self-protection. That the only purpose for which power can be rightfully exercised over any member of a civilized community, against his will, is to prevent harm to others. His own good, either physical or moral, is not a sufficient warrant.[39]

According to this principle, we may only justifiably interfere with another in order to prevent harm. The harm principle would then justify the criminalization of acts where there are clear harms to others, such as arson, murder, or rape: 'the criminal law aims at preventing harm'.[40] These harms are often understood as *other-regarding,* as harms regarding others. Victimless crimes are understood as *self-regarding,* as harms regarding only oneself. Victimless crimes may include drug possession or speeding. They are not other-regarding harms and, as such, are not covered by the harm principle. The harm principle only appears to justify other-regarding harms as crimes.

Not unlike legal moralism, the harm principle has difficulty accounting for a similar group of crimes, such as drug and traffic offences, but for different reasons. Legal moralism has the difficulty of accounting for crimes that may be considered *mala prohibita*. The harm principle has the difficulty of accounting for crimes that are self-regarding, or victimless. Perhaps interestingly, many *mala prohibita* crimes are also self-regarding. Legal moralism and the harm principle offer two very different approaches to criminalization, but both fail to account for a similar group of widely endorsed crimes.

A key issue is what we understand by *harm*. While it is fairly clear that many physical acts may embody harms, such as murder or assault, it is much less clear whether other activities, such as emotional distress, should count as well where relevant. While it is not difficult to imagine cases of emotional abuse that would be criminalized by the harm principle, it is also clear that not all cases of emotional hurt would be criminalized. For example, the fact that Cindy hurt the feelings of David is not itself a clear case of criminalization. Perhaps another was hurt by my dislike of his painting. This is not to say that emotional distress cannot play an important role in identifying harms but rather that they are insufficient and perhaps unnecessary.

We might also question the relevance of harm. The fact that Cindy has harmed David is not itself reason to punish Cindy. One reason is because we may consent to harm. An illustration is a prize fighter in a boxing match. Or a surgeon conducting an invasive operation. We may prefer to argue that it is a harm to autonomy, or domination by another, that is a more useful idea.[41] This alternative overcomes some of the problems with the harm principle, but not all. For example, there remains the problem of being able to account for self-regarding crimes. The question will be whether there are crimes I might commit without being under the domination of others. Self-regarding crimes may play such a role and pose a genuine challenge for this approach.

The lesson learned here is that our discussion of crime and punishment should not presuppose that all crimes are immoral or that all crimes are harms, or at least harms to others. These issues will arise again in the following chapters.

The plan for this book

This book is divided into three parts. The first part will focus on four general theories of punishment: retributivism, deterrence, rehabilitation, and restorative justice. This will be followed by the second part of the book, which will examine three 'hybrid' theories that attempt to bring together two or more of the general theories discussed in Part 1. The hybrid theories discussed will include the mixed theories of John Rawls and Herbert Hart, negative retributivism, expressivist and communicative theories of punishment, and the unified theory of punishment.

The book will conclude with a third part composed of case studies. These studies focus on many of the most important topics concerning the philosophy of punishment, such as capital punishment, juvenile offenders, domestic abuse, and sexual crimes, such as rape and child sex offences. The aim here is to help explain how the various theories considered in the first two parts relate to real practical problems across a wide range of important cases.

My aim is primarily to alert readers coming to the subject for the first time of the leading theories of punishment and their ability to speak to important case studies. A further ambition is to shed light on the rich variety of theories of punishment. There is no one theory of 'retributivism' or 'deterrence'. Instead, these names identify a family of theories that bear specific resemblances. Finally, I hope to impress upon readers the need for further work both in the philosophy of punishment more generally and, specifically, in the area of pluralistic, hybrid theories of punishment, which I believe are most promising. While every theory may have certain drawbacks, each theory also offers an important contribution to how we should think about punishment. A theory that could unite these contributions could hold great promise for the future.

One important contribution of this work concerns the theories of punishment, but a second contribution lies in various implications for policy. I believe it is important to understand punishment as a practice informed by theory. Each chapter will speak to different implications for practice, although the policy implications will be brought together in the conclusion.

Now let us begin our journey of exploration together and see if it is possible to cast light where there is much darkness.

Part 1

General theories

There are at least two ways that we might think about theories of punishment. The first is to consider each theory as an individual theory with a core principle. Our focus then concerns identifying theoretical approaches and considering their acceptability in terms of factors such as coherence but not empirical findings. A second alternative is to examine each theory of punishment by how well it speaks to practices in light of evidence.

The first and second parts of this book contain seven chapters that consider each theory in terms of core principles and coherence. The final third part of this book will take up four different case studies relating to practices. This division is important as it may be that some theories may be found highly coherent as a theory, but yet impractical. When we critically analyse any theory of punishment, it is useful to be aware of these two different, although related, standpoints.

In this first part, we will examine more traditional theories of punishment. These theories will include retributivism, deterrence, rehabilitation, and restorative justice. Each theory will be discussed individually within its own chapter. While these theories may be understood in light of a single aim or principle, each is also perhaps surprisingly complex. This part will set the scene for Part 2, where we will consider various attempts to defend 'mixed' hybrid theories of punishment that bring together elements from different theories we will consider in Part 1.

1 Retributivism

Introduction

Retributivism is perhaps the most familiar and most misunderstood theory of punishment.[1] It is important to note that retributivism is not vengeance, nor is it any one single position. Retributivism is a rich, venerable tradition with a variety of supporters who each defend different retributivist variations. The aim of this chapter is to shed light on precisely what marks out a retributivist theory from other theories of punishment, as well as highlight the most important varieties of retributivism.

What is retributivism?

Defining retributivism is both simple and complex. It is a simple task as two interrelated concepts are at the heart of most retributivist theories. Yet, this task is complex because different theories understand these concepts in very different ways.

Desert and proportionality form the conceptual core of most retributivist theories. Retributivists claim that criminals *deserve* punishment *in proportion* to their crime. There are many senses in which persons may be said to deserve something. For example, a hardworking student may be thought to 'deserve' good marks or a criminal deserves to leave prison early due to good behaviour. In both these cases, someone deserves some result based upon a view of *merit*. However, we also use 'desert' in a negative sense. We might claim that someone deserves to lose his political office because of incompetence, or perhaps we say that a person deserves punishment because she committed a crime. In these cases, someone deserves some result based upon *demerit*.

Retributivists give desert a central place, but only to the latter sense of desert as demerit, or what we might call *retributivist desert*. Someone is thought to have desert not merely on account of his committing a *wrongful* act, but on account of his committing an *illegal* act. There are many actions that are wrong, but not punishable because they are not illegal. For example, lying or adultery may be wrong. Both actions betray the trust of others.

We may discourage or look down upon people who tell lies or cheat on their partners. However, unless either involves breaking the law, it may be wrong, but it is not illegal. Punishment is only justified as a response to crime in relation to desert.[2] Perhaps all crimes are wrongful acts. However, not all wrongful acts are crimes, as cases such as lying or adultery may illustrate. When we punish someone because he *deserves* to be punished, we are punishing him because he deserves punishment on account of his performing an illegal act.

We do not punish people simply by virtue of the fact they have committed a wrongful act. Retributivism punishes criminals for the wrongful acts they performed: retributivism is *backward*-looking. We do not punish a criminal for what we think she might do tomorrow, but what she has done. We look backwards in time to a past action. It is what happened in the past that might justify punishment and not what might happen sometime in the future. Retributivists find consequences irrelevant. If we want to know what someone deserves, then we must look to his past action.

Retributivists endorse a conception of proportionality in addition to desert. The two concepts are interlinked. We punish criminals not only because they are deserving of punishment, but we punish them *in proportion* to what they deserve. Desert is clearly of central importance for retributivists as it not only indicates *who* we might punish, but it also informs us of *how much* we might punish. When we know no more than that someone deserves punishment, it does not tell us how much punishment is justified for this person. For example, if all we knew was that a person had broken a law, then we might find that person deserving of punishment but lack any clear idea of how much punishment is deserved. If we had more information – such as that the person had murdered someone – we gain a clearer sense of how much punishment might be deserved. So punishable desert is not only something that a criminal possesses, but something she possesses in degrees: the more desert, the greater the punishment.

We can now get a better sense of not only where retributivists agree, but also about where they might disagree. A retributivist theory will have a particular position on desert and proportionality whereby punishment is justified for persons who deserve it and the severity of punishment is in proportion to what these persons deserve. A murderer and a thief might both deserve punishment on account of their each being a criminal. However, the murderer may be deserving of a more punitive punishment on account of his having greater desert for his more wrongful crime.

Retributivism is not vengeance

Retributivist punishments are sometimes misunderstood as a form of vengeance. We punish criminals *because* they have committed an illegal action; the law is avenged when criminals are punished to the degree they deserve. This commonplace view is mistaken. An example may make this plain.

Perhaps the most classic version of retributivism is found in the Code of Hammurabi's *lex talionis*, more commonly known as 'an eye for an eye and a tooth for a tooth'. On this view, a criminal deserves punishment in strict proportion to the harm he causes others.

When we see statements such as 'an eye for an eye', it may look like vengeance. However, the *lex talionis* has two characteristic features that distinguish it and other retributivist theories from vengeance. First, punishment is an act of public justice. When we punish someone for taking an eye or a tooth, we do so because the criminal has broken a law. She is punished by her community as a just punishment for a violation of law. The *lex talionis* does not endorse private acts, such as my attacking others on a whim in the name of punishment. Instead, a wrong must be committed that demands redress from the criminal justice system. There must be a law broken and justice is dispensed in public.

Second, retributivist punishments have limits. On the one hand, if you take someone's eye, then it is unjust to kill you – or ritually disembowel you. You are to be punished in proportion to the degree that you deserve. On the other hand, vengeance is something I seek against individuals who harm me personally. It is easy to lose all sense of proportion when carrying out a punishment on someone who injured me or those I love. As a community, we might be appalled by the thought that a murderer should be executed. Nevertheless, we might also easily sympathize with the victim's family and their support for the murderer's death.[3]

These two features of retributivist punishment distinguish it from *vengeance*. Vengeance is an act of private justice without limits: I seek vengeance when I desire to injure another; I injure another to a degree I am satisfied with and not only to what he may deserve. Retributivist punishment is an act of public justice within limits: we seek retribution when we desire only to punish someone to the degree he deserves according to public laws and procedural justice. Punishment is only justified when it is deserved, not when it satisfies private anger or bloodlust. Retribution is clearly not vengeance.[4]

We might ask next if retributivism is the opposite of vengeance, namely, mercy. Many retributivists are opposed to mercy or pardons. For example, Michael Moore says:

> But retributivism goes further. As a theory of a kind of justice, it *obligates* us to seek retribution through the punishment of the guilty. This means that officials have a duty to punish deserving offenders and that citizens have a duty to set up and support institutions that achieve such punishments.[5]

The retributivist argues that criminals deserve punishment on account of their wrongdoing. If they deserve punishment, then justice demands we punish. We do injustice if we fail to punish criminals, because they then do not receive what they deserve.

It is unsurprising to find some retributivists uncomfortable with mercy and pardons. Both are often an attempt to bring about the best consequences from a situation, a perspective most retributivists reject. For example, the South African Truth and Reconciliation Commission has been criticized by many retributivists because the Commission did not punish those who testified that they had broken laws, often performing quite serious offences. Simply saying sorry is insufficient: we should expect the criminal to make more of a sacrifice and suffer some kind of pain; otherwise, we may view his apology as insufficiently sincere.[6] Some degree of mercy can be acceptable, but only within certain limits and as long as some degree of punishment is administered.

This view is certainly coherent. A retributivism that argued against punishing deserving criminals might find itself in trouble. The problem is not consistency, but its relation to future public policy. There come times when greater good is achieved in pardoning a criminal than punishing him. Retributivists will respond that this may be so, but it does not justify failing to punish deserving persons. Retributivists are not consequentialists.

The question becomes how wedded retributivists are to the idea we must punish the deserving. If a situation arose where freeing a murderer would avoid a bloody revolution, should we make an exception? Kant famously tells us that 'if justice goes, there is no longer any value in human beings living on the earth'.[7] It is better for the revolution to take place because we meted out justice, than avoid it through injustice. Consequences are irrelevant, even in some troublesome cases. Of course, not all retributivists agree, but only because they believe consequences matter once their importance moves beyond a certain threshold.[8] Nevertheless, retributivism is not vengeance nor easily compatible with mercy.

Moral responsibility and wickedness

What does it mean to say that a person *deserves* punishment? Thus far, this has been understood in the simplest of terms: a person deserves punishment on account of his performing a criminal act. This is true, although retributivist desert is more complicated than this, as I will now explain. We have seen that retributivists recognize that a punishment is deserved if in proportion to what is deserved. Desert is something we possess in degrees and some criminals will be more deserving of punishment than others. The problem is ascertaining the amount of punishment a person deserves.

Retributivist desert relies upon a notion of moral responsibility. Whether or not we are deserving of retributivist punishment depends upon our degree of moral responsibility. We are morally responsible for our free choices. If a criminal intends to murder Alice and acts on his intentions, then the criminal is morally responsible for her death. He deserves punishment in proportion to his responsibility. Now take a second example. If a criminal intends to steal money from Brian and acts on her intentions, then she is morally responsible for this theft. The thief likewise deserves punishment precisely because of her moral responsibility for a criminal act. Suppose that in both cases each criminal plans his or her crime with an equal amount of preparation. If both are equally morally responsible for planning their crimes, then we might think that they each share equal desert and should be punished in equal severity. This is precisely how we might understand retributivist punishment given what we have seen thus far, but this would be a mistake.

For retributivists, it is not only the case that we punish someone on account of her moral responsibility, but also on account of her committing a wicked act. Let me explain. I am morally responsible for an act when I commit the act freely: it is an action I have chosen for myself. This is different than causal responsibility. If someone pushes me into you and you drop your phone, then I am causally responsible for your dropping your phone. I am not morally responsible.

The distinction between causal and moral responsibility may become clearer if we consider the difference between self-defence and murder. In both cases, Andrew may be seen holding a bloody knife over the dead body of Bob. Whether Andrew is causally or morally responsible for Bob's death is crucial to determining if Andrew deserves punishment. If Andrew stabs Bob in an act of self-defence, then Andrew is causally responsible for Bob's death. In this case, Andrew is causally responsible because he caused Bob's death: Bob would have lived if Andrew did not defend himself. However, Andrew is not morally responsible because he did not intend to harm Bob. This is because Andrew only stabs Bob in self-defence. Bob might have lived if Andrew did not defend himself, but Bob would never be in this situation if he had not first threatened Andrew's life. If Andrew did not stab Bob in self-defence and Bob's death was intentional, then Andrew is *both* causally responsible *and* morally responsible for Bob's death. Andrew is causally responsible for Bob's death on account of his stabbing Bob. Andrew is morally responsible because he intended to harm Bob. The distinction between causal and moral responsibility is crucial because retributivists punish a criminal's moral responsibility for his act. It is not enough that a person stabs another person. What matters is the killer's moral responsibility for his crime. The fact that Andrew killed Bob does not entail that Andrew is a murderer. It is centrally important whether or not Andrew is morally responsible for killing Bob.

Our gaining clarity on the difference between causal and moral responsibility is important, but does not explain the full retributivist picture. It is not enough that I be morally responsible for a criminal act. The murderer and the thief may both be equally responsible for their crimes, all things considered. The retributivist will not want to punish them both equally. Instead, the retributivist will want to punish the murderer more than the thief. The reason is because retributivists do not merely punish persons to the degree they are morally responsible for committing a crime, but rather to the degree they are morally responsible for committing a wicked action. This moral responsibility is the measure of punishable desert.[9]

Immanuel Kant provides us with an illuminating example:

> whatever undeserved evil you inflict upon another within the people, you inflict upon yourself. If you insult him, you insult yourself; if you steal from him, you steal from yourself; if you strike him, you strike yourself; if you kill him, you kill yourself.[10]

We punish theft, assault, murder, and other crimes as 'undeserved evils'. All evils are not equal. If they were, then we would punish thieves and murderers the same. As Kant makes clear, we punish these crimes differently: execution of a murderer may be justified, but not for thieves. The more *evil* an act, the more punishment it deserves. Murder and theft are both evils, but murderers face a more severe punishment than thieves precisely on account of murder being a more evil act than theft.

We seem to have solved our problem. Retributivists punish criminals in proportion to their desert. Retributivist desert is clearly complex, although it has a clear structure. Desert flows from an action. It pertains to violations of the law, not immorality outside the law. We have desert when we are morally, not causally, responsible for breaking the law. We are more morally responsible for actions that are wicked, rather than less wicked. So when the murderer intentionally executes the death of his victim, the murderer deserves punishment because he is morally responsible for a wicked and illegal act. We punish the murderer with a view towards the degree of evil in his act. Retributivist desert is far from a simple notion, but we can still identify its central structure.

The problems with desert

A new series of problems arises with the solving of the last problem. This section will focus on three major problems, namely, the problem of punishing evil, the problem of amoral crimes, and the problem of knowing a criminal's intentions. I will take each in order.[11]

The problem of punishing evil

The first problem is that retributivists punish criminals to the degree they deserve. How much is deserved corresponds to the wickedness of the crime. The problem is ascertaining wickedness. Let us suppose that all crimes are wicked and leave aside the question of whether any crimes are amoral. Can we make sense of the thought that some crimes are more evil than others? If this is a non-starter, then we cannot punish the wickedness of crimes and retributivism fails.

For one thing, the immorality of crimes must be comparable. We must have a gold standard by which we can assess the *wrongness* of crimes.

Without such a standard, we will be unable to ascertain how we should punish crimes differently, if at all. The problem is that we live in an age of pluralism. Modern societies are characterized by citizens adhering to different and reasonable conceptions of the good. Whose morality do we use to measure the wrongness of crimes? Mine? Yours? We are unable to use both because then inconsistencies in our moral views will lead to injustices in our acceptable punishments. At most, we need a singular vision of morality that offers us some standard by which we can rank the wrongness of crimes. At the very least, we need a common moral standard that coherently brings together the moralities held by the community's members. The problem is that it seems unfair to assert one view of morality over others even if this makes the criminal law more consistent, and it is difficult to see how competing views of morality can be unified if these views are truly different. The task of simply 'punishing evil' is more complicated than it may first appear. This is not least because we each understand this idea in sometimes very different ways.

The problem of amoral crimes

A second problem is that it is unclear how retributivists should best distinguish punishable evils from non-punishable evils.[12] If we punish criminals for their actions in response to the wickedness of their act, then it would seem we are actually punishing wickedness instead of illegality. This is a problem for retributivism because a theory of punishment must address illegal acts and such acts do not always amount to wickedness.[13]

Most crimes are both illegal acts and widely considered to be immoral. Examples might include murder, theft, rape, and assault. These acts would be immoral even if legal. Such acts are often classified as *mala in se* crimes. *Mala in se* crimes are different than so-called *mala prohibita* crimes. *Mala prohibita* crimes are wrongful only in virtue of being illegal. These are crimes which are not clearly immoral. It must be said that philosophers disagree widely on what crimes, if any, are *mala prohibita*. The more common examples include traffic offences, drug offences, prostitution, and perhaps treason.

Retributivism has an easy time with *mala in se* crimes, such as murder. The retributivist punishes murderers for breaking the law and in proportion to the wickedness of their act. *Mala prohibita* crimes cause a real problem for retributivists because while they might punish persons for committing *mala prohibita* crimes, retributivists cannot do so in proportion to the wickedness of the act.

For example, let us consider *mala prohibita* crimes such as traffic offences. Imagine a motorist is caught driving faster than the speed limit on a lonely, country road. The motorist has clearly broken the law and, thus, she has committed a wrong. However, is the act *immoral?* Perhaps we might think so if the motorist sped at considerable excess of the lawful limit or if she demonstrated a lack of due concern for the safety and well being of others. We might then think she is wrong whether or not a law is broken. Yet, let us suppose the motorist is an off duty police officer well trained over many years at high-speed driving, perhaps practising her driving skills. What serves as the uppermost safe speeding limit on this particular stretch of road will differ between a common motorist and the motorist well trained in high-speed pursuits. The only wrong in this case is the fact the motorist sped above the legal limit, not that she endangered others or showed them a lack of due concern. In this case, speeding is a *mala prohibita* crime: it is wrong only because it is illegal. The retributivist who wants to punish the off duty police officer because she broke the law cannot set the punishment in proportion to her wickedness because none is present.[14]

Actions that are crimes, but not immoral, then pose a real problem for retributivist accounts.[15] The question then becomes whether any options are available for retributivists to overcome this problem. One solution is to change the laws so that all crimes are both illegal acts and immoral. Thus, perhaps we legalize the use of drugs and availability of prostitution. We might continue to impose penalties on miscreant drivers, but perhaps remove traffic offences from the criminal law and include them elsewhere, such as in tort. However, until the law is changed substantially so that it better accommodates their penal theory, retributivists will continue to have the problem that retributivism does not fully accommodate the criminal law and perhaps many of the *mala prohibita* crimes we would want punished.[16]

A different strategy is to claim that no crime is *mala prohibita*, strictly speaking.[17] This view claims that it is unwise to evaluate crimes individually in terms of their morality. Perhaps it is the case that certain crimes, such as traffic offences, are not wicked acts *in themselves* and so appear to be *mala prohibita* crimes. This may not be the best perspective. Instead, if we understand our laws as serving a common good, it is then wrong to violate them because they are our laws and they serve the common good. In this light, all crimes are both illegal and wrongful acts although some crimes are more wrong than others. This strategy appears to serve the retributivist well. The retributivist already claims some crimes are more wrong than others, such as murder being a more wicked act than theft. One problem with this perspective is that critics may reject the view that suspect *mala prohibita* crimes truly serve the common good. A second problem is that retributivists require some moral standard to justify general criminalization, but also to determine the different degrees of moral wrongness of each crime. This is a problem of legal moralism discussed previously. Either all crimes are wrong in equal measure and, in turn, demanding equal retributivist punishment for petty thieves and murderers alike or we require some further moral standard to distinguish crimes that are minor from crimes that are more serious. Either way, the strategy of claiming no crime is *mala prohibita* may run into serious problems.

The problem of ascertaining criminal intentions

In order to impose retributivist punishments, we must ascertain the moral responsibility of criminals with some certainty. It is not enough that we know that Victoria stabbed Louise. We must discover Victoria's moral responsibility. How can we do this? If we could read Victoria's mind at the time she stabbed Louise, then we might be best placed to discern Victoria's moral responsibility. Of course, we are unable to read each other's minds. We cannot know with certainty precisely what is Victoria's moral responsibility because we cannot know her intentions in committing a crime with any certainty. This problem is spelled out well by Kant in an important passage:

> The real morality of actions, their merit or guilt, even that of our own conduct, thus remains entirely hidden from us. Our imputations can refer only to the empirical character. How much of this character is ascribable to the pure effect of freedom, how much to mere nature, that is, to faults of temperament for which there is no responsibility, or to its happy constitution, can *never* be determined, and upon it therefore no *perfectly* just judgments can be passed.[18]

We cannot make perfect judgements of the moral responsibility of others. The best we can manage is to make an educative guess based upon the empirical evidence.

Whilst the question of ascertaining a criminal's past mindset may appear unimportant, nothing could be further from the truth. It is the case that we believe the murderer who kills impulsively rather than from deliberate premeditation is a less dangerous offender. We believe that circumstances and character defects which affect a criminal's autonomy also affect his punishable desert. So it matters if the criminal is a child as he is thought incapable of making fully autonomous decisions. It also matters if aggravating or mitigating circumstances are present. Aggravating factors are often thought to include provocations relating to disability, race, religion, and sexual orientation; mitigating factors are often thought to include factors such as the impact on third parties and whether a crime was committed under duress.[19] No such factors may excuse the wrongdoing or the need for punishment. Instead, the point is that a criminal's moral responsibility matters for us in determining appropriate punishments. We cannot avoid this problem. The issue then is how best to address it.

Retributivists have been aware of this problem since Kant, proposing several solutions. One solution is behavioural. This view claims that how we act is the product of our intentions. When someone buys a newspaper or drives her car, she is acting precisely how she intended. In order to know her intentions at any given time, all we need to do is note her actions. This once popular view has since been largely discredited. An example may help to explain why. If someone gives you flowers, what are his intentions? Is it a sign of friendship or something more? Is it a sign of sympathy or a random act of kindness? How do we know that the act is not mistaken? Mistakes happen all the time and not least in criminal justice. If Betsy receives flowers from Jonathan, it may be because Jonathan intended Betsy to receive the flowers. However, it may be that Jonathan did send Betsy the flowers, but mistook her identity: Jonathan actually wants Claire to receive the flowers, but mistakenly thinks Betsy is her name. We need to read Jonathan's mind to know if his actions accurately reflect his intentions. When mistakes happen, we are back in the thick of the problem: actions are no more a precise tool to help us unlock the intentions and moral responsibility of others.

A second solution is more pragmatic. It combines an examination of what we *do* with an attempt to discover the underlining reasons *why* we do what we do. We see countless examples in trial dramas and popular detective television shows. Was Mrs Jones murdered and, if so, by whom? The detective's task is both to discover who had the physical opportunity to murder Mrs Jones, but also to discover who had the *motive* to murder her. A motive is not the same as intention. Both motives and intentions cannot be known with precision. The difference is that the existence of motives depends upon empirical evidence, whereas the existence of intentions does not. I may have the intention to eat a sandwich or steal a bicycle, but if I do not act on my intention then there is no evidence of my having a motive to perform either act. For this reason, detectives try to uncover empirical evidence that presents an explanation of why it is that the accused is morally responsible for a wrongful act. If someone accused of murdering another had the opportunity and benefited from the death, this evidence helps us estimate whether or not the accused had intended to murder another. It may not be conclusive, but this mixture of both noting physical movements and possible reasons why someone might have been the last to see the victim alive without witnesses after midnight, etc. is seen as the best *pragmatic* attempt we can make to ascertain the moral responsibility of another for wrongdoing.

It must be said that this second attempt has much in its favour. Our courts convict persons *beyond reasonable doubt*, not beyond all possible doubt. We guess the moral responsibility of alleged wrongdoers because we both cannot know it for certain and because we believe finding persons morally responsible for the actions important. An example may make this clearer. Suppose Andrew and David are both arrested for assault. Andrew was caught on CCTV cameras instigating a fight between himself and another person. David assaulted a person who he genuinely believed had just robbed an elderly woman. Andrew and David both assaulted innocent people and should be held to account. However, we would not punish them equally. Instead, we would punish Andrew more than David. Andrew is more guilty for performing the same crime on account of his being more in the wrong.

David was wrong to misidentify his victim. Perhaps David deserves punishment. Yet, by all accounts, David assaulted his victim in a last minute, albeit mistaken, attempt to apprehend a criminal. David was not intending to harm anyone until he was led to think someone had robbed an elderly woman. Andrew was wilfully attempting to harm someone. Both actions are wrong, but clearly Andrew's action is much worse.

Of course, whether or not this decision is correct will depend on our best judgement of the evidence: does the CCTV camera really prove Andrew is looking for a fight? Do we have reason to accept David's testimony that his crime was the result of an honest case of mistaken identity? Retributivists and most non-retributivists would argue that this guesswork is intractable given the problem of intentionality, namely, our inability to know the intentions of others with certainty. What people intend to do matters and we make our best guess as to these intentions. Our courts perform this task countless times every day since the origins of the trial. This epistemological problem of knowing another's desert is real, but it is intractable *and* manageable as our courts demonstrate.

There is a third solution retributivists offer to the problem of knowing the intentions of others: retributivist sentiments, such as resentment, indignation, remorse, blame, and guilt.[20] This view claims that the law reflects essential characteristics of our emotional makeup. We feel guilt, blame, and other emotions. We blame others for actions we feel are wrong. When we blame others, we want them to face up to their wrongdoing, possibly requiring sanctions. So we know how to set punishments in proportion to what criminals deserve because the proper amount is found in our hearts: we know *intuitively* through the proper use of our sentiments what a criminal deserves. We then avoid the worry we need to read minds.

The problem with this solution is that even if it were true that most, if not all, persons possessed retributivist sentiments, it is far from clear how this solves the problem at hand.[21] In order for us to have a meaningful understanding of the link between desert and proportional punishment, we will all have to possess the same strength of blame, guilt, and other emotions, which is highly doubtful.[22] For example, most, if not all, people regard murder as the most serious of crimes. However, reasonable people disagree on whether execution or alternative sanctions are most appropriate. Retributivist sentiments may lead reasonable people to substantially different ideas about punishment.

The discussion thus far has focused on problems and attempted solutions to the issue of whether or not we can discern the intentions of others. We need to know what others intended in order to understand the amount of moral responsibility. This discussion is epistemological. A related worry is metaphysical, concerning whether moral responsibility exists to be discovered. Some critics of retributivism have charged that the theory is false because criminal behaviour is a product of the social environment rather than a criminal's free choice.[23] If socio-economic conditions shape the available choices for me, my choices may well become limited to more criminal options than if my conditions were different. The argument is not that the environment determines all behaviour, only that it is responsible for some of it. Our moral responsibility is less when our environment is an important factor. Whether or not this is a real problem for retributivists will depend on the empirical evidence. There is evidence to suggest that gender, age, socio-economic conditions, and other factors largely beyond one's control are more likely to be present in certain offenders. However, these are probabilities, not certainties. A space for moral responsibility is still left for the retributivist. His problem is knowing how much there is to find.

Making punishment fit the crime

We have discussed the importance of both desert and proportionality for retributivists. This led us to consider the importance of moral responsibility and ascertaining a criminal's intentions in order to know the amount of his punishable desert. Now let us suppose that we know how deserving a criminal is of punishment. How do we determine how much punishment he deserves? There are several different ways retributivists determine punishment in relation to desert. This list is not exhaustive and these ways are combinable.

The guilty should suffer

Why think guilt entails the infliction of pain? Most retributivists either claim that punishment must cause pain or avoid the question altogether. However, if punishment is painful, we still need an argument why it is that we are justified in causing pain to others, including the guilty. When a person performs a crime, he has broken the law. Retributivists not only punish someone for breaking the law, but in proportion to their wrongdoing. Retributivists punish criminals for their wrongful acts, causing them pain, but too often find it unnecessary to justify this practice beyond the view that criminals should suffer for their guilt. Herbert Hart defines retributivism as 'the application of the pains of punishment to an offender who is morally guilty'.[24] One retributivist, Leo Zaibert, argues further that the true core of retributivism is the view that punishing the deserving is 'intrinsically good'.[25]

It seems clear that this link between evil deeds and painful punishment is found in most major religious traditions, traditions that have surely informed our conventional thinking about crime and punishment. For example, the Bible is replete with any number of passages that make clear a connection between evil deeds and painful consequences. St Paul tells us that: 'God will be the just Judge of all the world. He will give each one whatever his deeds deserve ... he will terribly punish those who ... walk in evil ways ... He will punish sin wherever it is found'.[26] We find God punishing those who do evil to the degree they deserve. Of course, in this example, God's punishment is distributed on Judgement Day when the world comes to an end. His punishment is not given to us today in our earthly existence, but awaits us upon our death. In some respects, retributivist punishment is a more complex theory that attempts much that is set out in the passage above, such as punishing us for our evil deeds to the degree we deserve. However, neither adequately sets out why pain is necessary. The claim is that pain is a necessary response to evil actions because God has decreed it. Whether or not we accept this claim is a matter of personal faith. However, with retributivists, that we must fight evil with pain for its own sake seems equally an article of faith.

Strict equality

Classic retributivists, such as Kant, argue in favour of strict equality between the evil in our criminal act and the pain of our punishment. Recall the passage we discussed earlier by him that 'whatever undeserved evil you inflict upon another within the people, you inflict upon yourself ... if you kill him, you kill yourself'.[27] The argument is not simply that what we do unto others should be done to us. It can be formulated differently, namely, the wickedness of crime is *equal* to the harm of punishment. We, thus, repay an evil act with evil.

It is first worth pointing out that a standard criticism of strict equality is false, namely, that it endorses overly harsh punishments.[28] Strict equality demands that I am punished only as much as I deserve, no more or less. It is not lenient because it does not justify a weaker punishment than I deserve. Yet, it is also not harsh because it does not justify a punishment greater than I deserve. By definition, strict equality retributivists cannot justify harsh punishments. It may be the case that strict equality may justify punishments we find objectionable, such as the death penalty. However, if we can demonstrate that a criminal does not deserve capital punishment, then we can prove that strict equality does not endorse punishments we find objectionable.[29]

There are some problems with strict equality worth noting. First, it is unclear that the wickedness of crimes and their punishments are of a similar character. The evil of crime and its punishment seem two different things. Crime is an evil that ought not be done, whereas punishment ought to be done as a matter of justice. Another way of putting this point is to argue that crimes and punishments are different in character for a different reason: what can serve as a crime and a punishment differ. For example, it is a crime to rape another or engage in bestiality with an animal. However, the acts of rape and bestiality are crimes, not punishment: no one claims we should rape prisoners or engage in animal abuse. So the *varieties* of wickedness that are crimes are different *in kind* from the varieties of punishment we use in response to crimes.

A second problem is that it is unclear why two wrongs should equal a right. If both crime and punishment are evil, then it seems we might opt for less evil in the world and forgo punishment and, thus, bypass retributivism and choose a different response to crime.

Another problem is more practical: do states impose punishments that criminals deserve? Some philosophers have argued forcefully that they do not.[30] A common feature of all modern common law systems is plea bargaining. In plea bargaining, the accused admits guilt for a lesser offence, receiving a lesser punishment than she would otherwise 'deserve', all things considered. The state justifies this on consequentialist grounds: in coming to an agreement between the state and the offender, a trial is avoided, as well as taxpayers' money and the courts' time. In fact, far less than 10 per cent of all criminal cases result in a full trial. All retributivists have broad misgivings over plea bargaining and pardons. In these cases, the criminal does not receive his just deserts: he is not punished to the degree his crime deserves.[31] This is most acute for strict equivalence retributivists as we find that in the vast majority of cases criminals are punished less than they deserve. Perhaps strict equivalence proponents must argue for all criminals to stand trial, spiralling the costs of criminal justice. The fact is that modern common law states are highly unlikely to conform to this demand. Thus, not only does strict equality suffer from a number of problems already highlighted, but it is also impractical.

A final problem is the impossibility of ascertaining strict equality. This problem takes two forms. First, it is perhaps arguable that strict equality entails executing a murderer, but what is entailed in punishing a thief or a con artist? Do we steal our money back from the thief? Do we force the con artist into a trick? How do we punish the rapist if raping him is unacceptable to us? Strict equality is unhelpful beyond language like 'eye for an eye', 'a tooth for a tooth', or a 'life for a life'. When we ask about punishing the overwhelming majority of crimes, such as burglary, theft, rape, and others, we lack answers. The second problem pertains to our previous discussion of intentions. If we can only have our best guess of another's desert, then we may have a good sense of how deserving another is of punishment. However, strict equality does not demand that we merely discern a ballpark estimate of criminal desert. Instead, it demands that we accurately ascertain desert: we do the criminal an injustice if we believe his desert too little or too much as in both cases we will fail to punish his crime with a punishment that is in strict proportion. Strict equality is a position that retributivists no longer defend due to these many concerns.

Desert within limits

The view that has taken strict equality's place as the retributivist position of choice can be called 'desert within limits'. Desert sets an upper ceiling on the severity of punishment, although punishment need not ever be set at this maximum amount and may well fall below. We punish persons to the degree they deserve within certain limits. This view rejects our ability to punish with strict equality, as well as the ability of philosophy to tell us *exactly* how much punishment is justified. For example, if someone assaults another in the street, these retributivists will argue that a given range of punishment may be justified. It is not the case that 354 days in prison is *less* just than 355 days in prison. Such narrow distinctions are beyond penal theory. Instead, what we can do is we say that perhaps more than 400 days' imprisonment is too much and a sentence of less than two weeks' imprisonment too little, depending upon the circumstances. A range of acceptable punishments are available: no one acceptable punishment is less justified than another. On this view, retributivism justifies a range of potentially equal just punishments for a crime above a threshold and below a ceiling.

The promise of this perspective is its acknowledgement of the need for some discretion. If we are punishing persons to the degree they deserve, then we need the discretion to account for the many particularities of a specific case. It would be a mistake to set the punishment for all assaults as a single sentence and force it on all convicted assaulters. The mistake is that setting out in advance the punishment of others may not cohere with what they deserve. If persons are not getting what they deserve, then the punishment is not retributively justified.

One problem with this view is that it is unclear why we should accept limits in the first place. If what matters is a criminal's desert, then it seems pointless to set limits on how he might be punished *independently* of assessing his desert. We might argue that whether a car thief should earn five years imprisonment should be determined by an assessment of his desert and not the use of discretion within a pre-set range of options.

A second problem concerns how clearly lines may be drawn. For example, G. W. F. Hegel argues that retribution can aim for nothing more than 'an approximate fulfilment'.[32] So perhaps a retributivist cannot argue with confidence that a criminal deserves only 100 days in prison, no less and no more. Instead, retributivism justifies an approximation, such as three to six months. We are to work out for ourselves which specific amount within this justified range is most appropriate for an offender given the particular circumstances. But the problem is this: if we cannot do better than offer an approximation, then where are lines to be drawn? Perhaps sentences between three and six months are justified, but how are we to determine that two months would be too few or seven months too many from the standpoint of retributivist desert? There may be many pragmatic reasons to draw lines of different sorts. We might worry that like cases are treated too differently. But what is *too* different if approximations are the best we can offer? This is not a problem for other theories of punishment. For example, a deterrent theorist might find that only punishments within a specific range best ensure deterrence. How do we know which range best ensures desert satisfaction? This problem of retributivist approximation is about the 'intrinsic uncertainty' concerning the relative justice and injustice of borderline cases.[33] This is not an argument against retributivism, but a problem for how we draw lines between what is 'deserved' and what is not.

Pay back

A different retributivist position holds that when we punish a deserving criminal, the criminal 'pays back' an owed debt stemming from his crime. The view that criminals repay their crimes in being punished may derive from retributivism's Latin roots, *re* and *tribuo*, meaning 'to pay back'.[34] We see this as well in how we speak of criminals: we claim that we want to see them 'pay' for their offence.

The trouble with this view is that it is difficult to make sense of punishment as repayment beyond a metaphor. For example, how does a criminal 'pay back' anyone else when serving six months imprisonment for a victimless crime? All retributivism demands is that a criminal be punished for his crime to the degree he deserves. The criminal does not owe a debt as such. It is then difficult to see how punishment might serve as a repayment for what he owes.

Unfair advantage

Other retributivists claim that we punish criminals to the degree that they deserve in order to remove their unfair advantage. Most of us obey the law and this constrains our interactions. The criminal chooses to avoid such constraints and take advantage of his disobeying the law for his own benefit. For example, the criminal may choose to ignore laws protecting property and break into my home to steal my possessions. The thief has benefited from breaking the law: he has stolen my possessions. Punishment should aim to remove this unfair advantage he unlawfully enjoys.

A problem with this view is that it is not always clear that criminals enjoy any advantage in committing crimes, especially *mala in se* crimes. We would not want to say that the rapist or the murderer is enjoying an advantage over others. Instead, we would claim that they do harm to themselves in choosing evil, becoming a person of defamed character.

The position that we should endeavour to remove unfair advantages is more defensible if it claimed no more than that criminals should be punished for illegal acts. We all are obliged to follow our state's laws. Those who choose to disobey our laws act unfairly and should be punished. This view can be defended, but not on the grounds that criminals are enjoying a privilege in choosing evil. Even a liberal may admit that our laws should be designed to best enable all citizens to flourish, even if the laws constrain what we are permitted to do. However, this view is more defensible because it does away with the position we should remove unfair *advantages* with the removal of *unfairness*. Thinking of retributivist punishments as removing unfair advantage continues to appear problematic.

Annulment

A variation of the view that punishment should remove an'unfair advantage claims instead that punishment should annul crime. This view has been attributed to Hegel, although it is questionable whether he truly endorsed it.[35] Nevertheless, we can find passages where Hegel at least appears to endorse such a position. For example, Hegel says: 'The cancellation of crime is *retribution* in so far as the latter, by its concept, is an infringement of an infringement'.[36] The argument is that retributivist punishment is not merely a *response* to crime, but a *cancellation* of crime. We annul crime when we punish it properly.

The general idea does have something appealing about itself. When a criminal breaks the law, he does something wrong. Punishment should fix the damage caused and restore what was lost. Indeed, Hegel refers to the punishment of crime as 'the restoration of right'.[37] If we did not punish crimes, criminal actions and lawful actions would live side by side. That is, there would be no substantive difference between lawful and unlawful acts if neither were punished. When we choose to punish, we choose to prioritize lawful acts over crime; we defend our rights in punishing those who violate them.

The problem with this view of retributivism as annulment is that it seems impossible to enact. Perhaps a thief who steals our purse might return it to us intact and undamaged. Perhaps someone who broke our fence can restore it to its previous condition. Beyond a small handful of cases, talk of 'annulling' or 'cancelling' crime seems more metaphoric than real. How do we 'cancel' murder when we cannot bring the dead back to life? Why think we can 'annul' an assault on me when no one can reverse the pain I feel in recovering from treatment and weeks lost in recuperation? If a woman is impregnated by a rapist, how exactly can such a horrific experience be 'cancelled'? There is something appealing about punishment reversing time, allowing us to live life again as if a crime had not taken place. The problem is that once crime has occurred, it might be dealt with but probably not reversed entirely. Perhaps we may restore rights, but we cannot turn back the clock.

Proportional retributivism

It is particularly common for retributivists to argue that retributivism sets punishment in proportion to crime, but that it does this in a particular way. They claim we should rank separately crimes and punishments in terms of 'value', punishing a crime with the lowest value with the punishment having the lowest value, and then likewise with other values of crimes.[38] For example, Jeffrey Reiman says:

Proportional retributivism, then, in requiring that the worst crime be punished by the society's worst punishment and so on, could be understood as translating the offender's just desert into its nearest equivalent in *the society*'s table of morally acceptable punishments.[39]

The problem is that how punishments get chosen as possible penalties for crimes is not performed in a retributivist way. As Reiman points out, the appropriate punishment for a crime is not chosen on account of the criminal's particular action as such. Instead, punishments are selected in accordance with considerations entirely alien and indifferent to the criminal's individual act. That is, society may choose punishments that are most 'morally acceptable' to them. However, it may well be that a criminal deserves a punishment that is not acceptable to the society. Perhaps the society can then justify punishing the criminal differently than retributivism demands. Nevertheless, we cannot claim to be retributivists while refusing to punish criminals to the degree their crimes deserve. Whether or not proportional retributivism appropriately links crime and punishment seems more an issue of luck.

An example may make this worry more clear. Suppose we list six acts as crimes, such as murder, rape, freedom of expression, assault, illegal parking, and arson. We then list six different punishments, such as torture, death, lifetime imprisonment, 15 years imprisonment, 10 years imprisonment, and £50 fine. These lists include crimes we might find objectionable and would not criminalize (e.g., freedom of thought) as well as include punishments we might find objectionable and would not impose on offenders (e.g., torture). We next rank them each most serious or severe to least serious or severe. For example, we might rank crimes by increasing seriousness beginning with illegal parking and moving to more serious crimes such as theft, assault with a weapon, and murder. We might also rank punishments in a similar way, such as starting with a monetary fine and leading to lifetime imprisonment.

Proportional retributivists next link together the most serious crimes with the most severe punishment through to the least serious and severe crimes and punishments. In this case, we link the least severe crime – illegal parking – with the least severe punishment – a monetary fine. The result is that illegal parking should be punished by a fine. We also link the most severe crime and punishment on our lists to determine that murder should be punished by lifetime imprisonment. Similarly, we link crimes and punishments between these two extremes in the same way. The attractiveness of this approach is that proportional retributivism is able to provide us with a clear method of linking acceptable crimes with acceptable punishments. We will avoid imposing unjustified crimes and overly harsh punishments because we can remove them from our lists before linking proportionate crimes and punishments we accept. There is perhaps much to be said for this position.

I hope that these illustrations help highlight the key problem with proportional retributivism, namely, that it is not clearly a retributivist theory of punishment. Retributivists link punishment with crime due to proportionality and desert. The connection between crime and punishment is internal: the degree of justified punishment is found in the desert of the criminal. This internal connection is lost with proportional retributivism. Do we punish a rapist with 15 years imprisonment because he *deserves* it? No, we punish him in this way because rape is the second most serious crime and 15 years imprisonment the second most severe punishment. If we added treason to the list ahead of rape, then rapists would merit a different punishment. The relationship between crime and punishment is external, beyond the strong link between desert and punishment that characterizes retributivism. We may still be persuaded by the claims of so-called 'proportional retributivists'. My point here is merely to say that this view does not merit the name 'retributivist'.

Negative retributivism

This brings us to a final perspective: negative retributivism. I will discuss this view in greater detail in chapter 5, but a few words can be said here first. This chapter has argued that retributivists claim a link between desert and proportionality: call this *the standard view* of retributivism. A majority of retributivists adhere to this view, although this chapter has also stressed that retributivists understand the relationship between desert and proportionality in several different ways. This view of retributivism is sometimes called 'positive' (or 'moral') retributivism.

A different view is 'negative' retributivism. Negative retributivists reject the link between desert and proportional punishment, but accept the view that desert is a necessary condition of punishment. They argue that punishment is only justified if someone deserves to be punished. However, the *severity* of punishment may be determined by factors beyond desert, such as favourable consequences. In this way, negative retributivists adopt only half of retributivism's traditional core: negative retributivists agree that we can only punish deserving persons (and not the innocent), but they reject the need to endorse proportionality in substituting different considerations in its place. This is an important break from traditional retributivism where 'the consequences of punishment are irrelevant'.[40]

As a result, a positive retributivist might punish a murderer more than a thief because the murderer is more deserving of a more severe punishment. The negative retributivist might also punish the murderer more than the thief, but on non-retributivist grounds, such as the need to protect the public or deterrence. Thus, both retributivisms might endorse similar punishments, but with different justifications. Likewise, both retributivisms might endorse quite dissimilar punishments. For example, a negative retributivist might punish a thief more than a positive retributivist if the safeguarding of public property necessitated disproportionate punishments for their protection, over and above what the thief would deserve otherwise. More importantly, the positive retributivist *must* punish a deserving criminal: if the criminal is not punished, then he will not receive what is deserved. Negative retributivists are not compelled to punish deserving persons: they need only *not* punish *un*deserving persons.

Negative retributivists avoid the problem of how to link crime and punishment through desert by taking the back door: they deny that any such link need exist. However, there seems a case to be answered given that most of us do think murderers deserve greater punishment than thieves precisely because greater punishment is deserved. Therefore, a criminal's desert should determine his just punishment. Avoiding the difficult question of how we decide such matters does not make the problem disappear.

Conclusion

It should now be clear why retributivism is both the best known and perhaps most misunderstood theory of punishment. It is best known because of its clear relationship with Biblical justice and perhaps also with our common sense or our everyday intuitions about justice. We believe criminals should be punished for what they have done in proportion to the evil they have performed. However, retributivists have a complex understanding of desert, proportionality, and how these lead us to justifying punishment, often taking any number of different forms. Each view has its shortcomings, but it does not take away from retributivism's primary hold on us today: any theory of punishment that permitted the punishment of the innocent would be implausible. Retributivism offers one important approach to explain why this is the case concerning the centrality of desert. The problem is how best to determine it. This problem leads to a further difficulty of determining whether retribution 'works'. This may yield as many answers as there are retributivist theories of punishment.

In the following chapters, we will examine competing theories of punishment. Each can be seen as a response to retributivism, often borrowing from it. All contemporary theories of punishment will attempt to show how they too punish only the deserving and without employing harsh punishments. We will now consider what these theories are and how well they perform this task.

2 Deterrence

Introduction

Deterrence has traditionally been understood as the primary alternative to retributivism. Both have been at loggerheads for literally centuries. It is easy to see why. Retributivists give special attention to a criminal's desert for a past injustice: it is primarily a backward-looking theory of punishment. Deterrence is primarily a forward-looking theory of punishment: deterrence proponents give special attention to deterring future criminality. Therefore, deterrence offers us a very different focus and understanding of the purpose of punishment. This chapter will clarify the leading theories of deterrence to determine their promise and potential problems.

What is deterrence?

Deterrence theories of punishment claim that the general justification of punishment is deterrence. Deterrence proponents argue that a key feature of punishment should be its ability to make crime less frequent, if not end. Punishment that merely harmed criminals and lacked any clear beneficial effects may even be seen as cruel. Instead, punishment may be justified on account of the good consequences that it makes possible. These may include deterrence of criminality.

Deterrence proponents have traditionally argued that people are deterred by the threat of punishment. Many classic defenders of deterrence have been utilitarians. Generally speaking, utilitarians argue that we seek pleasure and avoid pain. The threat of punishment is a pain to be avoided. Punishment deters because we want to avoid the pains of punishment. For example, David Hume argues:

> 'Tis indeed certain, that as all human laws are founded on rewards and punishments, 'tis suppos'd as a fundamental principle, that these motives have an influence on the mind, and both produce the good and prevent the evil actions.[1]

Utilitarians often assume that individuals are naturally selfish. We are influenced by external influences, not least social influences including the threat of punishment. The idea is that punishment may have a deterrent effect upon us because we are naturally selfish and we would normally choose to avoid the pain of punishment. We choose to be law abiding after making a rational choice calculus: the burdens of potential punishment outweigh the benefits from crime.

Deterrent punishment helps realize an important good. The political community has enacted a criminal law. If the criminal law is just, then it is right that we encourage others to act in accordance with it and avoid criminality. Punishment can play a positive role in protecting the security of us all in deterring potential criminals.[2] This idea has its roots in Plato's writings:

> It is appropriate for everyone who is subject to punishment rightly inflicted by another either to become better and profit from it, or else be made an example to others, so that when they see him suffering whatever it is he suffers, they may be afraid and become better.[3]

This defence of deterrence is shared by a great many today. For example, Ted Honderich argues that punishment 'may be acceptable simply because it deters'.[4] Acceptance of deterrence may lie in the beneficial consequences it might produce.

Deterrent punishments can take several forms, such as general or specific deterrence. General deterrence is often understood as the public threat of punishment and specific deterrence as the individual's experience of punishment. An alternative view of this distinction is between *macro-deterrence* (general deterrence) and *microdeterrence* (specific deterrence).[5] Macrodeterrence concerns society in general. It asks how we might best construct deterrent punishments for society at large. This analysis focuses on the crime and steps that could be taken to deter persons from crime. Macrodeterrence judges success on the basis of how well punishment acts as a general deterrence.

Microdeterrence focuses on the criminal. It asks how we might deter an individual from crime. This view finds expression in a brief essay by John Stuart Mill: 'You do not punish one person in order that another may be deterred. The other is deterred, not by the punishment of the first, but by the expectation of being punished himself'.[6] Microdeterrence judges success on the basis of how well punishment acts as a specific deterrent for particular individuals.

Macrodeterrence and microdeterrence offer different perspectives on how we might approach the construction of deterrent punishments. However, these different perspectives need not translate into conflicting viewpoints. Instead, the two should be understood as working together in approaching the same project from different angles. Furthermore, they may overlap so that general and specific deterrence may be achieved together.

The way we construct deterrent punishments may take several forms, such as fear, incapacitation, and reform. The first form is the traditional understanding of deterrence. Deterrent punishments are public threats: individuals are deterred from criminality by the fear of threatened punishment if they engage in criminality. This fear of threatened pain is what motivates individuals to remain law abiding. If the public is sufficiently afraid of threatened punishment, then the public will not offend.

The second form of constructing deterrent punishments is *incapacitation*. This view, first argued for by William Paley, has a long history as well.[7] The incapacitation approach argues that the criminal can be said to be deterred from criminality by virtue of his becoming imprisoned. For example, the idea is that all potential criminals have something in common: they are not imprisoned. Whatever prison's deterrent effects upon the general public, prison has an undeniable deterrent effect on imprisoned criminals: they cannot commit crimes while imprisoned. The incapacitation approach does suffer from at least two serious problems. The first is that it may compel us to imprison everyone. If our desired goal is to deter as much crime as we can and no imprisoned person can commit crime, then we can deter more crime by imprisoning more people. Moreover, we can deter all crime when we imprison (virtually) everyone.[8]

This position is highly objectionable because incapacitation is not reducible to punishment, nor vice versa.[9] Recall that we should understand punishment as a response to crime: punishment must be of a person for breaking the law. The first problem for incapacitation is that it might justify the imprisonment of innocent persons in order to prevent future crime. The second problem is that criminality does not stop at the prison gate: criminals can and do (and perhaps always have) committed crimes within prisons. Such crimes include assaults and abuse of controlled substances. Not only might incapacitation insufficiently guard against objectionable implications, but it rests on a mistake about *the geography of crime*, namely, that crimes are not confined to public places or private homes, but they may take place in prisons as well. Criminality is possible both within and outside prisons. A deterrent theory of punishment must recognize this fact about the geography of crime, a feature too often overlooked and unnoticed.[10]

A final form that deterrence might take is reform. Future criminality might be deterred because criminals have become reformed. I will highlight this further understanding of deterrence as reform in the next chapter.

Deterrence and crime reduction

Deterrence is about crime reduction, but not all crime reduction is evidence of deterrence. This is because deterrence is one approach amongst many to reduce crime. One method of crime reduction may be the rehabilitation of offenders. Rehabilitated offenders are reformed and refrain from future criminality, which assists crime reduction efforts. But this is not deterrence. Deterrence theories aim to reduce crime by deterring potential criminal offenders. They are deterred where they choose against crime because they desire to avoid punishment. Crime reduction may be a result of deterrence, but deterrence is not the only method for achieving crime reduction. It is important to recognize that deterrence is one of many penal strategies for achieving crime reduction because it highlights that there may be significant differences in how we approach crime reduction. So if there was evidence that crime has been reduced over a period of time, then this is not necessarily evidence that crime reduction was a result of deterrence. Deterrence may always aim at crime reduction, but not all crime reduction is a result of deterrence.

Deterrence and desert

The problem most commonly associated with deterrence is the problem of punishing the innocent: deterrence should be rejected because it could justify the punishment of innocent persons. This problem is frequently used by retributivists to argue that retribution should be preferred over deterrence because only retribution takes criminal desert seriously. Let me explain this debate further.

Retributivists argue – in what we might call *the standard view* – that punishment should be distributed only where it is deserved. Retribution is a deontological theory in that punishment is not justified by its effects, but desert. Deterrence is instead a consequentialist theory whereby punishment is justified where it has specific consequences, such as a deterrent effect. This difference gives rise to a disagreement about how we justify the punishment of criminals. One criticism of deterrence is that, as Hegel argues, 'to justify punishment in this way is like raising one's stick at a dog; it means treating a human being like a dog instead of respecting his honour and freedom'.[11] For critics like Hegel, deterrence fails to honour people in failing to offer them reasons for good citizenship and avoidance of criminality.

We might respond that this criticism misses its target. Deterrence does offer reasons to citizens to refrain from criminality: if citizens engage in crime, the state threatens to impose punishment. Nor need this be problematic where citizens believe. Deterrence proponents might also claim that retributivists are no better. Both declare that criminals will be punished in advance. One important difference is that deterrence proponents believe that the threat of punishment may have a deterrent effect. We should expect potential criminals to reconsider participating in criminal activity to avoid the possibility of punishment. Retributivists may accept a similar analysis. While retributivists might argue that the severity of punishment is not set with a view of any future deterrent effect, retributivists may still claim that the *wrongness* of a crime should weigh on the conscience of potential criminals and contribute to their reconsidering any criminal activity. Deterrence proponents are mistaken to believe that the only deterrent effect to be found is in the threat of punishment and not the gravity of a crime's wrongfulness.

Deterrence proponents might reply that its aim is to reduce criminal activity by rendering it sufficiently unattractive. One relevant factor will be the threat of punishment, but a second factor will be the criminal act itself. Citizens may find criminal activity unattractive because they wish to avoid the possibility of punishment, but also because they agree with the laws governing their relations. Cesare Beccaria says:

> What are the true and most effective laws? They are those pacts and conventions that everyone would observe and propose while the voice of private interest, which one always hears, is silent or in agreement with the voice of the public interest.[12]

The result is that perhaps deterrence does aim to manipulate the incentive structure for citizens in order to reduce crime. No plausible theory of punishment claims that criminal activity is desirable or good. If punishment could be used to reduce crime by winning the agreement of citizens and deterring potential criminals, then these should be compelling arguments in its favour.

This raises a deeper concern often raised by retributivists against deterrence. Let us accept that the reduction of crime is desirable or even good. The traditional argument against deterrence is that it might permit the punishment, or even execution, of the innocent. The objection is as follows. Deterrence proponents believe that punishment is justified, at least in part, by its deterrent effects. If these effects were obtained by punishing the innocent, then punishment would be justified because it would have a deterrent effect. If deterring potential criminals is what matters, then this does not rule out our only punishing criminals. The objection is that we should never punish the innocent for crimes they did not commit. Deterrence is an objectionable penal aim because it might justify punishing innocent people.

This concern is not lost on leading proponents of deterrence. In fact, it is difficult to find any major figure who accepts the possibility of punishing the innocent under any circumstances: the worry that deterrence approaches would lead to the punishment of the innocent is largely a criticism about deterrence approaches and not a policy that deterrence proponents espouse. All place clear limits on how deterrence should be pursued. Examples abound. Plato argues that the criminal should receive 'due punishment for the wrongdoing he commits'.[13] Fichte similarly claims that 'in a well-governed state, no innocent person should ever be punished'.[14] Bentham likewise rejects the punishment of the innocent.[15] Beccaria is a possible exception. He argues it is necessary to execute an innocent person if his death was 'the *only* real way of restraining others from committing crimes'.[16] However, this is not much of a concession to critics of deterrence approaches if we believed that such cases might be so rare as to be virtually non-existent.

We might then argue that deterrence theories are at best impure. Each would appear to accept some retributivist core that punishment must first be deserved before it can be punished and never imposed on the innocent. The difference would then appear to be that deterrence theories link the severity of punishment with expected future effects rather than the gravity of a crime's wrongfulness. If true, then these deterrent theories might be understood as *negative retributivist* theories of punishment. Negative retributivists argue that desert is necessary, but not sufficient for punishment. Punishment is distributed where other non-desert factors obtain.[17]

Deterrence proponents need not accept that their 'deterrence' theories are in fact a species of retributivism. Another compelling perspective is the following.[18] The state issues threats: if citizens perform a crime, then they will be punished for it. The state then punishes those persons who have failed to heed such threats.[19] So the state only punishes those persons who have failed to obey its threats and, thus, the state aims to deter without punishing the innocent. The state punishes to make good on its original threat to punish crimes: these threats would lack substance if the state failed to make good on its promise. Only those who break the law are subject to punishment: 'The threat is addressed to each individually, and each is punished because he, individually, chose to ignore the threat; the others, and their potential behaviour, are irrelevant'.[20] This understanding of deterrence punishes only the guilty, but not on grounds of desert. Deterrence theories can avoid justifying the punishment of innocent people.

One final consideration is criminals who resist deterrence: *the problem of the undeterrable.* Retributivists, on the standard view, would punish the undeterrable because punishment is deserved. Future consequences are irrelevant. This is untrue for deterrence, where future consequences take centre stage. The undeterrable are not a major problem for theories of macrodeterrence: while some may not be deterred, punishment may be justified where it leads to reductions in crime for the general population. The situation is different with the microdeterrence of an individual offender. If a person is genuinely resistant to changing his behaviour in response to any deterrent efforts, then specific deterrence would fail in like cases. The problem of undeterrable criminals raises an important difficulty for microdeterrence accounts. If certain persons cannot be deterred, then punishment is not justified because it will not have any deterrent effect on them. Punishment might only be justified on grounds of macrodeterrence were it possible to have a deterrent effect on others, or the deterrable.

Deterrence and difference

Deterrence theories of punishment aim to deter potential criminals from criminality. Our focus is on constructing a suitable deterrent for members of a political community. This is a consequentialist approach: the deterrent proponent aspires to secure a particular consequence, namely, reduced criminality. The target is the political community and this raises several potential problems concerning *the problem of difference*.

The first potential problem is that we cannot hope to find any *single* punishment that might have the same deterrent effect for everyone everywhere. A penal threat may have a greater effect upon you than me. There are several reasons why this is the case. One reason is that deterrence is specific to local social conditions: what works as a deterrent in one political community may lack a similar effect in other communities. So a punishment may have a different deterrent effect or none at all in different political communities. Furthermore, this problem may not merely exist between political communities, but it may also exist within political communities. Call this *the problem of domestic difference*. Some social groups within the same political community may respond differently to the same deterrent threats. A second reason why deterrent punishments may differ between communities is that deterrence is linked with particular crimes and these crimes may differ from one community to the next. Therefore, deterrent punishments for crimes may not hold universally where there is disagreement between different political communities on what is included within the criminal law. This is only a problem for a global theory of deterrent punishment: deterrence may only be a genuine possibility within a political community.

The second potential problem is that what may deter today may not deter tomorrow. This is *the problem of time and changing effects*. Whatever knowledge we have of deterrent effects is always knowledge of the past: the owl of Minerva takes flight at dusk.[21] The fact that some were deterred last year or even yesterday may be no guarantee that we can expect a similar number to be deterred today or next month. The deterrent power of punishment constantly changes over time in response to social conditions. Therefore, the deterrent potential of any punishment is always in flux and subject to constant change. One problem is that this potential may only be known after the fact; the deterrent potential of present punishments is always a matter of guesswork to some degree. We can never say that any one punishment is always best to maximize the deterrence of potential criminals for any crime. This is because we can only guess at likely future effects and these effects are subject to constant revision.

The use of the same punishment may have different deterrent effects in different communities and be subject to constant change over time. These issues highlight the deep complexity associated with deterrence and the challenges for presenting global theories of deterrence. These concerns do not entail that we cannot know whether there are deterrent effects from the threat of punishment, but rather that such knowledge is complex and difficult to acquire.

The data on deterrence

Deterrence proponents offer a theory of punishment linked to empirical claims. They argue not only *that* punishment should be designed to bring about deterrence, but that punishment *has* a deterrent effect. Deterrence is an evidence-based approach to criminal justice. So what do the data reveal?

The big problem for deterrence theories is that punishment does not appear to have much, if any, confirmed deterrent effect.[22] There is much disagreement about the best measures of deterrence and indications of success or failure, but several conclusions have become established in recent years concerning criminals who have been imprisoned. Many reoffend upon release. For example, most criminals who are imprisoned receive sentences of 12 months or less. Approximately 60 per cent will reoffend and often within weeks of release.[23] One study of American prisoners released since 1994 found that two-thirds were arrested for a serious misdemeanour or felony within three years, and half of these were reconvicted for new crimes. The study concluded that 'no evidence was found that spending more time in prison raises the recidivism rate'.[24]

These results have been confirmed in several international studies which have also cast doubt on whether there is any link between time served and reoffending.[25] For example, the British Prime Minister's Strategy Unit has concluded that 'there is no convincing evidence that further increases in the use of custody would significantly reduce crime'.[26] Increasing prison sentences may be popular with the public, but the evidence is that such policies place greater pressures on taxpayers for no substantive improvements upon recidivism rates. The public may often support 'tough on crime' policies whereby penal tariffs rise ever higher, but such support lacks sufficient evidence that it works. The main consequence is much higher costs without improvements in crime reduction.[27]

Perhaps surprisingly, even threats of severe punishment have not been conclusively shown to possess a deterrent effect, and decreased offending has not been strongly linked with increasing the severity of punishments.[28] One example is California's so-called 'Three Strikes and You're Out' law. This motto refers to baseball where a batter is 'out' after receiving three strikes. Anyone convicted of a third strike-eligible crime faces a minimum 25 year imprisonment. This is irrespective of the seriousness of the crimes committed. It might be expected that – even if an unreasonable policy – such a high penal tariff would have some clear deterrent effect, but the findings are surprising. The deterrent effect appears small and is estimated at about 2 per cent or less.[29] The policy has led to an explosion in the prison population and contributed to the further problem of prison overcrowding.[30] Thus, even fairly severe threats of punishment have not conclusively demonstrated a clear deterrent effect, but these penal experiments have contributed to ever higher costs for little, if any, public benefit.

A common criticism is that imprisoning criminals makes them better criminals. For example, criminals may be thought to become transformed into *criminal labourers* through imprisonment: the 'professional' thief, for example. Some claim that imprisonment may even be *criminogenic* because it may contribute to more crime and not less.[31] The contributing problems are that imprisonment often leads to offenders 'losing their jobs, their homes and their families'.[32] While we would expect those with the longest prison sentences to be most likely to reoffend, this is not supported by most evidence. Most released prisoners will reoffend, but these persons often serve sentences of less than one year. Recidivism rates drop for all criminals serving more than one year in prison: the longer a criminal is imprisoned, the less likely he is to reoffend upon release. This may have more to do with the crimes associated with longer sentences and the greater professional support these inmates can expect to receive, as well as the age of offenders upon release. It is worth noting that criminals given suspended sentences and community sentences reoffend less often than criminals imprisoned for under a year.[33] If our aim is to reduce crime rates, then the use of prison may be counterproductive. This may be counterintuitive: we might expect the burdens of imprisonment to deter better than community service, but deterrence proponents must support policies that best meet their preferred penal goals. If alternatives to prison work best, then these alternatives should be endorsed.

None of this need deny that crime rates have ever fallen. Instead, the issue is that where we find lower crime rates there are often non-deterrence factors to account for such changes.[34] For example, there is evidence that crime rates may be linked to the number of males aged between 15 and 24 years: the greater the number of males, the higher the expected crime rates.[35] There is also evidence that increased economic insecurity leads to both rising crime rates and a greater public fear of crime. It has been claimed that 'individuals who are worried about their economic stability may be more likely to fear criminals, who could further threaten their increasingly tenuous economic positions'.[36] Furthermore, Steven Levitt and Stephen Dubner argue:

> It is true that a stronger job market may make certain crimes relatively less attractive. But that is only the case for crimes with a direct financial motivation—burglary, robbery, and auto theft—as opposed to violent crimes like homicide, assault, and rape. Moreover, studies have shown that an unemployment decline of 1 percentage point accounts for a 1 percent drop in nonviolent crime.[37]

One clear result is that a strong job creation strategy ensuring low unemployment rates is not only good economics, but a good criminal justice policy leading to lower crime rates and lower public fear of crime.

Not all studies have failed to find substantive deterrent effects. However, these studies often conclude that these effects are modest at best. For example, the results often reveal that the effects of deterrence upon crime rates is at most between about a 2 to 5 per cent decrease in crime following a 10 per cent increase in the prison population.[38] If this is true, then prison may have an identifiable deterrent effect. However, the effects do not appear large and come at a significant cost to taxpayers.

Judging success

Discussions about the data on deterrence inevitably raise important questions about what constitutes 'success' for any deterrence theory of punishment. We have at least three options:

(1) Deterrent theories of punishment aim for any deterrent effect.
(2) Deterrent theories of punishment aim for any substantial effect.
(3) Deterrent theories of punishment aim for a complete effect.

The first option is too weak and the third is too strong. The first option claims that the aims of deterrent punishment are satisfied where *any* deterrent effect may be identified. This is too weak. Suppose we have two different punishments. The difference between them is that one punishment is known to deter a small handful and the other punishment lacks any known effect. The deterrence proponent would seem compelled to prefer a punishment with *any* deterrent effect over an alternative that *lacked* any effect. But would this remain true if a very small effect were only made possible by way of inflicting great pain? The deterrence proponent is not a retributivist: she does not link a punishment's severity with what is deserved, but rather what has a deterrent effect. But this is not quite right. Deterrence proponents argue that deterrence is a central justification of punishment. Therefore, deterrence should not have a mere negligible presence, but it should play a clearer role in punishing. If deterrence is the justification of punishment, then it must also play some clear – and not merely tangential – role. Deterrence is *reductivist*: its goal is the reduction of crime. A deterrent approach that can promise no more than little, if any, reduction in crime is not much worth its name.

The third option is too strong. While we may hope that a great many will be deterred from criminality, we cannot expect our hope will be realized. There is a little appreciated fact about crime that I call *the fact of crime in society*. It is a fact that any society will have crime if it has a criminal law. This fact is not always recognized by proponents of deterrence. For example, Johann Gottlieb Fichte argues:

Punishment is not an absolute end ... Punishment is a means for achieving the state's end, which is public security; and its only purpose is to prevent offenses by threatening to punish them. The end of penal law is to render itself unnecessary. The threat of punishment aims to ... never be necessary.[39]

However noble its aim of seeing punishment wither on the vine one day, it is pure fantasy to believe that crime will ever disappear so long as we are governed by the rule of law.[40] Laws are not made to be broken, but are broken inevitably nonetheless by carelessness as well as design. There is little point in creating *a utopia of crimelessness*, but much promise in aspiring to restrict the fact of crime in society as best as is possible. Penal theorists may disagree on the ultimate justification of punishment, but they should all prefer less crime and lower recidivism.

The fact that crime is ever present does not mean we should accept crime however it is found. Deterrence proponents should not be satisfied with punishments with negligible deterrent effects nor aspire to full or 'perfect' deterrence. Instead, deterrence proponents defend deterrence as a substantial consequence of justified punishment. This leads us to endorse the second option. A successful deterrence theory is one that can demonstrate a substantial deterrent effect. So what would such an effect look like? It is difficult to pinpoint any specific figure, but surely 2–5 per cent falls far below any plausible indication of a 'substantial deterrent effect'. Nevertheless, our knowledge about the deterrence effects, if any, for any crime is 'exceedingly thin'.[41]

Deterrence, intuitions, and knowledge limits

Many deterrence proponents naturally assume that punishment has a deterrent effect notwithstanding contrary findings by existing studies. For example, James Q. Wilson says:

People are governed in their daily lives by rewards and penalties of every sort ... To assert that 'deterrence doesn't work' is tantamount to either denying the plainest facts of everyday life or claiming that would-be criminals are utterly different from the rest of us.[42]

It is assumed that we, the community, know the laws that govern us. Ignorance of the law is no defence from future punishment.[43] It is also assumed that the burdens of punishment should outweigh expected benefits from possible criminal activity. Where this obtains, individuals engaged in a cost-benefit analysis will rationally choose to avoid crime. It would be irrational to commit a crime where the costs outweigh expected benefits. The deterrent effect of punishment is intuitively true. Evidence to the contrary is opposed to our most basic intuitions about criminal justice. Or so deterrence proponents may argue.

There are many reasons why this intuitive justification of deterrence is problematic. First, there is little evidence to suggest that criminals weigh costs and benefits in the way many deterrence models assume.[44] Criminals appear to rely on little more than guesswork about their possible likelihood of arrest and conviction.[45] But this is not all. In short, deterrence may assume too much. Michael Davis says: "'Deterrent' does not have any relation to actual or probable crime without assumptions about the rationality of criminals, the efficiency of police, the likelihood that the penalty will not itself make the crime glamorous, and so on'.[46] How many people would have stolen a car last week, if the laws had been different? How many people were deterred from any crime because of any specific legislation? If punishment deters criminals, then it might be possible to have some idea about how to answer these questions. Yet, such answers remain elusive.[47]

For example, deterrence presupposes knowledge about crimes, possible sanctions, the likelihood of arrest and conviction. There are many reasons to believe these articles of faith do not cohere with reality. First, only a few citizens will have knowledge about even a majority of crimes and perhaps no one knows them all. If citizens are to conduct a rational choice assessment weighing the costs and burdens of criminal activity, then they must have satisfactory knowledge about what counts as criminal activity. Most lack this knowledge. Punishment fails to serve its deterrent function where citizens do not know what is criminalized. Perhaps punishment might have a more limited deterrent function on a crime-by-crime basis. For example, many may be unaware about the full range of property crimes, but many will know that murder is criminalized. Punishment may only have a deterrent function for those crimes that citizens have sufficiently satisfactory knowledge about. The problem is that citizens lack such knowledge about most crimes.[48] Citizens cannot be deterred from crimes that they are unaware of.

Second, citizens lack knowledge about most crimes *and* they lack knowledge about possible sanctions for most crimes. This is perhaps a more serious problem than the first. While citizens may not know all crimes, they might still identify a plentiful core acknowledging arson, burglary, murder, and theft amongst others. However, their knowledge of what possible sanctions would relate from a conviction for any of these crimes is even worse. I have lectured on criminal law and punishment in several countries and before many distinguished audiences: not once has anyone been able to correctly identify the tariff for arson for any jurisdiction.[49] Can you? This is despite the fact that all recognize arson as a serious crime. If academics, lawyers, and policymakers are unsure about how arson might be punished, then there is reason to believe the lay public would perform no better. The problem is that punishment cannot have a deterrent effect where citizens do not know how their crimes might be punished.

Third, suppose we possess satisfactory knowledge about crimes and their possible punishments. We would still require satisfactory knowledge *in addition to this* about the likelihood of our arrest and conviction. The facts are startling: the majority of crimes are unsolved. Murders have the highest detection rates, but these are often no better than about 80 per cent. Do you know the likelihood of your being arrested or convicted for benefit fraud or illegal trading? Or for any crime? Punishment cannot have a deterrent effect where citizens do not know crimes, how their crimes might be punished, the likelihood of arrest for crimes, nor the likelihood of punishment.

There is a further issue concerning imprisonment. Many prisoners remain imprisoned beyond their official release date. There are an estimated 2,500 prisoners in the UK alone in this position. The justification is that they remain imprisoned because they have been found to remain a threat to the general public.[50] It is unclear whether or not this improves future deterrence for crimes that may involve imprisonment. On the one hand, this may be relatively unknown by persons potentially affected and so not enter into risk calculations about engaging in crime. On the other hand, the possibility that a prison sentence represents a minimal term and may be for life could have a potential deterrent effect if it is communicated effectively to persons potentially affected. It is perhaps shocking how little effort governments expend on informing the public about possible criminal sanctions. Whatever the reality of deterrence, there is a clear need for improved communication between governments and their citizens to better educate them about criminal punishment.

Many deterrence proponents claim that it is at least intuitively true that punishment has a deterrent effect. We have seen that few studies have shown any substantial deterrent effect. Furthermore, there is little reason to believe that citizens could be deterred by punishment for most crimes. This is because citizens lack sufficient relevant knowledge necessary for deterrence to obtain. Citizens do not know most crimes, know less about possible punishments for crimes, and know little, if anything, about the likelihood for arrest and conviction. It is clear that there is a need for greater communication about such matters with the general public to improve their knowledge in these areas. The intuitive evidence for deterrence seems limited to persons with perfect information about crimes, punishments, and other factors that no one has in fact. The conclusion to be drawn is not that deterrence is impossible, but rather that it is substantially more difficult to determine and perceive than we may initially recognize. Nevertheless, there remains something attractive about a society where crime reduction works, all things considered. But whether crime reduction should be achieved through deterrence or an alternative approach is another consideration.

Should government deter?

Consider the proper role of government. Should government deter? This concern may take many forms, such as whether governments should endorse some alternative justification of punishment. I do not want to address such matters here, but instead focus on a very specific concern that is often overlooked in discussions about deterrence. Surprisingly, this concern arises within the writings of John Stuart Mill, an advocate of deterrence. He offers the following worry: 'the preventive function of government, however, is far more liable to be abused'.[51] Perhaps governments should deter. The problem is this power is most likely to become abused.

Let me address this worry in the following way. It may be argued that a central task of any government is enforcing its laws. The government will have a clear interest in addressing criminality. Deterrence is one way of addressing criminality: governments should address criminality by deterring it, leading to crime reduction. One classic objection to deterrence is that governments fail to treat their citizens with the dignity that they deserve. Deterrence measures may lead governments to treating their citizens as a means to some goal rather than an end in their own right.

We might reply that we use people as a means all the time.[52] For instance, we use taxi drivers to take us to our destinations or we use waitresses to serve us our meals and so on. The question is not whether we use others, but rather whether we use others in a justifiable way.[53] There is a difference between paying another for a consensual service and demanding someone is imprisoned. Nevertheless, this difference does not reflect a problem with the respect of dignity for the imprisoned. Respect can be secured in our ensuring a person is only imprisoned for criminality: no person need be treated merely as a means by deterrence theories of punishment. Thus, deterrence can address people as moral agents and deterrence need not be understood as little better than addressing people like animals.[54]

Mill's worry is not that deterrence denies dignity to others, but that deterrence is more liable to abuse by governments than alternative theories of punishment. Recall that there is a link between the justification of law and the justification of punishment: *there can be no justified punishment for an unjustified law*.[55] If laws are justified, then it becomes possible to justify punishment for criminality. One problem is that governments may use greater threats to deter persons from violating unjustified laws. This might make a bad situation much worse.

Let me explain this point further. Suppose, following Cesare Beccaria, that deterrent punishments should aim to 'make the strongest and most lasting impression on the minds of men, and inflict the least torment on the body of the criminal'.[56] If our aim is to make the biggest impression with the least damage to the criminal, then perhaps our use of punishment should aspire to mislead the public into believing punishments are much worse than they are. This brings us to a famous illustration by Jeremy Bentham: 'If hanging a man *in effigy* would produce the same salutary impression of terror upon the minds of people, it would be a folly or cruelty ever to hang a man *in person*'.[57] The *effect* from punishment is of crucial significance for deterrence proponents. If this effect might be gained without harming anyone through punishment, then such an alternative may prove tempting. Deterrence does not aim to be cruel, but to reduce crime, and such an alternative might fulfil this ambition.

Beccaria argues that 'it is better to prevent crimes than to punish them'.[58] If this is true, then the state may be tempted to broadcast mock punishment in attempts to mislead the public. But this need not be the only result. Instead, governments might attempt to reduce crime without resorting to misleading the public. One reason would be concerns about the likely impact of the public gaining knowledge about any deceit. Mock executions may prove effective where the public are deceived, but backfire catastrophically where the public learn the truth about such matters. Many governments have moved to a greater emphasis on strict liability with the easier convictions this approach brings, albeit for often relatively minor punishments. While governments have many reasons to reduce crime, most do not appear to run afoul of Mill's warning about the likelihood of the abuse of power in the pursuit of prevention strategies. This does not conclusively prove that government should deter, but instead offers some evidence to believe that Mill's warning is not a deciding objection against deterrence.

Conclusion

This chapter has considered the problems and prospects of deterrence approaches. The problems are considerable. First, there is little evidence that deterrence works in any substantive sense. Most studies show limited, if negligible, effects for even severe threats of punishment. Second, there is little evidence that intuitive judgements about deterrence hold much water. These judgements rest upon various assumptions about the knowledge people have about criminal justice that they do not possess. Where we find reduced crime rates, there are often other factors that seem best to explain these changes.

There is also a curious paradox. The public strongly support a 'tough on crime' approach despite a lack of evidence that this approach has any significant beneficial effects. In fact, voters are more likely to vote for candidates who claim a 'tough on crime' policy even where those voters might otherwise favour alternative approaches, such as rehabilitation. Deterrence theories of punishment claim justification because they lead to crime reduction. The problem is that the evidence is inconclusive at best and perhaps even counterintuitive.

There are also clear prospects. The fact that conclusive evidence is lacking does not entail that no evidence can be found, but only that the jury is still out. People may have limited knowledge about criminal justice, but so then we might rely on a more modest understanding of how deterrence might apply. The threat of punishment is clearly one possible factor for potential criminals to desist from engaging in crime. Moreover, crime reduction is desirable: we would prefer a society with less crime to others, all things considered.

The project of deterrence may prove more challenging to offer than its defenders have claimed, but it remains an approach to punishment of real importance.

3   Rehabilitation

Introduction

Rehabilitation is the major alternative theory of punishment to retribution and deterrence. Its popularity has decreased over the last few decades. There was an explosion in interest from academics and public policymakers during the 1960s, which began to decline in the late 1970s. This fall in interest is partly explained by the public's growing impatience concerning conclusive findings that rehabilitation was more effective than other punitive approaches at crime reduction combined with the concern that rehabilitation is too lenient. Rehabilitation theories have been making a comeback, sometimes now referred to as the 'New Rehabilitation' although the aims and methods are broadly similar.[1]

This chapter will examine the leading approaches to rehabilitation and why its proponents believe it is a compelling theory of punishment. We will then consider the available evidence on our ability to rehabilitate offenders. While rehabilitation theories continue to offer us a fresh approach, its promise remains unfulfilled and its possibility is potentially suspect. These challenges may encourage us to understand how we might improve this important project rather than jettison it altogether.

What is rehabilitation?

A rehabilitation theory of punishment holds that punishment should aim at the reformation of offenders and assist their transition from criminal to law abiding citizen. Rehabilitation is successful where criminals come to reject crime out of choice.

Rehabilitation theories of punishment attempt to address a central problem in criminal justice. The great majority of imprisoned criminals will be released eventually.[2] So what next? How do we best ensure they do not reoffend upon release? Other theories of punishment appear to have relatively little to say about this issue. For example, retributivists might say that the point of punishment is to punish and not to reform.[3] Criminals should not receive help from us, but they should be punished by us. Deterrence proponents aim to deter: if punishment were seen to *help* offenders, then it might lose some of its deterrent power because punishment might be viewed as beneficial and desirable rather than something to be avoided.

Rehabilitation takes a very different position. We may believe that punishment should teach offenders a lesson. Consider the following illustration. A young adult commits a crime and is imprisoned for several years after conviction. This offender may suffer from several major obstacles. The first is that his employability skills may suffer while in prison. While in prison, the offender is unable to maintain and update his skills and training. Furthermore, time in prison is time removed from important social networks, such as family and friends, that may prove crucial in assisting lawful reintegration into life outside prison. Over time these social networks may become fractured further and some offenders may struggle to receive effective mentoring and support. Finally, time in prison is more generally time removed from 'normal life'. What was familiar may become unfamiliar upon release. Some critics may argue that these problems are the fault of the offender or that they contribute to the deterrent effect of his punishment. The rehabilitative theory of punishment asks us to confront important questions. Does retribution punish criminals twice through the added disadvantages endured upon release? Is the only purpose of punishment to make criminals suffer or is it instead to reduce crime? Is punishment an injustice inflicted upon criminals? How might punishment contribute to less injustice overall?

There are at least two general ways of conceiving rehabilitation The first is a deontological approach to rehabilitation, or *deontological rehabilitation*. This approach says that we should rehabilitate offenders because it is just. We do not aspire to rehabilitate offenders because it may save us money or reduce crime, but rather because each individual has moral importance and we should make every reasonable attempt to assist offenders in the transformation from criminal to law abiding citizen. Most proponents of rehabilitative theories of punishment defend a second approach to conceiving rehabilitation, namely, a consequentialist approach to rehabilitation or what we might call *consequentialist rehabilitation*. This approach says that we should rehabilitate criminals because we will all be better off. Consequentialist rehabilitation is a reductivist position: rehabilitation aspires to achieve crime reduction. Our discussion of rehabilitation will focus specifically on rehabilitation as a consequentialist approach.

Reformation is achieved where criminals understand the wrongness of their past actions and choose against further criminal activity. Part of this reformation will include some acknowledgement of regret. It is difficult to conceive criminal reformation without including some measure of regret. This is because a criminal who continued to approve of his past criminal activity cannot be said to have become reformed into seeing the error of his ways.[4] A criminal must regret her crime in order to achieve rehabilitation: rehabilitation requires a changed mindset, a new change of heart.

Letting a thousand reforms bloom

The goal of rehabilitative theories of punishment is simple: the reformation of criminal offenders. But how best to reform offenders? Rehabilitation proponents offer a myriad of different forms through which reform might be facilitated. These forms are often thought to address crime and its causes, or as oft stated by former British Prime Minister Tony Blair, 'Tough on Crime, Tough on the Causes of Crime'. I will consider the most common forms.[5]

One form of rehabilitation is therapeutic. Many criminals require therapeutic treatment. The idea is that delivering needed treatment addresses root causes behind a person's criminality: we should expect criminals to not reoffend upon release where these causes are removed. This therapy may take various forms. The first is in treatment for criminals suffering from drug and alcohol abuse. This is a major problem for most offenders. Between one-third to half of all new prisoners in England and Wales are believed to be problem drug users where drug-related crime alone costs £13.5 billion.[6] Most juvenile offenders have drug and alcohol problems as well. Attempts to reduce alcohol and drug abuse have led to lower reoffending rates in most cases.[7] The success of treatment programmes for drug and alcohol abuse has been encouraging.

Offenders may also require treatment for mental health problems which are often complex. Some have found up to 90 per cent of offenders suffer from mental health problems.[8] Several different approaches may be offered including cognitive behavioural therapy (CBT) and similar high intensity programmes. These help provide support for offenders suffering from this common problem which often may become worse when offenders are imprisoned. These programmes are most effective where the offender is able to receive assistance outside prison where possible. Such efforts may save the taxpayer approximately £20,000 per case.[9] A continuing problem is that most offenders will receive little support, leaving these problems to continue. Offenders rarely receive the support they need post-imprisonment as they attempt to reintegrate into society. One study found that women were 36 times more likely to kill themselves after imprisonment.[10] There is clearly a need for rehabilitation in prison and outside elsewhere.

A newer form of therapy is the use of recreational therapy, or therapeutic recreation. The idea is that offenders may become rehabilitated through interaction with others in recreation, such as art projects and sports. For example, some studies indicate that 'the arts can have a significant positive impact on offenders, especially in building self-confidence, self-esteem and social capital'.[11] Offenders may better address any anger and aggression through the self-expression that the arts facilitate.[12] Furthermore, sports promote working with others to achieve shared goals and receive mutual recognition through teamwork. These activities may help offenders positively reconnect with others and turn away from crime.

The emphasis on treatment is sometimes criticized as the problem of 'medicalization' of crime.[13] For example, Bertrand Russell says:

> I merely wish to suggest that we should treat the criminal as we treat a man suffering from plague. Each is a public danger, each must have his liberty curtailed until he has ceased to be a danger. But the man suffering from plague is an object of sympathy and commiseration whereas the criminal is an object of execration. This is quite irrational. And it is because of this difference of attitude that our prisons are so much less successful in curing criminal tendencies than our hospitals are in curing disease.[14]

The idea is that crime should not be treated as a moral failure, but an illness to be cured. Offenders engage in criminal activity because they are 'sick': crime is a medical problem, a pathology. This criticism overlooks the fact that there are many risk factors associated with criminal offending that may be addressed most effectively through treatment programmes. The target of the criticism is the ideas that, first, all crime can be cured through treatment and, second, all crime should be cured through treatment. Medical professionals can be of great assistance to rehabilitation efforts and improve our crime reduction efforts. The question is whether all crime is best addressed through treatment or a combination of treatment with other punitive measures. There is also the further question of whether these approaches may command public confidence in the criminal justice system.

Improved education and training is a second form of rehabilitation. Most offenders lack qualifications and employability skills. Studies have found about half of male prisoners have been excluded from school previously with two-thirds possessing the reading ability of an eleven year old or worse. Furthermore, nearly 70 per cent were unemployed.[15] If criminals are not retooled and better equipped to succeed in the market, then they run a risk of remaining unemployed and potentially returning to criminal offending. There is a need to help criminals develop new work-related skills. Many prisons have addressed this need by training criminals in skills such as bricklaying, engineering works, industrial cleaning, painting and interior decorating, and woodworking. Additional skills taught may include anger management. Getting offenders back into work is key to tackling future reoffending. Promoting job creation is more than a good economic policy: it is a good criminal justice policy, too. Improve employment prospects and crime reduction may become far more likely.[16]

A final form of rehabilitation is mentoring schemes aiming at sustainable social reintegration. An offender who has gained treatment for any drug or alcohol abuse and learned new employability skills will stand a better chance of avoiding future offending. However, there remains a need to provide further counselling sessions with a social worker or probation officer to ensure a smooth transition back to society. Reintegration is a crucial transition for offenders. Many lack the support networks that might best assist this transition. This will bring further costs to the rehabilitation of offenders, but the savings from successful crime reduction should more than offset these costs.

Rehabilitation approaches are often used in combination. Many criminals share a broadly similar profile consisting of a lack of education, unemployment, financial hardship and debt, drug and alcohol abuse, mental health problems, a lack of adequate housing, poor life skills, and weak family networks.[17] These difficulties will not go away on their own and punishment may exacerbate an offender's sorry plight. Imprisonment may serve as a personal disaster in ensuring that an offender's skills and life prospects fall further behind others. The problems that offenders face are not always isolated and may be treated in tandem, such as unemployment and financial hardship. Rehabilitation proponents seem to get right that punishment must be sensitive to the fact that it may contribute to an offender's reoffending if we fail to address specific contributory causes. Our failure to rehabilitate offenders through punishment may lead to further reoffending. Is this a price worth paying? The answer will depend on which theory of punishment we find most compelling.

Rehabilitation as punishment

It may be tempting to argue that rehabilitative theories of punishment are not theories about punishment at all. This is because punishment often involves the imposition of something painful, or so it may be said, and such a feature is lacking in these cases. While it is true that recidivism rates are often too high, offenders must be punished and not pampered. Perhaps short prison terms may increase the likelihood of reoffending.[18] This does not prove the case for rehabilitating, but perhaps sentencing is not punishment enough.

The public have become sceptical and perhaps even cynical about whether rehabilitation is an appropriate response to punishment. This is because rehabilitation is sometimes considered to be 'too soft' an option. Perhaps there is merit in providing some forms of rehabilitation, but this may not be welcome where our choice is either rehabilitation or prison in some cases. Politicians know the political truth that being 'tough on crime' is a winning electoral strategy for all voter groups and even those groups that favour penal alternatives. The attempts by some politicians to address predictably the popular appeal of ever more punitive punishments has led to an increase in the use of mandatory sentencing policies. A problem with these policies is that offenders are unable to apply for parole where they would gain regular access to a parole officer to monitor their social reintegration upon release. Those who need help most receive the least help: this is bad policy if our goal is to best ensure successful reintegration and rehabilitation.[19] Proclaiming to be tough on crime may be playing popular politics, but it may be bad criminal justice policy depending upon the associated costs.

While it is tempting to see rehabilitation as incompatible with punishment, this view is incorrect. Punishment is best understood *as a response* to crime. Theories of punishment are then theories about how best to respond to crime. Rehabilitation is one of many possible responses. Punishment is also best understood as involving some sort of loss. It is clear that rehabilitation theories meet this standard as well. A criminal sentenced to imprisonment and a criminal sentenced to hospital treatment share a similar loss in terms of their freedom of movement and association, amongst other potential losses. Nor is it clear that imprisonment is less enjoyable than enduring hospital treatment, all things considered. Rehabilitation may challenge our initial beliefs about the nature of punishment, but we are wrong to believe rehabilitative theories of punishment are not theories of punishment. Rehabilitation is one possible response to crime from many alternatives.

The role of morality

The relationship between moral education and rehabilitation is strong for many rehabilitation proponents. For example, some argue that rehabilitation should include 'the inculcation of moral principles'.[20] Criminal rehabilitation is a moral reformation project. Criminals will become rehabilitated once they become satisfactorily aware of their crimes as moral wrongdoings. Punishment may morally educate criminals and it is for both their good and the public good. The idea is that criminals commit crimes because of a lack of moral education: if this is addressed, then crime reduction should follow.

The best exponent of this view is Jean Hampton:

> Thus, according to moral education theory, punishment is not intended as a way of conditioning a human being to do what society wants her to do (in the way that an animal is conditioned by an electrified fence to stay within a pasture); rather, the theory maintains that punishment is intended as a way of teaching the wrongdoer that the action she did (or wants to do) is forbidden because it is morally wrong and should not be done for that reason.[21]

The aim of punishment is not to condition offenders, but to morally educate them: crime should be avoided because it is morally wrong and not merely to satisfy our social mores. Our task is to educate criminals about their wrongs as moral wrongs.[22] We must convince criminals that they should desist from crime through education.[23] This project best honours victims in confirming that a victim was wronged and criminals in addressing them as moral agents.[24]

Admittedly, this view accepts that the laws commanding punishment are justified in some moral sense.[25] If they were not, then moral education might be counterproductive to crime reduction efforts and the purposes of rehabilitation. One major problem is that not all crimes are immoral and not all immorality is criminal. There is then a *justice gap* between those crimes where moral education may be a relevant possibility and those crimes for which it is not. This gap highlights incoherence between rehabilitation as moral education and the criminal law how we find it, wherever we find it. We might require fairly radical revision of our criminal law in order to close this gap. This is a major problem too often overlooked by rehabilitation proponents who wrongly assume that legal moralism is correct and that all crimes are largely reduced to various acts of immorality.

Rehabilitation as moral education is consistent with the use of imprisonment for criminals. For example, Hampton argues that 'pain is the way to convey that message' and prison may be appropriate.[26] Pain plays a role in moral education in communicating moral boundaries to offenders. Punishment may serve a similar purpose as an electric fence for animals: 'The pain says "Don't!" and gives the wrongdoer a reason for not performing that action again'.[27] Punishment as something painful helps criminals reflect on the moral reasons for their incarceration. Imprisonment may possess an educative effect in presenting us with time for necessary reflection on the moral wrongness of our past crimes. Punishment promotes a choice: the choice to avoid law breaking.

One concern is that this view of rehabilitation might lead to the problem of punishing the innocent. Citizens may lack satisfactory moral awareness about the immorality of crime that may leave them susceptible to future crime. If punishment has a moral educative effect, then we might believe it justified to punish the innocent now to best guarantee they never offend later.

This objection fails. Rehabilitation as moral education does not target all immorality: if it did, then it would recommend punishment for telling white lies. Instead, we punish immorality that is criminalized. This is a problematic view as we have already noted. But the point is that we punish crime alone. Rehabilitation does not lead to the punishment of the innocent.

This is perhaps a minor victory given the larger problem that rehabilitation as moral education is wedded to two positions that are themselves deeply problematic. The first is that crime is reducible to immorality. How to educate a criminal about the moral wrong of a non-moral illegal act? The second is that punishment possesses or may possess an educative effect. This second problem rests on empirical facts about rehabilitation that are complex and somewhat inconclusive, requiring principled commitment from government and sensitivity to the individual needs of offenders. This latter issue may raise further questions of its own.

The problem of individualization

It is often said that similar cases should be treated broadly similarly. For example, suppose there are two people convicted separately for similar, but unrelated, thefts. It may be tempting to argue that both thieves should receive similar, if not identical, punishment. This could be justified on retributivist grounds: each thief possesses broadly similar desert and so deserves broadly similar punishment. This could also be justified to promote general deterrence: similar punishment is necessary to communicate a clear deterrent message to potential future thieves.

One potential problem for rehabilitation proponents is that a rehabilitative approach could theoretically warrant very different treatments of virtually identical criminals. While both thieves may have committed broadly similar crimes, their circumstances may be very different. Perhaps one thief may benefit from treatment for drug abuse to best ensure he avoids future offending and the second thief does not. Rehabilitation is tailored to the needs of offenders in light of their crimes. The potential problem is that the same crime may be handled in very different ways. This is because the rehabilitative needs will differ across all offenders.

A related worry is how differently offenders may be treated. Suppose a petty thief and a murderer are convicted and we must determine their rehabilitative punishment. Suppose further that the petty thief suffers from a variety of problems, such as drug and alcohol abuse, unemployment and financial hardship, and weak social support networks. The murderer does not have any of these problems. If rehabilitation is tailored to an offender's needs, then the petty thief might appear to demand more punishment than the murderer.

It is interesting to consider first why this might be a problem before turning to how a rehabilitation proponent could respond. It is testament to the deep pervasive grip that retribution has achieved in recent decades that our first reaction might be to say it would be grossly wrong to punish the petty thief more than the murderer because the murderer deserves greater punishment even if he does not have greater rehabilitative needs. The problem is that what a person may deserve in terms of retribution may differ widely from what this person may require to become rehabilitated successfully. The two may be at cross-purposes such that what is deserved is counterproductive to successful rehabilitation. Rehabilitation proponents ask us to make a choice between punishment without potential concern for future consequences and punishment that aims at effective crime reduction in favour of the latter strategy.

Is rehabilitation deterrence by another name?

We may wonder about the distinctive difference between deterrence and rehabilitation. Both have the aim of crime reduction and both judge success by the results. While these theories share common aspirations, they have achieved them in different ways. For example, deterrence is not always rehabilitation. If an offender is deterred from crime, the reason may be that she is fearful of possible punishment. She decides against crime because she doesn't want to endure the punishment, but not because she believes criminal activity should be avoided anyway. Evidence of deterrence is not necessarily evidence of rehabilitation.

The key difference is in how results are achieved. Deterrence attempts to convince us to avoid crime out of the fear of punishment. Rehabilitation attempts to convince us to avoid crime because we should not perform crime. John Mabbott brings out this point well: 'a man who abstains from crime from fear of punishment is not reformed'.[28] Where people avoid crime out of fear, this speaks to deterrence theories of punishment. Rehabilitation theories of punishment speak to cases where people avoid crime because they have no desire to perform crime.[29] Both rehabilitation and deterrence aim at crime reduction. Their difference is in approach and they are distinctly different.

Does rehabilitation work?

We have examined several considerations regarding the definition of rehabilitation, its many forms, and other factors. But does it work?

Rehabilitation aims at crime reduction and we may wonder if rehabilitation efforts reduce recidivism. The results are promising, but remain uncertain and inconclusive. It is widely acknowledged that most countries lack a clear national strategy at implementing rehabilitation programmes and that rehabilitation is rarely made a priority. The programmes that exist are often run on a small scale, such as a pilot scheme. Furthermore, recidivism rates offer a partial picture. Most crimes are unreported and only a minority lead to conviction. We can only consider how rehabilitation appears to work in this minority of cases in those instances where rehabilitation is used. So our ability to comment with greater confidence on the potential success of rehabilitation programmes is limited given the shortfall of available data.

The data available appear to present encouraging news. Rehabilitation works. Studies have found that reconvictions may be reduced by 5–10 per cent through a targeted rehabilitative treatment programme.[30] Rehabilitation programmes have the potential to be roughly twice as effective as deterrence. Rehabilitation efforts must involve a clear strategy for targeting those most at risk to be most effective. For example, reoffending is 'closely entwined' with housing problems and drug and alcohol abuse.[31] This strongly suggests that we should not consider reoffending in isolation from other factors if we desire effective crime reduction.

Intensive intervention shortly after offenders are imprisoned and extra support after release may make a big difference.[32] This is because offenders often require support: punishment may only confirm that help is needed in overcoming problems regarding substance abuse or securing a sustainable livelihood through work and acquiring housing. Further delays in addressing these needs may only make achieving these goals more difficult. Additionally, support is required post-release to ensure that offenders make a successful transfer back to society. Furthermore, offenders become more likely to reoffend the more often they have committed crimes. Early intervention efforts could lead to impressive results where factors contributing to reoffending are addressed. These efforts are best directed to offenders under 21 years: roughly two-thirds will be reconvicted within 24 months.

Media commentators have occasionally placed blame for criminality on the so-called breakdown of the traditional family. The argument is that the traditional family helps inculcate social norms of behaviour that benefit children. People from different backgrounds have a disadvantage because they may be less likely to accept these norms and at greater risk of criminal behaviour. It is true that prisoners are far more likely to have been in care at some time in the past, including about half of all prisoners under 25. However, prisoners who have previously been in care are a minority overall and form about 25 per cent of the prison population.[33]

Some have pointed to the problem of the *responsibility deficit*.[34] It is thought to afflict so-called 'troubled' families. They are defined by unemployment, mental health problems, and where any children are out of school. These are all high risk factors for criminal and other anti-social behaviour. One approach to this problem is providing these families with specialist support from a family liaison officer that may help them address various needs. It is estimated in the UK that there are approximately 120,000 families potentially affected. Providing £400 million in funding is believed to lead to savings of £8 billion for taxpayers through reductions in crime and need of punishment, in addition to avoiding the need of placing children in care. Rehabilitation programmes are promising, but they need investment and political commitment.

The management of successful rehabilitation programmes leads us to the new question: how best to incentivize rehabilitation efforts? One common policy recommendation is to pay for results. Those organizations that can demonstrate the best recidivism results should receive cash rewards. This incentive will lead to competition between rehabilitation organizations on how best to deliver criminal rehabilitation. Or so the argument goes.

There are at least two ways to measure success. The first is to consider the number of criminals who have become reformed and offer organizations a cash incentive per reformed offender. A second method is to reward organizations that demonstrate higher percentages of reformed offenders and provide the biggest pay outs for the best results. We might distinguish these two methods as the 'individualist' approach versus the 'group' approach.

Both methods run into a similar problem. Organizations adopting either approach will be more likely to accept lower risk offenders because these will more easily reap rewards. It is easier to perform better on either approach where offenders are less costly to reform, where cost is understood in terms of time, use of experienced staff, and facilities. Neither approach will desire large numbers of higher risk offenders because they will be less likely to become reformed. This will lead to fewer reformed criminals on the individualist model and lower success rates on the group model.

This problem is best addressed by offering different rewards for different categories of offenders. The reform of higher risk offenders could be linked to greater cash incentives for rehabilitative organizations following an individualist approach. These firms will then be armed with satisfactory incentives to rehabilitate offenders of different types. This solution is unavailable for organizations judging success by recidivism rates, or the group model, rather than a reformed offender by reformed offender basis, or the individualist model. This is because high risk offenders will be less likely to become reformed than low risk offenders. The inclusion of high risk offenders would lead to potentially worse recidivism rates. If we were to judge success through monetary or other incentives, then organizations should be rewarded for each individual reformed and not their overall success rate. Moreover, the reward for reforming an offender should relate to the offender's risk. One important starting point is to begin with the number of persons who do not reoffend within six months. This would address a significant number of reoffenders that would have a major positive impact on crime reduction.

The problem of the unreformable

We have already discussed the problem of the undeterrable in the previous chapter. There is a similar problem of the unreformable, or those resistant to rehabilitation.

One issue is whether the unreformable should be punished. Imagine that someone has performed a crime for which she should be punished. If rehabilitation were our goal and someone could not be reformed, then should she not be punished? We must have genuine certainty that such a person were truly beyond possible rehabilitation. If we have this certainty, then it is unclear why the death penalty would never be justified. The argument is that someone beyond the possibility of rehabilitation may pose a constant danger. For example, Jean-Jacques Rousseau argues that 'there is not a single wicked man who could not be made good for something. One only has the right to put to death, even as an example, someone who cannot be preserved without danger'.[35]

It is especially important to highlight the difficulty of achieving such certainty about the future possibility of rehabilitation for any offender. We may be able to identify risk factors for offending, such as drug and alcohol abuse, but not everyone with risk factors engages in criminal activity. Criminal profiling is more an art than a science. Declaring any person beyond possible rehabilitation is a judgement we should resist.

A further issue is whether there are people we should not reform. Some may agree that sexual offenders may be rehabilitated, but they should not be in favour of some alternative punishment like the death penalty.

This position rests on a mistake about the relative dangerousness of sexual offenders. Studies demonstrate that non-sexual offenders will be three times more likely to reoffend over a four-year period than sexual offenders over a twenty-year period.[36] If it is true that we may be unable to declare with sufficient certainty that it is impossible to rehabilitate another, then this offers a compelling reason to provide some effort to rehabilitate offenders if we defend the rehabilitation theory of punishment.

Conclusion

This chapter has explored rehabilitative theories of punishment from several different angles. One general conclusion is that the results are encouraging, but inconclusive with further investment and political commitment required. For example, John Dewey says:

> If it be argued that most criminals are so hardened in evil-doing that reformatories are of no use, the answer is twofold. We do not know, because we have never systematically and intelligently tried to find out; and, even if it were so, nothing is more illogical than to turn the unreformed criminal, at the end of a certain number of months or years, loose to prey again upon society. Either reform or else permanent segregation is the logical alternative.[37]

Rehabilitation works best when it is targeted, properly resourced, and supported by a clear political commitment. Furthermore, we have seen evidence that intensive early interventions to tackle criminal offending may lead to improved results.

There are several ways in which rehabilitation efforts may be improved. The first is to make better use of existing resources. Prison officers are an underutilized source of great potential. They serve on the front line working directly with imprisoned offenders and are 'the most influential people in the lives of inmates'.[38] More prison officers should become Personal Support Officers offering mentoring and monitoring of offenders beyond their present role. This will require additional training and remuneration, but the potential pay-off is tangible.

A more clear strategy designed to tackle crime by youth and young adults is a second way that rehabilitation efforts might be improved. Criminals caught in a trap of reoffending most often begin their criminal careers as youths or young adults. Crime reduction for this age group will help bring about lower recidivism rates provided that programmes are specially tailored to address their specific needs.

Rehabilitation is about the reform of offenders to engender crime reduction. Most proponents consider the use of rehabilitation as a form of punishment, as a programme that offenders participate in while imprisoned. But why think offenders are always best rehabilitated in prisons? Why not think reform possible in other settings? There is also the important issue of public confidence. Criminal justice policy need not only lead to positive results, but receive public support. The problem is that rehabilitation does not have wide support for the most serious violent crimes. Rehabilitation is promising, but perhaps as a strategy for only some offenders at most.

4 Restorative justice

Introduction

Restorative justice is a distinctive alternative to rival theories of punishment. All theories of punishment justify the use of imprisonment under certain circumstances. While there may be disagreement about these circumstances, both retributivists and others will agree that there are cases where prison is justified. Restorative justice is an exception. Many proponents identify restorative justice with penal 'abolition' – calling themselves 'abolitionists' – to draw attention to their desire to provide an alternative to sentencing and the potential future abolition of prison. This distinctive, even radical, alternative offers a major challenge to traditional approaches to punishment. This chapter will examine this alternative as an alternative theory of punishment and consider its effectiveness as an approach to crime reduction. We will not consider the use of restorative justice in other contexts, such as in Truth and Reconciliation Commissions or as a process employed *in addition* to punishment.[1]

What is restorative justice?

'Prison works', or so declared former British Home Secretary Michael Howard in 1993. This optimistic view about the use of prisons as an effective punishment has come under increasing scrutiny. One reason is the spiralling costs. The cost per prisoner each year is estimated to be about $23,876 in the US and £39,600 in the UK.[2] A second reason is high re-offending rates upon release. Prisons have sometimes made more likely future reoffending: prisons may contribute to increasing crime and not crime reduction. An alternative punishment that could yield better crime reduction at reduced costs could be a compelling new approach. Restorative justice claims to offer such an approach.

Restorative justice aims at the 'restoration' of offenders, victims, and the wider community. The idea is that a relationship between them is damaged through criminal offending. This requires a process that may help restore the common bonds of association damaged by crime through shared communication and not imprisonment. Restoration is neither a private affair between offenders and victims nor only a public matter between offenders and the state. Offenders, victims, and the community all have a stake in addressing crime through restoration. Punishment should include all who are stakeholders in justice. Restorative justice is one attempt to allow the participation of all key stakeholders in the consideration of punishment. Each has an interest to see crime addressed effectively and so each should have a voice. The result aimed for is the restoration of the relationship between offenders, victims, and the community that is mutually satisfactory. Restorative justice is a forward-looking approach with a problem-solving orientation. So how best to restore what has been damaged or lost in a proactive and supportive way?

Restorative justice offers an alternative approach to the use of trial and prisons. First, restorative justice proponents advocate the restorative conference instead of the trial. They argue that trials are about winners and losers where each side attempts to defeat the other.[3] Restorative justice proponents argue that our goal should not be adversarial, but dialogue and mutual understanding. Everyone should win, if possible. Second, restorative justice offers an alternative approach to the use of prisons. While no theory endorses the use of prison for every crime, restorative justice never endorses imprisonment for any crime. Restorative justice proponents are often called 'abolitionists' because their approach calls for the abolition of prisons. The restorative process is about reconciliation and repair, as well as the transformation of offenders: some have understood restorative justice as 'transformative justice' as a result.[4] Restoration is *reductivist* in that it aims at crime reduction.

Restoration normally takes the form of a *restorative conference.*[5] Conference participants include the offender, support officers, members of the local community, and any victims. Together, they share in a process to collectively resolve how best to address the aftermath of a crime and its future implications as parties with a stake.[6] Each participant seeks to engage in a constructive dialogue and mutual understanding within a structured context. The idea is that greater mutual understanding will bring parties closer together rather than pull them further apart.

Relevant parties are those that can be said to *have a stake* in the specific offence. Restorative justice is determined by parties who are not impartial, aside from the facilitator who conducts the conference. These parties are *stakeholders* in their each having a stake in the offence. Restorative conferences are a *stakeholder society* in miniature.[7] The idea is that justice is served where each party with a stake has confidence in the outcome. Problems arise where not all involved are satisfied with the conference results.

Restorative conferences require the full consent of each participant along with the offender's acknowledgement of guilt: the centrality of remorse is essential to the process. This is because offenders cannot seek restoration where they fail to acknowledge their responsibility for their need of restoration. Not unlike rehabilitation, offenders cannot be restored unless they accept their guilt and express remorse for their crimes. Their apology is at the heart of restoration. This requirement is unique to restorative justice: we need not admit guilt when fined or imprisoned, for example.[8] Restoration requires offenders to take responsibility for their crimes within the unique context of the restorative conference.

All conferences are mediated by a trained facilitator operating under a body, such as the Restorative Justice Council.[9] Offenders retain access to legal representation, but they are to speak for themselves. Restoration requires parties to engage each other constructively and with genuine honesty within a supportive environment in order to agree to a contract that the offender must fulfil in order to become 'restored'. Restorative contracts are agreed on in about 98 per cent of restorative conferences. The restorative contract states the conditions that must be met by an offender in order to become 'restored'. Typical conditions include treatment for drug and alcohol abuse or mental health problems, anger management therapy, the payment of compensation to victims and others, and community service. All contracts normally include the expression of remorse by the offender. If the offender fails to abide by the terms of the contract, then there may be real consequences. One consequence is that a new contract is drawn up with much less favourable terms for the offender. A second consequence is that the offender may be formally charged and brought to trial with possibilities including imprisonment. Offenders have many reasons to abide by the terms of their contract including the fact that their situation will become much worse and restoration made more difficult.

The structure by which restorative conference participants agree to contracts with offenders is purposefully vague, but within a clear framework. The idea is that restorative justice is bottom-up and not top-down.[10] The restorative process should be guided by the particulars of a specific case instead of abstract legal precepts. Indeed, it is thought that a major obstacle to restoration is the abstract nature of many criminal proceedings. This is because the courtroom environment is sometimes perceived as cold and adversarial, a place where victims may receive unsympathetic and even hostile cross-examination. Criminal proceedings may appear to victims to be aimed at concealment and not revelation. Crimes may have deep and sometimes profound emotional and other effects on victims that may receive insufficient attention. Restorative justice seeks to address this problem through the use of mediated conferences. It offers an informal approach to addressing crime and its causes. We should note that responsibilities do not rest solely with the offender and his acknowledgement of remorse. The community has responsibilities as well in engaging with him to support his restoration.

Restorative conferences aim at restoration. But what is restored? Proponents claim the restoration of the offender's dignity, restoration of a shared communal bond, and prevention of future injustice.[11] Offenders are restored from criminals to reformed and reintegrated fellow citizens. Furthermore, the victim receives acknowledgement that she is not merely the victim of a crime, but someone who was wronged and by an offender seeking to make amends. The idea is that restoration – understood in these ways – contributes to crime reduction. Offenders acknowledge guilt and seek amends with victims and the community alike tailored to the circumstances of each individual case at a fraction of the cost of imprisonment.[12]

Restorative justice may take several forms, and its flexibility to handle diverse cases and needs is believed to be its advantage over alternative theories of punishment in addition to potential monetary savings. Additionally, restorative justice facilitates criminal justice that may respect parties as stakeholders and without need for a criminal trial.

Is restorative justice 'punishment'?

Critics have claimed that restorative justice is not a theory of punishment.[13] One reason is that restorative justice rejects the use of prison for offences. A second reason is that offenders permitted to participate in restorative conferences may not receive a criminal record if they satisfy the terms of their contract. Restorative justice is perceived as an alternative to theories of punishment (and not a theory of punishment in its own right) because there is no justification of prisons and no criminal records for offenders. Punishment without prisons?

This criticism is mistaken. Punishment is not reducible to imprisonment alone. Not all criminals must be imprisoned if they are to be punished. Punishment and prisons are different even if they may overlap. The objection cannot be that punishment and imprisonment are the same because *all* theories of punishment may justify alternatives to prison. For example, retributivists may argue an offender deserves no more than a fine for a minor crime. Or a deterrence proponent may argue a criminal should not be imprisoned because general deterrence is best sought by other means. And so on. It is a mistake to argue that restorative justice is not a theory of punishment because it justifies an alternative to prison.

Instead, perhaps a more subtle criticism is that restorative justice is an incomplete theory of punishment. The idea is that a complete theory of punishment would offer an account applicable to all crimes. The problem is that restorative justice offers us a partial account that is applicable to some crimes, but not all crimes. This problem arises for two reasons. First, virtually no proponent of restorative justice argues that it is applicable in all cases. Restorative justice is advocated primarily for relatively minor crimes committed by juvenile offenders. Virtually no one argues for restorative justice conferences instead of prison for offenders who have committed serious crimes. This is not to say there is any disinterest in offenders offering compensation and apologies to victims, but that restorative justice as an alternative to prison is a proposal for non-serious crimes alone. Our choice is between restorative justice or prison with the aim of making imprisonment less likely and for the most serious offenders only. While restorative justice offers an alternative model to imprisonment, it does not rule out the use of prisons altogether.[14]

Critics may believe that restorative justice is not then a complete theory of punishment because it does not speak to all cases, but instead it may be part of a larger general theory that will include a view to the justification of imprisonment in certain cases.[15] Further evidence is that imprisonment is a possible option for when offenders fail to satisfy contracts agreed in restorative conferences. For example, the leading proponent of restorative justice, John Braithwaite, says:

> the message the restorative justice conference should give is that it is better to put your best self forward at the bottom rung ... because if you don't, you will end up going through this again, and next time it will be a bigger production, and the conference will be more demanding.[16]

Conferences do not become ever more demanding *ad infinitum*. Where offenders fail to honour their agreements, imprisonment becomes an option. Restorative justice proponents believe that restorative conferences are preferable to imprisonment in many cases, but not necessarily preferable in all cases. Critics who argue that restorative justice is not a theory of punishment because it rejects the justification of punishment make a mistake: restorative justice proponents need not reject the use of imprisonment in all cases, but only the commitment to alternatives to prisons where possible although this argument is not defended by these proponents.

Restorative justice may offer an incomplete theory of punishment, but it is a theory of punishment in a further sense. We saw in the introduction that punishment is a *response* to crime. Restorative justice is a theory of punishment as a response to crime. This response is to enable restoration. We may prefer some responses to crime than others, but still acknowledge that restorative justice is a theory about punishment even if we prefer more punitive alternatives.

Is restoration rehabilitation by another name?

Restorative justice is a theory of punishment.[17] Is it a distinctive theory of punishment? Specifically, what is the distinction between the rehabilitative theory of punishment and restorative justice? They may appear to overlap perhaps too much at first glance. For example, both aim at the reformation of offenders. The problem of criminality may have many causes and our addressing these causes may help to reform offenders turning them away from future crime. Different offenders will have different needs and the support required may vary across persons. The question is whether rehabilitation and restoration is a distinction without a difference. This is an important criticism to raise because it may help highlight the distinctiveness of restorative justice.

Rehabilitative theories of punishment argue that punishment is justified through its reforming offenders and reducing crime. This is performed in the context of often removing offenders from society and using the prison or other secure facility and employing professionals to address the needs of offenders. Rehabilitation is offender-centric.

Restorative justice works very differently and it adheres to different goals. First, restorative justice aspires to find non-prison options to facilitate offender reform. One reason is because of general scepticism about the positive results from rehabilitation within prisons and the belief that better results may be found when using alternatives to best target specific problems. Second, restoration is community-centric, not offender-centric. The goal is not only to reform offenders, but restore damaged bonds of trust and respect within a community. We aspire to restore a relationship between members of a community to their collective satisfaction agreed through a contract and guided by a trained facilitator. Victims, their families, and the wider community matter. Or we might say that restorative justice is stakeholder-centric because restoration aims to restore a relationship between those who have some stake in a specific crime and its outcome as members of a relevant community.

Restorative justice is not rehabilitation by another name. Each offers distinctive approaches in pursuit of different goals, but both include the reform of offenders.

The role of victims

A traditional problem with theories of punishment concerns the role of victims. Punishment is not merely offender-centric, but addressed to offenders alone. The idea is that offenders may have wronged a victim, but the crime is a public wrong and should be punished by a public body. The problem is that victims may come to feel like bystanders in their cases. Others lead the debate on the rights and wrongs in a case shaping penal outcomes. The victims may become disengaged or even tangential to the punishment of crimes that were public wrongs against them. Victims may come to feel victimized twice: the first time by the offender, the second by the criminal justice system.

There is growing recognition for the need to bring victims back into the heart of the criminal justice system. The issue is how best to achieve this goal. It is instructive to consider how this problem first arose. The idea that victims may seek vengeance against offenders has no place in most legal systems. Legal justice is a matter of public justice: the state, not the victims, takes an interest in public wrongs where it determines guilt and penal options. This is called victim displacement because the victim is replaced by the state. John Gardner says:

> we seem to have lost sight of the origins of the criminal law as a response to the activities of *victims*, together with their families, associates and supporters. The blood feud, the vendetta, the duel, the revenge, the lynching: for the elimination of these modes of retaliation, more than anything else, the criminal law as we know it today came into existence.[18]

The displacement function of modern legal systems addresses an important concern while raising others. It is perhaps obvious that a system that gave victims the only say about criminal justice outcomes might be subject to abuse and inconsistency. If private citizens determined penal outcomes, then this would raise concerns about possible intimidation and nobbling by offenders and their supporters. For example, some argue that judges should decide cases without a jury where the trial runs a risk of jury nobbling.[19] Victims who are more vulnerable to intimidation may become more likely to be victimized on account of their being perceived as soft targets. If we believe that it should not matter whether the victim is 'a sinner or a saint', then we should be concerned about protecting victims from possible further victimization.[20]

Furthermore, if sentencing were left to the sole discretion of victims, then similar cases might not be punished similarly. This is because we, as victims, may be moved towards very different outcomes. Some of us may choose a purely punitive result while others might prefer making a deterrent example of an offender or focusing on an offender's reform. The principle of proportionality says that punishment should be proportional to the crime. There are many ways that proportionality might be determined. One way is to argue that punishments should be proportionate to retributivist desert. A second is to say that punishments should be proportionate to general deterrence or a third to an offender's rehabilitation. Perhaps punishment might be proportionate to an offender's restoration. Whichever we choose, proportionality would differ by individual judgement treating like cases unalike. Consider Taliban-like justice. Victims and their families have the choice of either agreeing to a state-sanctioned punishment or forgiving offenders altogether. Thus, some criminals receive no punishment while others have lost their hands or even their lives for the same crimes. This situation finds punishment transformed into a kind of lottery where penal principles may be abandoned by personal discretion or even individual taste. There are good reasons against offering the victims the only say on penal outcomes.

These concerns to protect victims and ensure fairness for offenders have set the horizon for the displacement function in the criminal law. This function is to remove the victim from having the only say on penal outcomes. This argument – namely, that the victim should not have the only say – does not offer conclusive grounds for the position that the victim should have *some* say: while it may be problematic to give victims the only say, there may be good reason to give them some say in penal outcomes. After all, *the victims may claim a stake in the outcome.* For example, Nils Christie argues:

> The victim is a particularly heavy loser in this situation. Not only has he suffered, lost materially or become hurt, physically or otherwise. And not only does the state take the compensation. But above all he has lost participation in his own case. It is the [state] that comes into the spotlight, not the victim. It is the [state] that describes the losses, not the victim.[21]

The victim is too often marginalized despite her non-consensual inclusion at the coal face of criminal justice. There have been growing calls to better address this problem and 'rebalance the criminal justice system in favour of the victim and the community so as to reduce crime and bring more offenders to justice'.[22] In short, this is an issue about how we maintain or improve results with increasing public confidence. It is thought that the best way to improve public confidence is to include victims more effectively in the criminal justice system.

Restorative justice is argued to be a compelling approach to addressing this problem. Early results are strongly encouraging, which suggests that the approach may lead to improved crime reduction. We will discuss this matter below. Most importantly, restorative justice has been highly popular with victims thus far. Victims are centrally involved in the process and they have a say in the contract agreed with offenders in restorative conferences. Moreover, this is done without the victim having the only say in the conduct of meetings or the penal outcomes. So the reasons for victim displacement are adhered to while allowing victims a greater voice in proceedings.

Restorative justice offers one approach to improving public confidence. This raises the question of how best to assess public confidence. We should note that a deontological approach, such as retributivism, may be uninterested in public confidence.[23] What matters is that justice is done and not that it is popular. We punish the deserving in proportion to what is deserved and not what brings the greatest pleasure to the greater number. Nevertheless, if public confidence matters, then how should it be best achieved? One approach might be to argue if the criminal system wins the approval of the most citizens. Restorative justice offers a second approach: public confidence is best achieved where outcomes win the best approval from all those *with a stake* in outcomes. The second approach is preferable to the first approach. One reason is that it is possible that a system bringing the least approval from victims, offenders, and those with a stake might bring the greatest approval to the greater number. The idea that those with a stake should matter most sends the message that if the penal outcomes have won the approval of those most involved then this is a weighty reason that those of us much less involved and with a smaller stake, if any, should give our approval, too.

Only restorative justice best guarantees the approval of direct stakeholders, not least because all are involved. Unsurprisingly, politicians on both sides of the Atlantic and beyond have become more favourable to the use of restorative justice because it may improve public confidence while improving crime reduction and lowering costs. Put bluntly: if the outcomes are good enough for those involved, then they should be good enough for the wider public. Improved distribution of relevant information is the key to this strategy of winning public confidence. The public may only arrive at this view if they are properly informed about the confidence that stakeholders have in restorative justice. If they don't know, then there remains a significant challenge in confronting the media's often alarmist misrepresentations of crime and its effects.

Restoration is believed to be a promising way to tackle the so-called *justice gap*. This is the space between reported and unreported crimes. The majority of crimes are unreported. One worry is that this may be caused by the unwillingness of victims to report crimes. Restoration recommends itself as a way to win greater confidence among victims which, in turn, may lead to more victims coming forward to report crimes. Restoration also aspires to winning greater confidence and, in turn, support from the community. This is because those with a stake in penal outcomes may be invited to participate in a restorative conference. These persons may include friends and family as well as neighbours and support networks. These groups report very high satisfaction with restorative conferences. The hope is that victims and the wider community will both have greater confidence in the use of restorative justice which will lead to improved relations between the public and the police as well as a greater likelihood that crimes will be reported.

One potential criticism is that our giving stakeholders a say in outcomes may lead to a lack of consistency in how similar types of crimes are addressed. It may appear to be justice by lottery.[24] But how do we understand 'consistency'? If consistency is understood as the agreement by stakeholders guided by a trained facilitator, then consistency across cases is achieved. All cases are treated consistently in aiming to ensure restoration. We tailor our contract to each particular case, which may make direct comparisons difficult. Restorative contracts are fair where each consistently addresses restorative needs.

We should note that restorative justice does not have a monopoly on bringing victims back into the heart of criminal justice. There has been growing use of *victim impact statements* (or 'VIS'). These are statements presented in court that detail how a crime has affected victims and their families. Their purpose is to help the court determine the punishment for an offender post-conviction. The idea is that discretion should move towards more punitive sentences where victim impact is more severe.

VIS have had an awkward reception by the courts. While politically popular, the courts often adhere to the view that the impact on victims may be accounted for in sentencing, but never the victims' opinions on what the particular punishment should be in any outcome. So it may be appropriate to state that a crime has had a potentially devastating effect on a person's recovery, but never appropriate to opine on how many years in prison would be satisfactory from the victim's point of view. It is for this reason that these court statements are genuinely *victim impact* statements and not *victim opinions on appropriate penalties* statements. While restorative justice may offer us a theory of punishment that brings the victim back into the heart of criminal justice, there are alternatives such as the use of VIS. It is perhaps intuitively compelling that the impact on relevant victims may have bearing when determining punishment as a response to crime. This is not to say that these statements should be the only or the primary determinant. Indeed, we may often understand the seriousness of crimes in relation to their potential harms to victims already.

Community sentencing

Restorative justice proponents recommend the use of alternatives to imprisonment to improve restoration between offenders and their communities. We must endeavour to create the conditions for restoration supported by public confidence. Punitive rehabilitation is sometimes held as a practical ideal. Our response should be rehabilitative to remove the risk of future reoffending, but it must also be sufficiently punitive or the public may find our penal responses unsupportable.

Community penalties are one approach to offering so-called punitive rehabilitation. Community penalties may take many forms, such as educative and employability, social reintegration, and/or treatment including the participation in a restorative conference.[25] Educative and employability forms include education and training, especially basic skills like improved literacy and numeracy. Many offenders lack employability skills and one way to tackle this problem is to demand they attend training programmes to acquire this knowledge. Educative and employability forms of community penalties may also take shape as compulsory unpaid work.[26] There is a strong link between unemployment and reoffending.[27] Compulsory unpaid work offers offenders the opportunity to gain new workplace experience to further support future employability.

Community penalties may also take the form of social reintegration, such as curfew and residence requirements as well as community supervision and electronic monitoring. These penalties permit offenders to continue benefiting from any social support networks within specified restraints until they are restored and permitted to move freely. The idea is to improve their reintegration through monitored support.

Finally, community penalties may take the form of treatment. This approach includes the use of behaviour programmes and treatment for substance abuse as well as abstinence programmes. Drug and alcohol abuse is prevalent for many offenders and treatment is necessary to address risks to offender health and future reoffending. There may also be the need for behaviour programmes, such as anger management classes.

Community penalties may take these three forms individually or in combination.[28] An offender may become registered in mandatory treatment for substance abuse and have a curfew as well as unpaid community service. These opportunities are community-oriented insofar as the punishment is served within the community. The benefit to offenders is that it helps offenders build and create support networks, and it benefits taxpayers as a much cheaper alternative to imprisonment. Community penalties are penalties in that they may have a punitive element, such as limitations on free movement or association plus mandatory attendance at treatment centres or unpaid work. The benefit to offenders is to improve their employability and reduce their risk of future offending. Community penalties may be a mode of restorative justice in that they focus on the causes of crime and not only the crime itself in dialogue with offenders. This requires flexibility, but not necessarily inconsistency although it may be difficult to satisfactorily compare cases.[29]

A lack of satisfactory public confidence is perhaps the biggest problem facing community penalties. There is evidence that about 60 per cent of the public find community sentences a 'soft' option.[30] Reasons for public dissatisfaction may include empirical findings, such as one recent study which found that about 40 per cent of offenders breached curfew orders, such as Anti-Social Behaviour Orders (ASBOs).[31] There is always the temptation for politicians and policymakers to tailor criminal justice to issues prioritized in the media instead of addressing the priorities of those with a stake in social restoration.[32]

There have been attempts to address the problem of public confidence. One idea is to rename existing measures to better sell them to the general public. Community penalties are newly understood as forms of 'justice reinvestment'.[33] Community penalties already include unpaid work, but now this is rebranded *community pay back* to draw greater attention to its punitive potential. This new language is thought to better capture the spirit of unpaid work by offenders as a 'pay back' to the community through their labour for their crimes. Community pay back has become an increasingly attractive option for policymakers who are keen to use community penalties instead of imprisonment where possible, but without losing public confidence if possible. These efforts include some attempt to ensure some public visibility of offenders performing unpaid labour to generate public confidence in the punitive nature of community penalties.

A second idea on how to better promote community penalties is to appeal to their effectiveness. For example, community penalties are believed to reduce reoffending by 14 per cent. The use of similar measures for youth offenders have seen 43 per cent reductions in the frequency of offending. Greater effectiveness is achieved at lower costs. It is claimed that community penalties may deal with four times more offenders as prisons at 40 per cent of the cost.[34] This should not be surprising. A major problem for offenders is the combination of unemployment, housing problems, and weak support networks. Community penalties offer one method of restoration that may positively impact on employability, living arrangements, and building support.

Shame punishments

Perhaps the most controversial form of restorative justice is the use of so-called shame punishments. Gone are the days of placing criminals in stocks and left at the mercy of an angry mob. Shame punishments take very different forms today.[35] These forms include scrubbing sidewalks with toothbrushes, signs declaring 'Dangerous Sex Offender – No Children Allowed' on cars, or requirements to put photo advertisements in local newspapers that state the crime committed and asking relevant readers to seek help.[36] The idea is not to endanger offenders, but to instil a sense of guilt where it is lacking.

Shame punishments may take two forms. First, shame punishments may take the form of *disintegrative* shaming. These are cases where the purpose of shaming is to humiliate. Examples might include requiring convicted child sex offenders to wear t-shirts that state 'I am a child sex offender'. Such acts are disintegrative because they are likely to be counterproductive to an offender's reformation. Instead, offenders become vulnerable to violence and social links are severed rather than healed.

Shame punishments may also take a second form as *reintegrative* shaming. These are cases where shaming is used within a context of mutual respect aimed at restoration.[37] The idea is to instil a change of heart in offenders. It is important that offenders take responsibility for their crimes and be held accountable. The problem is that not all offenders understand their crimes as public wrongs. Reintegrative shame punishments are a method by which offenders may come to accept an important sense of guilt that makes possible their future restoration. But how to make offenders realize their guilt? Shame punishment proponents argue that the controlled and measured use of shaming may be one important tool to awaken guilt in those who have no guilt.

Opponents of shame punishments, such as Martha Nussbaum, acknowledge that:

> Shame ... goads us onward with regard to many different types of goals and ideals, some of them valuable ... It often tells the truth: certain goals are valuable and we have failed to live up to them. And it often

expresses a desire to be a type of being that one can be: a good human being doing fine things.[38]

Shame may play a positive role in bringing us to the recognition that we have fallen short. This awareness may even be painful for us. The point is that shame may play an educative role in helping us recognize guilt and this, in turn, may help facilitate our reformation. The idea is that reformation is possible where we are able to recognize our guilt.[39] Shame may play a positive role in select circumstances if managed in the appropriate way: 'shame and guilt can trigger one another'.[40]

Shame punishment has many critics. Not all restorative justice advocates believe shame punishments are compatible with restoration. For example, Andrew von Hirsch argues that restoration should never humiliate offenders. Instead, they must be able to endure their punishment 'with dignity'.[41] This objection rests on the understanding of all shame punishments as affronts to personal dignity. The idea is often conjoined with the view that criminals should be treated as an ends and not a means to secure any social policy. The problem with shame punishment is that it uses persons in the wrong way in pursuit of alleged lofty political purposes.

These criticisms correctly capture the fragility of using shame in public policy. Shame may yield positive and negative effects. For example, shame may lead to stigmatization, making bad situations worse by endangering future restoration. Or shame may invite the public to 'discriminate and stigmatize' offenders.[42] A further objection is that reintegrative shaming may necessitate overly harsh punishments in order to shame.

There are several issues arising from these potential objections. The first is that shame is absent from criminal justice: we should not bring it into the fold through shame punishment. This argument rests on an important mistake. As the US Supreme Court has noted, 'virtually all individuals who are convicted for serious crimes suffer humiliation and shame, and many may be ostracized by their communities'.[43] Shame is already a part of our criminal justice system. For example, many job applications have prospective employees note if they have any past convictions. This may be used in decisions against hiring former offenders no matter how advanced their reformation. Offenders may be stigmatized in this way: shame is a part of an offender's punishment to some degree. So it is not a conclusive argument against shaming punishment to say that shaming does not have a place in our criminal justice system already. It is a different argument to claim that punishment should never have a shaming element. This position is difficult to imagine. Unless we agree that employers cannot discriminate on the basis of past convictions then offending will carry some significant element of shame in addition to the experience of indictment and a public trial.

Shaming is not the purpose of reintegrative shaming: restoration is its goal. The point is not to humiliate, but to give offenders a wake up call where it may facilitate restoration. This point is brought out well in the famous case involving a mail thief, Shawn Gementera.[44] Gementera had been convicted of repeated offences and it was becoming more serious. He was convicted for stealing mail and failed to satisfactorily recognize the wrongness of his actions because he did not see how his actions victi-mized others. He agreed to hold a sign stating 'I am a thief. This is my punishment' as an alternative to certain imprisonment. The US Court of Appeals stated:

> Criminal offenses, and the penalties that accompany them, nearly always cause shame and embarrassment. Indeed, the mere fact of conviction, without which state-sponsored rehabilitation efforts do not commence, is stigmatic. The fact that a condition causes shame or embarrassment does not automatically render a condition objectionable; rather, such feelings generally signal the defendant's acknowledgement of his wrongdoing.[45]

Shame punishment addresses the problem that not all offenders accept responsibility for their crimes. Shame punishment is an attempt to instil guilt where it is lacking in the absence of constructive alternatives. The goal is to help offenders recognize their wrongdoing as *theirs* and not make more difficult their reformation. This goal is to be achieved through shaming: it must be punitive and public, but not humiliating.

We might also argue that shaming may form some part of most punishments to some degree, but we should endeavour to permit shaming to no more than what is necessary within a supportive context. Shaming need not be entirely objectionable where it is reintegrative and restorative, not disintegrative and counterproductive to reformation. This is an argument about the purposes and appropriate methods of shaming. Shaming takes many forms. Perhaps it is a verbal warning from a police officer instructing us to obey speed limits. Does this not help bring many of us to reconsider our actions and drive more carefully? Or perhaps shaming should be controlled within specific contexts. For example, John Braithwaite argues: 'It is not shame of police or judges or newspapers that is most able to get through to us; it is shame in the eyes of those we respect and trust'.[46] If our goal is to help offenders understand their crimes as wrongs, then some contexts may better facilitate this goal than others. The use of a restorative conference bringing together relevant stakeholders may bring about some feeling of shame where family members and friends are engaged in a discussion of an offender's behaviour. Such acts may seem exciting for offenders when they falsely believe they are at a safe distance from possible discovery, but foster a sense of shame and remorse when brought out in the full light of day. Reintegrative shaming need not be in public or involve stigma in order to bring about a change of heart and facilitate reformation in certain cases. Restorative justice seeks to win both the minds and, importantly, the hearts of all. Reintegrative shaming is one approach to restoration that attempts just this.

These arguments rest to some degree on empirical facts, such as that reintegrative shaming is possible and perhaps additionally that shaming does not render restoration less likely to succeed post-shaming. If shaming made restorations more precarious and/or less likely, then this would offer strong grounds for restorative justice proponents to oppose shame punishments. Shame punishments seek justification through their good consequences. We must have some evidence to believe such consequences flow from shame punishments in order to determine their full context for justification. This case is not yet made.

The limits of restorative justice

Restorative justice is believed to be constrained by the limits of its applicability. These limits concern the identification of the community to be restored, the participation of victims in restorative conferences, and satisfying public confidence. Each will be taken in turn.

First, there is the problem of community. Restorative justice aims at a restoration of the damaged relationship between an offender and the wider community. But which community and who are the relevant members? It has been noted by some, such as Andrew Ashworth, that 'the concept of restoring the community remains shrouded in mystery, as indeed does the identification of the relevant "community"'.[47] The normative idea of 'community' is the product of a contested narrative that lacks any fixed group boundary.[48] This fact is presented forcefully by Bhikhu Parekh: 'Cultural communities are constantly exposed to, and having to change in response to, each other, and can no longer define and maintain their identities as they did before'.[49] Identities are not forged within a cultural vacuum, but within the world where identities may conflict or overlap. Indeed, we often possess 'multiple belongings' among different social identities.[50] Which are relevant for the purposes of restoration? How might we confirm whether restoration is achieved?

While the idea of social and political identity is complex, this does not present deep problems for restorative justice. Restoration must be flexible to address the needs of multiple conceptions of communities. For example, Ashworth says:

> If the broad aim is to restore the 'communities affected by the crime', as well as the victim and the victim's family, this will usually mean a geographical community; but where an offence targets a victim because of race, religion, sexual orientation, etc., that will point to a different community that needs to be restored.[51]

The fact that different communities may be relevant in different circumstances is not a problem of imprecision concerning restoration, but a strength of the restorative approach. The strength is that our focus is on addressing the need to restore damaged social relationships. We need only draw our attention to how restoration might be best achieved given the particulars of a specific situation.

Primary attention should be directed to relevant stakeholders. These are persons who have some stake in a crime and its outcome. They may include offenders, victims, neighbours, friends, and others. Their relevance is that they have a stake in restoration. We judge success by the satisfaction of stakeholders that restoration has been achieved. The idea of a 'community' may be open-textured, but this assists restorative justice in its ability to be applied with flexibility.

Second, there is the problem of victim inclusion. Restorative justice aims at a restoration of a damaged relationship between an offender and the wider community, including victims. Some have argued that restorative justice proponents face a problem concerning addressing the restoration of victims and the public interest. Ian Edwards says:

> Restorative conceptions of criminal justice focus on conceptions of crime as being an offence against a specific individual victim, as a violation of individual rights. But the public nature of crime requires more of the offender than the mere restoration or visceral satisfaction of the victim. The problem lies in defining the relationship between the public interest and the victim's interest, a relationship that is as yet insufficiently articulated.[52]

I believe this problem is directed at a mistaken conception about restorative justice. Properly understood, this approach addresses a need to restore damaged relationships. The presence of victims may play an important role, but it must be emphasized that damaged relationships are often not a private affair between victim and offender in that many others may have a stake in outcomes including the local community and the public interest. We look to restore what has been damaged and not only concerning the victim, however central the victim's position may be in proceedings. Nor need we find any problematic tension between the victim's interest and the public interest. Restorative conferences often include victims, offenders, and members of the community. They agree to a contract together and not separately with offenders with the assistance of a trained facilitator. Together, they may come to amend their recommendations in forging a common agreement. The interests of all may be preserved through constructive and structured dialogue.

Restorative justice does not require victim participation. This is an issue for several reasons. First, many crimes are victimless. If restorative justice were only applicable to restoring relations between offenders and victims, then many crimes would have to be dealt with by some other approach because they are victimless. Such crimes may include drug offences and traffic offences. While crimes may lack victims, they do not want for relevant stakeholders from the relevant community. Restorative conferences are applicable for addressing victimless crimes.

Second, there is the problem that some victims may not want to be involved. Or victims may be unable to become involved for some reason. This problem raises important worries. Restoration is about repairing a damaged relationship between more stakeholders than the victim alone, but the victim may play some central role in the restorative process. Restoration may become more difficult where victims are discouraged, unwilling, or unable to participate in some meaningful way. It is clear that a restorative conference may still move forward and be a success without the involvement of any victims, but less clear how this might be best achieved. The need to improve public confidence in restorative conferences is crucial: if the public accepts and endorses their use, then victims may become more willing to participate in these conferences when the need may arise.

This brings us to a third problem: this is the problem of public confidence. This is a real obstacle to the more widespread use of restorative justice. It is widely recognized that restorative justice may be (or should be) inappropriate for use in all cases and specifically inapplicable for serious crimes.[53] Restorative justice is primarily used for crimes involving youth offenders rather than adults.[54] Public confidence is lacking in many cases because of the perception that restorative justice is a soft option for these crimes. The objection is that restoration may be an appropriate response to youth crimes or minor crimes like shoplifting, but insufficiently punitive to address more serious crimes such as a violent assault or murder.

One route to improving public confidence is to improve the public's knowledge about restorative justice and its potential effectiveness. We will consider its effectiveness in the following section. There is ample evidence that public criticisms directed at criminal justice outcomes are inversely related to their knowledge about particular cases. In short, the more the public learn about any specific situation, the more likely they are to agree with its outcome. A major concern is that the public have a too limited understanding about criminal justice in general. The public's knowledge about criminal affairs is often gained through the media or word of mouth. The result is that the public may form opinions based upon misrepresentations and incomplete knowledge. If their understanding about restorative justice and its effectiveness were improved, there is much reason to expect greater confidence in the use of restorative justice as an alternative to traditional theories of punishment.[55]

Suppose that the public may come to have confidence in the use of restorative justice for many crimes. It is an open question whether public confidence in restorative justice will translate into a motivation to participate in restorative conferences. One problem is the widely noted decline of social capital in countries like the United States, the UK, and elsewhere. We now tend to 'bowl alone' with steep declines in attendance at club meetings and family meals.[56] People are turning away from face-to-face group forums and toward more private pursuits. This fact of declining public participation presents problems for more issues than restorative justice, and perhaps even the robust health of democratic institutions.[57] Public participation may be desirable for many reasons, but there must also be some clear plan for how it may be fostered and maintained so that it is sustainable. If citizens would rather disengage from public affairs than choose to participate, then there may be problems with implementing policies, such as restorative justice, that require participatory interest. This compounds the problem for restorative justice: it must both improve public confidence and become a more attractive forum for public part-icipation. Restoration aims to restore damaged community relationships: if few in the community want to become involved, then this undermines the project of restoration.

There is a second problem concerning public confidence and restorative justice. Suppose that the public had broad confidence in restorative justice. Suppose further that the public was sufficiently motivated to participate in restorative conferences where necessary. The problem is that virtually no one advocates the use of restorative justice for all cases. For example, virtually no advocates argue that we should use restorative justice instead of impri-sonment for violent sexual offenders or murderers. Restorative justice is then an approach to punishment for some crimes, but not all. The concern is the lack of public confidence in using an alternative to prisons for violent offenders. But let's suppose that restorative justice is applicable to all crimes. The problem is that it may not be applicable in every case. This is because restorative conferences aim at agreement of a contract that offenders must honour. If they fail to honour their contracts, then prison becomes a possi-ble last resort. Restorative justice aims to replace the use of prisons as much as possible, but it may not be possible for restorative justice to be the only alternative in every case. Imprisonment may become necessary in some circumstances. The lack of public confidence in non-penal outcomes for serious violent crimes is another problem. Restoration is a noble project that may command our best efforts, but perhaps more an ideal than reality.[58]

There is a third problem. Guilt is at the heart of restorative justice: the possibility of restoration requires offenders to take some responsibility for their crimes. One issue for critics is who has the right to demand offenders to own up to their criminal wrongdoing. Some argue that only victims may make these demands from their offenders.[59] The idea is that offenders have wronged victims and apologies are offered to victims in return. But why believe that offenders owe an apology to victims alone? This suggests that offenders do not need to apologize for victimless crimes, which is implausible. Moreover, if we accept the view that restorative justice aims at restoring a damaged public relationship, then apologies may be demanded by all who have a stake in the crime and its outcome.

A second related issue is whether the state should be in the business of demanding apologies from offenders. The worry is that state coercion is inappropriate for matters of conscience: we should oppose 'compulsory compassion'.[60] Conscience must be left to individuals, not the state. We fail to honour criminals where we coerce them on matters such as this.[61] The idea is that there may be strong incentives for criminals to cooperate. For example, we might offer restorative conferences instead of imprisonment on condition that offenders acknowledge their crimes. Critics worry that such incentives may coerce offenders into situations against their better judgement. However important we find apologies, they must only be for the right reasons. Moreover, some are concerned about the absence of a trial, the lower standard of evidence, the lack of an appeal, and the worry that apologies may be nothing more than empty gestures as offenders merely learn to say the 'right' things to receive lighter treatment betraying restoration.

The criticisms miss their mark. One reason is that the offender is free to change his mind during any restorative conference. For example, John Braithwaite says:

> Conferences should never proceed in cases where the defendant sees him, or herself, as innocent or blameless; they should not become adjudicative forums ... It is critical that defendants have ... a right to terminate the conference at any point that they feel moved to deny the charges being made against them. That is, at any point up to the signing of a final agreement defendants should have a right to withdraw, insisting that the matter be either adjudicated before a court or dropped.[62]

The offender's acknowledgement of guilt is central to the success of restoration. But restoration is only possible with the commitment and agreement of relevant stakeholders. Offenders may remove themselves from restorative conferences at any time. A second reason why these criticisms are unsuccessful is because restoration is secured through the agreement of a contract. The evidence that relevant parties are satisfied about future restoration is the high satisfaction victims, offenders, and others have after participating in a restorative conference. We may not accurately read the minds of others, but if victims and affected communities are satisfied by the attempts to repair damaged relationships by offenders on terms agreed between them then this offers strong reason to believe restoration is no empty gesture. Furthermore, there is no problem concerning appeal because the contract is to be agreed between those involved. It makes little sense to appeal a contract that you helped author and freely consented to accepting. Finally, there may be a lower bar for evidence and this is how it should be. This is because restoration is a constructive dialogue and not an adversarial trial.

Perhaps these problems highlight a new strategy for winning greater support for restorative justice. Restorative justice has two central claims.

First, punishment should restore damaged relationships. Second, punishment should be understood as non-imprisonment because this best facilitates restoration. Restorative justice punishes while reducing imprisonment.[63] These claims point towards a new question: why think restoration only possible without the use of prisons? If restoration is our goal, then why limit the methods by which it can be achieved?

Consider the idea of punitive restoration. Imprisonment may make restoration more difficult in most cases, but it need not do so in every case. If there are cases where prison may play some useful role in helping make restoration possible, then prison may form a part of the restorative solution. For example, employability skills and treatment for specific problems may form a central part of a criminal's reformation and subsequent restoration. These issues may often be best dealt with outside imprisonment, but it is unclear why secure facilities, such as a prison, could never serve a useful purpose in assisting reformation and restoration in some cases. Prisons provide various opportunities to offenders such as working in the kitchens, gardens, and recycling facilities in addition to both factory and assembly workshops where woodworking and textiles or training in construction, such as bricklaying, painting, and decorating and other skills are taught.

Prison may support restoration in some circumstances and it may increase public confidence in select cases. Limited applicability is a problem for restorative justice. Perhaps there would be greater public confidence where part of a restorative contract might include the possibility of prison, such as a suspended sentence pending the completion of a contract.[64]

Does restorative justice work?

Restorative justice has been highly promising in the limited contexts in which it has been employed. It is popular with both victims and offenders. About 85 per cent of victims are satisfied with the restorative process among those who have taken part. A majority of offenders choose to participate in restorative conferences where available. Preliminary findings show that the restorative justice approach leads to roughly 25 per cent less reoffending than alternatives. Restorative justice is more effective and at significantly less cost. One study found that the use of restorative justice saved £9 for every £1 spent.[65]

There are several reasons that may explain why restorative justice offers improved results. For example, there are several risk factors associated with reoffending, including substance abuse, housing problems, and unemployment.[66] Effective crime reduction must include some strategy for addressing risk factors and restorative justice is designed to fulfil this need. Offenders may be required to seek treatment or undergo education and training where these risk factors are present. These factors often have a heavy presence. For example, a recent report found that among persons arrested, approximately 12 per cent were problem crack or heroin users.

Four-fifths claimed to have performed a crime over the past week and almost one-third claimed to commit crimes daily. Drug-related crimes are costly and estimated to be £13.5 billion in England and Wales alone. The evidence from many studies suggests that non-prison alternatives are often more beneficial to tackling drug and alcohol abuse.[67] Restorative justice may better reduce crime where several risk factors are present with the savings to taxpayers that crime reduction brings.

Weak social networks are strongly associated with reoffending. Restorative justice aims at repairing and rebuilding these networks for the benefit of the affected community. Restorative conferences facilitate members speaking their own language in ways that have best meaning for them beyond the dry atmosphere of the courthouse.[68] We may expect the involvement of our community and support networks to better assist restoration because of the influence these groups often have on us. It has been argued that 'the closer the adjudicators and enforcers are to the offender, the more likely they are to be effective in bringing about the desired changes in behaviour'.[69] Restorative justice offers such a solution through the use of the restorative conference. Together, these reasons present much optimism for restorative justice and its future use.

The preliminary results are promising, but they are also inconclusive. John Braithwaite acknowledges: 'Most of the data are limited to a small range of outcomes; we are still awaiting the first systematic data on some of the dimensions of restoration'.[70] He continues:

> So restorative justice at the moment is an adventure of research and development, where the research is proving tremendously encouraging in some ways, discouraging in others. As we use empirical evidence to repair this leaky ship at sea, we should be careful about being too sure about a plan for the voyage.[71]

The success of restorative justice may lie in its flexibility to address specific crimes and their causes in a targeted way. We require further study and greater utilization of restorative justice to gather evidence of restorative justice's promise in more areas of criminal justice. These efforts will require a clear national strategy, which is often lacking, to direct future policy. This strategy must include some clear thinking about what it means for offenders to become restored in practice and how expectations may be effectively managed. For example, most offenders believe that restoration is complete when punishment is served.[72] Should this be true? Or should some offenders be restricted from some forms of employment temporarily or perhaps for life post-punishment? Should offenders post-punishment report their location to the police or a public database? Would these moves facilitate restoration or demarcate its limits? We require clarity on questions like this when creating an effective future national strategy. The answers we give will be influenced by how we conceive restoration and the importance we give it.

Conclusion

Restorative justice is a new alternative to traditional theories of punishment. While penal theories may disagree on several matters, they all endorse the possible justification of prison. Restorative justice does not. The preliminary results are promising although more research and further application are required before we may arrive at a more clear assessment of its wider effectiveness beyond its current usage. This will require a clear strategy and investment. The focus on restoration and not mere rehabilitation enables the approach to address the needs of the offender as well as those of the victim and wider community. Thus far, it has proved popular with participating stakeholders, but more work must be done to win over a more hesitant public.

Restoration appeals to the idea of holding offenders and the community responsible with accountability. Stakeholders come together in constructive dialogue to agree how restoration may be possible. Offenders take responsibility and they are held accountable, but the community has a responsibility also to engage with offenders and help determine the conditions for future restoration.

Restorative justice rejects the use of imprisonment as an obstacle to restoration. While prisons have their problems, they may also have their uses. There may be strong grounds for restorative justice proponents to no longer view criminal justice in terms of restoration or imprisonment, but instead in terms of restoration alone. Prison may have a place in assisting restoration in some cases. If restoration is our goal and we desire flexibility in how it is achieved, then it may be a mistake to omit prisons. Moreover, restoration and imprisonment may become combined as punitive restoration where we have greater options in hand and perhaps improved public confidence. Perhaps the only barrier to this move is that restorative justice may have to lose one source of its distinctiveness – its rejection of imprisonment – to improve restoration. Time will tell whether this is one recommendation too far.

Part 2
Hybrid theories

The first part considered the more traditional theories of punishment, where each has a single goal or principle. This second part will now consider 'hybrid theories' of punishment. These are alternative theories that bring together different elements of the theories in Part 1 into new combinations. We will discuss the 'mixed' theories of Herbert Hart and John Rawls including negative retributivism, expressivist and communicative theories of punishment, and the 'unified' theory of punishment with its idea of punitive restoration. These hybrid approaches will each be discussed individually in their own chapter. In Part 3, we will discuss how the several theories of punishment speak to practice.

5 Rawls, Hart, and the mixed theory

Introduction

We have considered several theories of punishment that advance a specific goal. Retributivists believe punishment should be distributed to the deserving in proportion to what is deserved. Deterrence proponents believe that punishment should deter and rehabilitation proponents believe punishment should reform offenders. Restorative justice advocates believe that punishment should aim at restoring damaged relationships and without using prisons. Retributivism, deterrence, rehabilitation, and restorative justice offer general theories of punishment.

This chapter will examine two important contributions by John Rawls and Herbert Hart on how we might understand a *mixed* theory of punishment. They argue that punishment has a mixed justification that brings together two or more penal goals. The hybrid nature of mixed theories of punishment renders them distinctive to general theories of punishment. These theories are attempts to bridge general theories of punishment and harness their combined theoretical power. However attractive, mixed theories of punishment raise new problems that may lead us to question their serving as a plausible alternative to non-mixed theories. We will survey the contributions of Rawls and Hart to consider the potential prospects and problems that mixed theories present us, including the theory of negative retributivism.

Rawls on punishment

John Rawls is widely recognized as the greatest political philosopher in at least a generation. His *A Theory of Justice* revolutionized the field and remains highly influential.[1] Rawls's novelty also extends to his arguments concerning punishment. He recognized that retributivists and their critics were not only in disagreement, but each was talking past the other.[2] Rawls believed it was possible to bring each side together if these approaches were structured in the right way. While his arguments broke new ground, they have received much criticism and most leading commentaries neglect Rawls's important contributions to this subject.[3] So while there are perhaps few explicit adherents of Rawls's views, there is an important new position set out that has led the way to the now popular view of so-called *negative retributivism*. This section will examine Rawls's arguments on punishment before turning to their later development in the work of Herbert Hart and the development of negative retributivism.

Rawls addresses punishment in an early and important essay entitled 'Two Concepts of Rules'.[4] His aim is to make a distinction between, first, the justification of a practice and, second, the justification of particular actions within a practice.[5] To justify a practice is not to close off the justification of actions within it: the two should be thought of separately. Rawls uses punishment to illustrate this distinction.

The two dominant theories of punishment at this time were utilitarianism and retributivism. Utilitarians justify punishment with reference to the beneficial future consequences.[6] Retributivists are understood to justify punishment on the grounds that 'wrongdoing merits punishment'.[7] Traditionally, utilitarianism and retributivism were believed to clash. How is it possible to *both* justify punishment in terms of its future effects *and* criminal desert? The worry is that punishments which may best bring about beneficial future consequences may not necessarily be linked with desert. The project of justification based on future consequences is different from the project of justification based on past crimes. Utilitarianism and retributivism appear to be incompatible at first glance.

Rawls argues that they are not incompatible, but instead address different questions concerning the justification of punishment. He says: 'utilitarian arguments are appropriate with regard to questions about practices, while retributive arguments fit the application of particular rules to particular cases'.[8] These questions are different. Their difference is also the possibility of their combination. Rawls believes that utilitarianism and retributivism address different questions and that together they offer a coherent mixed theory of punishment. He argues:

> One question emphasizes the proper name: it asks why *J* was punished rather than someone else, or it asks what he was punished for. The other question asks why we have the institution of punishment: why do people punish one another rather than, say, always forgiving one another?[9]

One question concerns why punish *this* criminal; the second question concerns why punish *any* criminal. The first question is about distribution of a particular practice addressed by retributivism. The second question is about the justification of punishment as an institutional practice addressed by utilitarianism. Any plausible theory of punishment must address both questions. Rawls's novelty is to argue that a theory of punishment may be a *mixed theory* combining two seemingly incompatible general theories of punishment.[10]

Punishment concerns legal questions, and the law should be approached from two different viewpoints, namely, the legislator and the judge. Rawls argues that the legislator looks to future consequences and the justification of the larger legal enterprise. However, the judge looks to the past to determine whether we are justified in selecting a particular person as a criminal. These two viewpoints of law do not represent a confusion, but point towards a common project. Rawls says:

> The answer, then, to the confusion engendered by the two views of punishment is quite simple: one distinguishes two offices, that of the judge and that of the legislator, and one distinguishes their different stations with respect to the system of rules which make up the law; and then one notes that the different sort of considerations which would usually be offered as reasons for what is done under the cover of these offices can be paired off with the competing justifications of punishment.[11]

Utilitarianism and retributivism may not only be combined in a plausible and compelling theory of punishment, but they contribute to an attractive theory of law. The justification of an overall practice is different from the justification of actions within a practice.

Or is it? We might reject this distinction on the grounds that utilitarians offer more than a theory about the justification of a practice. For example, utilitarians might argue that the distribution of punishment should be determined with reference to consequentialist considerations, such as promoting the greatest happiness of the greater number. Or we might reject the distinction on the grounds that retributivists offer more than a theory about the distribution of punishment within a justified institutional framework. Retributivists might argue that the institution of punishment should be justified on grounds of distributing just deserts. While Rawls may offer one perspective on how utilitarian and retributivist considerations may be brought together under a single mixed theory of punishment, Rawls is wrong to claim that neither utilitarianism nor retributivism offers a theory of punishment and its distribution separately.

Rawls considers and rejects these objections. He denies the claim that retributivists advocate an institutional theory of punishment. Instead, Rawls argues that retributivism addresses the distribution of punishment only and highlights the important issue that punishment should never be distributed to the innocent.[12] Rawls takes it that plausible utilitarian theories of punishment assume that the innocent should never be punished, but must recognize that a focus on consequences alone leaves utilitarians vulnerable to the charge that their theory of punishment would justify punishing the innocent.[13] Each view of punishment appears to assume the presence of the other and each is incomplete separately. Not only is it *possible* to bring utilitarian and retributivist theories together in one coherent mixed theory of punishment, but they *should* be viewed together.[14] Utilitarianism and retributivism assume and require each other.

This fundamental distinction may rest on a mistake. The mistake is to suggest that a *retributivist* or *deterrent* theory of punishment is impossible because each fundamentally addresses different, but compatible questions which must be brought together in one single mixed theory to support a plausible theory of punishment. We have already considered retributivism and deterrence in chapters 1 and 2. While these theories have shortcomings, it is inaccurate to conclude that neither offers some complete theory of punishment. Of course, it is a separate matter whether either retributivism or deterrence offers the most compelling theory of punishment. But both can and do address the justification of punishment and the justification of the distribution of punishment. It is a mistake to argue contrariwise.

The more interesting philosophical issue is not whether retributivism and deterrence may each offer a theory of punishment, but rather whether they offer a coherent mixed theory of punishment in combination. Rawls argues any theory of punishment must address two questions about justification concerning the institution of punishment and the distribution of punishment. Utilitarianism addresses the first justification and retributivism the second. So each view may address these different questions and it is possible to bring them together. But is this a coherent theory?

There is a central problem at the heart of Rawls's mixed theory of punishment.[15] There is an unresolved tension between crime reduction and retributivism that renders the theory incoherent. The utilitarian justification of the practice of punishment addresses the issue of why we should have a penal system. Utilitarianism looks to the beneficial future consequences arising from crime reduction. These future consequences are manifested in non-utilitarian distribution of punishment to guilty persons. The tension is this: if individual punishments are distributed solely on the basis of retributivist desert, then Rawls is assuming a system whereby each offender deserving punishment will lead to crime reduction. For example, an offender is on trial and correctly found guilty. He is then punished for his crime because of his guilt. Utilitarianism plays only the role of justifying the legal system, but it does not justify how the legal system chooses people to punish and which punishments they receive. This question of what is distributed to whom within the practice relates to retributivism. But then what work is utilitarianism doing in fact? If no offender is punished in order to contribute to beneficial future effects, then why claim that the criminal justice system is justified as a system because it *does* have such effects? It is uncertain how mixed Rawls's mixed theory of punishment is, in fact. It might appear broadly retributivist in practice, if not theory.

One move available to Rawls is to claim much more than what he says about how utilitarian features might play a role in his theory. For example, Rawls distinguishes the institution of punishment from distribution of punishment. However, he might argue that the institution of punishment includes the *proportionality* of punishment. Retributivism plays the role of ensuring only the guilty are punished, but utilitarianism would then play the role of determining how much punishment the guilty will receive. Rawls might then avoid the central tension in his mixed theory of punishment by more explicitly endorsing *negative retributivism*. We will consider this view of punishment shortly. Before we continue, it is helpful to examine Hart's attempt to offer his own Rawlsian-inspired mixed theory to see whether or not this theory is more successful.

Hart on punishment

Herbert Hart primarily addresses punishment in his landmark work *Punishment and Responsibility*.[16] Hart's account is inspired by Rawls's attempt to offer a mixed theory of punishment. Similarly, Hart claims to offer a theory of punishment that exhibits 'a compromise' between distinctly different approaches to punishment.[17] The problem with traditional debates concerning punishment is that they rest on a mistake. Commentators are mistaken to claim 'there is one supreme value or objective (e.g. Deterrence, Retribution or Reform) in terms of which *all* questions about the justification of punishment are to be answered'.[18] Anyone who argues that all such questions may be answered by one particular penal objective over-simplify the complexity of punishment.[19] Hart says: 'theories of punishment are not theories in any normal sense' where each offers claims about why punishment 'should or may be used'.[20] Punishment is a feature of our society. How should punishment be best understood?

Rawls argued that a mixed theory of punishment should address the justification of punishment and the justification of the distribution of punishment. Hart develops this model further. He says:

> What is needed is the realization that different principles (each of which may in a sense be called a 'justification') are relevant at different points in any morally acceptable account of punishment. What we should look for are answers to a number of different questions such as: What justifies the general practice of punishment? To whom may punishment be applied? How severely may we punish?[21]

These three questions are broadly understood to address the definition of punishment, the general justifying aim of punishment, and the distribution of punishment. We considered the definition of punishment in our general introduction and claimed that punishment should be understood as a response to crime. Hart correctly highlights the problem of the *definitional stop*, namely, that the definition of what we consider punishment is distinct from its aims.[22] Therefore, our view of punishment as a response does not lead us to any one view of what the best aim of our response to crime should be.

Hart's distinction between the general justifying aim of punishment and the justification of its distribution is presented in the following way:

> Retribution in the Distribution of punishment has a value quite independent of Retribution as Justifying Aim. This is shown by the fact that we attach importance to the restrictive principle that only offenders may be punished, even where breach of this law might not be thought immoral.[23]

Retribution as the justification of distributing punishments says that we may only select the deserving for punishment. Retribution as the justification of punishment as a legal institution says that punishments must be proportionate to what offenders deserve. Retribution means different things when considered from different perspectives.

The idea is that no single view of punishment captures all relevant aspects of punishment on its own. A more compelling view of punishment will bring together seemingly different penal considerations within a mixed theory of punishment. This theory will be coherent because there need not be any clash between different penal justifications employed at different levels. For example, the justifying aim of punishment cannot be *both* retribution and deterrence. But there is no incoherence with a theory whose justifying aim of punishment is deterrence and its justifying distribution is retributivist. This is because who we should punish and how much they should be punished are different questions. There is no necessary contradiction in different penal goals addressing different questions.

Hart follows Rawls in arguing that different penal goals may address different penal questions and that certain goals best address certain questions. Again, similarly, Hart shares the distinction between the judge and the legislator when we consider the construction of a theory of punishment: the judge looks to particular cases in the past while the legislator takes a larger view in looking to the future.[24]

It is unclear where Hart's mixed theory of punishment advances Rawls's mixed theory much further. While Hart helpfully offers insight into the different questions addressed by punishment, he follows Rawls in the mistaken view that different questions demand different penal perspectives. The fact that there are three different questions to address does not clearly rule out the theoretical possibility that they may be all addressed by a single theory of punishment. For example, retributivism can offer a theory of punishment as we saw in chapter 1. We may prefer some alternative theory of punishment, but it is not clear that no general theory of punishment is plausibly possible. This claim appears to claim too much in its enthusiasm to present a mixed theory that can capture punishment in a more complex way by bringing together retribution and other penal goals into a coherent theory. Perhaps this theory is preferable. But others are possible even if less compelling. Hart appears to admit as much in his discussion of retribution.

While he admits that it can answer the three questions about punishment he raised earlier, Hart calls such a 'thoroughgoing' variety of retributivism 'simple', 'crude', and 'severe'.[25] The argument is that it is possible to offer a coherent general theory of punishment modelled on a single view, but these attempts are less compelling than a mixed theory that speaks to more penal considerations. So Hart need not disagree with our criticism.

Hart concludes by arguing that the most compelling theory of punishment will hold that punishment is proportionate to the gravity of the crime, the justifying aim of punishment is retribution, and punishment should be understood within a utilitarian framework.[26] This position has a strong resemblance to Rawls's theory of punishment. Hart's explanation for why a utilitarian framework is important is as follows:

> any theory of punishment purporting to be relevant to a modern system of criminal law must allot an important place to the Utilitarian conception that the institution of criminal punishment is to be justified as a method of preventing harmful crime, even if the mechanism of prevention is fear rather than the reinforcement of moral inhibition.[27]

Hart argues that our modern understanding of retribution and utilitarianism rests on the older distinction between *mala in se,* where crimes are criminal because they are morally wrong in some sense, and *mala prohibita,* where crimes are criminal because they are legally prohibited.[28] It is then not always possible to address crimes as moral wrongs, but it is possible to punish crimes as legal wrongs.

This view of punishment runs into a significant problem identified by Douglas Husak:

> A system in which a subset of deserving offenders should actually be punished may have a different general justifying aim than a system that endeavors to punish every deserving offender. But if the issue of whether the deserving should be punished is to be classified as a question about distribution, as seems likely, I believe that Hart is mistaken in holding that consequences are irrelevant to distributive concerns.[29]

The problem is that the distinction between the justification of punishment and the justification of its distribution may not be as sharp as Hart claims. If each offender is punished solely in terms of her punishable desert, then how is retribution *not* part of the aim of punishment in fact? We might only claim the justifying aim of punishment is consequentialist when we distribute punishment solely to the deserving where we hold that punishing the deserving because it is deserved *also* contributes to the promotion of separate consequentialist considerations. If this is true, then beneficial consequences arise as a side effect of a retributivist theory of punishment. If desert does the work, then why should consequentialism receive the credit?

Both Rawls and Hart attempt to offer a new account of punishment. This account is a mixed theory of punishment. Both highlight the fact that punishment is a more complex issue than previously understood and that punishment should address more questions than its definition. Both attempts run into similar problems concerning how each seeks to 'mix' its theory. Neither offers any clear compelling argument for how their theory is a coherent mix of multiple penal goals as presented, but they do point towards a more promising view of punishment that has attracted much attention in recent years. This is the theory of negative retributivism and we will turn to it now.

Negative retributivism

Rawls and Hart may have been unsuccessful in their attempts at offering a mixed theory of punishment bringing retributivism and consequentialism within a compelling framework. Nonetheless, their efforts at bridging different theories of punishment have not been in vain, because they have inspired others to improve upon their original project.

Perhaps the most widely held mixed theory of punishment is now commonly known as *negative retributivism*. We previously saw in our examination of retributivism in chapter 1 that retributivism was defined as the view that punishment is distributed only to the guilty and in proportion to their guilt. This view of retributivist punishment was then identified as *the standard case* because it is the classic view of retributivism that its adherents have defended in the past. The standard view of retributivism is also understood as *positive* retributivism. It is positive insofar as this theory of punishment positively links desert to both the distribution of punishment and its severity. Positive retributivists justify punishment for the guilty alone and in proportion to their guilt.

Negative retributivists argue for a view of punishment where desert plays an important, but less central role. They argue that we should distribute punishment to the deserving, but the severity of punishment is linked with consequentialist considerations. The view is attractive because it appears to avoid specific problems. One problem it avoids is the problem of punishing the innocent. Negative retributivists argue that we punish only the deserving. This mixed theory of punishment can never justify punishing an innocent person. A second problem is where our judgement to punish or not to punish may yield beneficial consequences: we may want a theory of punishment that is satisfactorily responsive to future beneficial consequences where possible. If punishments are distributed only to the guilty, but the decision to punish and the judgement of how much to punish were determined with a view to the consequences, then such a mixed theory may prove compelling.

This highlights a specific distinction between positive and negative retributivism. Desert is necessary and sufficient for positive retributivism.

Desert is necessary because positive retributivists may only punish the guilty and never the innocent. Desert is sufficient because positive retributivists punish with a view to an offender's desert alone and other considerations are irrelevant. We punish the deserving because they have desert; we punish the deserving to the degree that they deserve.

Desert is necessary, but not sufficient for negative retributivism. Desert is necessary for the same reason that it is necessary for positive retributivism. Punishment is only distributed to the deserving because they possess desert for both positive and negative retributivists. However, desert is *not* sufficient for determining whether we should punish a deserving person for negative retributivists. While we would only punish the deserving because they have desert, we need not punish the deserving where we are guided by other considerations instead. For example, suppose that our negative retributivism justified the distribution of punishment to the deserving and it justified punishment on grounds of general deterrence. This understanding of negative retributivism would not justify the punishment of the innocent: all persons punished must be guilty. Nevertheless, the fact someone deserves punishment is not enough to justify our distributing punishment to him: we would only punish where his punishment served the aims of general deterrence.

Negative retributivism is a mixed theory of punishment because it is able to combine retributivist desert with other perspectives on punishment. This theory may appear compelling because it avoids punishing the innocent while remaining flexible to take advantage of future benefits. Negative retributivism may be a coherent mixed theory because it 'justifies punishment in terms not of its contingently beneficial effects but of its *intrinsic* justice as a response to crime; the justificatory relationship holds between present punishment and past crime, not between present punishment and future effects'.[30] There is a difference between the link to the past and the connection to the future. There may be good reason to ensure that all persons liable to be punished have some link to a past crime, but decide against deserved punishment because it is outweighed by important future effects that we value. For example, suppose that punishing a deserving person would lead to little social benefit (however this is understood) and would damage social trust between citizens. This situation could be avoided through issuing a pardon. A pardon does not deny the desert of the pardoned, but rather it denies the imposition of punishing. Negative retributivism could justify pardons on these grounds and so it may be sensitive to promoting beneficial consequences but never at the cost of punishing the innocent. Positive retributivism, or the standard view of retribution, would be unable to justify pardons. The deserving should be punished even if this contributed to political instability and civil war.

One problem with negative retributivism is a problem we have seen with other mixed theories: it draws too sharp a distinction between the justification of punishment and its distribution that may be untenable. Perhaps the consequences should matter. The problem is that if desert alone may be so central to the determination of who we may choose to punish unlike all other considerations, then why should desert play no clear role whatsoever in the justification of punishment? It seems odd to claim that desert plays the only role in one arena, but perhaps none in any other. Negative retributivists might respond that desert does play a role in the justification of punishment, namely, that only the deserving can be punished. Perhaps desert is insufficient to ever tip the balance in favour of our punishing a deserving person. But desert does have a central role to play and that role is selecting all persons we might punish.

However, this reply raises a second problem with negative retributivism. Punishment may involve different considerations. We have already noted the worry that the distinctions drawn may be drawn too sharply. For example, if we only punish the deserving to the degree they deserve, it is unclear how our acts of punishment could contribute to a non-retributivist general justifying aim of punishment.

Now let's consider the issue in light of negative retributivism. The justification of punishment may be different from its distribution, but how different are they in fact? So we might imagine someone claiming that punishment should be distributed only to the deserving where this contributes to beneficial future effects. Note that this understanding of negative retributivism shows that this mixed theory of punishment is essentially a form of *rule utilitarianism*, and perhaps with all the concerns that rule utilitarianism attracts.[31] Rule utilitarianism is broadly the view that we should pursue the greatest happiness for the greater number within the constraints of set rules. The traditional objection is that the justification for the rules that constrain desired consequences may differ from the justification for why we should pursue these consequences. If the consequences are justified, then why be constrained by rules unless this constraint best supports pursuit of preferred consequences? So why limit the conditions for punishing with a view to deter others where the conditions may not contribute to improved deterrence? Or if the rules chosen to constrain our practices have such priority, then should we look to follow these rules alone?

Perhaps one reply is to say that we simply find the flexibility of negative retributivism attractive. This prize may come at the heavy cost of theoretical underdevelopment and incoherence. It is not enough to claim punishment has different questions so we *can* answer them in different ways. Punishment is a practice and it demands some coherent account for why different questions *should* be addressed in particular ways. Negative retributivists owe us a more compelling account of how the different features relate to each other and not only how each feature addresses distinct, but related, questions.

Furthermore, negative retributivists should acknowledge that their mixed theory of punishment is broadly rule utilitarian. This understanding may place how we view negative retributivism within a new light and it may cause us to query more critically the relation between how the means and the ends of punishments are coherently justified. We do not want for explanations of their differences. But, if the means and ends of punishment broadly understood as the constraining rules and overall general justification of punishment are unrelated, then it becomes difficult to find negative retributivism more than intuitively compelling.[32] Perhaps there is good reason to distribute punishment in a particular way and a different good reason to justify the practice of punishment. What we require is some third reason to justify how these reasons come together, if negative retributivism is to be a theoretically coherent theory of punishment.

Conclusion

This chapter introduces the first of several attempts at offering a hybrid theory of punishment. A general theory of punishment rests its justification on a particular aim. A hybrid, or mixed, theory of punishment aspires to justify punishment on the basis of more than one aim. These theories are intuitively attractive because there is often something compelling about each major view of punishment. For example, there is something compelling about the retributivist focus on the necessity of desert, not least for avoiding the problem of punishing the innocent. Likewise, there is also something compelling about the focus of deterrent or rehabilitative views on crime reduction: we might want a theory of punishment that made crime less likely rather than more likely over time. The problem is whether or not we can enjoy both goods at the same time. Traditional proponents of (positive) retributivism, deterrence, rehabilitation, and restorative justice have argued we cannot. A choice must be made.

Rawls and Hart offer important first attempts at how we might understand a mixed theory of punishment that brought together more than one penal goal. They argue it is possible to bring retributivist desert and other penal considerations within a hybrid theory. Such a view has the attraction of addressing the importance of desert while remaining flexible to respond to maximizing beneficial future consequences. The problem is that these attempts are unsuccessful; their promise is more mirage than concrete. This is because the conceptions inadequately address their problematic internal coherence.

The theories of punishment offered by Rawls and Hart find some expression in negative retributivism. All three hold that retributivist desert is necessary for punishment. Negative retributivists claim that desert is not sufficient for punishment and that the potential beneficial consequences are relevant. The problem is once again internal coherence. Perhaps we find it intuitively attractive to say that all punishment must be deserved, but not all the deserving should be punished and that consequences matter. But we must have some plausible explanation for how these different parts with different approaches are meant to hang together in a theoretically coherent way.

This chapter begins our exploration of new approaches to considering punishment as a hybrid theory bringing together different considerations into one coherent view. We shall see whether the expressivist theory or unified theory of punishment fare any better in the next two chapters.

6 Expressivism

Introduction

Expressivism is a theory of punishment that has swiftly grown in popularity over recent years. Some critics have called it 'the latest fad in the philosophy of punishment'.[1] Expressivists challenge a longstanding feature of most thinking about the criminal law. For example, the former US President John Adams once said that the law is 'deaf as an adder to the clamours of the populace'.[2] The idea is that citizens should be ruled by the impartial and objective rule of law rather than public sentiment. It should not matter how the public feel about a case, but only how the rule of law might apply to it. Justice is about what is right and not always what is popular.

Expressivists argue that punishment should be understood as the expression of public disapproval. Punishment, and especially imprisonment, is not the mere infliction of pain but a statement of denunciation. It is this expressive character of punishment that justifies punishment. Expressivists defend linking punishment with public approval. Justice can be about what is right and popular. After all, criminal justice policy should command popular support in democratic societies to justify the use of coercion against offenders and to justify the large costs to the taxpayer. Furthermore, expressivism offers a new *hybrid* theory of punishment and alternative to the approaches by John Rawls and Herbert Hart examined in chapter 5. Expressivists argue that punishment may address several penal goals through its expressive character, including retributivist desert, the promotion of general deterrence, and offender rehabilitation.

This chapter will begin with an examination of expressivism's roots and include discussion of more recent attempts to revise and improve expressivism, principally, the communicative theory of punishment. Expressivists raise several important considerations that are often overlooked by other theories of punishment and this has helped contribute to their increasing popularity.

What is expressivism?

The idea behind expressivist theories of punishment is simple, but elusive. Expressivists, following Lord Denning, claim that: 'The ultimate justification of punishment is not that it is a deterrent, but that it is the emphatic denunciation by the community of a crime'.[3] Punishment is not merely something that happens to criminals, but it is something that the public communicate to them. Crimes are those activities that the public denounce, and the formal statement of their denunciation is punishment.

Perhaps the most famous classic exponent of expressivism is the Victorian judge James Fitzjames Stephen:

> The sentence of the law is to the moral sentiments of the public in relation to any offence what a seal is to hot wax. It converts into a permanent final judgment what might otherwise be a transient sentiment ... the infliction of punishment by law gives definite expression and solemn justification to the hatred which is excited by the commission of the offence.[4]

Punishment gives concrete expression to the public mood in a structured way. Public anger towards crime is not always unjustified. Punishment is the expression of *justified* public denunciation pertaining to a criminal offence. Expressivists make a distinction between public anger *simplicitor* and public anger in relation to crime. Offenders are punished for crimes alone and their punishment gives expression to the public mood. Therefore, punishment expresses not mere public hatred, but justified public hatred that relates to crimes.

This link between punishment and public denunciation is understood as *the expressive function of punishment*.[5] Expressivists make a distinction between punishment and penalties which we noted in the general introduction. Punishment is understood as imprisonment, and penalties are non-prison sanctions, such as monetary fines and community sentences. For expressivists, punishment is different in severity and character from penalties:

> To define punishment as hard treatment inflicted on a person who has offended against a legal rule, by an authority constituted by the relevant legal system, is to miss an essential element of punishment as distinguished from a mere penalty such as a parking ticket. That element is its symbolic significance.[6]

Punishment is symbolic as imprisonment; prisons are 'a clear case of punishment in the emphatic sense'.[7] Prison physically separates the offender from the community's everyday life. Offenders have violated moral values affirmed by a community in its legal system and are 'unfit to continue living among us'.[8] This separation of the offender from the community speaks to the significant disapproval held by the community for an offender's crime. Punishment 'tells the world' that an offender 'had no right to do what he did' and 'his government does not condone that sort of thing'.[9]

These claims may seem more metaphorical than realistic, but expressivists reject this criticism. Punishment highlights those activities with official government disapproval.[10] The public may understand official disapproval through punishment. There is no good reason to believe that punishment expresses official approval under normal circumstances. Punishment should be understood as a megaphone whereby the public make clear their denunciation of criminality.[11]

Expressivist theories of punishment are deserved and proportional. Disapproval focuses on the crimes committed. We express condemnation of acts and not the individuals who perform them: punishment expresses disapproval of crimes and not persons.[12] Expressivism is also proportional. Some crimes command greater public denunciation than others. Expressivists are able to differentiate the just punishments for crimes whether they are murders, thefts, or others through the strength of public disapproval addressed in each case. We may all believe that murders should be punished more severely than thefts, all things considered. Expressivists argue that this judgement is correct because we condemn murder more than theft. It is not about how much punishment may be 'deserved' for particular crimes, but how strongly we, the public, disapprove them. Punishment should be related to the strength of our condemnation: 'Pain should match guilt only insofar as its infliction is the symbolic vehicle of public condemnation'.[13] Expressivism claims to account for other penal goals beyond desert and proportionality which we will address below.

Expressivist theories present us with a powerful and compelling new understanding of punishment. Before we turn to a more critical appraisal of its supposed merits, our attention should focus first on an important new development within expressivism that attempts to build a more robust and satisfactory view of how we should conceive punishment as expressivist. This new development is the communicative theory of punishment championed by Antony Duff and others.

The communicative theory of punishment

One view of expressivism is that punishment expresses public denunciation to offenders. Expression is unidirectional from the public to the offender. A second view of expressivism is the communicative theory of punishment. This approach argues that expression is communicated in two directions in a call and response. First, we express our public disapproval to offenders through punishment. This is our declaratory call where our denunciation is expressed. Second, offenders then communicate to the public some expression of their remorse. This is their communicative response to our declaration of disapproval. Communicative theorists argue that punishment is not merely our expression of disapproval, but a communicative dialogue between the public and offender.[14] We communicate our disapproval; offenders communicate their remorse. The communicative theory offers this novel revision of classic expressivism.

Communicative punishment aims at the reformation of offenders. Antony Duff says:

> If he is convicted, his conviction communicates to him (and to others) the censure that he has been proved to deserve for his crime. He is expected (but not compelled) to understand and accept the censure as justified: to understand and accept that he committed a wrong for which the community now properly censures him. His trial and conviction thus address him and seek a response from him as a member of the political community who is both bound and protected by its laws.[15]

Punishment is understood as imprisonment, or hard treatment. Prison provides offenders with an opportunity 'to examine their souls' as time is served.[16] Prison offers a space for reflection and reformation. It is expected that offenders will eventually view their imprisonment as justified although this is not forced onto them. Offenders need not become reformed to be released from prison after the end of their sentence. Nevertheless, punishment aims at enabling reformation while offenders are in prison.

Time spent imprisoned should not be a pleasant experience in order to best benefit offenders. Punishment as imprisonment intends some degree of suffering. For example, Duff argues: 'Punishment aims to inflict something painful or burdensome on an offender for his offense ... Nor are this pain and this burden mere unintended side effects of a procedure which is not designed to be painful or burdensome'.[17] Some degree of suffering is important instrumentally in ensuring that punishment 'go deep with the wrongdoer and must therefore occupy his attention, his thoughts, his emotions, for some considerable time'.[18] So punishment should take time so offenders can satisfactorily reflect on their crimes.[19] Offenders should not only be apologetic, but endure 'secular penance'.[20] This is because, for Duff, 'a (mere) apology cannot heal the moral wound done by the wrong'.[21] Imprisonable crimes require penance, not only apology. Offenders receive a clear expression of public disapproval for their crimes in enduring punishment and offenders communicate their penance, not merely their apology, in serving time. Punishment is justified as a form of expressive communication between the offender and the public.

A central idea is that prison best ensures criminal reformation through penance. This account is philosophical: we speak of prisons *as they should be* and not *as they are found*. Duff says:

> Such an objection would have force if my claim were that the familiar kinds of hard treatment punishment which are salient in our existing

penal systems actually serve to induce repentance and self-reform, but that is not my claim … My claim is rather that suitably designed and administered kinds of hard treatment should, and in principle could, serve those aims … [I]t does not depend on proof that our existing penal systems serve those aims.[22]

Duff does not overlook the fact that present realities often fail to live up to our expectations. The idea seems to be that we have a duty to ensure our prisons improve so that our expectations are met rather than abandon prisons in search for some alternative. Duff notes that prisons 'will often fail' to secure their proper aims and their relative 'success is highly unlikely'.[23] But the fact that prisons do not satisfactorily support criminal reformation today should not lead us to reject the use of prisons for criminal reformation in future on this view.

The communicative theory of punishment justifies punishment as a two-way expressive dialogue between the community and an offender leading to the offender's repentance and self-reform. It is a paternalistic theory aimed at criminal reformation.[24] The importance of repentance is its self-reformative power. Through imprisonment we come to recognize the need to act differently in future.[25] Hard treatment, such as imprisonment, is necessary to ensure this message is communicated effectively to offenders. Offenders repay their *apologetic debt* to the society in serving time in prison for their crimes. Time served is a concrete act communicating apologies through repentance.

Duff is the leading exponent of the communicative theory of punishment and other major figures have defended broadly similar theories centring on the expressive and communicative elements in justified punishment. One important example is the idea that the primary aim of punishment is *censure*.[26] Andrew von Hirsch argues that offenders must recognize and accept their blameworthiness for crimes. Censure is addressed to the victim, the offender, and the community. It is addressed to the victim by acknowledging her hurt in sentencing the offender. Censure is addressed to offenders by communicating a call for remorse in relation to harm caused. Finally, censure is addressed to third parties, such as the community, in giving reason to avoid an action *as a wrong*. Punishment as censure communicates recognition of a wrong and the acknowledgement of hurt as well as the need for remorse and healing. Punishment is justified by the communicative nature of legal punishment.

The communicative theory of punishment is a development of expressivist theories of punishment. For communicative theorists, the purpose of imprisonment is twofold. First, it gives expression to our feelings of public denunciation towards a crime. Second, it provides an opportunity for offenders to look deep within themselves and grasp the error of their criminal ways by communicating repentance and self-reformation paying back their apologetic debts to the community. Punishment looks back to the crime performed and ahead to the future repentance of offenders bringing different penal goals together in a hybrid theory of punishment.

What is expressed?

Expressivists argue that punishment has an expressive character in communicating public denunciation of crimes. This may take any number of forms including the expression of 'attitudes, sentiments, resentment, revenge, emotions, respect, indignation, and disgust'.[27] If punishment is expressive, what is expressed?

One understanding of punishment as expression is *punishment as metaphorical expression*. To say punishment is an 'expression' of disapproval is to view punishment as a metaphor for the disapproval community members may share. Punishment is not the embodiment of public denunciation, but it is a metaphor for it. To punish is to say we strongly disapprove of your crime – and we mean it![28] This view is attractive insofar as it is compelling to view justified punishment as an institutional response to crime that conveys disapproval. Few prisoners believe that punishment is a sign of public *approval* of their crimes.

There are two potential problems with this position. The first is that the justification of punishment as expressivist may give punishment 'undesirable glamour'.[29] Punishment is not a celebration of our condemnation, but an institution of some regret. We may be justified to punish offenders for their crimes, but we may wish that punishment were unnecessary because crimes had not occurred. Expressivism may be thought to give significance to matters that ought not receive such attention, such as public anger or vindictiveness.

The second potential problem is that expressivism appears little different than retribution in practice. Both may claim punishment condemns crime and that punishment should be more punitive in proportion to the wrongness of a corresponding crime. Expressivism has even been said to be a servant of retribution.[30] There seems little difference in fact between retributivism and expressivism from this perspective. One difference is that retributivists would argue that deserved punishment in prison need not have a reformatory effect; communicative theorists would argue that retributively deserved imprisonment has this effect as a form of secular penance. We will turn to this claim later.

Note that the problem here is about the distinctiveness of expressivism and not its plausibility. Perhaps retributivism and expressivism justify strikingly similar punishments for the same crimes on similar grounds. This is the problem of expressivism collapsing into retributivism and not necessarily an argument against expressivism as a potentially compelling theory of punishment. So while punishment as a metaphorical expression of public denunciation may not be unique to expressivism per se, this is not an argument against the view that such a metaphor lacks meaning or is completely unfounded if we accepted retributivism. Metaphorical expressivism is retributivism by another name.

A further issue is this: if punishment metaphorically symbolizes disapproval, then might *any* theory of punishment accept this view? For example, rehabilitation theorists or restorative justice proponents can also accept that punishment may have some symbolic significance as a form of disapproval. Punishment as a metaphorical expression is a view all theories might accept to some degree. Again, this is the problem about expressivism's lack of distinctiveness. Disagreement will remain on the role that expression should play. But should we link punishment with metaphorical symbolism? Or should punishment be grounded on a more secure foundation?

A second understanding of punishment as expression is *punishment as emotional expression*. This view takes punishment as expressing widely shared emotional responses to offenders. The problem here is determining which emotions, if any, are most appropriate for a compelling theory of expressivist punishment. There appear to be three leading views. These are that punishment is the expression of public anger, fear, or disgust. Let's examine each.

One view is that punishment should be understood as an expression of public anger. For example, Feinberg argues that punishment expresses 'a kind of vindictive resentment'.[31] Punishment is the manifestation of our justified anger: we punish offenders because we are angry about their crimes. Our anger must be justified: we do not punish persons merely because we dislike them, but because we denounce crimes. There is something perhaps prima facie appealing about this view. Many of us are unhappy about crimes, and punishment is one manifestation of our collective displeasure.

There are several problems. First, not all anger is relevant. Public anger may take many forms including anger towards particular individuals, groups, or towards behaviour. Not all such anger counts for expressivist punishment because punishment is related to crimes alone. Anger arising from different sources does not figure in expressivist punishments. The problem is that expressivist punishment gives voice to only some public anger and not others. This might not be a problem if punishable public anger were all public anger above some threshold. We might argue that only anger above this level is strong enough to warrant criminalization and punishment. But it is unclear that public anger works like this. So there may be public anger directed towards persons and non-crimes that is above some threshold, not unlike justified public anger towards crimes. We might still argue that only public anger that is justified can become a foundation for expressivist punishment. However, notice then that it is not the fact that punishment expresses public anger which does justificatory work, but the fact that punishment is justified on some other ground. It is perhaps this other ground – such as retributivist desert – that appears to justify expressivist punishment and not the expression of public anger per se. Expressivism is rendered either incoherent or irrelevant.

A second problem is that punishment should not be linked to vindictive sentiment. Expressivism becomes shorthand for 'we strike you because you struck us and we wish to express our collective anger'. Punishment may still symbolize our disapproval, but perhaps other sentiments play, or should play, a more central role. But a further issue is whether criminalization should be based upon public anger. Is illegal parking criminal because it stirs public anger? If true, then this is partly an empirical claim. So where's the evidence? Rather than ground claims on the intuitions of any particular author, expressivists should endeavour instead to provide evidence that public anger plays the role they assume in justifying punishment to better convince critics.

Perhaps instead punishment should be understood as an expression of fear.[32] The more we *fear* crime, the more we *punish* it. This understanding is more attractive in relation to some crimes rather than others. So it may make sense to say that the public fear murder and rape and this explains why these crimes are punished severely. However, problems arise when we consider many other crimes. The public may fear many things. Perhaps there is deep fear of an alien invasion from a hostile planet. Or there is fear about the future coming of Armageddon. Not all things feared are to be punished. Moreover, not all things feared above a certain threshold command punishment. Instead, punishment must be an expression of justified fear on this view. If true, then expressivist punishment is justified not on account of fear, but because it is justified on some other ground, such as retributivist desert. Again, expressivism appears either incoherent or irrelevant.

Finally, a third view is that punishment should be understood as an expression of our disgust of crime. The idea is that the public express their disgust for crimes in proportion to the severity of justified punishments. We do not merely dislike murder, but are disgusted by it. Punishment is the expression of our revulsion to the criminal offending.

One important concern is the problematic nature of disgust. This is well documented by Martha C. Nussbaum. She argues that disgust is both unreasonable and unreliable as a guide for public policy-making. Disgust is unreasonable because it embodies unrealistic fantasies about contamination and threats to purity.[33] When we argue that a practice should be prohibited because it is disgusting, we seek to prevent ourselves or society from contamination relating to this practice. Therefore, the use of disgust establishes hierarchies: it characterizes its opponents as not merely wrong or unfavourable, but revolting or beyond the pale.[34] Disgust is stigmatizing. Furthermore, disgust is unreliable because we lack any clear unified picture of how best to determine the disgusting via disgust. This is not to argue that we can never agree on what we find disgusting, but instead that we can usually find some more reliable alternative. For example, many people may view child sex offences with disgust, but we might similarly come to justify its criminalization by understanding child sex offences in terms of their harmfulness or violation of rights. The problematic nature of disgust does not entirely rule out its usefulness for law in full. Nussbaum accepts that disgust may play some positive and constructive role in the justification of laws against nuisance or obscenity, but its role is largely restricted to this sphere because of its problematic nature.[35]

A second problem is that we do not punish all acts that yield public disgust, but only those acts which are crimes. I genuinely find egg mayonnaise disgusting. This may be a reason to avoid spreading it on my food, but not a reason to punish its manufacturers and distributors. Disgust is an unreliable guide to understanding criminalization and punishment because not all crimes are crimes vis-à-vis their being disgusting. We may wish to punish illegal parking with fines and those in contempt of court with possible imprisonment although neither appears disgusting. We see once more that expressivism ultimately appears to rest on a foundation of retributivist desert in fact and that what is expressed does not appear to do much justificatory work beyond having a metaphorical presence.

Punishment as an expression may take several forms whether metaphorical, public anger, fear, or disgust. Each view runs into some significant difficulties. This is about *what* punishment expresses. Another issue is *who* expresses what by punishment. First, there is the problem of whether the community can speak with one voice. Expressivists argue that punishment expresses a 'message' of public disapproval.[36] The idea is that punishment communicates one message and not several messages.

This view runs into an important objection raised by Hart:

> it is sociologically very naive to think that there is even in England a single homogeneous social morality whose mouthpiece the judge can be in fixing sentence ... Our society, whether we like it or not, is morally a plural society; and the judgements of the relative seriousness of different crimes vary within it far more than this simple theory recognizes.[37]

Expressivist punishment is thought to communicate a message of public disapproval. Hart's claim is that the community does not often 'speak' with one voice, but many. Any message 'expressed' is likely to be a collection of voices that may share in disapproval of a crime, but for different reasons and give expression a cacophonous character. This is the problem of multiple meanings for expressivist punishment. Any expression may contain multiple meanings that may not always cohere. The satisfactory expression of public denunciation to offenders may be undermined by the problem that any such expression may communicate multiple and even conflicting meanings. If this expressed communication is incoherent or lacking sufficient clarity, then offenders will not receive the intended message of public disapproval in their punishment. So expressivism may fail in its task even where there are messages of public disapproval expressed.

Expressed messages may also be open to interpretations by listeners. This is the problem of unintended meanings.[38] For example, punishment may be designed to express public disapproval of a crime, but be understood in different ways and express different meanings. Not all offenders may 'get the message' that their imprisonment is justified and they have a responsibility to refrain from future offending. Instead, it may be difficult to manage what messages are received by offenders, if any.[39]

Of course, expressivists are not unaware of these problems. For example, Duff readily acknowledges that 'we should ... recognize an irreducible diversity of values'.[40] He adds: 'We should not hope to find any single criterion, or neat set of criteria, of criminalization' to address what kinds of wrong are to serve as public wrongs deserving punishment.[41] The 'message' we express to offenders through punishment may be a bundle of statements and values rather than the communication of any one particular view. This need not render our expression incoherent, but it might contribute to a lack of clarity. Recall that expressivist punishment is more than a declaration of public disapproval, but the communication of moral disapproval: offenders are to receive a message that the public denounce their crime and that their punishment is justified. Punishment says more than we don't like what you did, but it should speak to the justice of punishment because of what you did. The problem is that punishment may send a signal of public disapproval, but lack any clear indication of the more precise reasons in support of this disapproval. So perhaps Duff and others are correct that every penal expression contains a bundle of values. There remains the problem that punishment may express multiple and perhaps conflicting meanings and unintended meanings. This renders problematic the ability of punishment to perform its expressivist tasks. Expressivists must say more about how punishment may best address these difficult challenges to be more compelling.

Punishment is said to express public disapproval relating to crimes. This understanding addresses empirical facts about the public and their views about crime. Consider what is called the theory of public perception about punishment. This theory states that the public will perceive punishments as too lenient the less they know about the particulars of a case. However, the more that the public know about an individual case, the less likely they are to find an offender's punishment lenient.[42] The problem is that most people lack information about most cases. A theory of punishment that says that it should be linked with public disapproval may be too punitive. This is because greater knowledge may be more likely to lead to a better judgement about sentencing, including greater recognition of any relevant mitigating factors. If those who lack such knowledge tend to support more punitive punishments than others, then the former may be said to support punishments that are too severe. Punishments that express actual public denunciation may tend to be too harsh and, in turn, lack satisfactory justification. Expressive punishments that are controlled for poor public knowledge about particular cases might justify punishments that the public *would* express *if only* they knew all relevant considerations.[43] The problem here is that once again the justification of expressive punishment is reduced to retributivism. What matters is whether a punishment is fittingly deserved and not how it relates to real or imagined public denunciation.

Expressivists argue that punishment is justified as an expression of public denunciation. But a denunciation in relation to what? The links between punishment as an expression of public anger, fear, or disgust run into several related problems. None is strongly connected with criminalization. For example, if not all things feared above some threshold are criminal and warrant punishment, then we must look elsewhere for a more satisfactory account. Perhaps punishment may be understood in some *metaphorical* sense as expressing public disapproval. It remains to be seen what role disapproval plays that retributivist desert cannot.

Expressivism and legal moralism

Most expressivists endorse some version of natural law and legal moralism.[44] Punishment is justified as an expression of public denunciation relating to wrongdoing that is criminal and immoral. For example, Duff accepts that 'my argument fits within the Natural Law tradition'.[45] Elsewhere he notes: 'As in the criminal law, so with morality'.[46] Duff adds that 'positive laws and legal systems must be justified and criticized by reference to moral notions which are internal to the concept of law itself; these moral notions are essentially, not contingently, related to the existence of law as law'.[47] This view does not deny that 'unjust laws may still be law' even if 'defective or perverted as law'.[48] Nor is this perspective unique to Duff's expressivism.[49]

We have already considered a pressing problem for theories of punishment that accept legal moralism in this book's Introduction. Recall the distinction between *mala prohibita* and *mala in se*. The former are wrong in virtue of being criminal; the latter are wrong independently of their being criminal. Examples of *mala in se* crimes might include theft and murder. Examples of *mala prohibita* crimes are more controversial, but often include so-called victimless crimes such as drug and traffic offences. The problem for legal moralists is that if not all illegality is related to immorality then legal moralism is an unsatisfactory account of the criminal law. This is because legal moralism fails to address much of the criminal law. Any theory of punishment that accepts legal moralism will only be able to speak to some crimes and not all.

Expressivists respond to this criticism by arguing that the distinction between *mala prohibita* and *mala in se* is drawn too sharply. Duff approvingly cites Jeremy Bentham: 'the acute distinction, between *mala in se*, and *mala prohibita*: which being so shrewd, and sounding so pretty, and being in Latin, has no sort of occasion to have any meaning to it: accordingly it has none'.[50] For Bentham, this is a distinction without a difference. The mistake is that crimes are publicly declared wrongs. The status of crimes as public wrongs is confirmed by the possibility of their punishment.[51] These wrongs are selected for criminalization by the public. Crimes are 'pre-legal' wrongs in the sense that they are understood as public wrongs *first* and criminalized *second*.[52] It is not the case that crimes are criminalized first and understood as public wrongs afterwards. So crimes are 'wrongful prior to and independently of their criminalization'.[53] Crimes would not have their status if not understood to be wrongful initially. Duff argues:

> The truth in Legal Moralism is that criminal law is properly focused on wrongdoing ... Its error is to claim that criminal law should focus on wrongdoing as such, thus implying that we are criminally responsible simply as moral agents: we still need to identify the particular kinds of moral wrongdoing that are, in principle, the criminal law's business.[54]

The criminal law may be understood to 'enforce morality' in the sense that crimes are public wrongs that are 'inconsistent with the central moral values of the political community'.[55] Punishment is an expression of public denunciation of crimes as wrongs, and which aspires to the moral reformation of offenders.[56] This is because, for Duff, 'If no one could ever be morally dissuaded ... there would be no room for, no point to, a criminal law'.[57] Legal moralism may be reinterpreted to overcome traditional objections. Expressivist theory of punishment may accept legal moralism, but this need not entail we reject expressivism. Call this reinterpretation of legal moralism 'new legal moralism'.

New legal moralism denies that criminalization arises from two different sources, moral and non-moral. It is able to overcome objections to traditional understandings of legal moralism because new legal moralism rejects even the possibility of *mala prohibita* crimes. Its success comes at a cost. The problem with new legal moralism is that it reduces all public disapproval to an expression of moral wrongfulness. The attractiveness is that disapproval is a feature of all punishable crimes. New legal moralists must argue that moral wrongs are co-existent with relevant public disapproval of crimes. The problem is that this may be untrue. Not all objects of public disapproval are crimes or should be criminalized. Perhaps all crimes are objects of public disapproval: the problem is that its being an object of public disapproval is insufficient. Nor is it clear that all objects of public disapproval are wrong beyond their being a target of disapproval. For example, the public may disapprove of non-citizens owning too large a share of domestic media sources. But, if criminalized, it is unclear how even justified public disapproval has any necessary connection with morality.

New legal moralism overcomes objections to legal moralism through a transformation towards a view about the legal enforcement of *public disapproval*, not public morality per se or at least in any straightforward sense. This is not a denial that morality may influence – even strongly influence – criminalization. Hart is correct to say: 'Has the development of the law been influenced by morals? The answer to this question plainly is "Yes"'.[58] The concern is that this reply to objections aimed at legal moralism overcomes them by ultimately shifting from a focus on immorality to public disapproval.

Let us turn to a further problem concerning the nature of the public for all versions of legal moralism. The problem is that they conceive of the public as singular and not pluralistic. For example, Feinberg says:

> At its best, in civilized and democratic countries, punishment surely expresses the community's strong disapproval of what the criminal did. Indeed, it can be said that punishment expresses the judgment (as distinct from any emotion) of the community that what the criminal did was wrong.[59]

Punishment is an expression of *the* community's shared view about a crime's wrongfulness. Democratic citizens affirm a common 'political morality' in their criminal law.[60] Duff argues: 'The law "prohibits" murder, rape, and the like because such conduct is wrongful in a way that properly concerns the law – wrongful in terms of the shared values of the political community'.[61] Together, we speak as one voice in expressing our disapproval of crime.

The problem of the public is that our disapproval may not arise from any single moral view. Legal moralist approaches, following Hart, may 'only apply to a society marked by a very high degree of homogeneity in moral outlook, and where the content of this homogeneous social morality can be easily known'.[62] These approaches run into significant problems where such homogeneity is lacking, or where it is present but not easily perceived. We might believe that society is characterized by the fact of reasonable pluralism in political society. John Rawls argues that 'a modern democratic society is characterized not simply by a pluralism of comprehensive religious, philosophical, and moral doctrines but by a pluralism of incompatible yet reasonable comprehensive doctrines. No one of these doctrines is affirmed by citizens generally'.[63] Citizens attempt to form an overlapping consensus through the use of public reasons in a political conception of justice.[64] Perhaps legal moralists might argue that society speaks not with one voice, but instead from a shared overlapping consensus and political conception of justice. This may be one fruitful alternative to overcoming objections.

There remains the problem of whether 'we' can be said to express any particular view. This is because the content of the criminal law is beyond any individual and the public have a 'pervasive lack of knowledge on sentencing matters'.[65] Douglas Husak argues: 'Criminal statutes have multiplied exponentially; no living person can be aware of more than a tiny fraction of them'.[66] He explains:

> In my state of New Jersey, which is fairly typical in most respects, the Motor Vehicle and Traffic Regulations span some 180 pages of dense text. Although the applicable statutes are relatively easy to find – especially now that they are freely available on the Internet – I daresay that almost no one is aware of the content of the regulations that pertain to him.[67]

If no one knows most, and not all, criminal laws, then how can it be understood as the expression of any shared public morality? The criminal law cannot be such an expression where those doing the expressing don't know much of its content. Nor is it likely that this would be substantively different if legal education improved given the vastness of the criminal law especially in recent years. It is then difficult to know what it would mean for the criminal law to be expressive in the ways in which expressivists claim where none of us possesses anything close to a complete knowledge of the criminal law.[68]

Is expressivism a theory of punishment?

All expressivists, including communicative theorists, argue that punishment has an expressive character which justifies punishment. Crucially, expressivists understand 'punishment' as 'imprisonment', or 'hard treatment'. Their claim is that punishment as imprisonment is not merely hard treatment, but rather 'symbolic acts of censure'.[69] Expressivist theories of punishment are best understood as theories of justified imprisonment. This is because they often do not explicitly address the justification of non-prison forms of punishment, such as penalties or community sentencing. Expressivists have a narrow focus on the response to some crimes, but not others, depending upon which may be imprisonable.

The problem for expressivists is that their view of punishment may be incomplete. Suppose their view is roughly correct. Only a minority of crimes lead to convictions and only a small minority of convictions lead to imprisonment. An expressivist theory of punishment is a narrow theory that addresses only a relatively small number of criminal cases. This renders most crimes beyond the purview of expressivists. Expressivism is perhaps only a partial and incomplete theory of punishment that directly speaks to a minority of cases; it is a theory about imprisonment.[70] While such a project has great value, readers looking for a theory of punishment that can satisfactorily account for how we should respond to all crimes should perhaps look elsewhere.

This problem could be easily avoided. Expressivists argue that imprisonment is justified as the expression of public denunciation. Prison is an emphatically declared message to all that makes public disapproval become concrete. Potentially, we could accept this picture and argue further that non-prison punishments, such as community sentences and fines, are also concrete manifestations of public disapproval. These punishments might be less emphatic, but the crimes are less serious. Nevertheless, the fact that a punishment might be less emphatic does not prove that it is not an expression of public denunciation. Expressivists accept that public denunciation admits of scales whereby some crimes are punished more than others as an expression of greater disapproval of some crimes over others. Murderers are punished more severely than burglars because the former receive greater public denunciation for their crimes. There is nothing inconsistent in saying that expressivism justifies punishment understood as both hard treatment and penalties. This move would permit expressivists to offer a theory more applicable to more crimes. Perhaps they would still want to offer an explanation as to why imprisonment is different from other forms of punishment. Perhaps punishment as communicative expression plays some central role in this narrative. Nevertheless, there is still a clear space and perhaps a clear need to consider non-prison alternatives as expressive communications, too.

Is expressivism a mixed theory of punishment?

Expressivists, including communicative theorists, argue that punishment should fulfil several penal aims: punishment is expressive, retributive, and reformative.[71] First, expressivism shares much in common with retributivism.[72] Some have claimed that expressivists are part of a 'retributivist revival'.[73] Expressivists, such as Duff, argue that punishment 'must ... be understood in retributive terms'.[74] Offenders should be punished because they are deserving on account of their wrongdoing. Similarly, von Hirsch claims that punishment should be proportionate to 'the gravity of the criminal's conduct'.[75] Retributivist desert plays a central role in expressivist theories of punishment. Only the guilty may be punished.

Second, expressivism conceives punishment in more than purely retributivist terms.[76] Retributivists punish offenders for their past crimes without regard to future consequences. Expressivists argue that punishment is both deserved and 'also a path towards reform and rehabilitation'.[77] Punishing deserving offenders in proportion to justified public denunciation can contribute to their reformation through repentance: we want 'to persuade offenders that they should repent'.[78] The idea is that a repentant offender is a person who recognizes his crime as a public wrong and this recognition enables his reformation. Offenders owe an apologetic debt to us because of their crimes.

The expressivist position on offender reformation is consistent with deontological rehabilitation. Offenders should be rehabilitated because it is just and not because it might be instrumental to the pursuit of consequentialist goals. Reformation must make some genuine attempt to persuade offenders that their crimes were wrongs and should be the object of regret. We attempt to rehabilitate offenders because it is just and not with a view to crime reduction: crime reduction is perhaps a welcome side effect, but not our primary goal. This is because to prioritize crime reduction would be to treat offenders as a means to an end which expressivists reject.

Finally, expressivist punishments also possess a deterrent element. It is sometimes a bit unclear and perhaps too readily assumed that expressivism might contribute to deterrence. For example, Feinberg argues that 'punishment no doubt would also help deter killers'.[79] Punishment as the expression of public denunciation communicates a message to offenders and also potential offenders in reaffirming the public's commitment to identify crimes as public wrongs that demand imprisonment. Potential offenders hear this message, too. Punishment is an expressive message that seeks to engage others to dissuade them from future offending.

But expressivism is more than mere deterrence. Or perhaps it is more accurate to say that it possesses a crime reductive element, but not a deterrent element. Expressivists aim to reduce future offending through reformation and the declaration of crimes as public wrongs, but not fear and penal threats. We should act lawfully because we recognize such behaviour as acceptable and avoid crime because it is wrong.[80] We should avoid crime because we reject it and not because we only wish to avoid the threatened burdens of potential punishment. We may achieve crime reduction in the long term through reinforcing our shared public values.[81] Duff says: 'Punishment should be understood, justified, and administered as a mode of moral communication with offenders that seeks to persuade them to repent their crimes, to reform themselves, and to reconcile themselves with those they have wronged'.[82] Punishment is persuasive as a form of hard treatment because the use of prison 'can assist the process of moral self-reform' and not only just deserts.[83]

Expressivists, including communicative theories, offer us a hybrid theory of punishment. They understand punishment, following Alfred Cyril Ewing, as 'expressive of society's moral condemnation': expressivist punishment '*teaches* a moral lesson in order to *reform* the criminal and *educate* the public, this contributing to the reduction of crime'.[84] Punishment is deserved and rehabilitative through the moral education of offenders through imprisonment. Expressivists argue that punishment addresses multiple penal goals, such as retributivist desert, offender rehabilitation, and future crime reduction through the expressive character of punishment. Expressivism may be understood as a hybrid theory of punishment for these reasons.

It is a separate question whether expressivism succeeds as a hybrid theory of punishment. So expressivism may be conceived one way, but amount to a general theory in fact. Punishment is determined with respect to public denunciation. Offenders are punished no more or less than the public believes satisfactory to effectively express disapproval. Perhaps the punishment of crime may contribute to crime becoming less attractive to some and so have a deterrent effect. Perhaps imprisonment provides a space for offenders to reform themselves. These claims offer no evidence that expressive punishment possesses a hybrid nature. Our public disapproval need not have a deterrent or rehabilitative effect to remain justified. Extra-retributive goals are welcome potential benefits arising from punishment, but they do not play any clear central role. If deterrence or rehabilitation were improved by punishing offenders more severely than justified by public disapproval, then expressivists would not punish more punitively.

It is worth noting that a retributivist could offer a similar 'hybrid' account. She might argue that offenders should be punished because it is deserved and in proportion to desert. But she might add that punishing the deserving may deter others from crime. Punishment could also give offenders space for reflection and personal reformation contributing to future rehabilitation. Punishment is retributivist, but it could be reinterpreted in a hybrid way by claiming that other penal goals might be addressed, too. We should note that these other goals play no substantive role in the distribution or severity of punishments. A less charitable critique might suggest that the retributivist has done no more than theorize that other penal goals might be realized, but not that they are likely to happen. The same might be said about expressivism and this is perhaps clearest when we consider the role that prisons play for expressivist theories of punishment.

The problem of prison

One problem for expressivist theories of punishment is that there is little, if any, evidence to suggest that prisons can be most helpful in serving these additional goals of deterrence and rehabilitation. We have seen previously that sentences of 12 months or less are associated with high rates of reoffending. If prison is meant to be a place for reflection and reform, then there is little clear evidence that it serves these functions better than alternatives. Perhaps prisons fall short of some realistic ideal. It seems problematic to claim that a particular theory of punishment is more compelling than others, in part because of empirical facts that do not obtain. It is more than a question of non-ideal reality: any social institution might be said to fall short of normative benchmarks. If we have no persuasive reason to believe that prisons do or can serve a reformatory role better than alternative sanctions, then this is a powerful argument against expressivist, including communicative, theories. Prisons play the only role in attempting to bring about goals that are often much better achieved by alternatives. If an expressivist theory of punishment is to contribute to crime reduction and rehabilitation, then the means through which these goals are to be achieved must be reconsidered.

One problem is whether prisons are necessary for the expression of public denunciation. Many have argued that they are not. For example, Bernard Williams observes:

> The idea that traditional, painful, punishments are simply denunciations is incoherent, because it does not explain, without begging the question, why denunciations have to take the form of what Nietzsche identified as the constant of punishment, 'the ceremony of pain'.[85]

Punishment may express denunciation, but this is not a reason why all denunciations should be expressed through punishment. We might be able to express denunciation in other ways. Indeed, we can 'exact retribution ... without denunciation' and 'denounce a crime without retribution indeed without punishing at all'.[86] So why punishment?

Perhaps our denunciation may take the form of mere words instead of some punitive sanction. Hart says:

> The normal way in which moral condemnation is expressed is by words, and it is not clear, if denunciation is really what is required, why a solemn public statement of disapproval would not be the most 'appropriate' or 'emphatic' means of expressing this.[87]

If our aim is to communicate public disapproval to offenders, then public statements may serve this purpose in some contexts. Prison is perhaps one particular emphatic method of embodying our denunciation, but it is not the only method. In fact, we might claim that the use of words – such as a stern verbal warning – is a superior method of expressing public censure for wrongdoing where appropriate. For example, R. G. Collingwood argues:

> The most perfect punishments involve no 'incidental' pains at all. The condemnation is expressed simply and quietly in words, and goes straight home. The punishment consists in the expression of condemnation and that alone; and to punish with a word instead of a blow is still punishment. It is, perhaps, a better and more civilized form of punishment.[88]

The argument here is not that imprisonment is never satisfactory for expressivist punishment, but instead that imprisonment need not always be the only satisfactory expressivist punishment. The problem with expressivist theories of punishment is that their scope is too narrow. If our goal is to effectively express and communicate public disapproval to offenders for wrongdoing, then this may take more forms than prison. If imprisonment is justified in some part because it is expressive of public denunciation, then why only imprisonment and not alternatives?

The problem of unrepentant offenders

A problem for communicative theories of punishment is the problem of the unrepentant offender. The communicative version of expressivism is distinctive: punishment is more than an expression of public disapproval; punishment is also the repentance that offenders communicate back to the public. Repentance plays a central role in the distinctiveness of communicative punishment. One problem is whether prisons are the best means to this goal, discussed previously. A second problem is what to do about those who are unrepentant. If repentance is a goal, then should the unrepentant remain imprisoned until a change of heart is confirmed?

This problem is expressed well by Michael Tonry:

> When the communication is unnecessary because the offender has already come to understand the wrongfulness of his act, and to regret it, hard treatment should be unnecessary. Likewise, if the offender is incorrigible, communication cannot succeed, and if the process is the goal, there is no point.[89]

One issue is this. If punishment as imprisonment is justified to effectively communicate a message to offenders that brings about their repentance, then we might argue that offenders should be able to enjoy early release where repentance has been achieved. Perhaps early release is not justified where repentance is not achieved. Note that punishment aims at reformation through prison as the expression of public disapproval: we punish in proportion to disapproval to bring about a change of heart and not only to reform. There is then no injustice in offenders serving full terms in proportion to public disapproval where repentance is not achieved. However, it might be counterproductive to continue punishing an offender who had already repented because it would involve early release.[90] Furthermore, prison is perhaps the institution least likely to bring about successful repentance. Prison may intuitively appear to succeed in its role as expressing public disapproval, but it might undermine its other goals such as repentance and reformation. Thus, communicative theorists, for Tonry, 'felt obliged' to develop theories of punishment 'in which, for use in the real world, they themselves did not really believe'.[91]

The problem of the unrepentant offender is not unnoticed by expressivists. Duff argues:

> But how can his punishment reconcile him to his victim or the wider community if it is obvious that he is unrepentant and unapologetic? ... The offender has been subjected to what would constitute an appropriately reparative apology if he undertook it for himself. His fellow citizens should therefore now treat him *as if* he had apologized ... He might not have paid the apologetic debt that he owed ... But something

like that debt has been exacted from him, and those who exacted it should not treat him *as if* the debt has been paid.[92]

We treat offenders *as if* they have repented *even where they have not*. There are several reasons for this view. For example, offenders should not be punished more than necessary to communicate deserved public censure. Offenders are subjected to communicative dialogue that they are free to accept or reject during their imprisonment. Duff notes: 'Even if she remains unrepentant at the end of her punishment, this does not render the attempt to persuade her pointless or unjustified'.[93] We are justified in punishing the offender, but it is up to the offender whether or not she elects to repent.

The problem with this argument is that secular penance is reduced to a fiction. Communicative theorists argue punishment is a communicative dialogue between offenders and their community. Both expressivist and communicative theorists argue that punishment expresses public denunciation, but only communicative theorists argue that penal expression moves in two directions. The first is the expression of public censure in punishing offenders and the second is the offenders' communication to the community expressing repentance. So communicative theorists claim punishment does not merely express disapproval, but includes repentance. The problem is that repentance performs no clear role in fact. If it does not matter whether any offender repents and all repentance is at minimum assumed, then what is the clear difference between retributivists and communicative theorists? Is the difference little more than that the latter *assume* that offenders repent through serving time in prison? We may argue that criminal repentance may be an important penal objective, but then we should expect it to play some central role. A theory that says it's justified because offenders repent and they repent because it's assumed by the theory is not compelling. It is perhaps even tautological: justified imprisonment is communicative because we assume offenders communicate repentance in being imprisoned, or it's communicative because we assume communication. The offender need not say or do anything. Furthermore, there is no evidence that repentance is best served through imprisonment. If communicative theorists believe punishment has or should play some communicative role enabling repentance, then they should champion alternatives to prison instead that better secure repentance.

We saw earlier that expressivism might be understood in many different ways, but perhaps it is best understood in a metaphorical sense. Punishment is metaphorically like the manifestation of the public declaring their disapproval with one voice. Likewise, communication might be best understood in a similar metaphorical sense. Punishment is metaphorically like the manifestation of public disapproval, but also metaphorically like a manifestation of the offender's repentance and regret for his crime. We re-imagine the prison cell as a reflective space. Parents may send troublesome children to their room, interrupting any plans to do otherwise, in order to force them to reflect on their wrongdoing to bring about reflection and repentance. Prison may be seen to play a similar role in aiming to enable offender reformation. But if this is important, then the most satisfactory sanctions will be those that serve this goal best. If imprisonment, whether real or imagined, cannot best serve this goal, then communication is perhaps best understood as metaphorical.

Judging success

We have discussed different ways of understanding expressivist theories of punishment and their potential limitations. Now how might we judge their success? It is difficult to see how an expressivist theory may help us determine punishment. Michael Cavadino and James Dignan argue that 'instrumental denunciation cannot justify any particular level of severity of punishment; nor can the penal system "give a lead" to public opinion about the rights and wrongs of how people should behave'.[94] So how to determine how much denunciation is justified?

What we might expect from the public does not often match what the public report. The problem is that how 'we' believe the public would respond to cases is often unsupported by the facts. Take public confidence in the police, for example. We might expect ethnic minorities to have much less confidence than the majority group. But this is not always true. One recent UK study found that 52 per cent of White respondents rated the local police as doing a good or excellent job compared with 59 per cent of respondents from Black and minority ethnic groups.[95] Such findings suggest that the public may not always express the concerns we expect them to have.

We may further question public competence. For example, about two-thirds have reported that they believed crime had risen, with 35 per cent believing it had risen 'a lot' despite the fact that crime had decreased.[96] The public believed crime was rising despite all evidence to the contrary. The explanation for public ignorance is perhaps unsurprising: those most likely to believe crime is rising claim to read either a non-national newspaper or none at all.[97] The public may often be poorly situated to express justified denunciation because they lack sufficient information. If the public lack knowledge about criminal matters, then the expression of disapproval may be inaccurate or incomplete. An expressivist theory of punishment that defended punishment as a justified expression of public disapproval has the problem that, first, the public's attitudes may differ significantly from the expressivist's expectations and, second, the public's attitudes may lack satisfactory knowledge about the relevant subject matter that may render problematic their ability to offer the kinds of justified expressions of censure that expressivists claim for them.

Conclusion

Expressivists argue that punishment as imprisonment is justified as an expression of public denunciation directed towards a crime. Punishment may be understood metaphorically as the embodiment of public disapproval, but it is unclear how it can serve as a distinctive view of punishment. Not all public anger is directed towards crimes and so only some public anger is relevant. The public generally lack satisfactory knowledge about criminal justice that may render their judgements at least somewhat problematic. Furthermore, communicative theorists argue that punishment has an expressive character and that expression works both ways from the community to offenders and back again. The problem here is that the communication to be expressed by offenders back to us need never take place. Punishment is communicative because offenders are understood *as if* they return communication to us irrespective of whether or not they do, in fact. In short, we might find the general motivating idea – e.g. that punishment can be seen to 'express' public disapproval of crime – intuitively attractive, but be unsatisfied with how this idea has been translated into practice.

Herbert Hart says that 'we do not live in society in order to condemn, though we may condemn in order to live'.[98] Perhaps punishment is characterized as a form of publicly sanctioned disapproval. This might be said about any theory of punishment and not only expressivist theories. Nor is it clear how expressivist understandings of denunciation differ significantly from retributivist understandings of desert. The biggest challenge then for expressivists is not that their theory of punishment is ultimately not compelling, but that it is not satisfactorily distinctive.

7 Unified theory

Introduction

Hybrid theories of punishment attempt to bring together two or more penal goals. They oppose standard views that demand we choose between existing options: for example, either we must side with retributivists or deterrence proponents because there is no middle ground. The common problem for hybrid theories is theoretical coherence. This is because different penal goals may pull in different directions. Retributivist desert may recommend punishments that may be counterproductive to general deterrence. Many have argued that hybrid theories are unstable at best and incoherent at worst.

The unified theory of punishment is a unique attempt to bring together several different principles of punishment within a single and coherent approach.[1] The problem is not that we must choose whether punishment must aspire to ensure offenders receive just deserts or how they might be restored, but how these goals can be satisfied in combination with other penal goals. The unified theory of punishment is ambitious: it aspires to offer a compelling 'grand unifying theory' of punishment bringing together the best elements from each view of punishment without being subjected to standard objections.

This chapter will examine the case for a unified theory and how it might succeed where other theories have failed. I will argue that the unified theory is not only possible, but it is perhaps the most compelling theory of punishment available. Only a unified theory can best address the complexity that confronts theories of punishment and can command widespread support as punitive restoration.

Why a unified theory of punishment?

The philosophy of punishment is at a crossroads. Judges and legal practitioners stand opposed to many academic philosophers and legal theorists. How sentencing is considered in courtrooms is perhaps starkly different from how it is understood in many lecture theatres. Judges and legal practitioners operate within sentencing guidelines that include references to several different penal goals. One issue is whether punishment is able to address multiple goals within a coherent theory; a second issue is whether a theory of punishment should address multiple goals.

The Model Penal Code continues to have a profound influence on sentencing guidelines in the United States, Canada, Britain, and elsewhere.[2] The Code was originally published in 1962 by the American Law Institute to assist national and state legislative bodies revise and better codify criminal codes. Each legislature had been left to draft individual codes and this led to the problem of divergence across all areas of criminal law. The Code is an attempt to arrive at sentencing principles that might improve coherence across codes.

The Model Penal Code recommends that sentencing guidelines address multiple penal goals. Section 1.02 says:

> (2) The general purposes of the provisions governing the sentencing and treatment of offenders are:
>
> a. to prevent the commission of offences;
> b. to promote the correction and rehabilitation of offenders;
> c. to safeguard offenders against excessive, disproportionate or arbitrary punishment;
> d. to give fair warning of the nature of the sentences that may be imposed on convictions of an offence;
> e. to differentiate offenders with a view to a just individualization in their treatment.

The Model Penal Code recommends that sentencing guidelines address multiple penal goals, such as prevention, rehabilitation, proportionality, desert, and publicity. The Code was later expanded to include the goal of restorative justice as well.[3] Punishment should be preventative and contribute to crime reduction; it should enable offender rehabilitation; punishment should never be disproportionate nor arbitrary; it should be proportionate to the individual case; and punishment should satisfy publicity in being publicly known in advance and avoid retrospective criminalization. The Model Penal Code's multiple penal goals approach was reaffirmed in the Sentencing Reform Act of 1984 creating the United States Sentencing Commission.[4] The Act states:

> The court, in determining the particular sentence to impose, shall consider–
>
> 1   the nature and circumstances of the offense and the history and characteristics of the defendant;
> 2   the need for the sentence imposed–

A to reflect the seriousness of the offense, to promote respect for the law, and to provide just punishment for the offense;

B to afford adequate deterrence to criminal conduct;

C to protect the public from further crimes of the defendant; and

D to provide the defendant with needed educational or vocational training, medical care, or other correctional treatment in the most effective manner.[5]

These sentencing guidelines have exercised a profound influence in the US, UK, and beyond. Most guidelines have since stipulated that sentencing should be determined with reference to multiple penal goals. So, in fact, those who argue that punishment should adopt only one or two goals defend a view of punishment contrary to the guidelines courts use to fix punishments: accepting their less pluralistic conceptions of punishment may lead to a fairly radical and substantial revision of most sentencing guidelines in use today.[6]

Critics argue that the Code suffers from at least two problems. First, the Code is outdated because the criminal code has changed significantly since, which may require substantive revision of the Model Penal Code if it is to be relevant. Standard examples include the omission of various drug offences from the Code and changes to the law that have criminalized marital rape. Critics claim that these changes call for a fundamental rethinking of the Model Penal Code and require us to abandon the existing Code. Note that this criticism does not offer any specific reasons to abandon the view that punishment should address multiple penal goals. Instead, this criticism speaks to how a multiple-goals approach may be better applied to contemporary issues.

Secondly, critics argue that the Code is incoherent. This is because multiple penal goals may come into conflict. For example, a sentence that might best promote offender rehabilitation may not safeguard offenders from disproportionate punishment. Multiple penal goals serve a multitude of ends and cannot be brought together in a unified and coherent theory of punishment. Of course, the Model Penal Code does not attempt to offer any *theory* of punishment and so it does not defend any philosophical account of how punishment can and should adopt multiple goals. Instead, the Code recommends guidelines that incorporate the multiple goals that many criminal codes have already adopted. Even those generally supportive argue that its promise is in helping us reflect on the best distribution of punishment, but 'not about the justification of the institution of punishment'.[7] The multiple penal codes may appear to us as more of a 'laundry list' providing 'more illusion than guidance' in the absence of any clear framework.[8] Nevertheless, the Model Penal Code has found very few philosophers and legal theorists willing to defend it. The widely shared position is that a penal code must ultimately choose between penal goals. We should adopt either retributivism, deterrence, rehabilitation, restorative justice, expressivism, or the negative retributivism of Rawls and Hart because we cannot provide a coherent 'Grand Unifying Theory of Punishment'. Different theories cannot be combined across the board on so large a scale.

I believe this widespread rejection is built upon a mistake. Perhaps we cannot offer a unified theory that unifies retributivism, deterrence, rehabilitation, and so on. But we can defend a theory that unified multiple goals. The problem with the Model Penal Code is that it lacks a more compelling justificatory framework that may show how multiple goals may be brought together in a unified and coherent way.[9] This project is possible and I will present this case here. If we can provide a compelling framework for how multiple goals may coherently work together, then we might offer a major advance in our understanding of punishment and how philosophy may meet the demands of practice. I therefore side with the judges and legal practitioners. It has been noted by others that 'the philosophies of punishment, at least in their traditional form, are based upon a rather idealized and one-dimensional image of punishment'.[10] The unified theory of punishment offers an account of how such problems may be best overcome.

What is the unified theory of punishment?

The unified theory of punishment is a theory that unifies multiple penal goals in a single and coherent theoretical approach. The idea is not that different theories are compatible, but instead that different penal goals are compatible. The argument is that the different penal goals found across different theories of punishment may be combined within a unified framework. The project of the unified theory of punishment is to show how this combination is possible and compelling.

The unified theory of punishment has attracted many defenders.[11] Perhaps the best classic statement is presented by Hegel:

> Punishment, for example, has various determinations: it is retributive, a deterrent example as well, a threat used by the law as a deterrent, and also it brings the criminal to his senses and reforms him. Each of these different determinations has been considered the *ground* of punishment, because each is an essential determination, and therefore the others as distinct from it, are determined as merely contingent relatively to it. *But the one which is taken as ground is still not the whole punishment itself.*[12]

This cryptic passage may be understood to present at least two philosophical positions. The first is that retribution, deterrence, and rehabilitation need not be considered in opposition to each other. Instead, we should conceive them as different components of one unified theory of punishment that brings them together. The second position is that retribution, deterrence, and rehabilitation fit together in an unequal way. A unified theory of punishment will have a 'ground' that will provide a foundation, but not serve as 'the whole punishment itself'.[13] Hegel is the first to offer a unified theory of punishment where we attempt to bring coherent unity to multiple penal goals within a new framework. Our task is to provide a compelling view of how to structure this framework to unify multiple penal goals.

There have been several different proposals for how we might construct a unified theory of punishment since Hegel and most notably by British Idealists, including Bernard Bosanquet, F. H. Bradley, T. H. Green, and James Seth.[14] Each builds on Hegel's idea that punishment can and should bring together multiple penal goals in a unified theory. For example, Green says: 'It is commonly asked whether punishment according to its proper nature is retributive or preventative or reformatory. The true answer is that it is and should be all three'.[15] Green and the British Idealists reject the idea that different penal goals are mutually exclusive.[16] More importantly, they help us conceive of a compelling framework that can successfully unify multiple penal goals. Let me explain how this framework may be understood.[17]

Punishment is a response to crime. We must understand one in relation to the other. Furthermore, the justification of punishment *requires* the justification of crime. This point is worth highlighting: if we cannot justify a particular criminal act or omission, then we cannot justify its punishment. There can be no just punishment for an unjust crime.[18] If punishment is a response to crime, then criminalization must be justified for the punishment of crimes to be justified. Penal justice is linked with just criminalization within a just legal system.

Laws are necessary for the continuation of any political community.[19] This is because there will be inevitable conflicts between community members over time. These conflicts will require some agreed procedures for future conflict resolution.[20] These procedures form a legal system. Note that legal systems are not necessary because people are naturally antagonistic per se, but instead because conflicts are inevitable over time in any political community. This is the fact of member disagreement. A legal system is a necessary, but not sufficient, condition for future political stability. While every political community requires a legal system to resolve member disagreement over time, good laws alone may be insufficient for this purpose.

The criminal law aims at the protection of individual *legal rights*. Our legal rights are substantial freedoms worthy of protection for each member.[21] Each person possesses rights in virtue of their recognized political membership. This idea is based upon 'a political conception of justice that all citizens might be reasonably expected to endorse' and which 'can serve as a basis of public reason and justification'.[22] While the legal system aims to protect individual rights, not all rights have equal value. This is because some rights represent more substantial freedoms than others. For example, the right to life free from murder is linked to a more substantial freedom than the right to private property. If we were murdered, then we cannot choose to exercise private property rights. Some rights are more central to the protection of our substantial freedoms than others.

This is not to say there is any trade-off between rights such that we should tolerate less of some rights to enjoy more of others. Instead, all rights demand protection because rights give expression to substantial freedoms. However, some rights may have more central importance because the freedoms they safeguard make possible other rights. Again, the right to life free from murder makes possible further rights, such as liberty of conscience.[23] All rights have importance although some are more centrally important than others.

The protection of individual rights is conducted within a legal system, and it is a *system*. Laws are often enacted in a piecemeal fashion. Any legal system will lack full coherence, but every system seeks greater coherence. Where there is inconsistency or incoherence, we clarify our understanding of law and its application through political and judicial bodies to resolve these shortcomings.[24] Some rights may be more central to the protection of individual rights within the context of a legal system. This system does not exist for its own sake as some 'end-in-itself'.[25] Instead, legal systems exist fundamentally for the protection of the individual rights of its members. Community members must find satisfaction in their community and the legal system employed to assist the community's future continuity.

Crimes are rights violations that threaten the substantial freedoms protected by law.[26] Punishment is the response to crime. Punishment aims at the protection of individual legal rights threatened by crime.[27] The goal of punishment is not to make people morally good, but rather to provide for the protection of individual legal rights.[28] Punishment is about the protection of rights.[29]

This view of punishment is not unique to British Idealism. For example, John Stuart Mill argues that, for each of us, laws are 'the rules necessary for the protection of his fellow creatures, individually or collectively'.[30] Mill says:

> The only right by which society is warranted in inflicting pain upon any human creature, is the right of self-defence ... But our right to punish, is a branch of the universal right of self-defence; and it is a mere subtletly to set up any distinction between them.[31]

Punishment aims to protect us from crimes in a form of legal self-defence. Crimes present us with threats that punishment attempts to overcome. Mill's understanding of punishment has many substantial differences from unified theories of punishment.[32] However, his position is worth noting to highlight how others have similarly accepted some version of the view that punishment serves a protective aim.

Nevertheless, the British Idealists more specifically understand crimes as threats to individual rights that may require punishment to best protect these rights and safeguard the public from 'criminal conduct'.[33] Thus, Green argues that 'the justice of the punishment depends on the justice of the general system of rights' and 'the proper and direct object of state-punishment [is] ... the general protection of rights'.[34] Green says:

> a violation of a right, requires a punishment, of which the kind and amount must depend on the relative importance of the right and of the extent to which its general exercise is threatened. Thus every theory of rights in detail must be followed by, or indeed implies, a corresponding theory of punishment in detail.[35]

Punishment is only required where rights have been violated by crime. Crimes are punished differently, if at all, in relation to the importance of the right violated. Crime is a necessary, but not sufficient, condition for punishment. Crime must present some threat to our rights in order for punishment to become justified. Rights, criminalization, and punishment are interconnected.

Furthermore, punishment expresses a specific form of disapproval. Green says:

> [Punishment] is a disapproval founded on a sense of what is necessary for the protection of rights ... It is founded essentially on the outward aspect of a man's conduct, on the view of it as related to the security and freedom in action and acquisition of other members of society.[36]

Punishment is an expression of disapproval, but its character is distinct from expressivist theories of punishment. This is because unified theories understand disapproval in terms of 'penal right' and not 'penal morality'.[37] We punish in view of 'what is necessary for the protection of rights, not on a judgment of good and evil'.[38] The unified theory of punishment rejects legal moralism. We punish crimes because they are legal wrongs that threaten our legal rights. Punishment is about illegality, not necessarily immorality.

This view of punishment is held by other British Idealists. For example, James Seth argues:

> This view of the object of punishment gives the true measure of its amount. This is found not in the amount of moral depravity which the crime reveals, but in the importance of the right violated, relatively to the system of rights of which it forms a part ... The measure of the punishment is, in short, the measure of social necessity; and this necessity is a changing one.[39]

Several key features are highlighted in this compelling position. First, rights are substantial freedoms that are protected by criminalizing their violation. Second, punishment is a response to crime that is proportionate to the right violated in view of how best to maintain and protect rights. Some rights are more central than others. More central rights may require more severe punishment than less central rights. Third, crime is necessary, but not sufficient, for punishment. If the protection of rights does not require punishment, then it may be unnecessary. This view of punishment is open to the possibility of justified pardons where such a condition applies. Seth correctly argues that 'punishment is not an end-in-itself, but a means of ... protection'.[40] We never punish for the sake of it, but instead where it becomes necessary for the protection and restoration of rights. Punishment must always be 'undertaken in the interest of the ... individual'.[41] Fourth, we punish crimes as legal wrongs and not moral wrongs. We punish crimes and not immorality. This is not to say the two never overlap, but it is to say that our focus is on illegality and rights rather than morality and wickedness.

Finally, the relation between crime and punishment is not fixed, but it must be responsive to changing circumstances. This is because the relation between crime and rights is not fixed either. Our understanding of individual rights as substantial freedoms has changed over time and so has our view about crime. Crimes that may have once been subjected to capital punishment may no longer be criminal today. What has changed during this time is the view of a crime as a potential violation of a particularly central right that would require the most severe punishment in order to provide the best source of protection. If an act or omission does not present any threat to our rights that might require punishment in some form, then it should not be criminalized.

The unified theory of punishment *unifies* multiple penal goals. First, punishment is a response to crime. We cannot punish the innocent because they do not present any threat that may violate our rights as substantial freedoms. Offenders are deserving of punishment insofar as they must only be punished for their crimes. The unified theory of punishment adopts a more restrictive view of desert than retributivism where punishment is deserved for crimes and not necessarily immorality.[42] Not all moral failures are criminal and not all crimes are moral failures. Offenders may only deserve punishment when they have performed crimes.

Secondly, punishment aims to protect rights from criminal violations. Punishment is proportionate to the violation of right that is criminalized and gives rise for the need of punishment. Some crimes may require more severe punishments than others because rights that are more central are violated or threatened with violation. So punishment has a distinctive understanding of proportionality in view of rights protection.. Punishment *metaphorically* may be said to *express* the community's disapproval. The greater the threat to our rights as substantial freedoms, then the greater the punishment and the greater our disapproval of such crimes as manifest in the severity of punishment. The most central rights may require the most severe punishments which, in turn, may express in some sense our community's disapproval for such crimes.

Punishment may also address penal goals such as deterrence and rehabilitation within a more robust understanding of restorative justice. Proponents of restorative justice argue that crime damages community relations that should be restored. Community members including any victims engage with offenders in a restorative process to come to a greater collective understanding in an important alternative to sentencing. We have seen that this view suffers from some shortcomings. Restorative justice need not be an alternative to prison only, but a process that may be employed in tandem with imprisonment. Our choice need not be prison or restorative justice, but some combination of the two. Some commentators have argued for the benefits of restorative justice for victims of violent crimes and their offenders in prison environments.[43]

Punishment can and should restore what crime has damaged. Punishment aims at the protection of rights threatened by crimes and their restoration where violated. There are many reasons to believe that restorative conferences may have a positive impact on reducing recidivism with high public confidence and the satisfaction of victims and offenders. While imprisonment may not always be the best environment conducive to effective restoration, there is no reason to believe that it might never play some role. Punishment may best serve the aims of rights protection through incorporating some restorative justice element wherever possible. Instead of an alternative to punishment, we might argue that any punishment should employ restorative conferences as a default and not as an exception. This is not to say that restorative conferences must be used or always relevant, but instead to argue that they should become a standard part of all punishments. Restoration may require that a criminal accepts his punishment as deserved and proportionate.[44] The most effective route to criminal reformation is his ownership of wrongdoing.[45] Restorative conferences should often be one part of any punishment as a response to crime where it may help assist offenders accept responsibility for their crimes and how they should be held accountable.

Restoration may require more than these conferences alone, however, in order to best guarantee the restoration of rights in most cases.[46] Punishment is not justified by deterrence or rehabilitation. However, deterrence and rehabilitation may play some *secondary* role in justified sentencing.[47] If our goal is the protection of rights, then this task may be achieved in different ways depending upon the particular circumstances. We must first confirm that an offender has performed a crime. We then punish in proportion to the rights threatened by the crime. The particular form this punishment should take may address deterrent or rehabilitative penal goals insofar as they might contribute to the restoration and protection of rights within these proportional limits. Furthermore, the unified theory of punishment defends *punitive restoration*. Punishment aims at the restoration of rights. Restoration may require some punitive element to best secure the restoration and protection of rights, such as community sentencing, a suspended sentence, or imprisonment.

The unified theory of punishment may address desert, proportionality, deterrence, rehabilitation, restoration, and expressivism in a coherent and unified account bringing together these multiple penal aims. The Model Penal Code presents a list of multiple penal goals. The unified theory of punishment offers us a theory about how these different goals may be pursued within a single coherent framework. Crimes are legal wrongs against rights. Punishment aims at the restoration of our rights and this restoration may take multiple shapes to achieve these aims.[48] Punishment is a response to crime that responds best as a unified theory.

Is the unified theory a 'unified' theory?

The unified theory of punishment raises several questions. Perhaps the most pressing is examining how 'unified' the unified theory is, in fact. Is it a *genuinely* unified theory?

One potential criticism is that the unified theory is no more unified than the Model Penal Code. The Code has been described as 'principled pragmatism'. It is principled because it is inclusive of several attractive penal goals. These goals address multiple sentencing principles, such as that punishment should be deserved, proportionate, provide a deterrent, and rehabilitate offenders. The Code is also pragmatic. This is because it recognizes that these different goals may potentially clash. For example, the aim of proportionate punishment may clash with the aim of providing a strong deterrence. The solution is to say that judges should weigh these different goals together in determining sentencing. So is there any difference between this position and unified theories?

The problem with the Model Penal Code is that its principled pragmatism is insufficiently principled: we require coherent pluralism, instead. This is because the multiple penal goals form a list lacking a suitably robust framework that offers a sufficiently clear steer on how these goals relate to one another *within* the framework. Why should *any* of these goals be included? The answer seems to be that each is intuitively attractive on its individual merits. But this fails to address specifically how each might relate. Imagine making a cake combining only those ingredients that you enjoy individually. Following this procedure may not guarantee that all the necessary ingredients for making a cake are included. Nor is there any guarantee that the cake will be edible. Now imagine starting a company by inviting only those persons that you enjoy working with individually. This procedure may not guarantee that all the necessary tasks will be covered. Nor is there any guarantee that the company's members will work together suitably effectively. These examples centre on the problem of justifying a legal practice without sufficient consideration of how the individual parts coherently work together in support of the practice aims. This problem lies at the heart of the Model Penal Code.[49]

The unified theory of punishment overcomes this problem. It addresses desert, proportionality, and other penal goals because they come together within a larger unified framework. So we don't weigh up possible sentences in light of general deterrence versus desert and other penal considerations because we find them intuitively attractive individually. Punishment does not bring together multiple penal goals because it can, but because it should. Punishment is a response to crime that aims at the restoration of rights. Punishment addresses multiple penal goals in serving its aims. The unified theory of punishment is not a mere list, but coherent penal pluralism.

A second potential criticism is that the unified theory may punish to maintain the power of the state at the expense of its citizens. This is a criticism some have levied at other approaches which claim punishment is justified by its ability to maintain political order. For example, one view attributed to Emile Durkheim is that punishment symbolizes and expresses our moral judgements with the purpose of reaffirming some moral order.[50] We punish in order to protect and maintain this moral order that governs us all. Punishment is justified in reference to its 'social necessity'.[51]

The unified theory of punishment overcomes this worry as well. We do not punish to maintain and protect the rights of the state, but the rights of its citizens which demarcate their substantial freedoms. Punishment does not serve the interests of the state at the expense of the interests of citizens. Punishment is only justified insofar as it fulfils its aim of restoring rights from criminal violations and protecting the substantial freedoms of individuals.

The problem of coherence

The unified theory of punishment is a specific variety of a hybrid theory of punishment. Hybrid theories of punishment attempt to offer theories which address two or more penal goals. Unified theories attempt to offer an account that may address multiple penal goals in a unified framework. There are alternative hybrid theories that speak to multiple penal goals.

One alternative states that we should consider various penal goals within sentencing guidelines and we should choose the most severe punishment available. For example, it might be argued that 'the length of the sentence of imprisonment imposed on the defendant by the court shall be the longest of the four sentences derived'.[52] Suppose that desert, deterrence, and other views could each support different prison term lengths where deterrence supported the longest term. This hybrid theory of punishment would endorse deterrence. The idea is that all principles are satisfied where we support the penal goal that is most punitive.

There are at least two problems with this approach. First, we should draw a different conclusion. Why believe all principles are satisfied in choosing the goal that exceptionally supports more punishment than the others? If this hybrid approach is attractive because it shows how multiple goals might support a common position, then we should instead endorse a punishment that all multiple goals support. Justified punishment is punishment that meets some threshold and within a range that multiple goals may endorse. This approach should lead us to a different conclusion. So we should not support the greatest punishment possible from the viewpoint of any single penal goal, but instead any punishment that all penal goals might endorse.

A second problem with this approach is that it lacks unity. It has a view about how we might determine sentences using different penal aims, but it says little about why these aims matter. Moreover, punishment is not determined so to further any particular aim, but rather only to find some – or, indeed, any – support for punishing offenders as much as possible. So it is hybrid in the full sense of being a collection of penal goals without being unified in the sense of offering some clear unifying rationale for why these goals and how they might work together in a coherent approach. This is the problem we found with the Model Penal Code.

Another alternative hybrid approach argues that multiple penal goals should be used to determine punishment within the boundaries of a primary penal goal. One formulation is to say that no criminal should be punished more or less than she deserves. Deserved punishment will typically fall within some range of possibilities. We choose from these possibilities with reference to multiple penal goals. Our theory of punishment is then hybrid insofar as it may address multiple penal goals, but guided by a primary goal. Suppose desert might support a punishment of between two and four years in prison. We then consider how penal aims such as deterrence, rehabilitation, expressivism, restoration might apply in determining a more precise sentence. One worry is that different penal goals may lend support to different outcomes. Thus, deterrence might endorse a longer punishment than restoration. The response to this worry is that this problem does not represent an injustice. If any punishment between two and four years may be said to be 'deserved', then there is nothing unjust about choosing a punishment within this deserved range according to other principles.

The main problem with this view is that it does not offer a coherent unified theory of punishment. Perhaps there is no injustice in selecting any punishment within some range of deserved alternatives. What justifies the relevance of applying other penal goals? Why not flip a coin? This formulation may offer a view that may bring together multiple penal goals, but it lacks a satisfactory account for why multiple goals should figure into a compelling theory of punishment.

A second formulation is to say that punishment should defer to the greatest utility, understood as crime reduction. Different penal goals may conflict when balanced against each other in determining just punishments. We should navigate between them with reference to supporting those punishments that best reduce crime. Broadly speaking, this is a formulation offered by the Model Penal Code. The main problem with this approach is that its declared primary goal is not primary, in fact. For example, the Model Penal Code is governed by 'basic considerations of justice' whereby punishment is not 'excessive, disproportionate or arbitrary'.[53] So punishment must be determined within the bounds of justified desert first and then we consider how we might best enable crime reduction second. Punishment does not defer to the greatest utility in fact, but only within clearly prescribed constraints determined by desert. While this formulation may present itself as a unified theory, it bears close resemblance to negative retributivism as discussed in chapter 5 and with all the problems associated with this approach.[54]

There are two further possible objections. The first is about distinctiveness. How is the unified theory *not* retributivist? The objection might claim the following. The unified theory punishes crimes in proportion to what is deserved. Its understanding of desert may be distinctive, but many retributivist theories differ on their precise understandings of desert. So perhaps there is nothing unique about the unified theory of punishment offering a different view about desert and it is best understood as a retributivist theory. This objection fails because the unified theory punishes crimes in order to restore rights. Punishment is not deserved because a criminal has performed a moral wrong, but because of a crime. Furthermore, retributivists argue that punishment should be proportionate to what is deserved. However, the unified theory does not claim that punishment is proportionate to moral desert, but instead what is required to best enable the restoration of rights. Moral depravity does not determine criminalization or penal proportionality. The unified theory of punishment rejects retributivism because it rejects the idea that punishment must be proportionate to a crime's moral wrongness. The unified theory is both coherent and distinctive; it is not retributivism by another name.[55]

Finally, it must be noted that the unified theory of punishment is not a 'rights forfeiture' theory of punishment. These theories claim that punishment is justified where offenders forfeit their right not to be punished.[56] The unified theory does not claim punishment is justified when offenders 'forfeit' their right against punishment. First, offenders cannot be said to forfeit their rights when their rights are merely suspended and not terminated. If we were to forfeit a game, then we have lost: we have terminated our participation. But we do not terminate our rights, not least any rights against punishment, unless sentenced to death. We do not lose our rights when punished. On the contrary, justified punishment aims to protect and restore our rights. This may include imprisonment, but only as a last resort where alternatives are unsatisfactory. So offenders do not lose their rights in being punished although certain rights may be suspended where justificatory conditions are satisfied.

Another objection concerns the justificatory aims of punishment. For example, we might accept the complexity that confronts punishment, but reject the possibility that it can have any 'single meaning or a single purpose'.[57] So punishment may speak to different penal goals, but not under any one coherent framework: 'any attempt to build a single theoretical model of the causes, forms, and consequences of penalty would be misconceived'.[58] This objection is correct to claim that a significant problem for most standard theories of punishment is their inability to address the complexity of punishment from their single purpose. However, this criticism is directed only to retributivists, deterrence proponents, and others. It is not a criticism of the more recent and novel unified theory of punishment. We may agree that standard theories have run into this problem, but this is more reason to accept the unified theory precisely because it avoids this objection.

This chapter's presentation of the unified theory shows that this objection is misplaced. It is possible to conceive of a unified theory of punishment that brings together multiple penal goals within a single, coherent framework. Punishment may speak to different penal goals, but we must first establish a new justificatory framework. The unified theory of punishment demonstrates this possibility.

The problem of treating like cases differently

The unified theory of punishment may appear a target for the problem of treating like cases differently. The objection is that the criminal law should not justify different outcomes in broadly similar cases. The unified theory may coherently bring together multiple penal goals, but it cannot guarantee similar treatment in similar cases. For example, two offenders convicted for similar thefts may be punished differently so that the first receives more rehabilitation (e.g. perhaps greater drug and alcohol therapy) and the second more hours of community service. Like cases are not treated alike.

There are two problems with this objection. The first problem is that there is no evidence that punishing two thieves convicted of similar offences differently is a case where like cases have been treated differently. Punishment aims at the restoration of rights violated by crimes. This restoration must be tailored to individual circumstances. Suppose that the first thief engaged in crime to support his drug and alcohol dependency and the second engaged in crime because she did not expect to get caught. The punitive restoration and protection of rights may take different forms to best address these different cases. We should distinguish between crime and its circumstances. The *crimes* in both cases are alike: each thief is supposed to have committed broadly similar offences. The *criminal circumstances* in these cases are not alike. We punish crimes in light of their crime-relevant circumstances. The unified theory of punishment may justify different punishments for these thieves without treating like cases differently. This is because the criminal circumstances are not alike.

For the objection to succeed, it must show that different punishments would be justified for the same criminal circumstances. Of course, no one argues that there is one and only one fixed sentence for the great majority of crimes.[59] We don't say that all arsonists should be punished by eight years and not a minute more or less in every case. The individual circumstances of a case will matter and judges will have some discretion in sentencing to account for these circumstances. Punishment is an imprecise science at best. We should not expect our penal theories to offer any specific recommendations beyond a small range of potentially permissible tariffs.[60] A theory of punishment cannot declare that only one sentence is justified in all cases at all times, but it can claim that sentences within some fixed range are justified, to be determined in light of particular relevant circumstances and open to future revision. Therefore, we should reject the view that punishment should be inflexible. The problem with this is that punishment cannot be so precise in addressing even the same circumstances to say that only eight years in prison is justified for all arsonists in every criminal circumstance. Some difference is permitted within a fixed range to be determined in light of circumstances subject to future revision and judicial review. The unified theory of punishment is not subject to the objection that it fails to treat like cases alike.

The problem of relativism

The unified theory of punishment aims to restore rights violated by crimes. One implication is that crimes may warrant greater or lesser punishment depending, in part, on changing circumstances. Punishment must do more work in societies that are engaged in civil war. Crime may present a different amount of threat to our rights within different contexts. Furthermore, political societies may then punish the same crimes in the same individual circumstances very differently in some part due to possible differences in societal contexts. Crimes and punishments may significantly differ from one political society to the next. The potential objection is that the unified theory of punishment is open to a kind of relativism that is problematic and should be avoided. There should be broad congruence across different political societies on criminalization and punishment.

The unified theory of punishment rejects the necessity of broad congruence across political societies. This is not to argue that broad congruence is impossible or problematic, but rather to argue that it is not necessary for a legal system to be satisfactorily justified. Of course, some minimal conditions concerning the recognition of rights as substantial freedoms protected by law are required. However, different societies may understand this recognition and its protection by law in different ways. We should not expect every political society to converge on all matters of criminal law. Perhaps we might expect this if we believed that all political societies are governed by a particular universal morality that should guide how we criminalize and punish. We have already rejected this strong version of legal moralism. In the absence of a particular universal morality to play such a role, we should expect some differences to emerge between legal systems on criminal justice matters, and this need not be fundamentally problematic.

We have seen that the unified theory of punishment may punish the same crime differently in different circumstances. This does have clear limits. Hegel says:

> The fact that an injury to *one* member of society is an injury to *all* the others does not alter the nature of crime in terms of its concept, but in terms of its outward existence ... [I]ts *danger to civil society* is a determination of magnitude ... This quality or magnitude varies, however, according to the *condition* of civil society.[61]
>
> The very stability of society ... makes crime appear in a milder light, so that its punishment also becomes milder ... Thus, harsh punishments are not unjust in and for themselves, but are proportionate to the conditions of their time; a criminal code cannot be valid for every age ... A penal code is therefore primarily a product of its time and of the current condition of civil society.[62]

Crimes are punished in proportion to their threat to our rights. Crimes will pose a greater threat under some conditions rather than others. Punishment is a response to crime that may vary in severity and application depending upon circumstances. Therefore, the unified theory of punishment rejects the position that there must be any one particular punishment that is always best for any specific crime. This is not so much penal relativism as it is *penal realism*. Punishment must always be considered in context. It matters whether or not the state is in civil war or prosperous times of prolonged peace.

It is worth highlighting that many political societies acknowledge the importance that changing circumstances may have in determining justified punishments. For example, many societies have different penal codes for non-ordinary times where they are at war. Punishments are typically more punitive during times of war than prolonged peace. Punishments may also be modified in response to mass protest. One recent illustration is the case of the London riots that took place during August 2011. Sentences were increased for offenders about 25 per cent, attracting political support across party divisions and supported by public opinion.[63] It makes sense to increase the severity of punishment for crimes committed during mass public disturbances, such as riots, because the threat posed to individual rights becomes much greater than normal. People who might not otherwise offend may attempt to take advantage of the temporary chaos in the hope of not getting caught. Such a likelihood increases during times of public disturbance and so punishment must do more in order to best safeguard and restore our threatened individual rights.

Note that punishment reacts to *perceptions* about threats to rights. There is always the danger that this perception is mistaken. Call this *the problem of penal perception*. This is perhaps an increasing worry given that the public have become increasingly fearful of crime during a period where crime has reached historic lows and prison numbers have hit historic highs. The fact that the public's perception of crime's potential threat to rights may be mistaken is not a reason to reject the role that penal perception should play in helping to determine punishment for crime. Instead, this problem alerts us to the need to endeavour so to ensure that our perceptions about threats to rights are satisfactory and not a product of fear mongering, but rather evidence based.

Judging success

There are at least two potential problems concerning how we might judge the success of the unified theory of punishment. The first problem concerns its success in its own terms. The unified theory of punishment has the aim of the protection and restoration of rights. Those acts or omissions that represent some threat to violating rights may require criminalization. Crimes are punished to the degree that they represent some threat to violating rights. This understanding of crime and punishment best addresses criminal justice. First, it offers a compelling explanation for why the 'standard' class of crimes, such as murder, assault, or theft, should be punished. These crimes represent threats to violation of the rights of others. Our response is greater in proportion to the threat a particular crime represents when considering the full criminal circumstances. The unified theory would normally justify greater punishment for assault than petty theft and greater punishment for murder than either assault or petty theft. It is not the case that most categories of crime need always be punished more or less than others. For example, some thefts may require greater punishment than some assaults in consideration of the full circumstances. This view of criminal justice accounts for the full 'standard' class of crimes we would want to punish and it defends a view of proportionality that is compelling without recourse to legal moralism.

Secondly, the unified theory of punishment also offers a compelling explanation for why the 'non-standard' class of crimes should be punished, such as victimless crimes. These are punished not because they are evil, but because they represent potential threats to rights. Such crimes might include drug and traffic offences as well as prostitution. To be criminal, these must be understood as threats to rights as substantial freedoms. It may be argued that some drug offences do not pose such a threat. If so, then the unified theory would not justify criminalization or punishment. However, if it is possible to argue that individuals might not only act in ways that may threaten the violation of rights of others, but also of themselves, then this may offer a more compelling explanation for why some victimless crimes should be considered criminal. We do not say that an act is criminal because no one should be able to consent to it. Rather we argue that some acts are criminal because they violate rights. Therefore, slavery is wrong as the violation of individual rights and so consent is irrelevant for determining criminalization. Furthermore, illegal parking may not be wicked. However, where the specific regulations concerning parking are justified as protecting the rights of citizens, perhaps in terms of rights of free movement within practical constraints, then a breach of the law may require some proportional penal response. Traffic offences can and should be criminal where they serve the maintenance and protection of rights. This role may often be relatively minor which explains why these offences are often punished by penalties and overlooked entirely by most considerations of criminal law.

The unified theory of punishment has at least two further merits. Treason is the most severely punished crime in every jurisdiction from antiquity to today.[64] Whatever a society's most severe punishment, it is always and everywhere a possibility for convicted traitors. The question is why? Treason is not clearly immoral or wicked in every case. We may have a moral duty to engage in treason against some states. The best reason for criminalizing treason is that treason is a crime against the state. Again, this may not always be morally wrong. The crucial point is that if rights are maintained and protected by a legal system and treason aims to end this system, then treason represents a threat to all rights within a legal system. Therefore, treason may be punished more than any other crime. The unified theory of punishment can offer the best explanation for why treason may require the greatest punishment. This is not to say that it is always 'best' to punish traitors and to do so more severely than all others. This is because a legal system does not exist for its sake, but instead for the sake of citizens with the aim of maintaining and protecting their rights. Where a legal system fails in these areas, such a system may be deeply flawed and perhaps not fit for its purpose. So one merit of the unified theory of punishment is that it may best account for treason as the most serious crime.

A second merit is its position with respect to persons unfit for trial, but detained in institutions almost as if they were sentenced. Many theories of punishment require the presence of retributivist desert, such as retributivism, expressivism, and other views. They might claim that punishment is justified where it is deserved and there is a problem where persons cannot be held morally responsible for violence. Suppose there is a violent psychopath. He is genuinely suffering from psychopathic delusions that compel him to attempt killing innocent persons without provocation. He lacks culpability for his actions, but these actions present a clear danger to the public.

The unified theory of punishment might argue that the violent psychopath should be incapacitated regardless of culpability. His actions represent real threats to the rights of others. The aim of punishment is to restore and protect rights and so incapacitation may be required. It is unnecessary to convict and sentence the violent psychopath for murder. This is because it is unnecessary for us to say only murderers should be incapacitated to best maintain and protect individual rights.

The unified theory of punishment may be successful when understood in its own terms. It offers a compelling and coherent account of how we might understand criminalization and the punishment of crimes across standard and non-standard cases. The unified theory is successful where it restores and protects rights. Further evidence for its success would consist in its ability to promote crime reduction. We should expect fewer crimes and less serious crimes where crime rates fall. Additional evidence for the success of the unified theory of punishment may arise from the positive endorsements of restorative conference participants. Any theory that aspires to restore and protect rights should command the support of those who have a stake. Victims, offenders, and community members each have a stake in penal outcomes. Where they are satisfied with these outcomes, this is an important benchmark for judging success of the unified theory. If stakeholders are satisfied, then this offers a strong reason why others should also be satisfied with outcomes.

A second potential problem is whether the theory is successful on other terms. For example, one criticism of retributivist desert is that there are many different positions on moral responsibility and it may be very difficult, if not impossible, to determine approximately how much punishment is deserved in proportion to moral responsibility for any crime. Similarly, one criticism of deterrence is that we cannot guarantee that our punishment today will have the effect we predict in reducing future crime. So why think the unified theory does any better?

The unified theory does not run into this problem of *penal indeterminism* to the same degree. Retributivists have more substantial problems with determining punishments in relation to moral responsibility: moral responsibility is not always relevant and may be impossible to know. Likewise, deterrence proponents may never know how many potential crimes were effectively deterred by a penal threat: they can only measure crime reduction and not deterrence itself. The unified theory claims to restore and protect rights. This view holds that rights can be known. We may be mistaken about the identity of rights and no legal system can expect to be free from any criticism. However, if we can have some satisfactory grasp of what our rights are, then this is a more secure foundation than found in rival theories. It will always be a matter of debate and good judgement concerning how punishment might best fulfil its aim of maintaining and protecting rights, but this task – however relatively open-textured – is no less clear than other theories of punishment. Furthermore, we should not expect any theory to offer any precise determinations. All we might expect is that a theory may offer a more compelling argument than its rivals. So while we may err in how best to protect rights, we could never know if we do not err in punishing criminals retributively or to secure deterrence.

The unified theory of punishment supports punishments that best restore rights violated or threatened with violation by crimes. Note that this view justifies punishment only where necessary: if punishment is unnecessary to restore rights, then it is unjustified. Note further that this view has a clear position on the punishment of criminal attempts. An attempt may be unsuccessful in fulfilling some criminal goal, such as a murder or theft. While an attempt may not succeed in violating rights, punishable attempts must succeed in presenting a sufficiently substantial threat to rights in order to be punishable. This is intuitively compelling. We often punish criminal attempts less, but often lack some clear principle to explain why we punish attempts less in some cases and not others. The unified theory offers us a helpful solution. Where an attempt presents a sufficiently substantial rights threat, then the attempt is punishable. The punishment is proportionate to the threat presented by a criminal attempt. This need not always entail that criminal attempts merit reduced punishment because they failed to succeed in achieving some criminal goal. The unified theory helps us make best sense of cases like these. The unified theory of punishment endorses punitive restoration.

Finally, we should note that the unified theory of punishment supports the use of restorative justice in conjunction with imprisonment and including intensive supervision programmes. Conviction is legal confirmation of personal criminality, but it also is often confirmation that a person requires help *now*. It's often crucial to provide necessary support sooner rather than later. Again, conviction often confirms that a person is in need of help.

This need not entail swift justice as moving too quickly to court which might undermine any fair trial. This is because the overwhelming majority of cases never reach trial. Only about 6 per cent or less (and about 3 per cent in Scotland) receive a full court trial. All others are handled through plea bargaining and alternatives to trial. Time must be granted for all parties to examine the relevant evidence and present their best case in court. But those who accept their criminal guilt should not wait too long. It is essential that criminals come to acknowledge their criminal wrongdoing through taking responsibility by being held accountable. The sooner, the better. For example, intensive supervision programmes enacted early may 'dramatically' improve reducing recidivism rates fourfold.[65]

Another idea is using imprisonment more frequently in shorter sentences. Brief imprisonment may provide criminals with a 'cooling off' period. Of course, brief imprisonment is often believed to be criminogenic, ensuring reoffending is more likely. But this common problem in prison studies often overlooks significant facts that contribute to this specific concern. For example, prisoners may receive little, if any, rehabilitative support during terms of 12 months or less. This support is often directed to offenders with longer sentences instead. It is little wonder that offenders are likely to return to criminal activity post-release when too little is done about them. Over 90 per cent of offenders will avoid trial and most of these accept some form of plea bargain. This is a substantial number of people and we could redesign our criminal justice system to better assist offenders acknowledging their crimes and taking responsibility by being held accountable. We can achieve these goals through punitive restoration by expanding the use of restorative justice conferences as a more common feature of punishments to be used in conjunction with brief imprisonment where this might best enable the restoration of rights and their protection. Early intervention may often serve this goal effectively.

The unified theory of punishment helps us explain this goal has importance and sheds light on how it may be fulfilled. Prison as a cooling off period may serve a useful rehabilitative function by best securing more immediate alcohol and drug treatment as well as perhaps anger management and life coaching where appropriate. This cooling off period might also serve a useful deterrent function in signalling imprisonment as a more likely outcome, but also retributive and expressivist functions by indicating the seriousness with which the public views crimes. Finally, prison may serve a wider restorative function in better securing public confidence through punitive restoration. Prison may be redesigned to better ensure the restoration of rights violated or threatened by crimes.

Restoration need not require the absence of imprisonment, but may require its use on occasion. Prisons are expensive and often poor at reducing reoffending by offenders post-release. The unified theory of punishment does *not* recommend imprisonment where it would fail to best restore and protect rights. However, the unified theory does encourage us to consider new ways of ensuring that prison more effectively serves the aim of best restoring and protecting rights. A likely result is more brief prison terms where offenders receive immediate and intensive support rather than more longer terms in prison. While these brief terms will carry greater costs, they might also contribute to better results and be cost effective in reducing the need for longer prison terms. Brief prison terms might be served in one block or spread over time. One major problem in imprisoning offenders is that it may contribute to a bad situation becoming much worse. Many are unemployed and face financial insecurity. So one option might be to permit non-violent offenders to work during the day, but return to prison at night and perhaps on weekends. Offenders might then retain employment and maintain support networks while securing public confidence that they are being held accountable for their crimes through the loss of personal liberty while in prison. The unified theory helps explain not only why prisons should be avoided where possible, but also how they might become reimagined to better serve the underlying purpose that justifies their use as punitive restoration.

The stakeholder society

The idea of the stakeholder society may play a significant role in any compelling theory of punishment.[66] Many wonder about how to best tackle crime. We have already identified in previous chapters factors that are often associated with criminal behaviour. These factors include drug and alcohol abuse, unemployment, financial insecurity, housing problems, and past offending. There are other important associated factors, such as support networks of friends and family. Many offenders will share one or more of these factors although each case will be very different from the next. Criminal profiling is an imprecise art far removed from detectives depicted on the silver screen.[67] It is an informed guess about more likely findings. Nevertheless, it remains tempting to speculate about the criminal mind. This is relevant because insights into criminality may contribute to reduced crime and less need for punishment. We may further wonder how it is that crime rates have changed over time and how associated factors may have changed, too.

It is easy to overlook a common bond that these risk factors address. Crime is not necessarily a problem of drug abuse or unemployment although these factors may often be present. The unifying thread that brings together these factors concerns the individual's beliefs about his or her relation to others. The primary factor associated with likely criminal behaviour is the failure of individuals to see themselves as having a stake in their political community. Other associated factors become a concern where they contribute to a sense that someone lacks a stake.

The problem of failing to believe someone has a stake in the political community is often understood as a failure of political recognition. This is captured well by Hegel:

> When a large mass of people sinks below the level of a certain standard of living ... that feeling of right, legitimacy, and honour ... is lost. This leads to the creation of a rabble ... Poverty in itself does not reduce people to a rabble; a rabble is created only by the disposition associated with poverty, by inward rebellion against the rich, against society, the government, etc.[68]

Hegel identifies a group, the rabble, united by their shared disposition about how they relate to others. The rabble believes they are disassociated from others in their political community. This disassociation is based upon a sense of injustice: that they lack in some significant share of right, legitimacy, and honour. The rabble are united by the conviction that they are somehow divorced from lawful society; that the rules applying to all somehow don't relate to them because of this sense of political otherness.

Hegel's rabble may often be found amongst those in poverty, but this is not the only associated factor. Hegel is clear that 'an excess of wealth' may also contribute to a rabble.[69] The rabble is a state of mind, a mentality. Not all persons with associated factors will identify with the rabble although many may self-identify. Anyone may adopt the rabble state of mind whether rich or poor. However, the problem is not only how to prevent a rabble from arising in the first place, but how to bring about a change of heart and convert the rabble to believing themselves to have a stake. Hegel famously lacks any clear answer to either question although we might do better.

The idea of the stakeholder society is the idea that each individual citizen believes he or she has some significant stake in the political community and its continuation. This shared sense that I have a stake in the continuation of my political community may lead me to refrain from crime where possible. This is because the stakeholder society is a political community that satisfactorily attracts my interest and concern.[70] People will believe that any problems are best resolved within the system rather than without. Not everyone need be fully satisfied with any current political arrangement or oppose radical reforms. Instead, the essential concern is whether persons identify themselves as having a stake in the political community or not. Some may believe they do not have a shared stake and can 'opt out' in a position we might call political exceptionalism, which is rooted in alienation. Not everyone possesses a palpable sense of social belonging. Our challenge is to convince Hegel's rabble to 'opt in' where they remain unconvinced.[71]

One important route to helping individuals become more conciliatory to their political community is to honour our *recognitional debt* to them. This debt is the political recognition we owe fellow citizens. It is understood in terms of a shared political reciprocity.[72] John Rawls says:

> The least advantaged are not, if all goes well, the unfortunate and unlucky – objects of our charity and compassion, much less our pity – but those to whom reciprocity is owed as a matter of political justice among those who are free and equal citizens along with everyone else.[73]

Our perception is key to changing hearts and minds. Hegel's rabble is best addressed where they are convinced that they are not strangers to be pitied, but fellow citizens who deserve our respect. All members must enjoy some standard of reciprocity in order to best secure acceptance of the self-identity that comes with believing in possessing a stake in society. This is politically and legally realist in taking people as they are and predicting how they will respond to different situations.[74] The political community should ensure that its members do not view themselves as powerless, isolated, and disconnected if only to best guard against crime and the need for punishment.[75] The more members believe they have a stake in society, the less likely crime will occur. We have a responsibility to honour our recognitional debt to all and ensure that our political community is a place where all may share some stake in its present and future.

The idea of the stakeholder society offers an insight into criminality. It claims that failing to see yourself as having a stake is a primary factor associated with crime. If punishment is to be an effective response to crime, then punishment must aim to restore and protect our rights without undermining stakeholding. Offenders should accept responsibility for their crimes while coming to see their having a stake in society. We best reduce crime where all view themselves as belonging to a stakeholder society. There is compelling evidence that criminality is linked with a failing to see one's stake in the political community and its future.[76]

There are several ways we might promote stakeholding. Criminal justice policy must focus on reducing recidivism while improving public confidence. Most offenders will be eventually released if imprisoned. Our view must consider punishment with a view to life post-conviction and post-release.[77] Stakeholding is promoted where key contributing risk factors for social and political disassociation are effectively managed. This raises the importance of behavioural and employability programmes in addressing stakeholding.[78] This may require assistance with accommodation, skill building, financial advice, cognitive therapy, and behavioural support. There must be a more effectively managed post-conviction plan integrating penal management with addressing offender needs.[79]

These efforts may be assisted in several ways. Restorative justice conferences promote stakeholding. Offenders, victims, and community members come together to determine how offenders may restore rights. Each has a stake in the deliberative outcome premised on the offender's acknowledgement of his crime. Unsurprisingly, all parties regularly report high satisfaction with the process and its outcome. Restorative conferences have demonstrated promising crime reduction potential at a fraction of the cost of alternatives without sacrificing public confidence. The key to their success is the promotion of stakeholding where each has a stake in the outcome. These conferences may be reformed to permit more punitive possible outcomes where these may best secure the restoration of rights. Such conferences might be mediated by a magistrate or judge rather than a facilitator, depending upon the circumstances involved.

A second example is so-called 'community pay back', where offenders perform public tasks as part of their punishment. These may include voluntary work at charitable organizations and rebuilding the community. Examples of the latter may include cleaning graffiti, interior decoration of public buildings, and assisting public building maintenance and new construction. These forms of punishment are public and punitive without stigmatization. Offenders are encouraged to see themselves as having a stake in what they help maintain and create for public benefit.

A further example is the Certificate of Good Conduct issued by the US state of New York to reformed criminals.[80] It gives offenders the ability to seek work without automatic disqualification for having a past criminal conviction. The Certificate removes a large barrier that may prevent offenders from securing employment and furthering their stake in society. An alternative idea is to place time limitations for how long some offenders are required to acknowledge past convictions on applications. This might be limited to offenders without previous convictions or no more than two convictions. Or perhaps only relating to conviction for non-violent crimes. Perhaps first non-violent offences need not be acknowledged on applications at all. These measures might retain some obstacles to full future stake-holding, but without closing this possibility off permanently. They address the concern that if an offender must also face obstacles to employment, housing, and other areas for even minor crimes performed long ago in his past the possibility of full restoration may be inhibited and perhaps even denied. Such possibilities provide offenders with hope and a goal to pursue that may better inspire them to see themselves as having a stake in society.

These are only a few recommendations for how we might promote the idea of a stakeholder society. Of course, not everyone will see themselves as having a stake in society. Stakeholding requires individuals to *believe* that they have a stake in society.[81] It may be the case that some hold false beliefs about their relation to others. Call this *the problem of stake-holding beliefs*. This problem is a concern because citizens may be most at risk of criminal engagement. However, while criminal justice policy should aspire to crime reduction, it cannot deliver crime eradication. Moreover, there is no crime in failing to see oneself as having a stake. We punish crimes alone. Our goal must be to reduce crimes, but we cannot end crime without abandoning criminalization itself. If there is a criminal law, then there will be criminals. Our society is characterized by the fact of crime and it cannot be wished to disappear. But we can acknowledge, confront, and reduce crime more effectively. The idea of the stakeholding society paired with the unified theory of punishment offers the best approach to criminal justice.

The idea of the stakeholder society has a central relevance for any penal theory although its complete treatment would require a separate text and my discussion cannot be more than preliminary. The central idea presupposes that the political community is worth having a stake in in the first place. We have already seen that the conception of politics accepted by the unified theory of punishment is the idea that rights are understood as our substantial freedoms. Crime is the violation or threatened violation of our rights. Punishment is a response to crime that aims to restore and protect our rights through punitive restoration. We have also seen that there can be no just punishment for an unjust crime. The restoration and pro-tection of rights is best guaranteed within the political conception of the stakeholder society although the idea of a stakeholder society is not exclusive to the unified theory of punishment.[82] Finally, the promotion of stakeholding must be aimed at all members of a political community. It is not for offenders alone. The central importance for promoting stakeholding to offenders is that it fosters good citizenship, including crime reduction.[83]

Conclusion

We have examined the diversity in strengths and weaknesses for various theories of punishment both general and hybrid. Each contains something of importance. There is something intuitively compelling about a theory of punishment that might bring diverse and attractive penal goals together into a coherent unity. If a theory of punishment could address retributivism, deterrence, rehabilitation, restoration, expressivism, and perhaps more, then such a theory may prove more compelling than alternatives that address only one or two. The problem is how to conceive of such a theory and get the balance right where so many have got it wrong.

The unified theory of punishment proposed in this chapter is an important attempt to offer a compelling hybrid theory of punitive restoration that brings together multiple penal goals into a coherent and unified theory. While its presentation here is novel, its philosophical roots extend to Hegel, the British Idealists, and perhaps even earlier. The unified theory of punishment has been defended in different forms. The form explained and defended here is one of many possible forms.

Not only is a unified theory of punishment theoretically possible, it also makes best sense of our current practices.[84] A major problem of the Model Penal Code is not that it seeks to address multiple goals in sentencing, but its lack of a more robust and attractive theoretical framework that brings unity to its goals and illuminates punishment's primary goal of restoring rights within the context of a stakeholder society. This perspective helps us better understand where current practices might be reformed and conceive of new ways to achieve this end.

Philosophers looking to defend the most compelling theory of punishment that makes best sense of the world as we find it while pointing towards a bold new vision for criminal justice policy and political justice more broadly should accept the unified theory of punishment.

Part 3

Case studies

We have now completed our examination of seven theories of punishment *as theories*. We have viewed both general, more traditional theories of punishment and several hybrid accounts concluding with the unified theory of punishment. In this final part, we now consider how well these theories perform *in practice*. The practices that we will focus on now are capital punishment, juvenile offenders, domestic abuse, and sex crimes, such as rape and child sex offences. Each will be discussed individually in its own chapter.

8 Capital punishment

Introduction

Capital punishment (or 'the death penalty') is the most severe form of punishment generally permitted, where the convicted are executed. It is also the subject of intense debate about its justification and whether the state should execute its citizens. This chapter will begin by presenting background information about the use of capital punishment before turning to considerations of its justification. Perhaps one surprising result is that, often, any one penal theory may offer support to both sides of the debate. While it may be tempting to believe that accepting one particular theory of punishment commits its proponents to a single conclusion, we will discover that most theories may lead to split conclusions or be inapplicable. Some theories, such as the unified theory, are able to best account for why capital punishment may be justified if at all, and this chapter will attempt to illuminate why this is the case.

Background

Capital punishment has been practised by human societies from their beginning to punish a variety of crimes, such as murder, rape, adultery, sexual assault, treason and espionage, and stealing horses. The number of capital crimes (i.e. crimes punishable by execution) today is far fewer than in the past. For example, the Old Testament recommends several other crimes for execution, such as anyone who speaks blasphemy against God,[1] worshippers of Baal,[2] witches and wizards,[3] parents who let their children worship Molech,[4] anyone who curses his or her father or mother,[5] adulterers and homosexuals,[6] prostitutes,[7] and those who engage in bestiality, where both the person and the animal are to be killed.[8] Many of these Old Testament recommendations have become incorporated into Western legal codes over time only to be removed later. The execution of witches in Salem, Massachusetts, and elsewhere is one such example. The legal distinction between 'felony' and 'misdemeanour' has been thought originally to distinguish felonies as crimes punishable by death from crimes punishable by alternatives, although this is probably untrue.[9] The Athenian legislator Draco recommended that even minor crimes be punishable by death in ancient Greece. Legal codes have been changed much since, and one central reform has been the significant decline in crimes punished by death.

Many countries have abolished capital punishment altogether, including Australia (since 1984), Costa Rica (since 1877), Germany (since 1949), Ireland (since 1990), Vatican City (since 1969), and Venezuela (since 1863). Roughly thirty countries are abolitionist de facto countries: that is, countries which have legalized the death penalty, but have not used it in ten or more years. These countries include the Buddhist kingdom of Bhutan (since 1964), Guatemala (since 1983), and the Maldives (since 1952). More than a dozen countries have abolished the death penalty for 'ordinary crimes' – crimes taken place when not in a state of war: Canada (since 1976), Greece (since 1993), Israel (since 1954), and the United Kingdom (since 1965). Despite the great number of states that have abolished the death penalty in whole or in part over the last one hundred years, most countries continue to endorse capital punishment. These countries include China, Japan, Iraq, Iran, North Korea, and the United States. The international abolition movement remains a minority position in global affairs although it remains on the rise.

Nevertheless, capital punishment is a *global* phenomenon. All societies have legally sanctioned execution of criminals at some time and a majority continue to do so today. Moreover, the abolition movement is notably a relatively recent development and most abolitionist countries have rejected the use of capital punishment in only the last few decades. Those countries that have retained the death penalty all agree that treason and murder are capital crimes, but disagree on much else such as the crimes punishable by death and the acceptable methods of execution.

Much attention has focused on the United States in the literature on capital punishment: it is without doubt the best known and most studied case. Both the Federal government and most US states support the use of capital punishment. Today, there are nearly 3,500 condemned prisoners. These prisoners are almost all men.[10] More than 50 per cent are white, never married, and never finished high school. Most condemned prisoners had a prior felony conviction and were sentenced to death before the age of 30. While different states allow for various forms of execution, virtually all executions are by lethal injection. For example, only one person was killed differently (by electrocution) out of the 58 persons executed in 2004.[11] There is wide variation in the use of capital punishment by individual states. Since 1976, the five states that have executed the most offenders are Texas (477), Virginia (109), Oklahoma (97), Florida (71), and Missouri (68). Several states have executed only one person during this period, such as Connecticut and Idaho, or none at all, such as Alaska, New Jersey, and New York.

Now that we have considered some general background facts about the use of capital punishment in the world today, how can we make best sense of its justification? This is our focus for the rest of this chapter. We will examine justifications both for and against its use in order to gain better clarity on whether further abolition should command our support. It is also instructive to illuminate how different theories of punishment are able to address practices, such as capital punishment.

Justifications against capital punishment

Let's begin with arguments *against* the death penalty that claim it is unjustified. We will consider whether the state should have the right to kill its citizens. We will also examine the arguments against capital punishment put forward by restorative justice and the rehabilitative theory of punishment. In each case, we will see that the case against capital punishment is not as strong as we may think or even hope.

Does the state have a right to kill its citizens?

One common blanket objection to capital punishment is simple: the state does not have a right to kill its citizens. The business of the state is to protect and promote the well being of its citizens. This central task cannot be achieved by sanctioning the execution of citizens.

Perhaps we should first approach this objection by making a distinction. Before turning to whether the state may be justified to execute citizens, we might begin by examining whether the state is justified in making decisions that concern the life and death of its citizens. Several potential case studies spring to mind. Consider military interventions. The state must be aware that not all its soldiers may return alive from a military operation. This is a relatively uncontroversial example of the state being justified in taking decisions that may lead to the possible deaths of its citizens. There are several possible explanations, but let us focus on one important consideration: the state is justified in placing its soldiers in grave risk in order to protect and promote the general well being of its citizens. It may be that some might face grave risks in order to best secure the well being of others.

Suppose our state was under attack by an Evil State attempting our extermination.[12] Suppose further that Evil State lacks just cause and our state is entirely innocent. This would be a case of potential extreme emergency where doing nothing may lead to our massacre. The state would be justified on grounds of self-defence in sending its citizens off to battle in the knowledge that lives may be lost. The state is justified in making decisions concerning the life and death of its citizens, or at least in cases such as this if we accept we may have a right to self-defence.[13] While there is much more that may be said, this case helps clarify the central issue: the question is not whether the state may be justified, but under which conditions the state is justified. It is then a question of determining when, not if, the state may be justified. This does not settle whether or not the state is ever justified in employing the death penalty. We might accept the state may be justified in making decisions concerning the possible death of its citizens, but not accept its justification for criminals. One reason might be because the state is not responsible for any deaths incurred in the Evil State case. Capital punishment is a different case where the state intends to execute particular offenders. Why should the state be forbidden from intending to execute any offenders?

One objection is metaphorical: capital punishment is like state-sponsored murder. If murder is forbidden by the state, then the state should be forbidden from murdering its citizens. This objection fails. Take other metaphors: imprisonment is state-sponsored kidnapping or levying fines is state-sponsored extortion. Neither is accurate. Kidnapping and extortion are crimes that lack justification with innocent victims. An imprisoned burglar is not kidnapped, but convicted and punished for his crime. Nor is capital punishment akin to state-sponsored murder. The differences are significant. Consider murderers. Suppose we understand murder as the intentional killing of an innocent victim. Executing a murderer may be intentional, but it is not directed at an innocent victim. Capital punishment is not like state-sponsored murder.

Now return to the objection that capital punishment is unjustified because the state's role is to protect and promote the well being of its citizens. We may accept this understanding of the state's role without rejecting capital punishment. Protecting and promoting the well being of citizens need not require we protect and promote the well being of each citizen at all times. It may be the case that we might better promote the well being of citizens on the whole through executing murderers, such as where this might deter future murderers from engaging in crime. Accepting that the state should promote and protect the well being of its citizens need not commit us to rejecting capital punishment.

My purpose here is to clarify that acceptance or rejection of the death penalty may not be as straightforward as we might suppose in these preliminary remarks. We will now turn to a closer examination of how different theories of punishment might bear on the justifiability of the death penalty.

Restorative justice

Restorative justice aims at the restoration of damaged relations between offenders, victims, and the community. Most restorative justice proponents defend this approach as an alternative to so-called hard treatment, such as prison and capital punishment. Restorative justice opposes capital punishment by its nature.

One reason is that restoration seems beyond reach. A murderer has damaged relations between himself and his community through his crime. But how to restore what has been damaged? We cannot bring his murdered victim back to life. Restoration seems impossible in such cases. We are unable to restore what has been damaged where relations cannot be healed. Furthermore, the execution of the murderer would not promote restoration either. His status cannot be restored when he no longer exists as a member of our community. Restoration is about bringing parties together and not expelling members permanently. If the murderer is executed, then he cannot become reintegrated and restoration becomes impossible.

Restorative justice may appear to be an approach firmly opposed to capital punishment. However, this approach is hampered by the fact that its proponents often limit its application to relatively minor offences. Restorative justice is promoted for crimes such as vandalism, minor assaults, or harassment and not murder, treason, or grievous bodily harm. Some have argued that restorative justice should be employed for serious offences, such as domestic violence and sexual assault, but few argue for its use more broadly across all violent crimes.[14] So while restorative justice may appear opposed to capital punishment in principle the problem is that most of its proponents do not believe it is applicable for offences that might be punished by capital punishment. If restorative justice is inapplicable for murderers, then it does not offer a strong case against the justification of the death penalty.

Perhaps the general popularity of restorative justice is based upon the belief that its application should be limited to more minor offences because the related offenders are most capable of reform and restoration. Those who commit more serious offences, such as murder, may be less capable of restoration. Or so the public might believe. Perhaps the reasons for this are that the murderer's plea for mercy should fall on deaf ears or that hardened, violent criminals are unworthy. Whether or not these reasons are justified, restorative proponents have been effective in rethinking punishment for a broad range of offences, but not murder. Restorative justice may prove a fruitful approach to punishing murderers, but it is untried and lacks a compelling narrative that might win over public support for its use.[15] So we might recognize that restorative justice is opposed to capital punishment, but accept that capital punishment may be justified in some cases because restorative justice is inapplicable.

Rehabilitative theories

Now consider rehabilitative theories of punishment. This approach also appears opposed to capital punishment. If our goal is to reform offenders, then the death penalty is unjustified. This is because we cannot reform criminals through execution. This point is captured well by Jean Hampton: 'killing someone is hardly an appropriate technique for educating him'.[16]

Rehabilitation, unlike restorative justice, has been promoted as a theory of punishment applicable to all offenders. Some proponents argue we have a duty to rehabilitate all offenders, including murderers, so that they may become productive members of society again. For example, Eric Cullen and Tim Newell believe there is a strong case for the rehabilitation of murderers.[17] They conducted a study of murderers sentenced to life imprisonment in England and Wales. They found that murderers often make for model prisoners. This is because their good behaviour in prison is often better than many others. Murderers should not be executed because they are not beyond reform. Instead, Cullen and Newell recommend a maximum sentence of about 12 years as the lowest the public might tolerate. Their findings may be controversial, but they direct us to a powerful argument. Virtually all murderers kill once. Reoffending rates are amongst the lowest for any type of offender. Murderers may also demonstrate better behaviour in prisons. These characteristics do not apply in many cases. Of course, there are well known cases of murderers who have killed multiple victims and who would present a danger to the public if released. But there is a clear case for the use of rehabilitation for those murderers who would not and do not reoffend in future. If murderers are capable of reform, then the need for execution may become less and the case for the death penalty lacking.

So rehabilitation may support opposition to the death penalty because it may be shown that many offenders, including murderers, may be capable of reform. But what about offenders who are not? Rehabilitative theories claim the purpose of punishment is to rehabilitate. One main concern has always been the problem of offenders who are incapable of rehabilitation. Suppose we accept that executing murderers does not facilitate rehabilitation.[18] This is only a problem where rehabilitation is possible. If someone could be rehabilitated and we executed her, then we may have contravened our rehabilitative goal. Capital punishment may not oppose rehabilitation when it is not a possibility. This conclusion need not require us to execute persons we believe are incapable of rehabilitation. We might argue that such a judgement is not something we may determine with certainty and should be avoided for this reason. We should not judge anyone beyond future rehabilitation.[19]

Nevertheless, we must have some way of knowing how successful we might be at rehabilitating offenders. Otherwise, we would lack evidence for rehabilitating anyone in the first place. So we must develop some ideas about the possibility of the future rehabilitation for offenders. Or so we might argue. If we were able to confirm that rehabilitation was beyond the capability of some offenders, then the goal of rehabilitation loses much of its force. It becomes more difficult to argue that we should not execute otherwise deserving offenders for their crimes because we should attempt their rehabilitation where we know this task impossible beyond doubt. Perhaps we rehabilitate all those we can, but those we cannot are a different case. So we could accept rehabilitation as the best theory of punishment while also accepting that the death penalty may be justified in those cases where offenders cannot be rehabilitated.

There are several justifications against capital punishment we may find attractive, but each has been found wanting. The argument pursued here is that the different approaches considered thus far do not necessarily commit us to opposing capital punishment. Thus, we might accept rehabilitative theories and oppose capital punishment, but my point is that not all who accept these theories need oppose it. Theories often do not lead to any clear conclusion against the justification of the death penalty. This does not mean that it is justified, but rather that the case against it may be more elusive than we might suppose.

Justifications in favour of capital punishment

We will now turn to arguments that offer possible justifications in favour of capital punishment. The goal will be to demonstrate that the case in favour may be as elusive as the case against. Capital punishment may not offer obvious conclusions on either side. Nevertheless, we may gain better clarity for how the conclusions we draw may become more convincing.

Executing murderers and human nature

One argument in favour of capital punishment is that it is how human beings have traditionally responded to violent crimes, such as murder. There is some truth in this claim as all peoples either live in states that permit the death penalty now or at an earlier time.

There are some major flaws in this claim, however. Several practices have existed since the earliest human societies, such as human sacrifice, slavery, and patriarchy. Some of these practices continue to this day. The mere fact that a practice exists or has existed is not a reason to claim that it is an irreducible part of human society. This is true even where a practice has existed for a considerable time. Social mores are subject to change, even on a global scale. For example, those practices that are legally permitted today may not be so tomorrow.[20] Once human enslavement and sacrifice were widespread; now each is condemned wherever it is found. The mere *fact* of a social practice does not speak conclusively to its *merit*, even if it is a long-standing practice. If someone argues that 'this is the way we have done things', then we might reply that it was about time they stopped.[21]

Therefore, the fact that all societies have justified capital punishment is not conclusive evidence that any society should justify it. Philosophical justification requires argument. It is centrally important to explain *why* capital punishment may be justified and not merely *that* many societies have permitted it in the past.

Religious justifications

A second argument is that capital punishment is justified on theological grounds. For example, it might be claimed that the only justification we may require is that execution is endorsed by God. One problem is that religious beliefs are matters of personal faith that will differ between individuals and even those sharing the same faith. It is unclear how we might choose between such accounts. Paradoxically, it may even be blasphemous to claim to have such knowledge at all.[22]

The Bible has been used to offer a religious justification of capital punishment. There are several passages that lend support to this view. For example, Genesis states that 'any man who murders shall be killed'.[23] We also find several passages that support different conclusions. One example is the story of Cain also found in Genesis. After murdering his brother Abel, Cain is banished and not executed for his crime.[24] A second example is found in the Gospel of Matthew. Jesus is reported to have said that the law of Moses may have justified a life for a life, but we are now to follow a new law where we are to avoid violence, turn our cheek when we are slapped, and love our enemies.[25]

These passages are not meant to end the deep controversy about whether Christians or others should support capital punishment. Instead, their purpose is meant to demonstrate that whether the Bible justifies capital punishment is itself controversial. This is true even in cases where we might least expect to find it.[26] Nor is this treatment of religious justifications meant to be exhaustive. However, we may similarly find reasonable disagreement across many religious believers. This evidence suggests that religious justifications on capital punishment may not lead to any single conclusion. This is not to argue that such justifications cannot be made to support capital punishment. Nevertheless, my claim is that religions do not often lend themselves to only one side of the argument whatever these religions may be.[27] So even if we accept a common religion, this need not require us to always arrive at any one conclusion about whether the death penalty is justified. It is obvious that any religious justification will be problematic from the standpoint of non-believers or those who accept different faiths. So the fact that some believe there is a religious justification in favour of capital punishment is unsatisfactory. This is especially the case when we consider such justifications within the context of the pluralism in beliefs and values that is embedded within our political communities today.

Retributivism

Retributivists argue that criminals should be punished to the degree they deserve. Most retributivists argue that murderers deserve death for their crimes. The most famous example is offered by Kant in a passage we have considered before:

> whatever undeserved evil you inflict upon another ... you inflict upon yourself. If you insult him, you insult yourself; if you steal from him, you steal from yourself; if you strike him, you strike yourself;

if you kill him, you kill yourself ... [E]very murderer – anyone who commits murder, orders it, or is an accomplice in it – must suffer death.[28]

The argument is much more than mere 'life for a life'. Criminals are punished to a degree proportionate to the value of their wrongful act. Murderers commit the most wrongful act of all. All human beings possess infinite worth for Kant. The only punishment that is proportionate to the gravity of the crime is the murderer's life because only this also has infinite value.[29] Murderers should be executed because only their death is proportionate to the gravity of their wicked crime.

This argument may be restated in different terms. Retributivists argue that the punishment must be proportionate to the crime. Murder is perhaps the most grave crime. It should be punished to a degree commensurate with its gravity. The death penalty is justified as the most severe punishment for the most grave crime. The result is that we don't argue that the death penalty is justified for murderers because we should punish in terms of a 'life for a life'. We punish the worst crime with the most severe punishment. It is only a coincidence that both the crime and its punishment include deaths. Capital punishment is justified for murderers because they are suitably proportionate in value. Note that this would not hold if we believed that another crime were more serious or another satisfactory punishment more severe.[30]

A different argument claims that our rights are not absolute and each has limits. For example, we might argue that a clear limit is where we violate or threaten to violate the rights of others. Some argue that substantial violations may lead to substantial losses: '[i]f I violate the rights of others, I thereby lose the same rights. If I am a murderer, I have no *right* to live'.[31] This view has its admirers even amongst deterrent theorists, such as John Stuart Mill:

> I confess it appears to me that to deprive the criminal of the life of which he has proved himself to be unworthy – solemnly to blot him out from the fellowship of mankind and from the catalogue of the living – is the most appropriate ... mode in which society can attach to so great a crime the penal consequences which for the security of life it is indispensable to annex to it.[32]

Murderers do not merely deserve a severe punishment in proportion to their wicked act, but they do not deserve to live at all. This argument is based on a view of desert. What someone deserves is linked to what he has done. In exceptional cases, he may not deserve to live and capital punishment is justified.

Retributivists have several different arguments for how the death penalty may be justified. However, retributivism may also offer arguments against its justification. We may accept that murderers might deserve capital punishment in principle, but not in practice. For example, we might argue that murderers deserve the most severe punishment because of their responsibility for this wicked crime. The problem is that many murders occur in circumstances where aggravating and mitigating factors are present. The murderer may be correctly found guilty of murder, but fail to possess the full responsibility we might require to warrant execution. Relatively few murders are the product of premeditated plans and many are perhaps best viewed as crimes of passion. Where murderers are not fully autonomous and so not fully responsible, they might not deserve the full extent of possible sanctions. We may accept that the death penalty may be justified for some murderers, but not for all.[33] This argument does not rule out capital punishment at all, but it does remind us that not all murderers may be deserving of death, narrowing significantly the number of persons that may be executed.

Some retributivists argue that capital punishment should be rejected because of its unjust distribution. There is well documented evidence that ethnic minorities are disproportionately sentenced to death in the United States.[34] A White murderer is less likely to be sentenced to death than a non-White murderer. The evidence of racial disparity in capital sentencing was a major factor in the landmark 1972 US Supreme Court decision in *Furman* v. *Georgia* that declared the death penalty unconstitutional.[35] Some retributivists would agree. Retributivists argue we should punish murderers in proportion to what they deserve. A system that failed to distribute punishment on the basis of desert cannot be supported by retributivism. The death penalty should be rejected by retributivists because it unfairly distributes punishment where murderers do not always receive their just deserts. Retributivists may accept that murderers deserve execution in principle, but reject the use of capital punishment in practice. We can be retributivists and fail to support the death penalty.[36]

A powerful objection to this argument rejects its conclusion. The conclusion is that no one should be executed because not all murderers who deserve it will be sentenced to death. If we don't distribute just punishment to all, then we shouldn't distribute it to any. The objection is that if the problem is that more deserving murderers should be sentenced to death then we should better ensure more are condemned. The retributivist conclusion we should draw is that we should distribute the death penalty to more deserving murderers rather than end the practice altogether. If murderers deserve death and not all are sentenced to die on arbitrary grounds, then the retributivist conclusion is that more should be sentenced and the distribution of punishment improved. Our task is to punish *more* of the deserving to the degree they deserve, rather than punish *none* of the deserving proportionately. This argument does not offer us a strong *retributivist* argument against capital punishment.

A more compelling retributivist argument against the death penalty is offered by Judge Jed Rakoff in *U.S.* v. *Quinones*:

What DNA testing has proved, beyond cavil, is the remarkable degree of fallibility in the basic fact-finding processes on which we rely in criminal cases. In each of the 12 cases of DNA-exoneration of death row inmates referenced in *Quinones*, the defendant had been found guilty by a unanimous jury that concluded there was proof of his guilt beyond a reasonable doubt; and in each of the 12 cases the conviction had been affirmed on appeal, and collateral challenges rejected, by numerous courts that had carefully scrutinized the evidence and the manner of conviction. Yet, for all this alleged 'due process', the result, in each and every one of these cases, was the conviction of an innocent person who, because of the death penalty, would shortly have been executed (– some came within days of being so –) were it not for the fortuitous development of a new scientific technique that happened to be applicable to their particular cases.[37]

This view accepts the idea that murderers may deserve capital punishment in principle. Retributivists argue that criminals must be punished to the degree they deserve. This requires that we have confidence that criminals *deserve* their punishment in fact. The problem is that we cannot be certain about their desert. Scientific advances in forensics, such as DNA testing, can prove beyond any doubt that a person is innocent. So we cannot be certain someone deserves capital punishment no matter how fair the trial or number of failed appeals against the conviction. If we cannot be certain about desert, then we should not punish. Retributivists may accept that murderers deserve execution in principle, but not in practice.[38]

One criticism of this argument may take the following form. Humans are fallible and mistakes are inevitable. The fact that we may be mistaken about someone's guilt does not mean that no one should be punished. If mistakes about murderers are possible, then mistakes about shoplifters are possible, too. Should we not punish anyone because mistakes are possible?

We may reject this criticism. Yes, mistakes may be made and so those wrongfully punished should receive reparation, such as compensation. We cannot return the time someone has spent in prison under a wrongful conviction although we may still make some substantial effort at making amends however difficult. The problem is that we can return fines paid or repair mistakes made, but we cannot bring the dead back to life. We cannot offer reparations to the dead for our mistakes.[39] So we may inevitably make mistakes about whether we punish the deserving in proportion to what they deserve. These mistakes may be condonable where reparations are possible. This is impossible where offenders are executed. Retributivists should reject capital punishment because mistakes are possible despite their best efforts and these mistakes cannot be repaired.[40]

This retributivist argument against capital punishment brings out an important distinction by Jeffrey Reiman: 'the moral question of whether the death penalty is a just punishment for murder is not the same as the moral question of whether it would be just for us to adopt the policy of executing murderers'.[41] This is a distinction with a difference. One question is whether capital punishment may be deserved for offenders, such as murderers. A second question is whether we are able to distribute this punishment to deserving offenders. So our task is not finished when we conclude that murderers and perhaps others may deserve the death penalty in principle. If it is ever justified, then we must have confidence that it can be distributed to those for whom capital punishment is justified. Perhaps many offenders executed deserve their punishment. The problem is that we lack any certainty that all deserve their punishment and we lack any means of providing reparations to those wrongly executed because they are dead. The death penalty may be a just punishment, but it cannot be a just policy. If we take desert seriously, we should not practise capital punishment.[42]

Most retributivists argue that capital punishment may be justified where it is deserved. The problem is that this argument runs into several difficulties and, ultimately, perhaps we should reject capital punishment on retributivist grounds.

Justifications for and against

We have examined several arguments for and against capital punishment. One aim has been to explain how theories may not lead to any clear conclusion. Many rehabilitation proponents may believe their position rules out capital punishment in all cases, but there are reasons to doubt this. Similarly, many retributivists may argue that their view is consistent with the justification of capital punishment and we have seen that there are reasons to doubt this conclusion, too. We now turn our attention to various theories of punishment that are often seen to be more relativist on the justification of capital punishment, as they are widely accepted to agree with either side. We will now see if such views will prove a more promising alternative to what we have seen thus far.

Deterrence

Does deterrence justify capital punishment? Perhaps nothing is more controversial than the empirical evidence about whether capital punishment is a deterrent.[43] Most statistical studies focus on its use in the United States. One widely criticized study claimed that each execution of a murderer led to between seven and eight fewer murders.[44] Studies have also concluded the opposite, namely, that executions may actually *increase* the number of murders. This is the brutalization effect.[45] The argument is that executing murderers does not contribute to general deterrence, but instead brutalizes the public to such violence.

Theories about whether the death penalty deters murderers are controversial. Less contested are the data about murder rates and US states that permit capital punishment, sometimes referred to as 'pro-death' states. These states have a noticeably higher murder rate each year than states that do not permit capital punishment. Their murder rates range from 5 to 40 per cent higher per 100,000 people. Nevertheless, there has been a sharp drop in the number of offenders sentenced to death in recent years. For example, there were about 300 offenders sentenced to death in 1997, but less than half that number were sentenced in 2004. Furthermore, more people have been removed from death row each year than sentenced to death since 2001.[46] These facts coincide with a drop in the national murder rate of over 3 per cent. So the murder rate has dropped nationally despite fewer offenders being sentenced to death.

Many believe these figures are evidence that capital punishment does not deter murderers. The murder rate has decreased as the death penalty has been used less. But this is not conclusive. This argument presupposes that potential murderers constantly revise their considerations about whether to murder based upon available information concerning the use of capital punishment. If the death penalty is used more, then more potential murderers will become deterred. A problem with this argument is its time horizon. Potential criminals do not revise their considerations within a vacuum. Their decisions are made within a context. More potential murderers may be deterred today as the use of the death penalty has decreased where they are influenced by its past use. More decide against committing murder because they have seen others executed for similar crimes in the recent past. The state need not still continually increase its use of the death penalty to deter murderers; its past use may have a deterrent effect on our present. So a decreased use of the death penalty and drop in the murder rate do not conclusively demonstrate that the death penalty does not have any deterrent effect.

But let's say we remain unconvinced. We believe that the evidence is conclusive: the death penalty does not deter potential murderers. There is a second objection we might raise. Most murders are solved cases although some are not. Only a relatively small number of convicted murderers in the United States will be executed if condemned. We might conclude that the death penalty has an inconclusive deterrent effect. Potential murderers may know there is a chance they may avoid conviction and a relatively small chance they might be executed if convicted. We might believe there is an inconclusive effect because the threat is insufficient and it should be more widely used to better test its deterrent ability. If potential murderers were significantly more likely to be executed upon conviction, then we would be better able to assess the potential deterrent effect that capital punishment may have.

A further problem concerns the decision-making of murderers. The standard view is potential criminals make a cost–benefit analysis: they weigh up the costs such as the potential punishment against the benefits such as the death of a person. If the costs outweigh the benefits, then the argument is that potential murderers will be deterred and will not murder. So for capital punishment to be a deterrent it must be too great a cost for murderers to bear. The problem is that many murderers do not engage in a cost–benefit analysis of this kind. For example, approximately 90 per cent of the most violent criminals fail to perceive their risk of apprehension or likely punishment.[47] If offenders fail to consider the relevant costs, then they may not play a substantial role in their decision-making about whether to commit a crime. Capital punishment may not be a deterrent because murderers do not weigh the relevant costs before acting. It is then difficult to justify capital punishment on the grounds that it deters in the absence of conclusive evidence and where relevant risks are not considered by murderers.

There is a larger problem concerning our ability to determine deterrence effects more generally. Empirical evidence may demonstrate crime reduction. We might then compare the number of murders in June last year with the number in June this year. So we can get a sense of whether crime is falling or not. But we cannot possess the same clarity about deterrence effects. This is because we cannot know how many people may have been deterred from committing any crime because of its potential punishment. First, we don't know how many were deterred from crime. How many potential bicycle thefts were prevented through deterrence this week in your local area? We may have some idea about the likely numbers and crime trends, but little or no idea about how many potential crimes would have happened if not deterred. Secondly, we don't know how many potential criminals were deterred from crime because of its likely punishment. Potential criminals may be deterred by many factors beyond possible punishment. These factors may include the guilt they might feel afterwards if they committed a crime. These persons may be deterred from committing crime, but they are not deterred by the threat of punishment. Penal deterrence is a theory of punishment that argues that punishment is justified as a deterrence: potential criminals may be deterred through the threat of punishment. The problem is that we must know how many were deterred by this threat and not other factors. We lack any conclusive information about this as well. All we can know is the number of crimes, not the number of potential crimes. Deterrence is justified to the degree it affects potential crimes, something beyond our knowledge. We cannot gather the evidence we need to make a strong case either way.

Some deterrent theorists have argued that capital punishment does deter despite the fact there is no empirical evidence to support the view. Execution *ought* to deter potential murderers and it is justified for this reason. Many have argued that it makes sense to think this. For example, James Fitzjames Stephen argued that '[n]o other punishment deters men so effectively from committing crimes as the punishment of death'.[48]

Perhaps the empirical evidence is difficult to find, but isn't it intuitively compelling anyway?

The most prominent such argument is the 'Best Bet Argument'.[49] We should bet on the fact that capital punishment deters even if we do not know for certain that it deters.[50] It works like this. If I bet that executions should be illegal on the grounds that the death penalty does not deter and I am wrong, then I save the life of the murderer while innocent victims will be killed. If I bet that capital punishment is acceptable because it deters and I am correct, then we execute the murderer and save potential innocent victims. Innocent people would die if capital punishment deterred and I disallowed it. Do I gamble that the death penalty should be illegal and risk additional murder victims or do I legalize the death penalty, killing murderers and risk saving the lives of additional murder victims? The 'best bet' is to err on the side of saving the lives of the innocent rather than the murderer. If the death penalty deters, we save extra innocent lives. If we are wrong, then there are no extra innocent lives to save, but we have killed murderers. Thus, Louis Pojman adds: 'If we value the saving of innocent lives more highly than the loss of the guilty, then to bet on a policy of capital punishment turns out to be rational'.[51]

There are two arguments we might offer in reply. One response is simply to claim that human lives are not something we should gamble with.[52] We are gambling with the lives of human beings by effectively taking bets on who might live and who deserves to die. Such gambling is wrong and we should reject this argument. A second response is that the best bet argument does not risk the lives of any murderers, but rather it takes their lives and risks that some good will come out of it.[53] We might want to bring about the best consequences within clear constraints. So we may want to decrease the number of murders, but refuse to execute murderers until we had evidence that it did deter future murders. This evidence is lacking and we should reject the best bet argument.

Cass Sunstein and Adrian Vermeule present a reformulation of the best bet argument. They argue that capital punishment is morally required as the best bet, if there are 'imaginable empirical findings' that support deterrence as a method of reducing murders.[54] Should there be some empirical evidence to support the view that we can reduce murders by executing murderers, then the state is morally required to save the lives of innocent people it has reason to believe it can save. The merit of this argument lies in how realistic we find these 'imaginable empirical findings'. If we think that gambling with the lives of murderers in the hope of certain consequences is acceptable, then Sunstein and Vermeule give us additional reason to support the best bet argument. However, these empirical findings are deeply suspect and clear data on how many potential murderers were deterred during a given week are impossible to come by. This restatement of the best bet argument does not avoid the problem of illusive empirical evidence that capital punishment has a deterrent effect on murderers.

Those who advocate the best bet argument claim a murderer's execution is acceptable, even if it fails to bring about positive consequences. Is this a deterrent view? Deterrent proponents are thought to argue for the value of a punishment judged on its positive effects. Yet, the best bet argument justifies executing murderers irrespective of any positive deterrent effects. It is true that they do so in the belief deterrence may take place. But it is not a deterrent view of punishment properly so called. Deterrence aims at deterring crime in order to reduce crime. We must not only have some reason to believe deterrence takes place, but also evidence that crime reduction is being achieved. For example, we could not argue a criminal justice policy had a deterrent effect where the available evidence is that crime has become more likely. Deterrence requires a positive consequence. The best bet argument is not committed to this and it is not then a deterrence-based view all things considered.

Now let us consider a different argument. Some deterrent proponents argue that deterrent punishment may be more humane than others. We should only punish offenders as much as necessary to deter others; this may be less than what offenders may deserve. For example, John Stuart Mill says: 'one of the strongest recommendations a punishment can have, that it should seem more rigorous than it is; for its practical power depends far less on what it is than what it seems'.[55] Deterrence concerns penal consequences. If punishment has a positive deterrent effect, then it is not necessary to punish offenders more harshly than needed. Moreover, if this effect might be produced without punishing anyone, then we should consider it. Jeremy Bentham says: 'If hanging a man *in effigy* would produce the same salutary impression of terror upon the minds of people, it would be a folly or cruelty ever to hang a man *in person*'.[56] Capital punishment is justified where it deters potential murderers. But mock executions are perhaps more justified if they have a deterrence effect because no one is harmed. The death penalty may deter without causing anyone's death and helping to prevent future murders.

There are at least two objections to this view. The first is that our concern should not be what is most humane for the condemned, but what best deters. Perhaps deterrence may justify less punitive punishments. This is not reason to prefer deterrence on deterrence-based grounds. We should prefer those punishments that best promote deterrence. So the issue of whether deterrent punishments may often be more humane is tangential. In any event, deterrence may also recommend punishments far more punitive than alternatives, too.

The second objection to this view is that it may be inhumane to stage mock executions. These events treat people as a means to certain consequences and under false pretences. We fail to respect the dignity of our citizens in purposefully misleading them about criminal justice in this way.[57] Furthermore, misleading the public runs the risk of undermining public confidence in criminal justice if this became known. Citizens may lose trust in the government to address crime and punishment. This approach to deterrence might lead to deterrence being undermined through the loss of public trust.

Deterrence has been believed to justify and reject capital punishment across several grounds. Many reasons are problematic on both sides. There is one final consideration. If you believe that capital punishment is justified because it is a deterrent, then would your position change if you were presented with convincing evidence that it did not? Or vice versa? I believe that most of us would not change our position in such cases. A study asked respondents for the reason they favoured or opposed capital punishment. The preferred reason in favour was that capital punishment was a deterrent; the preferred reason against capital punishment was that it did not deter. Respondents were then asked if they would change their position if offered convincing evidence to the contrary about assumed deterrent effects. Those who said capital punishment was justified because it deterred said that they would continue to support capital punishment because murderers deserve death. Those who believed capital punishment was unjustified because it did not deter argued that murderers did not deserve to die. The finding is that we may debate in terms of deterrence, but deterrence plays little role in our actual beliefs about whether to justify capital punishment.[58] Why argue in terms of deterrence? One suggestion is that this shrouds the debate with an 'objective' veneer: my view is not merely subjective moralizing, but based upon empirical evidence – or so the argument goes.[59] So we claim our view is moulded by facts about deterrence, but instead our view is actually linked to the values we attribute to capital punishment. Our judgement is not about whether deterrence is a factor; it is about whether we believe someone deserves to be executed for a crime. Call this *the problem of insincerity.*

The problem of insincerity is the problem of adherents not genuinely committed to the position they defend. This may be a particular problem for deterrence proponents. We have already considered findings where respondents say they support a position based upon the evidence about deterrence effects, but they actually support their position for different reasons. Deterrence proponents must consider a particular counterfactual: would they continue to defend some practice if the evidence about deterrence were very different? They must be guided by the best available evidence, if discernible, about how deterrence may be promoted. Additionally, deterrence proponents must continually revise their positions in light of new evidence. The sincere deterrence proponent will accept the position best supported by the available evidence even where this may lead to counterintuitive positions. If capital punishment best deterred thieves and an alternative sanction best deterred murderers, then the sincere deterrence proponent must defend capital punishment for crimes, such as theft, and not for others like murder. This position would be impossible for a retributivist, who would argue that murder is more wrong than theft and so theft should not be punished more severely than murder. But this should not be difficult for a defender of deterrence if he were sincere. This is because he supports the position best justified by the available evidence, if discernible, about deterrence effects. The problem is that the cost of his sincerity is acceptance of counterintuitive positions that are not merely hypothetical.

Deterrence does not clearly support or reject capital punishment. Its position is reliant upon the best possible evidence concerning deterrence effects. There are doubts about whether such evidence is possible to acquire. There are further doubts that people are sincere that deterrence plays any leading role in fact regarding whether they support or reject capital punishment. It is then unclear what genuine difference it would make to debates if we could acquire more satisfactory evidence about deterrent effects because other factors, such as deeply held values concerning punishment, appear to play a more fundamental role. If deterrence is not impossible to perceive, then it may be largely irrelevant.[60]

Expressivism

Expressivism does not offer any clear argument for or against capital punishment either. Expressivists argue that punishment is justified as the public denunciation of crime. The greater we denounce a crime, the greater its justified punishment. The question is: does expressivism justify public denunciation in the form of execution?

We have seen earlier that expressivism is retributivism by another name. We punish offenders because they are deserving of punishment. However, punishment is not merely something deserved, but it also represents an expression of our denunciation for a crime. That punishment is an 'expression' of our disapproval is perhaps no more than metaphorical. Retributivists justify capital punishment where they believe it may be deserved, such as in murder cases. We have seen that this argument is problematic because of problems concerning desert. If the idea that murders might deserve the death penalty is problematic, does the idea that punishment expresses public disapproval fare any better?

Expressivists are particularly unclear about whether their theory of punishment justifies the death penalty. Consider first the argument against capital punishment. Antony Duff argues:

> To execute someone is to say to him (and to ourselves) that he has wholly removed himself from human community – from the possibility of a continuing human life ... To execute such a person is to *place* him beyond redemption – beyond the very possibility of redemption.[61]

One purpose of expressivist punishment is to foster criminal rehabilitation. Punishment should start a communicative dialogue between the offender and his community that facilitates secular penance. The offender cannot engage in this dialogue if he were to be executed and this would render his potential rehabilitation impossible. Capital punishment should be rejected by expressivists, especially by those defending the communicative theory of punishment. This is because execution denies communicative dialogue.

This argument requires that there is some such process actually taking place. If there were no such dialogue, then its being denied by executing an offender need not be problematic. We have seen before that communication is largely assumed. We conceive of an offender's punishment as her secular penance: she need not communicate anything to anyone at any time in fact. The fiction of communicative penance does not promise a compelling argument against capital punishment because it would render secular penance impossible. We must have greater clarity about the fact of communicative penance to best argue that expressivism rejects capital punishment.

A further problem is that communicative theories of punishment may also appear to support capital punishment. This leads to uncomfortable acknowledgements. For example, Duff argues that capital punishment 'should not figure in any properly communicative system'.[62] He notes that his theory 'has no room for the death penalty', but that also 'the matter is not, however, that simple'.[63] Duff recognizes that it is not implausible for a murderer to believe that he can become best restored to his community by his death because of the gravity of his crime.[64] Duff ultimately opposes capital punishment because it permanently forecloses the possibility of an offender's redemption. This begs the question of whether his opposition can be maintained where we know restoration is impossible. Duff argues that this is a judgement we should not make because we might not know this with any certainty. While this may be true for many offenders, this may not be true for all.

Consider non-communicative theories of expressivism. Expressivism claims that punishment expresses public censure. Whether this penal theory justifies capital punishment will depend on how convinced we are that our censure of an offender's crime must take the form of his execution to capture the gravity of our public disapproval. Our disapproval is constrained by what is deserved. So we might strongly dislike a racist, but we may only punish her crimes, if any, and not her beliefs. Disapproval is reduced to desert. So our question is not about whether our disapproval is best expressed through capital punishment, but whether the death penalty is deserved by an offender. Expressivist arguments for or against capital punishment are arguments about what offenders deserve where expression plays little genuine role, if any. Therefore, expressivist theories of punishment may both argue for or against capital punishment depending upon the particular view of desert defended.

Note that the problem of desert is a problem for both retributivists and expressivists. So expressivists do not fare better than retributivists on this issue. The problem of desert is that retributivists argue that punishment must be deserved if it is to be justified. This requires that we know punishment is deserved if it to be imposed. Let us grant that it is possible a murderer may deserve capital punishment. The problem is not that we may be mistaken about desert, but rather that we would lack any remedy for mistakes made. The fact that we may be mistaken about criminal justice matters is not a reason to reject all punishment provided that mistakes may be rectified all things considered. Capital punishment involves the death of offenders and mistakes made cannot be remedied. Moreover, we know that we may be mistaken about the guilt of persons wrongfully condemned despite the fairness of a trial and appeals granted. New advances in DNA testing have proven innocence where all other methods may have failed. Capital punishment should be rejected for all offenders even if deserved because any mistakes are impossible to remedy. Similarly, it should be rejected for all offenders even if it were an appropriate expression of public disapproval because any mistakes are impossible to remedy. While expressivists and communication theories may be used to argue for and against capital punishment, they ought to oppose the death penalty although not necessarily for the reasons they advance.

The unified theory of punishment

The unified theory of punishment argues that rights should be understood as our substantial freedoms and they are protected by law in a legal system. Crimes are threats to our rights and punishment aims to restore rights threatened by crimes. This restoration may take many forms in the pursuit of restoration, rights protection, and crime reduction. The question is whether the unified theory may justify or reject capital punishment.

The unified theory aims at the restoration of rights. Recall that this occurs within the context of the idea of a stakeholder society. This is a view about society where each individual should believe he or she has a stake in the political community and its future. If the stakeholder society is to become a reality, then we should reject capital punishment. This is because capital punishment renders the stakeholder society impossible. Not everyone may come to believe he or she has a stake in society: the use of the death penalty whereby some are permanently removed from society may only confirm these beliefs and make stakeholding impossible for those executed and virtually impossible for some who are not.

It is important to note that the central problem is not that I may fail to believe I have a stake in society, but rather that I have threatened the rights of others through my crime. Punishment is a response to crime and not beliefs about stakeholding. So the question for us is not about my self-identity in relation to members of my political community. Instead, it is about my capacity for rights. T. H. Green has argued that only 'a permanent incapacity for rights' could allow us to permit capital punishment.[65] If I cannot possess rights, then punishment cannot restore anything for me as such. However, Green is careful to argue that 'it may be doubted whether the presumption of permanent incapacity for rights is one which in our ignorance we can ever be entitled to make'.[66] This is not an issue about an offender's desert, but his capacity for rights.

The judgement that someone should not possess rights may be controversial and subject to reasonable disagreement. The judgement that people have the capacity for rights is much less controversial.[67] If people have this capacity, then capital punishment breaches its purpose of restoring rights for all through terminating the rights for some. The unified theory rejects the death penalty. This position assumes that everyone has the capacity for rights. We might follow Green and argue that we should never judge anyone incapable of possessing the capacity for rights. Suppose we argue that someone does lack this capacity. This need not justify capital punishment in these rare cases. This is because we might believe the circumstances that might allow for someone to lack the capacity for rights would render such a person incapable of conviction. We might doubt that anyone lacking the capacity for rights should be found capable of conviction. The unified theory rejects capital punishment even where someone does lack the capacity for rights.

The rejection of capital punishment is conditional upon the political community satisfying some basic minimum of rights protection. If the political community is unable to satisfy this basic minimum, then capital punishment might be justified under these circumstances. Hegel offers a key insight: the more established and self-secure our political community, the less likely it will require harsh punishments and the death penalty should become unnecessary in time.[68] The idea is that crimes are threats to rights requiring punishment. These threats should never rise to the need of requiring capital punishment in order to best secure the restoration of rights. Therefore, following Alan Goldman, we might say that 'because capital punishment always exceeds the least restraint necessary to protect society from repetitions of harmful acts by convicted criminals, it is clearly ruled out'.[69] This view assumes that societal protection from crime through punishment need not require capital punishment.

But this may not always be the case. Suppose a political community is struggling to protect and maintain the rights of its members. Perhaps it is gripped in civil war. The same crime poses a greater threat in these fragile political communities than in those more securely established. It is not impossible to imagine circumstances where a sufficiently fragile political community may be justified in sanctioning the death penalty where this punishment is necessary to best protect and maintain rights within non-ideal circumstances. Note that the justification of capital punishment is possible only in non-ideal circumstances that are conditionally specific to sufficiently political communities.

The unified theory of punishment may offer the most promising approach to address such issues although further analysis is necessary.[70] It is clear that where minimal conditions are satisfied the unified theory rejects the use of capital punishment. However, there may be rare cases in non-ideal circumstances where it may be justified. The death penalty should be unjustified, but it may be justified under specific conditions.

Conclusion

Capital punishment is an issue that deeply divides many. One question is whether defending particular theories of punishment leads to justifying or rejecting the death penalty. This chapter has set out to show that most theories lack any clear answer for one side versus another. Most may be used to defend either side. This book has argued that the unified theory is the most compelling theory of punishment amongst those studied. The unified theory does not reject capital punishment in all cases, but it does draw the line more sharply than most others in only permitting its possibility under specific conditions in non-ideal circumstances. The justification of capital punishment may be more nuanced than we have first supposed, but we are still able to gain clarity, and the unified theory is perhaps best placed to provide this.

A second question is whether any of this matters in convincing fellow citizens to revise or reverse their positions. In his illuminating study of American public opinion on the death penalty, Samuel Gross says:

> For most Americans, a position on capital punishment is an aspect of self-identification. We say, 'I'm for the death penalty', the same way we say, 'I'm a Republican', or 'I'm a Red Sox fan'. In this long-standing debate, sides have been chosen, and the great majority are for it.[71]

The death penalty is an issue where we have often taken sides. It may be surprising that most penal theories do not take sides. So which side should we support? Which theory we defend might say more about which result we prefer rather than which theory best captures the problem of how best to punish murderers. Nevertheless, both sides may be theoretically possible, but only one theory appears to best address its justification and this is the unified theory of punishment.

9   Juvenile offenders

Introduction

When we think about punishment we tend to think about how it affects adults and not juveniles.[1] Questions about what a thief might deserve or the most appropriate punishment for murderers tend to assume the thief and murderer are adults. Many believe that an offender's age may justify different punishments for the same crimes. But why should youth matter and what difference should it make? Do juvenile offenders deserve different punishments?

This chapter examines the punishment of juvenile offenders. I will explain why justice requires different consideration given to youths and what this might look like. I will also challenge traditional conceptions about youth justice and how we should conceive punishment for non-adults. The idea of having a stake in society takes on central importance. Juveniles are in a transition to becoming full members of political society. One concern is how best to ensure that they see themselves as coming to have a stake in society as a means to tackle juvenile offending. This is best addressed by the unified theory of punishment which is based upon the idea of stake-holding. Furthermore, the unified theory best addresses relevant multiple penal goals within a coherent framework. We are able to make better sense of juvenile offending and its punishment. The unified theory offers us a compelling view about how this is best achieved.

What is a juvenile?

The idea of 'the juvenile' is relatively recent. This is perhaps best explained by improvements in record keeping: 'Compulsory registration of births was not introduced until 1836, and thus it was not until the 1850s that birth certificates would have been available for the purpose of determining whether someone qualified as a juvenile'.[2] It did not take long for new courts to emerge that tailored punishment specifically to juvenile offenders. The first was launched in the United States with the passing of the Illinois Juvenile Court Act of 1899.[3] It established the first separate court hearing cases involving juvenile defendants and it could sanction different penal outcomes. The aims of the court were not punitive, but aimed at rehabilitation.[4] The idea was that youth offenders require reformation. This idea of youth and the need for reformation is based upon the view that juveniles are in a developmental transition to adulthood: to be a juvenile is to be a non-adult. This background provides the framework for how juvenile offending is understood today.

A juvenile is a non-adult often less than 18 years old.[5] But why should age make a difference? Antony Duff says:

> we should understand 'juvenile' offenders to be those who are neither so immature that they can certainly not be held criminal responsible, nor so mature that they are certainly as fit as any other adult to be held criminally responsible.[6]

Juvenile offenders are persons who are not fully responsible for their crimes because of their immaturity. Put differently: 'to treat someone like a child is, roughly, to treat her as if her life is not quite her own to lead and as if her choices are not quite her own to make'.[7]

Youth are in a transition to adulthood. Perhaps many adults will share a similar lack of maturity and foresight. The issue is that we give all persons a reasonable life chance to acquire these traits by distinguishing between adults and non-adults in the criminal justice system. We do not have the legal expectation that persons below a set age limit will develop a more complete transition to adult maturity. So while some underage people might well be treated as if they were adults, they are the exceptions rather than the rule. Unless there are grounds for doing otherwise, all persons underage are treated as juvenile offenders.[8] Those who are above a set age limit may well lack full maturity as well, but they are the exceptions rather than the rule on that side of the legal border. Unless there are grounds for doing otherwise, all such persons are treated as adults.[9]

While there is little controversy surrounding the need for youth courts, there is wide variation between legal systems on who should be considered a relevant non-adult.[10] Legal systems often distinguish between children, juveniles, and adults. *Children* are persons who cannot be held criminally liable for their actions.[11] *Juveniles* are persons who may be held partially responsible and *adults* may be held fully responsible.[12] The age of criminal responsibility differs widely, especially in the United States. The Federal government holds that persons under 11 years old cannot be criminally liable. Individual states each accept considerable variation from 6 to 12 years. The age of criminal responsibility is 13 in France, 14 in Germany, 15 in Scandinavian countries, and 16 in Spain and Portugal. It is 10 in England and Wales and 12 in Scotland. Those under the age of criminal responsibility may not be held criminally liable, but there are some powers in place to address relevant matters arising. For example, children under

10 years old may be subjects of civil care and supervision orders in England and Wales, where children may be taken into care by a local authority.[13] So while children may lack criminal responsibility, there may still be sufficient reason for the state to intervene and perhaps have children put under state supervision.

The primary distinction between children and juveniles is that the former are incapable of rendering minimally satisfactory judgements about permissible actions. Children are persons who are 'genuinely at sea on the question of right and wrong'.[14] Juveniles are believed capable of minimally satisfactory judgements which might render them partly criminally responsible for any offences. However, these judgements are merely minimally satisfactory and not more substantially satisfactory where the latter might render them fully responsible for any crimes. The difference between them is a difference in degree. Minimally satisfactory judgement is necessary, but not sufficient, for possession of some partial degree of criminal responsibility that will never be more than incomplete. Only substantially satisfactory judgement may entail some degree of criminal responsibility that may be complete. For example, a youth and an adult otherwise similarly situated may possess very different degrees of criminal responsibility for the same crimes whereby the youth may never be found more criminally responsible for the same act all things considered.[15]

There are at least three reasons why juveniles are believed to fall short of full criminal responsibility. First, youth are believed to have underdeveloped cognitive abilities. This may impair their understanding of the consequences stemming from their actions. Second, juveniles are believed to have underdeveloped control mechanisms. Teenage years are often a time where we learn self-control and mature in our understanding about how we might work with others to overcome obstacles. Third, youth are believed to be developing their sense of self-identity and relationships with others. Juveniles are learning how they may see themselves as part of a societal fabric. This process of identity formation faces inevitable environmental pressures from family and peer groups that may often play a positive role, but not always.

Juveniles face several developmental challenges in terms of their cognitive abilities, control mechanisms, and self-identity where each may be fragile and relatively malleable. One prison governor is reported to have said: 'Adolescents are impulsive, confused about their own identities and relationships'.[16] Of course, adults may have these characteristics as well. But adults seem less excusable because we might expect them to have achieved a more satisfactory development after reaching a certain age. The idea of juvenile justice is the expectation that most juveniles will not achieve full responsibility.[17] We must then consider how justice should be managed for persons who are not expected to possess full criminal responsibility.[18] Note that this need not entail that youth are punished less than they may deserve. The fact they may not possess full responsibility for their crimes may justify a punishment less severe than what might have been retributively deserved if the youth had full criminal responsibility.

Much hangs on which side of the line a person finds herself. The categories of child, juvenile, and adult represent groups defined by age, but justified by other factors. Age is a crude, but convenient and broadly effective, means by which the law may pronounce clear judgements about whether a person may be held criminally responsible and which court is most appropriate. It is not that a person becomes significantly better developed in her own judgements about lawful conduct on the day she becomes 18 years old reaching legal adulthood. Instead, the significance of becoming 18 is that by this date she will be expected to be held fully accountable for her actions. There is often a legal significance attached to reaching a particular age, such as 18 years, and achieving legal adulthood. Its significance lies in the attached behavioural expectations from a legal point of view to be reached at that time. So the borders between child and juvenile as well as juvenile and adult are porous from the standpoint of the facts of development, but not law. While the law gives fixed determinations about when each stage is reached by attaining a particular age, different people may develop at different paces. This may warrant exceptional treatment for exceptional persons.

Punishing juveniles as if adults

Some legal systems permit juvenile offenders to be prosecuted and punished as adults. This is usually set within a clear framework that is rarely employed. For example, in the United States there are over 80,000 juveniles in residential placement on any given day. The following conditions apply:

A person may be tried as an adult if:

(a) a juvenile is charged with a violent felony or drug trafficking or importation offense and if the offense was committed after the person's 15th birthday;
(b) a juvenile possessed a firearm during a violent offense and the offense was committed after the person's 13th birthday; or
(c) a juvenile had been previously adjudicated delinquent of a violent felony or drug offense.[19]

This framework is not entirely unusual for other jurisdictions. A juvenile may be tried as an adult under specific conditions that normally include violence towards others, including use of a firearm. The main factor is not his responsibility or mature development, but rather the dangerousness of his alleged crime. Let us first reflect on this fact before considering a critique.

This idea about when youth may be punished as if an adult is more sympathetic to some theories of punishment than others. Deterrence proponents might argue that general deterrence is best secured by ensuring that all persons engaged in violent crimes are punished severely. The benefit that flows from general deterrence and future crime reduction through fear of strong punishment has priority over the cost of punishing juveniles as adults independently of any clear evidence that their capacity for judgement is satisfactorily advanced for non-adults. Expressivists, including communicative theorists, might argue major violent crimes are events to be avoided however possible. Their occurrence understandably commands widespread public condemnation. It is possible that juveniles may be punished as adults where this is necessary to convey justified public disapproval. Finally, a unified theory of punishment might claim that the actions of some juveniles may pose more substantial than normal threats to rights under exceptional circumstances that might warrant punishing juveniles as adults. Punishment is a response to crime that aims at the restoration of rights. There may be exceptional circumstances that give rise to the justification of treating some youth differently than most others in less exceptional circumstances.

So some theories may justify punishing juveniles as adults. It is unclear how far below the age of legal adulthood each might extend. Expressivism would require punished juveniles to be capable of understanding the message of public disapproval conveyed to them by the political community through punishment. Furthermore, some expressivists, such as communicative theorists, would additionally require that juveniles be capable of returning some communication of secular apology in reply. The unified theory of punishment is based around the idea of the stakeholder society. We punish with the aim of the restoration of rights in order to best maintain and protect rights. This is done with a view towards promoting stakeholding which includes the offender. The punishment of juveniles as adults should not make less likely her ability to realize her coming to have a stake in society and its future. This is a major constraint. If we believe that in most, if not virtually all, cases juveniles will be best served in being punished as a non-adult, then the punishment of juveniles as adults will be limited to exceptional circumstances that meet the condition that they best promote stakeholding for all including the juvenile offender.

These examples are meant to illustrate that perhaps expressivists and unified theorists might justify the punishment of juveniles as adults, but this would be limited to fairly exceptional circumstances within robust limitations where such punishment is understood to be deserved and proportionate. Thus, the punishment of juveniles as adults may be exceptional, but it must also crucially be deserved and proportionate.[20]

Nevertheless, the unified theory may offer a more compelling view because it remains unclear how expressivism differs from retributivism. Expressivists argue that punishment must be proportionate to what is deserved and justified as the expression of public disapproval. But are there cases where expressivists might argue punishment is proportionate to what is deserved, but unjustified because it does not express public disapproval? No, there are not and the two issues of retributivist desert and justified public disapproval are not distinctly separate. So it is unclear what precise contribution expressivism offers beyond what retributivism might offer us already. The unified theory does not run into any such problem.

The deterrence theory of punishment might justify the punishment of juveniles as adults on different grounds. The central importance for most deterrence theorists is how punishment might best promote deterrence. If deterrence may be promoted best by punishing juveniles as adults in some circumstances, then this may be justified. This need not be in exceptional cases only although widespread use might lead to public confusion about the expected penal threats issued by the state which would undermine general deterrence. One remaining problem is that it is difficult to know whether deterrence takes place. While we may measure the reduction in recorded crimes over time, correlation is not causation: the fact that crime is reduced is not necessarily evidence that crime reduction is a result of popular fear of threatened punishment if they chose to perform crimes. This fundamental problem about deterrence is one reason to prefer an alternative theory of punishment. A second reason is that we may reject the punishment of juveniles as adults in non-exceptional circumstances. This may be justified by deterrence, but not by other approaches including the unified theory as noted previously. A third reason is that deterrence may require us to punish juvenile offenders more than adults similarly situated for the same crimes. If juveniles are more likely to commit offences, then there is a need for punishment to have a greater penal threat in order to serve as a more effective deterrent. So deterrence proponents may justify greater punishment for juveniles because they require a greater threat to be deterred from criminal offending.[21]

Rehabilitation theories of punishment and retributivism present a somewhat different situation. Rehabilitation theorists argue that the goal of punishment is to help rehabilitate offenders. Some offenders will require more reformation than others. This need not be related to age. While juvenile offenders may have much more to learn, some adult offenders may be more difficult to teach on how to break from problematic behaviours. The rehabilitation of offenders should be tailored to their particular needs. The question is not so much about their age, but rather about their need to achieve satisfactory rehabilitation.

Similarly, retributivists argue that punishment should be proportionate to what is deserved. An offender's punishable desert is our central concern and not her age although this may impact upon her desert. It may be the case that juvenile offenders on the whole deserve less punishment than adults similarly situated for the same crime. But the reason is not that juveniles deserve less punishment because they are non-adults. Instead, the reason that any juvenile who is punished less than an adult similarly situated for the same crime must be because the juvenile possesses less punishable desert.[22] Ido Weijers and Antony Duff argue:

> It is thus plausible that juvenile offenders are often less culpable for the crimes that they commit than are normal adult offenders, and less competent to understand and participate in their trials than adults are supposed to be.[23]

Juvenile offenders may often possess less desert than adults similarly situated. This difference may arise where juvenile offenders lack minimal competence and, thus, lack similar desert. But the fact that an offender is not yet an adult does not entail he will always possess less desert than an adult.[24] Retributivists may justify the punishment of juveniles as adults where juveniles posses sufficient desert. Thus, rehabilitation theorists and retributivists might punish juveniles as adults, but this need not be in exceptional cases only and must be determined on a case by case basis.[25] This may provide an important reason to support an alternative theory, such as the unified theory of punishment, which would only justify such punishment in exceptional circumstances. Moreover, the unified theory does not run into the problems of possible cases where rehabilitative needs may require greater punishment than what is deserved or offenders who cannot be rehabilitated. Nor does the unified theory accept the problematic link between retributivism and morality.

Most legal systems acknowledge the importance of supporting a separate youth court for juvenile justice that is distinct from the criminal justice system that applies to adults. Nevertheless, there may be circumstances where juveniles are punished as if they were adults. The reasons may differ widely across various theories of punishment. However, it is clear that each may justify the punishment of juveniles as if they were adults under certain circumstances with some exceptions. There is also strongest support for the unified theory of punishment. This theory does not run into the problems faced by other theories while only justifying the punishment of juveniles as adults under exceptional circumstances.

Age and crime

There is a link between crime and the age of offenders. Richard L. Lippke says:

> Criminal offending is overwhelmingly the province of the young, with the vast majority of offenders consisting of those 16–35 years of age. Teenagers and young adults, while not altogether incapable of moral responsibility, are perhaps best viewed as moral works in progress.[26]

Consider the following facts about young offenders. About 40 per cent of all first time offenders are aged between 18 and 20 years.[27] Roughly 70 per cent of persistent youth offenders have been in contact with the police over the past year. Criminal offending tends to peak when offenders are in their teens or early twenties before soon tapering off. Criminal offending tapers off more slowly for more violent criminals.[28] This evidence strongly suggests that the most effective way to achieve crime reduction overall is to reduce offending by youths. Criminal offending is not only 'the province of the young', but the youth offenders of today compose most of the adult offenders of tomorrow. If we may reduce juvenile offending, then we may best reduce all offending.

A reduction in juvenile offending will contribute to fewer victims. Juveniles are both more likely to be offenders and victims than adults. For example, youth between the ages of 12 and 17 were twice as likely as adults 18 or older to be the victim of a violent crime.[29] In a study examining annual rates of violent victimization between 1993–2003 in the United States, the annual average rate for all violence per 1,000 persons was about 84 for juveniles between the ages of 12 and 17 and about 32 for adults aged 18 years or older. Rates of assault, robbery, serious violence, rape, and sexual assault were much less for those 18 years or older compared with youth between 12 and 17 years old.[30]

This speaks to a powerful truth in criminological research: most offenders share a broadly similar profile to their victims. The problem is not so much the dangerous stranger, but the dangerous neighbour or relative. The probability of being the victim of someone from a similar socio-economic background and ethnicity is high. There is also a high probability that offenders and victims will be similar in age and young. One study of victims aged between 12 and 19 years found that more than half of their offenders were perceived to be in the same age range and only about 20 per cent perceived to be 21 or older.[31] Juvenile offenders are most likely to engage in violent crimes against other youth.[32] Furthermore, younger teens are more likely to suffer violent crime at school than elsewhere.[33]

So why do juveniles offend? The standard view is that juveniles are more likely than adults to engage in risky behaviour, including criminal offending. The reason is that juveniles are generally less aware of the costs associated with potentially risky behaviour. Furthermore, juveniles are believed to be generally less aware of the likelihood of their incurring costs associated with their behaviour. Even where potential costs are known, their likelihood is dismissed. Juveniles may know they should not engage in offences, such as criminal damage or drug possession. The problem is that they may fail to acknowledge the risk of their behaviour by discounting the likelihood of their being convicted and sentenced for their crimes.

The common approach to the standard view is to improve education about risks. The idea is that juveniles might be less likely to engage in risky behaviour if they better understood the associated risks involved. The problem is that these efforts have met with limited success and not been found that effective. This is because youth may already understand the relevant potential risks. The issue is that they may remain unconvinced that the costs of risky behaviour might be imposed upon them.[34] Improved education about risks remains important, but it is insufficient. What is required is more efforts to convince potential youth offenders that there may be real consequences for them that are likely if they were to engage in criminal behaviour: 'Only when offending is seen to have more social costs than personal benefits will young people attempt to modify their behaviour so as to adapt to their current social situation'.[35] This is the challenge we face.

One idea about how to better convince potential youth offenders is through the lens of stakeholding. Youth must come to see the attraction about their coming to have a stake in society. Stakeholding is an idea about mutual recognition and reciprocity where we acknowledge others as fellow stakeholders. If we view ourselves as having a stake in society, then we may become much less likely to engage in criminal behaviour that may damage our stake and common rights. This perspective seeks to foster crime reduction through constructions of self-identity with others.[36] The stakeholder society is a political community where members choose to engage with each other to address common issues.

Stakeholding comes in stages. Children are persons who have a stake, but are unable to participate on minimally equal terms with other stakeholders. The child's relation to society is more akin to a patient rather than an agent. So while children are affected in substantial ways by the decisions made by the political community, they lack the ability to contribute on a minimally equal basis with others. Adults are those who may engage with other stakeholders on equal terms. Juveniles are at a transitional stage between children and adults. While juveniles have a stake and some ability for engagement, their stake and engagement ability are in a process of development. This process may breed a certain amount of inevitable frustration for youth as they acquire and develop new self-identities of themselves and their relation to others.

While there has been much research into the idea of recognition and how it may contribute to our understanding of criminology, there has been precious little attention into how we might best foster stakeholding to more effectively reduce crime. This is not too surprising. The idea of stakeholding originally addressed how we might better conceive corporate responsibility and strategic communications in the area of business ethics: we should understand various parties as stakeholders and this should contribute to new management structures for collective decision-making that are more democratic, transparent, and ethically robust.[37] Much work has centred on how corporate governance might be improved if we adopted stakeholder theory, but it has also extended further into other domains. For example, there has since been interest in how economic justice might be improved through stakeholding: the idea of the property-owning democracy defended by John Rawls is perhaps one important example of this.[38]

These accounts are useful for showing us how we might reform our inst-itutions, but much more research is needed into the social psychology and socio-legal project of fostering stakeholding for fellow citizens. There is a particular need for how we might best foster stakeholding specifically for juveniles.

Stakeholding comes in stages of development. While the stages may be sufficiently clear, their membership ages are not. Stage membership may differ from one society to the next. For example, one proposal is that membership is set in terms of children (0 to 14 years), juveniles (15 to 24 years), and adults (25 years and older).[39] This is one of many such ways that age membership might be attributed to each group. Its importance is highlighting the need for thinking beyond binary considerations of adult and non-adult, and developing further categories. For example, those who are children will lack some, if not all, criminal responsibility, and so this group deserves individual attention. Those who are adults may possess full responsibility, but they are not most likely to engage in criminal behaviour. These are reasons why this group deserves individual attention as well.

The more problematic category is the juveniles group. This is because they are most at risk. This is further complicated by the fact that this group will contain persons deemed legal adults and those who are not if defined as persons between 15 and 24 years. So there may be good reason to con-sider crime reduction policies within this broad category, but then tailored more specifically for 15 to 17 year olds and persons between 18 and 24 years. This need not require establishing new courts, but it will require new considerations about how to better address juvenile offending by both minors and young adults more effectively than we have. There are already procedures in place for children, juveniles, and adults to receive different treatment in most legal systems. These procedures should be reconsidered, specifically in terms of how stakeholding and restoration might be better promoted for juvenile and young adult offenders through punishment.

Juveniles and restorative recognition

Juvenile offending is an issue of central importance for any criminal justice policy. One major factor is that juveniles are most likely to be first-time offenders.[40] If offending can be reduced for juveniles, then this may yield major benefits in terms of greater crime reduction in general. Successive governments have initiated different penal experiments to best address juvenile offending through various piloted schemes.[41]

Restorative justice has received increasing attention as the approach of choice for confronting youth justice.[42] There are at least two reasons behind its popularity. The first is that most juvenile offenders commit non-violent crimes. Juvenile offenders are more potentially dangerous in the longer term where any future offending may become more serious if not satisfactorily addressed. But juvenile offenders do not commit many serious violent crimes when underage. There is greater public support for less punitive approaches, such as restorative justice, if it may effectively end non-violent criminality. Such support might vanish in cases where juveniles have committed more serious violent crimes. Restorative justice is less often used in such cases generally. A second reason behind the popularity of restorative justice for juvenile offenders is that it has been shown to be highly likely to reduce crime among adults. Fewer juvenile offenders often leads to fewer adult offenders in future. So restorative justice has become increasingly popular for juvenile offenders because it is likely to contribute to crime reduction in the longer term while its use is often confined to addressing non-violent offenders. Studies have found reoffending rates still high, but restorative justice for youths has been found to lead to far less reoffending than community sentences and about half as much as custodial sentences.[43] While such studies are inconclusive, the evidence thus far is promising.

Restorative justice aims to restore what crime has damaged between offender, victim, and the local community. This approach has proven widely popular for all participants and effective in reducing crime. However, the use of restorative justice for juvenile offenders raises specific issues. Juveniles are not adults and their parents may decide that they participate in a restorative conference on their behalf. Most victims who agreed to take part in restorative conferences are satisfied by the experience and its conclusion. There is less satisfaction for underage victims who have not agreed to take part, but participated because of the decision by their parent or guardian.[44] A similar problem may arise for juvenile offenders. Restorative justice becomes possible where offenders accept responsibility for their crimes. But what if participation is determined by the decision of a parent or guardian instead of the underage offender?

It is unclear how best to address this problem. On the one hand, restorative justice works best where all persons present who have a stake in the outcome come together to address how what has been damaged by crime may be resolved. So it is important that all parties choose to participate to ensure the process is successful. On the other hand, juveniles are not deemed fully legally autonomous. Their parents or guardians have a responsibility to protect and promote their interests. There may be inevitable conflicts on occasion between what a juvenile and his parents believe is the best response to an invitation to participate in a restorative conference. Many problems with restorative conferences are resolved by better management of likely expectations about the purpose of a conference, its conduct, and possible results. Perhaps the best way to address the specific needs arising in restorative justice cases involving youth is to take further measures to ensure that all potential underage participants and their parents or guardians receive additional support and information about likely expectations from participation. Juveniles may be unable to make fully informed decisions, but this is not a reason to be more diligent about ensuring they have as much information as reasonably advisable.

Restorative justice conferences for juvenile offenders often end with the agreement of a contract that the offender must fulfil. These contracts may include acceptable behaviour contracts, anti-social behaviour orders (ASBOs), curfews up to 90 days, and child safety orders for children under ten years old. The contracts are an acknowledgement of responsibility and accountability. Offenders often become more aware about how their actions have impacted upon others negatively with an action plan for how they might best restore what they have damaged. This may include financial contributions to repay any material losses.

Restoration appears to work well because it brings together relevant stakeholders to a crime and its penal outcome into constructive dialogue with one another. It is tempting to view its success as fostering a sense of recognition in juvenile offenders: they gain a sense of inclusive membership in the community through restorative justice. Recognition then plays a central role in making restorative justice a success. However, it is not recognition as such that has this role, but rather recognition *of a particular kind*. What counts is not only that I am recognized, but recognized *as a stakeholder*. Restorative justice conference members are persons with a stake in the decision.

The idea of stakeholding as *restorative recognition* best captures the specific form of recognition that plays such a central role in these contexts. This leads to practical results. One result is that contracts agreed to in restorative conferences should have regard to how they promote future stakeholding. A second practical result is there must be a greater focus on ensuring a satisfactory provision of support networks, such as family, friends, and local community. Youth offenders often lack such provision which may contribute to their failure to see themselves as future stakeholders.[45] Restorative recognition is better achieved where satisfactory support networks are available.

Finally, stakeholding is important for all members in a political community and not exclusive to non-violent offenders. Restorative justice proponents limit the applicability of their approach by rejecting the justification of hard treatment. Non-custodial sentences may not always command public confidence. There is perhaps a greater need for violent juvenile offenders to acknowledge their crimes and accept accountability for their actions in dialogue with fellow stakeholders. There is much potential benefit for victims, offenders, and others engaging in restorative dialogue. This may require a different membership, such as a magistrate or judge conducting the conference. The benefits of restorative conferences should not be limited to non-violent offenders only, but extended to potentially most, if not all, offenders. Furthermore, these conferences may warrant possible custodial sentences for violent offenders. This understanding of more punitive restorative justice is closest to the unified theory of punishment. If our aim is the restoration of rights, then we should not limit ourselves to non-custodial sentences where these may improve our ability to satisfy our penal aims.

Juvenile gender justice

The problem of crime is often a problem of males and crime. The difference between men and women is striking. The crime rates are broadly similar from around the ages of 12 to 13, but they rise only slightly for young women before dropping significantly from the age of about 21.[46] This is in stark contrast with young men. The male crime rate doubles at 14 years and then tapers off more slowly. There is also a major difference in crimes performed. For example, young women are more likely to engage in criminal damage or purchasing stolen goods when under the age of 16. Young men are also more likely to engage in these crimes, but also fighting, which begins to increase sharply in likelihood as they approach adulthood. Nevertheless, nearly 75 per cent of all youth crime is property related. Young men are four times more likely to engage in these crimes than young women.

The evidence about juvenile offending highlights an important fact often overlooked in relevant debates. Juvenile offending is largely a problem of crime performed by young men; adult offending is largely a problem of crimes performed by many young men later in life. There is a clear gender dimension to juvenile justice which we might call *juvenile gender justice*.[47]

There are many arguments given about why young women are much less likely to offend after their teenage years. One argument is the influence of relational factors, such as the responsibility for raising children, the positive impact of a new relationship or support from family and friends. For example, Monica Barry interviewed one women who had previously offended. She says: 'Reasons for stopping? Well the kids, know what I mean. To try and make a family ... [My daughter] had seen so much ... She hadn't seen the needle or nothing, know what I mean, but kids aren't stupid'.[48] This passage is suggestive of the importance of stakeholding. The change in this woman's life is she has come to view herself as having a stake in society because of the importance she gives to her responsibilities to her children. Her self-identification in constructive 'pro-social' relations to others is one important route to understanding herself as a stakeholder.[49]

Juvenile offending and the unified theory

The courts have generally adopted a multiple penal goals framework for the punishment of juvenile offenders. For example, some courts claims four goals should be pursued in these cases: the punishment of juvenile offenders; the reform and rehabilitation of juvenile offenders; the protection of the public; and the making of reparations by juvenile offenders to persons affected by their crime.[50] Punishment should be determined with regard to these different goals. Note the absence of any explicit inclusion of deterrence. This is explained by the decisions of many courts to find it unlawful for the purpose of youth punishment.[51] Deterrence assumes a cost–benefit analysis that is believed to be inapplicable for juvenile offenders.

One potential problem is that these goals may come into conflict with each other. The goal of reform may be undermined by the need to protect the public, for instance. Should we reject a multiple penal framework for the punishment of juvenile offenders because it is incoherent? The unified theory may best address this commonly used framework. The potential conflict between multiple penal goals is possible in the absence of a principled context which the unified theory provides. It argues that punishment is a response to crime that aims at the restoration of rights within the context of promoting stakeholding. Punishment may address multiple penal goals to promote the aim of restoring rights. Different penal goals are justified insofar as they help promote the aim of restoration. The unified theory has the flexibility to address this framework and it is able to best explain its justification. By contrast, other theories of punishment would insist on some alternative framework employing some, but not all, of these principles. For example, rehabilitation theorists might endorse the goal of rehabilitating juvenile offenders and communicative proponents may support payment of reparations, but neither may offer a compelling justification for how these multiple penal goals may be defended in a coherent theory which the unified theory provides us.

The unified theory best addresses the multiple penal goals often brought to bear on the punishment of juvenile offenders. The theory may also best account for the risk factors that may contribute to the need for punishment.[52] One risk factor is a troubled home life where the parents or guardians are regularly in contact with the police. This risk factor is linked with another: a lack of adequate housing or homelessness. The struggle for satisfactory accommodation may contribute to criminal behaviour in order to secure it. Other risk factors include drug and alcohol abuse and often undetected mental illness, such as manic depression or schizophrenia. These four risk factors for criminal behaviour are common for adults, too.

There are a further two risk factors that are specific to juvenile offenders.[53] The first is peer group pressure. Youth are engaged in the process of self-identity formation and their 'self-concept'.[54] This may make them more vulnerable to render poor judgements than adults. One way to tackle juvenile offending is to target leaders in peer networks, including gangs.[55] Changes at the 'top' may flow down to benefits at the 'bottom'. Youth may find some networks attractive because of their perceived importance in terms of social status. Networks that promote anti-authority attitudes, such as gang membership, may contribute to higher crime rates.[56] A second risk factor is poor performance or attendance at school, especially school exclusion.

Together, these six risk factors are united in illuminating a problem we have discussed previously: the problem of persons failing to see themselves as having a stake in society. If young persons are not in school with other students, then they may fail to see how engaging with others in a constructive environment may be conducive to their future. Lacking opportunities for lawful behaviour may provide incentives for creating opportunities for unlawful behaviour. Overcoming these problems is the project of helping ensure youth see themselves as coming to have a stake in society and its future. This is more than mere recognition, but recognition as a stakeholder. It is important that all juveniles see themselves as coming to have a legitimate stake in society.[57] Criminal justice policy should help remove obstacles to stakeholding where possible.[58] One finding is that crime reduction is better achieved through non-custodial sentences wherever possible and greater use of community penalties where juvenile offenders may have punishment tailored more to their individual needs.[59] The idea is that youth who view themselves as coming to have a legitimate future stake in society may find membership in peer networks, including gangs, that oppose legitimate stakeholding an unattractive option.

Punishment is a response to crime that often becomes necessary for offenders who lack positive support networks. This is no less true for juvenile offenders. It is important to help create and maintain such support to promote restorative recognition through stakeholding.[60] This sense is often lacking for many young adults. For example, one recent British study of over 2,200 persons between 16 and 24 years old found that more than a third 'do not feel part of their local community'.[61] One in five felt isolated 'most of the time' and about 10 per cent felt like an outcast. Nearly a third did not believe there was a future for them in their local area. The problem is that many youth feel some loss of control over their lives and future direction.[62] There is a central need to promote stakeholding and assist young adults in taking greater control over their lives by helping them to see themselves as having a future stake in society.

The unified theory of punishment occupies a unique position. It is best placed to defend the multiple penal goals that are often employed in determining punishments for youth. The unified theory is also best placed to explain the central issue behind the risk factors associated with potential future offending for adults and juveniles as a problem concerning stakeholding. The unified theory best accounts for the problem of youth crime as well as its flexible and effective punishment.

Conclusion

This chapter has examined the punishment of juvenile offenders. The issue is highly important because juvenile offenders are most likely to commit crimes and the youth offenders of today are often the adult offenders of tomorrow. We require an approach that might best address the specific issues associated with juvenile justice that promote an effective criminal justice policy.

The unified theory of punishment offers the most compelling theory for thinking about juvenile justice. Juvenile offending is often a product of a failure of youths understanding themselves as having a stake in society. This may be best addressed by promoting restorative recognition through shared stakeholding which the unified theory advances. Offenders engage with others to become more aware of how their actions impact upon others and receive assistance with forging and maintaining positive support networks. Juvenile offenders may be developing into legal adulthood. Punishment may become justified, but it should not contribute to creating further obstacles for offenders to view themselves as stakeholders. Instead, punishment aims at the restoration of rights and promotion of stakeholding for adult and juvenile offenders although each may require different treatment according to what restoration may require.

10 Domestic abuse

Introduction

Domestic abuse receives relatively little attention from most theories of punishment.[1] Discussions about criminal law tend to focus on serious crimes, such as murder or rape, but without acknowledging that domestic abuse is a serious crime as well. In fact, 'domestic abuse' is perhaps best characterized as a bundle of crimes united by the relations between an offender and victim. These crimes are not evils imposed upon us by some bogeyman, but those with whom we share intimate relations. Domestic abuse is a 'crime' unlike any other in its multifaceted nature and the intimate relations damaged. Some have likened domestic abuse to 'intimate terrorism'.[2] Moreover, it is a crime with many victims, affecting more lives than most crimes. Together, these are several reasons why any discussion of punishment *must* be able to address its relation to domestic violence.

This chapter will explain what is understood by 'domestic abuse' and the more compelling arguments about how it may be best punished. Many defend the use of restorative mediation frameworks to promote healing without recourse to criminal justice. Others argue that this sends the wrong message to abusers and severe punishment is desirable and perhaps required. I will argue for a middle ground of *punitive restoration* that is best advanced by a unified theory of punishment which aims at the restoration of rights and promotion of stakeholding. The unified theory helps illuminate how to navigate different circumstances that may require different outcomes within a coherent framework.

What is domestic abuse?

The most startling fact about domestic abuse is that it is not criminalized in many jurisdictions. Only a few jurisdictions have a specific offence of 'domestic abuse': domestic abuse is the 'crime' that everyone thinks they know.[3] Offenders are often prosecuted for committing other crimes, such as homicide offences, sexual or non-sexual offences against the person, or breach of peace.[4]

One reason for prosecuting 'domestic abuse' through other crimes is because it is perhaps best understood as a bundle of crimes and multiple wrongs. First, domestic abuse is foremost characterized by violence, particularly physical violence as well as emotional, physical, and sexual abuse. Domestic abuse is a violent crime involving victims. Second, domestic abuse consists of multiple violent acts; it is not so much a *single* crime as it is a *set* of crimes. Consider the situation of victims. One study in the United States found that over 60 per cent of male and female victims were either hit, slapped, or knocked down. About 25 per cent of male victims and nearly 55 per cent of female victims reported being grabbed, held, and tripped. Less than 1 per cent of male victims and more than 7 per cent of female victims were raped.[5] Domestic abuse is repeat violence that is physical and sometimes sexual. Domestic abuse is violence that may take several forms and often does. Citizens are more likely to be a victim of some form of domestic violence than burglary, mugging, or robbery. Moreover, domestic abuse victims are most likely to be victimized more than once. One study found that nearly 75 per cent of all domestic violence consists in repeat victimization.[6]

Third, domestic abuse is repeated violence of a relational nature; it is relational repetitive physical or sexual violence. Domestic abuse is violence between persons who are domiciled together. The abuse has a home-based 'domestic character'.[7] Not all violence in private homes is 'domestic violence'. What distinguishes domestic burglary from domestic violence is the particular relational connection between offenders and victims.[8] This connection is forged through shared intimacy, familial bonds, or a shared household. Those jurisdictions that have criminalized domestic abuse as a specific offence often include in their standards of evidence the fact of a relation of intimacy, familial bonds, or a common dwelling to capture the idea of the 'domestic' in 'domestic abuse'.[9]

This standard may often be effective at capturing some common fact about the relation between offenders and victims that is relevant to identifying domestic abuse. However, it does not best address the nature of the wrong. Suppose someone subjects another person to non-fatal physical abuse over a period of time where both persons are strangers to each other. Now suppose a second scenario where a husband subjects his wife to physical abuse over a period of time. The two cases are alike in every respect except the first case is physical violence between strangers and the second case is physical violence between a married couple. Now consider which you, the reader, believe is the worse set of crimes. Most, if not all, will argue that the second case is worse than the first. But why?

Domestic abuse is repeated violence of a relational nature. One element of its distinctiveness is that it is violence against persons to whom an offender owes special duties.[10] Special duties are different from general duties. General duties are owed 'generally' to everyone. Special duties are owed to some, but not all. Special duties arise in relation to the connections of intrinsic value, such as our shared intimate relationships. The duties we have to some may be different than the duties we owe all. Domestic violence is not only a violation of our general duties, but it is also a violation of our special duties. It is criminal for a stranger to commit battery against another; it *ought* to be *more* criminal for an offender to commit battery against another to whom he owes special duties. Domestic abuse is a distinctive set of crimes with victims to whom offenders owe special duties. There is perhaps nothing intrinsically 'domestic' about domestic abuse. Part of its distinctiveness is that it is about the violation of special duties we owe to some. Domestic abuse is a crime against those near and dear.[11] While it may often occur amongst persons that share a home together, this need not be true nor need domestic abuse always take place at a shared home.

Domestic abuse is a set of violent acts perpetrated against victims to whom we owe special duties. Some may find this definition surprising, and even perhaps shocking, because it is gender neutral. The evidence is clear: domestic abuse is a set of crimes where women are most often victims and men are most often offenders. Women are nearly 90 per cent of those victims experiencing four or more acts of domestic violence. Additionally, women are far more likely to be subjected to greater physical injury and sexual abuse than male victims. Domestic abuse is most often a set of violent crimes performed by men against female victims. Nevertheless, domestic abuse includes both men and women as its victims. Domestic abuse is not exclusive to either gender. Nor is domestic abuse exclusive to heterosexual relationships.[12] While most domestic abuse involves male offenders, domestic abuse must be understood more broadly.

One standard approach to criminalizing domestic abuse is to prosecute it as battery. While much domestic abuse does include physical violence that may constitute individual acts of battery, there is a major difference between the two that is clear. Battery is a crime that may be performed in a single action. An offender may be convicted and punished for battery that took place only once. Domestic abuse is a more violent crime because it is performed more than once over time. Moreover, domestic abuse may often take multiple forms of physical and sexual violence. It should be considered a more dangerous crime than battery not least because domestic abuse is often more than mere battery. So punishing domestic abuse as battery is problematic.

This criticism has not been unnoticed. There have been efforts to criminalize 'Coercive Domestic Violence'. This requires that the offender be found to commit two or more violent crimes.[13] This approach is correct to capture the fact that domestic abuse is a set of violent crimes composed of a bundle of violent acts. The approach also captures the fact that domestic abuse is often more than mere battery and a distinctive crime. However, domestic abuse is also more than a mere bundle. Domestic abuse is not any set of violent acts perpetrated over time, but systematic acts of violence where the whole is greater than the mere sum of its parts. That it involves violating special duties helps address this feature about domestic abuse that may be difficult to fully articulate.

Domestic abuse is a distinctive crime that is often recognized as criminal by citizens, but which has all too rarely been formally criminalized as a distinctive offence by many jurisdictions. This fact often rests on a misunderstanding about what is domestic abuse and how it should be conceived as a more serious crime than battery. In fact, domestic abuse is best understood as a set of violent crimes, which may help underscore its seriousness.

Justice and non-punishment

Some argue that the best way to combat domestic abuse is not through punishment, but through alternatives to criminal justice, such as support networks.[14] Criminal law is sometimes called a blunt instrument. The worry that some have is that it might also be counterproductive to achieving justice. The problem is that attempts to pursue helpful assistance through the criminal justice system may backfire. One reason for this is that many victims pursue these formal procedures after informal procedures have failed. The formal procedures of the criminal law may be alienating and frustrating for victims, from calling the police to the pursuit of prosecution and obtainment of protection orders.[15] Some argue that it might be preferable if victims pursued justice informally to avoid these concerns.

The challenge is the scale of the problem. For example, the effects on victims may be substantial. Studies reveal that victims of domestic violence are more likely to suffer from depression, anxiety, personality disorders, and post-traumatic stress disorder. These victims are also more likely to attempt suicide and engage in drug and alcohol abuse.[16] These effects are often unnoticed for a substantial time period. For example, research indicates that female victims are attacked about 35 occasions before seeking help. About one woman is killed each week by a current or past partner. Most domestic abuse is unreported to the police.[17]

The argument for informal procedures to best achieve better results focuses on the need to improve the informal procedures that many prefer and turn to in the first place. A central problem is that many victims may lack information about how to receive satisfactory informal advice and support.[18] There have been many efforts to improve the availability of information and resources to assist victims, including practical guidance to inform decision-making.[19]

A second reason in favour of informal procedures is that they may better address the problems of domestic abuse. Linda Mills argues:

> study after study confirms that arrest, prosecution, and incarceration do not necessarily reduce the problem of domestic violence and may even be making the problem worse … At worst, the criminal justice

system increases violence against women. At best, it has little or no effect.[20]

It may be surprising for some to learn that many victims do not want to see their partners imprisoned for domestic abuse. This is because many report that they want the abuse to stop; they don't always want their relationship with an abusive partner to stop.[21] Consider two research findings. One study found that about half of female victims choose to return to their abusive partners after they are discharged from shelters.[22] Another study of prosecutors found that most found about 60 per cent of the victims they represented were uncooperative during the prosecutions of domestic abusers.[23] While it is not true for all, a substantial number of victims – perhaps roughly half – prefer non-imprisonment in domestic abuse cases. They choose their partners over the often impersonal criminal justice system when asked to decide between them.[24]

Restorative mediation is often endorsed as the preferred informal means of addressing domestic abuse in cases where victims oppose the possible imprisonment of their abusers. Restorative mediation takes the form of groups, such as the Intimate Abuse Circle, which aim at restorative healing.[25] All participation is strictly voluntary and managed by an Intimate Abuse Assessment Team composed of mental health professionals. The findings are broadly positive, but remain inconclusive.[26] One benefit for those who favour this approach is the avoidance of the criminal justice system and possible sentencing of abusers. A second benefit is a clear focus on targeting the needs of offenders and victims to address the abuse by specialist professionals.

This approach to restorative justice is different from what we have considered before. Restorative mediation here is entirely voluntary and without penalties to offenders for non-compliance. Restorative justice requires voluntary participation where relevant stakeholders engage with each other to agree to a contract that the offender must fulfil or face more punitive measures. While restorative mediation and restorative justice over-lap in many respects, there is something more compelling about the latter. Domestic abuse is a most serious set of violent crimes over time. If restoration is to be secured, then it is important that the offender is held accountable for his crimes. This need not require the infliction of pain, but it should require a commitment to achieving restoration or face more punitive sanctions. If our goal is to restore what has been damaged, then there must be some more stable commitment to achieving this goal.

One alternative to restorative justice is abuser rehabilitation. This often takes the form of batterer intervention programmes. These programmes seek to reform batterer behaviour through cognitive therapy interventions, couples counselling, and other methods.[27] The focus is on close monitoring, and severe consequences for abusers should contribute to reduced violence.[28] Studies have found the effectiveness of these programmes inconclusive.[29]

This approach would be part of a rehabilitative theory of punishment. This would not then be an alternative to punishment as such, but an alternative to punitive sentencing where our object is to rehabilitate and reform offenders.

Consider this goal of offender reformation. One view is that it is best promoted by restorative mediation. Another view is that rehabilitative punishment or perhaps restorative justice is justified only where alternative non-punitive measures have failed. Suppose our preference was that an offender participate in mediation rather than sentencing because we desired the best means to the end of his abusive behaviour. Suppose further that these voluntary and informal procedures are ineffective. We might argue that informal procedures may be preferable for rehabilitation, but more formal procedures may become necessary later. So our view need not be that all formal procedures of criminal justice should be rejected by all. Many victims will prefer imprisonment for their abusers. Moreover, informal procedures may be ineffective and formal punishment, such as rehabilitation or restorative justice, may become justified where informal procedures fail.

The defence of informal procedures for some need not entail their use for all nor make informal procedures our only option. No one argues that there should never be punitive sanctions for domestic abusers. Our response to domestic abuse will always be open to the possible use of such sanctions. So the arguments for informal procedures are not a comprehensive response to the problem because they do not cover all cases and may not cover most. We may require a more robust theory about how best to meet the needs of victims and offenders while being open to the use of possible hard treatment.

Punishing domestic violence

Restorative mediation has received several criticisms. Some argue that we should prefer the enforcement of criminal law over informal procedures.[30] The argument is that mediation communicates the wrong message about the gravity of domestic abuse, namely, that our political community does not view it as a serious, violent crime. For example, the use of mediation and not punishment 'sends a message to both the participants and to society in general that domestic violence is either tolerable, or that both parties are responsible for domestic violence'.[31] The idea is that the criminal seriousness of domestic abuse requires severe punishment.

This expressivist view about domestic abuse links the gravity of this crime with the severity of its punishment. Note that retributivist desert is doing the work: crimes should be punished in proportion to their gravity. This reveals an important insight into retributivism. Perhaps only murder would normally be punished more severely than domestic abuse. This is because 'domestic abuse' represents a set of crimes that may often include some of the most serious violent crimes, such as battery and rape. Retributivists are perhaps most likely to deny the use of informal procedures for domestic abuse cases. The argument is this: if less violent crimes may warrant possible hard treatment, then domestic abuse is more deserving of it. Perhaps this would clash with victim preferences. However, the issue is not what victims prefer, but rather what punishment is most deserved. If we believe that domestic abuse victims should have a voice in the punishment of their abusers, then retributivism may often run counter to the preferences of many victims.[32]

The punishment of domestic abuse continues to be a work in progress. One problem is that domestic abuse is complex as we have noted above and it lacks a common legal definition.[33] In fact, domestic abuse was not criminalized at all until the late nineteenth century. The traditional response was that the state was unable to interfere in domestic matters.[34] This view has changed significantly. Many critics correctly recognized that too little action had been taken to address domestic abuse. One outcome is the now widespread use of 'mandatory arrest' laws in many US states. These laws empower the police to make warrantless arrests in cases of domestic violence. Unsurprisingly, these laws have contributed to large increases in the number of arrests pertaining to domestic abuse. However, there is no clear evidence that this policy has led to greater victim safety.[35] Moreover, this policy may run counter to the interests and preferences of relevant stakeholders.

One recommendation to better address victim preferences has been the use of a victim report.[36] Several courts permit the use of victim impact statements. These are statements that attempt to clarify the impact of a crime on a victim from the victim's perspective. Victim impact statements may only address the alleged impact of a crime: victim impact statements may not address any victim's sentencing preferences. The benefit is that these statements are thought to give more of a voice in the criminal justice system while leaving sentencing decisions with judges.

The idea of the victim report is that victims would provide the court with a statement about a crime's impact on them, but also concerning recommendations on sentencing. The victim report would permit victims who recommend imprisonment to make their view known. Likewise, it would allow victims who preferred non-custodial alternatives, such as restorative mediation, to declare their view as well. The outcome may be influenced by the victim report, in part, but discretion would rest with the judge. Sentencing guidelines may be upheld as victims gain a louder voice.

One potential concern is that the victim report might influence punishment beyond satisfactory bounds. Courts already may have regard to the evidence of dangerousness confirmed from victim impact statements. There is some controversy about the way that these statements are presented to the court.[37] The worry is that impacts may be presented in such a way that they persuade without convincing through appeal to our emotions rather than our reason. The idea that we should always divorce reason from emotion is rejected by many legal scholars and rightly so.[38] This is because our judgements about what is reasonable in a situation may rest on expectations about our emotional responses. Human beings are emotional beings, and we would miss something central to our humanity if we were to try to excise our sentimental relationships.

We may accept this view, but remain uncertain about victim reports improving sentencing decisions. One reason is practical. Judges may retain sentencing discretion with victim impact statements, but this may be lost with victim reports. This may not be true in every case. Suppose a victim recommends a custodial sentence, but the judge believes this is unwarranted. She may decide against the victim's recommendation. Now suppose a victim recommends a non-custodial sentence. My best guess is that any decision to imprison against the victim's preferences may be likely to be overturned on appeal. If the victim prefers non-custodial mediation, then why shouldn't we? So one reason to oppose victim reports is that they may be likely to undermine sentencing discretion. A second reason is that domestic abuse often has many victims, including children and relatives. There may be several stakeholders in how the abuse is addressed and concluded. Yet, it may be unclear how these voices may be heard as well.[39]

So while we might all agree on the seriousness of domestic abuse, there may remain much disagreement about whether criminal justice measures are necessary or desirable. There is a deep split amongst many victims about whether punitive sentences or mediation is most preferable. These preferences may be counter to what different theories of punishment might justify. This leads us to a potential problem of how we might defend a more comprehensive view about the punishment of domestic abuse that might better address this deep division.

Towards punitive restoration

Domestic abuse is a very serious crime. Our response should be proportionate, but does this require that it must always be severely punitive? No, it does not.

Recall that our rights represent our substantial freedoms. Crimes are best understood as rights violations. Punishment may be justified in response to crime. Punishment aims at the restoration of rights violated by crime. Punishment must be deserved and proportionate to the restorative needs of the rights under threat. This need not require punitive measures if non-punitive measures might effectively support rights restoration. Our goal is to restore and protect rights, not inflict pain for its own sake.

Domestic abuse is a serious violent crime that violates rights. This justifies the need for a response: punishment is this response. Punishment may take different forms depending upon what best promotes the restoration and protection of rights threatened by domestic abuse. The form that our penal response should take to domestic abuse ought to be informed by stakeholders in the outcome. This will include the offender, the victim, and others, including perhaps family members, close friends, and community members. Stakeholders should engage with one another where possible to agree how restoration is best achieved in their case.

The penal outcome may not include a custodial sentence and often imprisonment may make bad situations even worse. However, custodial sentences should not be rejected outright in any form. It is possible that the restoration of rights concerning stakeholders is best achieved through some use of imprisonment or a suspended sentence. This is one substantial difference between the unified theory of punishment defended here and most accounts of restorative justice. While these accounts of restorative justice reject the use of prison, the unified theory accepts its limited use where it may best help pursue the restoration of rights.

Our choice need not be between prison or non-prison, but perhaps some combination. For example, a brief custodial sentence may serve as a beneficial 'cooling off' period for abusers where they immediately receive some of the therapeutic assistance they require to end their abusive behaviour. This option of intensive sentencing may seem mistaken because brief imprisonment is strongly associated with high reoffending rates. However, brief imprisonment as currently practised lacks intensive efforts at offender reformation. Intensive sentencing is an option that may help offenders most when they are most in need.

Domestic abuse should be punished with the aim of restoring our rights. This may involve imprisonment, a punishment that includes some custodial sentencing element, or perhaps some alternative sanction. Our aim is to achieve rights restoration, but our restorative effort is also punitive; it is a project of punitive restoration. Punitive restoration places burdens on offenders in consultation with other stakeholders in the outcome.

The unified theory would deny abusers mediation that was purely voluntary and informal. This is because such an approach fails to address domestic abuse as a crime. The restoration of rights cannot be achieved by voluntary measures alone. The outcome is decided by persons with a stake in the outcome and not left to the victim alone. But it will include the victim in a more substantial way than either victim impact statements or victim reports might allow. Furthermore, the unified theory is flexible in how restoration may be achieved. It is a comprehensive approach that may justify the punishment of domestic abusers in terms of custodial and non-custodial sentencing.

Conclusion

The punishment of domestic abuse is a distinctive challenge. Domestic abuse is a complex crime best considered as a set of repeated acts of violence against persons to whom the offender owes special duties because of their relation. Domestic abuse is also one of the most serious crimes. One particular problem is how best to justify its punishment where many victims are divided. We require an approach that is suitably comprehensive so that it may address the complexity and seriousness of domestic abuse while also offering some compelling view about how to consider very different responses from victims about their preferences for how abusers are punished. This complexity is captured well by Katherine Baker:

> Women remain in relationships not only because they may be financially dependent on their partners or because they face a greater risk of violence if they leave; these women are often emotionally bound to their partners. Many battered women do not want to go. They want the violence to stop, and they want to feel safe, but they do not want to leave. Rather, they want to stay in a relationship with men whom they often continue to love, and with whom they share a life, a family, and a community. The legal presumption that one should walk away from a relationship because one gets hit reflects a remarkably anemic understanding of the emotional complexity of relationships.[40]

How best to address the complexity and diversity of opinions about domestic abuse?

This chapter has defended the idea of punitive restoration offered by the unified theory of punishment. Our goal should be the restoration of rights violated by domestic abuse determined by stakeholders in the outcome. This approach has the flexibility to address the complexity of domestic abuse crimes. The unified theory is also flexible on the appropriate form it should take to achieve this goal.

11 Sexual crimes

Introduction

Sexual crimes are amongst the most serious violent crimes, such as rape and child sex abuse.[1] While there is widespread support for severe punishment, there is general disagreement on its justification. Some retributivists argue that rape and child sex abuse are evil acts that deserve significant punishment on account of their wickedness. Other deterrence proponents argue that these crimes should be punished severely because of their relative dangerousness and the problem of serial reoffending. But which view is most persuasive? Is there a more attractive alternative?

This chapter will focus on the crimes of rape and child sex abuse. We will examine how both are defined in order to better understand their criminalization. We will next consider how satisfactory different approaches to punishing these crimes perform in light of the available evidence. One finding is that much of the evidence is relatively poor, but nevertheless consistent and perhaps even surprising. There is a compelling argument to be made in favour of the unified theory of punishment and its endorsement of punitive restoration.

Rape

Rape is defined differently across jurisdictions. In the United Kingdom, rape is the penetration with a penis of the vagina, anus, or mouth of another person without consent and where the offender does not 'reasonably believe' there is consent.[2] One notable feature is that only men can perform rape. This is because rape requires the unlawful penetration of another with a penis. Many other jurisdictions do not hold that rape requires unlawful penile penetration, including the United States. These jurisdictions permit rape where there is unlawful penetration using an object.[3] It is also notable that every case of penile penetration is treated as a case of sexual conduct. The law does not recognize acts of non-sexual penile penetration.[4] Nor need sexual conduct require an intention for erotic pleasure. There may be many reasons why persons consent to sex that are lawful and do not entail erotic desire.

Rape is often more than a single isolated crime, but may also include further 'sexual indignities', including physical abuse and sexual assault.[5] This is a feature it shares with domestic abuse. A second is that it is often a 'domestic' crime where victims are attacked at home or places familiar to victims. For example, rapes often occur at locations such as a victim's home or the home of friend, relative, or neighbour.[6] About 80 per cent of rape victims are under the age of 30 and half are under the age of 18 years.[7]

The criminal element of rape has changed in law over time. The traditional wrong of rape was the loss of a woman's chastity; the problem with rape was not conceived in terms of a loss of dignity.[8] Chastity had much value in traditional societies where sex outside marriage was punishable. One consequence was that there was no conception of unlawful sex within marriage.[9] While convicted rapists were often punished severely, the definition of rape does not capture how most conceive rape today.

Consent is now considered fundamental to the determination of rape: 'All that distinguishes [rape] from ordinary sexual intercourse is lack of consent'.[10] Consent often possesses a transformative legal power on our conduct. For example, 'consent can turn battery into surgery, murder into voluntary euthanasia, rape into intercourse, theft into donation, kidnapping into a vacation'.[11] For example, Duff says:

> What is morally wrong with rape is that it is a grievous assault on its victim's interests and integrity, not that it takes unfair advantage of those who restrain themselves (we do not show a rapist the wrongness of his deed by saying 'But suppose everyone did that?'); and it should be a crime because the law should protect members of the community against such assaults, not because the law should ensure a fair balance of abstract benefits and burdens.[12]

Duff argues that rape is a crime that assaults a victim's interests and integrity. We might restate this position in the following terms. Rape is a crime that threatens the fundamental freedoms of its victims and, therefore, rape is a violation of their rights that requires punishment. Punishment aims at the restoration of rights and the protection of our fundamental freedoms. This is why rape merits punishment.

The problem of rape is not that rapists may enjoy some unfair advantage over law abiding citizens. This is because there is no advantage in crimes that violate rights. The idea that rapists enjoy unfair advantages suggests that rapists acquire benefits through their crimes. This understanding of beneficial advantage is objectionable. The reason is that offenders do not benefit because they have no right to violate the rights of others in this way. Suppose Bill murders Steven in order to steal Steven's car. Bill benefits materially, but he does not benefit in terms of his rights. Bill's rights do not increase because he does not accrue additional fundamental freedoms.

On the contrary, his rights become threatened through his own act. This is because the legal protections he enjoys under a well ordered legal system protect both his rights and those rights belonging to Steven. Bill's crimes pose a threat to rights given legal protection which does nothing to further promote their protection in this case. So Bill may benefit materially, but he does not benefit legally because he had no right to murder Steven and steal his car. Nor does Bill benefit in terms of his rights by violating the rights of others. It is important to consider not material benefits as such, but instead benefits in terms that are legal and rights-based. Similarly, a rapist may engage in sexual conduct, but he cannot be said to benefit legally or in terms of rights promotion. Rape should be criminalized for many reasons, but not because rapists enjoy unfair advantages.

Rape requires the lack of consent. There are several reasons why this is the case. For example, one argument is to say that all penetrative sex is prima facie wrong and requires justification to be permissible.[13] First, sexual penetration exposes others to harmful risks, such as sexually transmitted diseases (STDs). Secondly, vaginal penetration carries the risk of unwanted pregnancy.[14] Sexual conduct may entail harmful and unwanted risks. Sexual conduct requires justification.

An attractive feature of this argument is that it helps to shift the burdens of proof in rape cases. So while rape requires the lack of consent, a significant problem is proving where consent is lacking. Traditionally, the burden of proof has been on victims to provide evidence that consent was lacking or withdrawn. Relevant evidence might include bruising or signs of physical struggle.[15] One major problem with this view is that it adopted a male-centric idea about self-defence often inapplicable. The law would assume that violence would be met with violence, but this is not always available or possible where victims may be overpowered by their offenders. The argument that sexual conduct requires justification shifts the evidential burdens from the victim having to demonstrate a lack of consent to the offender proving a reasonable belief that consent was present. While some may view this as a subtle difference, it is also an important innovation in how we might understand consent.

Consent is not always easily determinable. For example, Joan McGregor highlights the problem of mixed messages that may be expressed about consent to sex. She notes a study of university students in the United States where '39 percent of the students reported that they had said "no" once or only a few times when they intended to have sex with the person. The reasons for this behavior ... were: fear of appearing promiscuous, moral reasons, and what they called manipulative reasons, the desire to be in control'.[16] This study shows that a significant number of people may say 'no' to sex where they intend to say 'yes'. McGregor is correct to conclude that this study usefully reminds us that consent may not always be clearly expressed, but 'no' can never be understood as a consent to sex under any circumstances.[17] This is because 'no' never meets the minimal conditions for consent.

Consent is not easily determinable in other contexts. Antony Duff says:

> The sexual penetration of an unconscious person is not necessarily rape: it could be done with the person's consent, in a way that respects the person's autonomy. [The victim's] unconsciousness does, however, create a strong presumption that the penetration is rape – the penetration is in that sense a presumptive wrong.[18]

Duff's example raises the distinction between active and passive consent. Consider a 'standard' case of lawful, consensual sex where each person is alert and consent is acknowledged. This standard case is an example of active consent where consent is present and presently acknowledged. Inactive consent concerns cases where consent is present, but not presently acknowledged. An example of passive consent is lawful sexual penetration of an unconscious person with her consent and in a way that satisfactorily respects her autonomy.[19] Passive consent is less robust and may be a presumptive wrong requiring some additional evidence of justification. Nevertheless, the main idea is that consent may be present in different ways and this may further complicate the relation between rape and consent.

There are clear limits on the role that consent may play. For example, persons must be able to provide some intent to consent. Where someone is unable to consent to sexual penetration, this conduct may be rape. This does not entail that anyone intoxicated is unable to provide sufficient consent. But this does mean that someone too intoxicated or unconscious may be unable to consent. Such circumstances may constitute rape. Furthermore, people may be judged unable to provide consent to justify some conduct.[20] Consent must be possible and applicable.

Consent must also be secured without dishonesty. Rape by deception is where an offender deceives the victim in some respect in order to falsely acquire consent to engage in sexual activity. Suppose Anna will only consent to have sex with someone who shares her religious affiliation. Brian does not share her religious affiliation. But he falsely tells her that he does share the same affiliation and Anna agrees to sex. This is rape by deception. This is because Anna's agreement is acquired by Brian's intentional deception. Where agreement is acquired by deception, there is no consent.

Rape requires the lack of consent, but also a defendant's lack of a reasonable belief that his partner has consented to sexual conduct. Sex is not rape where the offender has a reasonable belief that his victim is consenting.[21] Rape by deception is rape because there is a lack of consent and the offender intentionally deceives his victim. Brian does not have a reasonable belief that Anna has consented to sex because he intentionally deceived her to acquire her agreement. His action constituted rape.

Sexual conduct might not be rape where the offender has a false, but reasonable, belief that his partner consents. These cases have been called 'rapes without rapists', where victims have not consented to sex, but there is no offender.[22] Nevertheless, these cases also require the justification for holding a reasonable belief that consent was given despite victims arguing that consent was denied, in fact.

One alternative view does not deny that a lack of consent should be central to the criminalization of rape. But it goes further to say that rape is more than a lack of consent: rape is also about a power imbalance between men and women. Rapes are often 'inflicted on those who have less social power by those who have more'.[23] The victims are most often women with less social power; the offenders are most often men with more. Part of what is problematic about rape should address this power imbalance. The power imbalance is not restricted to gender, but includes income. Consider one study from the United States on crime rates and annual family incomes. It found that persons on $7,500 or less were *twice* as likely to be a victim of rape or sexual assault than someone on an income of between $7,500 and $14,999, and *four times* as likely than persons on $15,000 or more.[24]

Should these considerations matter? This is unclear. Rape may represent the power imbalance that exists between men and women. This power imbalance becomes manifest in the violation of victims' rights. The wrongness of rape is linked with its violation of rights. It is unclear how the violation of rights is a separate matter from wrongful exercises of power. Furthermore, it is highly doubtful that rape should be understood as less serious where the victim has greater social power than the offender. Moreover, not all rape victims are women. These arguments do not deny the very serious and pressing gender issues often present in rape cases. However, they do suggest that the criminalization of rape is justified as the violation of rights. This may include some implicit acknowledgement of power imbalance while avoiding its shortcomings highlighted here.

Child sex offences

Child sex offenders may not be paedophiles, strictly speaking. Child sex offenders are persons who have raped or sexually assaulted a child. Paedophiles (or 'pedophiles') are persons who have sexual desire for children. The first is about behaviour; the second is about a state of mind. While many child sex offenders may be paedophiles, not all paedophiles are child sex offenders and vice versa. Paedophilia is commonly understood to be a psychiatric disorder that requires medical treatment through rehabilitation.[25] There is also research that child sex offenders may have mental disorders that might benefit from psychiatric treatment.[26] Our focus will be child sex offenders.

Child sex offending has a similar gender profile found with rape. Offenders are 97 per cent men and their victims are female in about 75 per cent of known cases.[27] Child sex abuse is rarely a single, isolated incident. Instead, child sex offending is often repeated over multiple acts of sexual violence against a child.[28]

Child sex offences are criminalized under the Sexual Offences Act in the United Kingdom, for example. This Act criminalizes all kissing and intimate touching between persons under 16 years. Criminalization rests 'on the understanding that there will not be a prosecution unless there is evidence of exploitation or abuse'.[29] Prosecutors may exercise discretion where such evidence is present. This task is complicated by findings that many persons under 16 have engaged in penetrative sex before the age of consent. Studies suggest that about 50 per cent of girls and about 35 per cent of boys under 16 years have had penetrative sex.[30] Child sex abuse is inclusive of cases where all persons involved may be underage. This fact is often overlooked.

The standard case of child sex abuse is sexual conduct between an adult offender and underage victim. There remains surprisingly little evidence for why child sex offenders engage in child sex offences. Perhaps one reason is that they have paedophilia. Perhaps a second reason is that child sex offenders derive satisfaction from exercising dominance over submissive victims. More research remains to be done to provide more conclusive evidence.[31]

Child sex offences are characterized by the absence of consent. Children are unable to provide legal consent to sexual conduct irrespective of any proclamations to the contrary. Consider the relation to rape. The presence or absence of consent is central to the determination of rape: there must be consent and reasonable belief that consent is granted. Child sex offences are easier to determine. This is because children cannot consent and so there can be no reasonable belief that consent has been granted under any circumstances. Therefore, we require evidence that sexual conduct has occurred. If so, then this is material evidence that a child sex offence has taken place. Indeed, we might argue that child sex offences are not so much characterized by the lack of consent as they are its legal impossibility.

Deterrence and sex crimes

How should rape and child sex offenders be punished? One argument is that we should defend the use of deterrence. Proponents of deterrence argue that punishment should act to deter future criminal offending. Such a view assumes that the threat of punishment may be sufficient to convince potential offenders that they should refrain from any offending. Rapists and child sex offenders must engage in cost–benefit analysis in order to be deterred. Furthermore, deterrence assumes our ability to have some knowledge about which policies may yield deterrent effects.

One problem for deterrence theories of punishment is that there are no reliable studies of reoffending rates available for sex crimes.[32] This problem is exacerbated by the fact of widespread under reporting of sex offences in general. For example, some studies have found that between 60 and 90 per cent of rape victims do not contact the police.[33] The available evidence is inconclusive, but broadly consistent. Only a small proportion of all recorded crimes are sex offences. For example, they may represent less than 1 per cent of all notifiable offences and no more than 2 per cent of all offenders convicted.[34] In the United States, the crime rate for rape or sexual assault per 1,000 persons or households was less than 1 per cent.[35] Similar findings have been found in the United Kingdom.[36] So the evidence is that relatively few arrests and convictions are for sex crimes, such as rape and child sex offences.

Rapists and child sex offenders have relatively low reconviction rates as well.[37] In fact, only murderers are reconvicted less often.[38] An American study found that about 5 per cent of male sex offenders and roughly 3 per cent of child sex abusers were rearrested for a new sex crime within three years of release.[39] Most empirical studies conclude that 'the probability of a serious sexual offender being reconvicted for a sexual (and also for a serious violent) offence is relatively low, even for those who have victimized children and have been at liberty for a considerable number of years'.[40] While sex offenders are less likely to be rearrested for any offence than non-sex offenders, sex offenders were more likely to be rearrested for another sex crime.[41] In addition, child sex offenders tend to receive relatively few reconvictions. However, they tend to be found guilty of more prolific crimes whenever convicted.[42]

These findings are suggestive of two tentative conclusions. First, most recent laws seem to assume that most sex offenders will reoffend. While the evidence is inconclusive, there is little evidence to support this contention. Second, deterrence is strongly undermined by the available evidence. Sex offenders are arrested, convicted, and reconvicted far less frequently than other types of offenders. It is difficult to justify punishment to promote deterrence given what evidence we have.

My argument is not that the evidence we have is conclusive. One central reason why rapists and child sex offenders appear to be less dangerous is because their reconvictions are comparably low. This fact masks the reality that securing convictions has been unsatisfactory for some time. We know that there are far more sex offences than there have been convictions for sex offences. The evidence is inconclusive because far too few sex offences enter the criminal justice system. Perhaps the true picture would look very different if far more sex offences were successfully prosecuted. Nevertheless, what evidence we have provides perhaps surprisingly little evidence in support of more punitive sentences based upon deterrence. If we understand 'dangerousness' in terms of likelihood of reoffending, the available evidence consistently indicates that sex offenders are among the least likely to reoffend.

Strict liability and penal borders

We have noted the problem of unsatisfactorily low conviction rates for sex offences. Efforts have been made to improve conviction rates through two policies. The first is to improve the availability and quality of information about sex crimes. The second has been to incorporate strict liability more often into the relevant criminal definitions. Strict liability has the advantage of removing the burdens of proving reasonable belief, consent, or intent to secure conviction. One example is the use of strict liability in the prosecution of child pornography where mere possession may constitute sufficient evidence for the crime. Prosecutions become easier to secure because all that needs to be demonstrated is that child pornography was in someone's possession.

One concern about the use of strict liability in this way is that the penal borders between child sex abuse and possession of child pornography is becoming blurred.[43] Their penal difference is becoming less distinct as possession of child pornography has its punishment increased substantially so that the two offences have broadly similar punishments. This has led to some criticism that their relative punitive equivalence is mistaken because the crime of actual child sex abuse is more dangerous than the crime of possessing child pornography that was produced by someone else's actual child sex abuse: this difference may be between active child abuse and passive child abuse. One response to these criticisms is that persons who possess child pornography contribute or participate in some important respect in the child sex crime. Perhaps a second response is that the possession of such images should be criminal because their production is unjustified and any satisfaction derived from viewing them amounts to wickedness. None of these arguments undermines the relevance of strict liability in these matters.

One argument in favour of using strict liability is that it is a legitimate policy to best promote and protect the central rights of children. Child sex offences are fundamental violations of the rights of children. The relevance of child sex offender recidivism to the importance of rights violated by child sex offending is not more than the relevance of murderer recidivism to the importance of rights violated by murderers. Strict liability measures may not be ideal, but they may prove instrumentally helpful in the legal system's goal of protecting our rights. A view of punishment, such as the unified theory of punishment, which defends the restoration and protection of rights is best placed to justify the use of strict liability policies such as this.

Proportionate punishment

What is a proportionate punishment for rapists or child sex offenders? First, we must note that no one justifies an 'eye for an eye'. Nor is it clear how it could be achieved. Some have noted that imprisoning offenders may subject them to sexual assault or rape.[44] But this is a problem to be addressed and not understood as a just punishment. If rape is criminal as a violation of a victim's rights, then it is difficult to see how it may be justified to violate the rapist in response. If our intuitions are unclear, we should ask: would we justify the state hiring someone to rape convicted rapists? Most will find the suggestion abhorrent. This is evidence that such a punishment is unjustified and inhumane. Furthermore, it is impossible to impose an 'eye for an eye' on child sex offenders. Such persons are no longer children and so any strict equivalence between their crime and our punishment is impossible.

Some support the use of capital punishment for some sex offenders. While rape has been punished by death in many jurisdictions, it has become increasingly rare in recent years. For example, it has been found unconstitutional in the United States since the late 1970s. The US Supreme Court ruled that the execution of rapists was 'grossly disproportionate' and constituted 'excessive punishment'.[45] The Court has also recently overturned an attempt to introduce the death penalty for child rapists on similar grounds.[46] It argued that execution is only deserved for crimes that include the death of victims. This provides some evidence that rapists and child sex offenders may be deserving of severe punishment, but also that there is a growing consensus for the view that death is not deserved. Much more must be said for why execution is warranted for crimes that do not involve death.

Some retributivists argue that rape is no worse than battery. Therefore, rape should not be punished more than battery.[47] The reason is that 'sex minus consent ... is sex nevertheless'.[48] Rape is also not about sex, but violence. For example, Michael Davis says: 'Rapists are seldom sex-starved. They tend to treat sex as a useful weapon to degrade their victim, to vent their aggression or to demonstrate their power. Rape is like other violent crimes'.[49] Rape is a violent crime little different from other violent crimes, such as battery. So not only should rape not be punished by execution, but it should be punished no more severely than crimes like battery.

One significant problem with this argument is that its analysis of the crime extends no further than the offender. It says that the offender in his attitudes and dispositions is similar to other kinds of offenders: therefore, his crime should not be punished much differently from them. This argument gets this wrong. The wrongness of crime should be understood in terms of its violation of the rights of victims. The victim should matter in our determination of criminal seriousness. Victims may be deeply affected by rape and child sex offences more profoundly than they are by battery. This provides a compelling reason to consider the crimes of rape and child sex offences as more serious and different in character than crimes like battery.

Another way that sex crimes have been addressed is through the launch of sex offender registers. There has been much campaigning by victim support groups for laws that require sex offenders to sign a public register that confirms their name with photograph, the sex crime for which they have been convicted, and their address.[50] This policy is sometimes highlighted as a case where moving too swiftly in response to strong public demand may lead to poorly crafted public policy.[51] There remain strong doubts about whether sex offender registers have contributed to positive results.[52] Three concerns have been raised.[53] First, local citizens may be wrongly assured that there is no risk to their child. Second, the policy may provide false reassurance to the public that the government is able to protect all children from child abuse. Both concerns are based upon the problem that most sex crimes are unknown and too rarely lead to conviction. Highly accessible information about any local sex offenders will only include those few sex offenders that have been successfully prosecuted. Sex registers may send out a misleading signal about the potential risks to local children. Furthermore, sex registers may send out a misleading signal about the political community's success in prosecuting sex offenders. This is because a community that lists only a few local registered sex offenders may appear to be a community with few sex offenders, but this may not be the case in fact.[54]

Third, there is a danger that disclosure schemes may undermine efforts to rehabilitate and reform sex offenders by raising further obstacles to their finding employment, adequate housing, and playing a positive role within the local community. High risk factors for future reoffending include offenders having difficulty with employment, housing, and finding a role for positive future contributions. Sex offender registers may make finding employment more difficult by providing employers with a reason against hiring convicted sex offenders in favour of others. Surveillance may contribute to several unintended consequences. In making it more difficult for convicted sex offenders to secure accommodation, it may become more difficult for the police to monitor them. Additionally, if sex offenders are to be released, but forbidden from playing any future role in their community, then they will be challenged to see a real stake in a legitimate future. This failure to promote future stakeholding may contribute to a greater likelihood of future reoffending. So while sex offender registers are designed to decrease dangerousness and recidivism, they may lead to counterproductive results if not managed properly. This is not to argue that sex offender registration has not produced any positive effects. One such effect is that it has helped ensure that known sex offenders are denied employment where they might exploit the vulnerability of children.[55] But, again, there is a real need for effective management to ensure beneficial effects are achieved instead of counterproductive outcomes.[56]

Punitive restoration

Some form of restoration may play a compelling role in criminal justice policy addressing rapists and child sex offenders. First, restoration may play a positive role for sex offenders. Sex offenders have been shown to respond well to treatment and the restorative approach is cost-effective amongst persons unlikely to reoffend.[57] This is also true for many child sex offenders.[58] Risk factors for sex offending include 'considerable anxiety, depression, and low self-regard'.[59] In addition, reoffending becomes more likely where these moods deteriorate. Whilst low self-esteem may not be a predictor of reoffending, it has been linked with initial offending.[60] Together, these factors speak to a problem concerning stakeholding. Sex offenders, such as rapists and child sex offenders, may often fail to believe they have a stake in society and its future. Punishment which held them responsible and accountable for their crimes, but which also addressed the restorative needs for future stakeholding, holds genuine promise as an effective and proportionate punishment.

Second, restoration may play a positive role for victims. Many victims may not want to participate in any such restorative setting. Nor might this be recommended in many cases. My argument is not that it should always happen, but that it should always be available to victims. This is because it may be a positive experience for victims who want to engage in restoration. Sex offending is a crime that is often between persons well acquainted with each other and only rarely is the crime perpetrated by a stranger.[61] Stakeholders in the penal outcome will often be known to one another. Victims often suffer from psychological and emotional harms in addition to physical harm.[62] Victims of sex crimes may not only feel dehumanized and degraded, but victims of 'soul murder'.[63] Restorative frameworks may play some positive role in helping victims overcome the significant harms they have suffered.

One significant problem is that restorative justice conferences may only be appropriate in a small number of cases.[64] The use of restorative justice instead of possible sentencing for all rapists and child sex offenders would never command public confidence for the foreseeable future. Instead, the 'recognized way of demonstrating that society takes something seriously' is to ensure some punitive element in sentencing.[65] This does not mean we should reject restorative measures; it only means we should support punitive restoration.

Punitive restoration is a more expansive and punitive use of restorative justice that may benefit victims and offenders alike.[66] Much research demonstrates that what most victims of domestic and sexual violence want is exposure of their offender as an offender and acknowledgement of the crimes perpetrated against them.[67] This is possible through a restorative process that aimed at the restoration of rights and the promotion of stakeholding. Such a process would incorporate the offender's acknowledgement of responsibility and a collective agreement about his accountability. This restorative process is *punitive* in that the contract agreed with the offender may include some measure of hard treatment, a suspended sentence, and/or intensive community sentencing. Punitive restoration may best address the needs of both offenders and victims in achieving justice through the restoration of rights.

Conclusion

Sex crimes such as rape and child sex offences are serious violent crimes. This chapter has explained how these crimes are understood and the central role that consent plays in criminalization. We have also considered different ideas about how these crimes are best punished.

There are compelling reasons in favour of the unified theory of punishment and the idea of punitive restoration. This approach is comprehensive in its scope and it avoids the many concerns that arise with competing theories of punishment. Punishment may be restorative and punitive as well as win the confidence of both stakeholders and the public. Imagination is required on how best to secure the restoration of rights. The relevant framework is offered by the unified theory of punishment and punitive restoration. Punishment may be deserved while contributing to crime reduction, criminal rehabilitation, and restoration, and provide some expression of public disapproval within a single, coherent and unified theory of punishment.

Conclusion

The unified theory of punishment

Crime and punishment are intrinsically interlinked. Rights are legal protections of our substantial freedoms. Crimes are violations of our rights and their threatened violation. Punishment is a response to crime. The goal of punishment is the restoration and protection of our rights. One consequence is that there can be no just punishment for a law that is unjust. This is because the justification of punishment requires the justification of the law violated. If acts or omissions do not violate our rights, then they should not be criminal.

This view about crime and punishment is best captured by the unified theory of punishment. It defends the idea that punishment may address multiple penal goals within a coherent and unified framework. Punishment need not be either retributivist, deterrent, or rehabilitative, but all at once. Punishment aims at the restoration and protection of our rights. The penal outcome justified is what best enables restoration to be secured. Punishment is addressed to the deserving in proportion to the violation that a crime presents to our rights. Some crimes present greater violations of our rights than others: murder should be punished more than theft for this reason. The form that punishment might take will be what best secures the restoration of rights.

The unified theory of punishment represents an important revision of restorative justice. Restorative justice is often proposed as a format for restorative healing independent of any penal considerations. For example, an offender might take part in a restorative conference after sentencing. Or restorative justice has been proposed as an alternative theory of punishment which rejects the use of imprisonment. Restorative justice has proved highly promising as a cost-effective alternative to competing approaches. However, it has lacked a clear national strategy, sufficient resources, and wide use beyond experimentation for juvenile offenders. One concern is that the non-punitive nature of restorative nature may inhibit its ability to secure greater effectiveness and public confidence for more widespread use.

The unified theory of punishment supports punitive restoration. Our goal is the restoration of rights. This may often require that we avoid the use of imprisonment where possible and only sentence as a last resort provided that doing so will be no worse than alternatives to securing the restoration of rights. Restorative agreements are more flexible and they may include more punitive elements, such as intensive community sentencing, suspended sentences, and the use of prison where necessary. Punishment is deserved and proportionate to the needs of restoration. This commits criminal justice policy to pursue effective crime reduction policies that deter and rehabilitate where possible. Punishment may be understood metaphorically to 'express' public disapproval in form and content. Finally, punishment aspires to the restoration of rights violated by crimes. The unified theory of punishment's idea of punitive restoration brings together multiple goals within a single, coherent penal framework.

The restoration of rights is best achieved through the promotion of the idea of the stakeholder society. The idea is that the most central risk factor of all for future offending is where someone does not believe that he has a stake in society and its future. Where we fail to believe we have such a stake, criminal activities become more likely. We may address multiple criminal risk factors at once through the promotion of stakeholding. This will include drug and alcohol treatment, educational opportunities, employ-ability training, and assistance with securing satisfactory accommodation. The improvement of each will contribute to the central goal of promoting citizen stakeholding.

Stakeholding informs the justification of punitive restoration. Crime violates our rights. Punishment is a response to crime that aims to restore our rights. It is important to include stakeholders in penal outcomes in the decision-making process wherever possible. This is precisely because these persons have a stake in these outcomes. Relevant stakeholders will include offenders, victims, and community members who may have some stake. Conferences should be conducted by a trained mediator, magistrate, or judge as appropriate. Together, stakeholders constructively engage with one another to determine how restoration is best achieved. Each conference requires that offenders accept responsibility for their crimes. Victims may be often encouraged to participate, but they need not. The best outcome is one that achieves restoration in the eyes of engaged stakeholders under conditions of mediated dialogue. The unified theory of punishment offers us a compelling and comprehensive approach that best addresses the punishment of crimes from theft to murder and beyond.

Sentencing guidelines modelled on the Model Penal Code often require judges to consider multiple penal goals when determining punishments for offenders. A common problem has been that these guidelines have lacked a compelling framework of philosophical justification. This framework is offered by the unified theory of punishment. Multiple penal goals may be pursued in a single, coherent framework when understood in terms of the unified theory of punishment.

Tough on crime

Punitive restoration may secure public confidence. This approach to punishment judges its success in terms of effectiveness in achieving the restoration of rights. One indicator of success is the satisfaction of relevant stakeholders. If those with a stake in penal outcomes have confidence in these outcomes, then this is a compelling reason why the public at large should share their confidence. Punishment is not about tailoring punishment to satisfy the offender or the victim, but instead ensuring punishment enjoys broad support across stakeholders however possible.

A second indicator of success is effectiveness in promoting crime reduction. The fewer crimes performed, the more likely that fewer rights have been violated – although this is a crude and imprecise indicator.[1] The public may be more likely to support criminal justice policies that are more effective at crime reduction than alternatives even where they may harbour desires for more punitive measures. Crime reduction may also contribute to further goods that might yield public confidence, such as cost savings. The most effective way to cut spending on criminal justice is to effectively reduce the need for criminal justice measures. If crime may be reduced, then there may be fewer costs required for punishment. Good criminal justice policy may contribute to greater economic efficiency. A good policy often pays for itself.

Punitive restoration endorses imprisonment where it helps promote stakeholding. Prison may be used more often for less time in a 'cooling off' period. Punishment often confirms that offenders require immediate support.[2] Greater efforts should be undertaken to provide intensive interventions for offenders where possible. For example, studies have confirmed positive and encouraging results from trials of brief but intensive targeted interventions in prison that have contributed to 'significant' improvements.[3] These intensive targeted interventions may be more costly in the short term, but they may reduce the need for longer sentences. They may also prove cost effective by contributing to crime reduction.[4]

Where imprisonment is justified, it could be better managed. Offenders are too often transferred between prisons that may be located far from their local communities. These communities are also those places where they may have the best support networks. Often these networks are weak, ineffective, and sometimes counterproductive. It is important that offenders are located in or nearby their local communities to enjoy most benefit from what support is available. New prisons should be built with a view to addressing expected future needs of offenders.

Support networks may be crucial to assisting their reentry to society post-release. The more that may be done to foster and improve these networks, the better. One recommendation is that prisons seek to constructively engage with members of an offender's support network in the local community. This activity may help improve what support they might offer to offenders post-release. This support may have a recognizable stake in an offender's reformation, too. A second recommendation is greater use of parole officers within prisons as support officers. These persons know many prisoners best and they are an underutilized resource within the prison service. More may and should be done to foster support and promote well being where possible.

A third recommendation is that offenders should retain any voting rights held prior to conviction. The reason is that this limited political participation is symbolic and substantive in the promotion of stakeholding. It is symbolic because voting is a formal recognition that the offender is a member of the community; he has a say in its affairs even from within prison walls, and his vote symbolizes his inclusion as a stakeholder. Voting is substantive insofar as it may help contribute to an offender connecting with the belief that he has a stake in society and its future. Critics may reject this idea on the grounds that voting may not lead to any such positive result. However, it should be clear that denying voting rights is likely to contribute to the opposite effect in symbolically confirming his suspension from society and promoting the idea that society is an other to him that desires separation. Such possibilities run counter to the promotion of stakeholding and the restoration of rights. It should be rejected for these reasons and criminals should retain voting rights.

Tough on the causes of crime

The causes of crime are often presented in a long list of individual risk factors. These include unemployment, lack of adequate housing, drug and alcohol abuse, financial problems, and mental health problems often not diagnosed. These factors are often isolated in studies and correctly found linked to increased risk for future criminal activity. Such perspectives do well to capture the trees, but they often fail to see the wider forest.

These risk factors have one element in common. This is the belief that I may lack a stake in society and its future. This is a belief: perhaps the difference between why two people otherwise similarly situated choose differently on whether to engage in crime or reject crime rests on a belief about whether he or she has a stake in society. If someone does not share this belief, then he becomes more at risk of criminal offending. The person who is unemployed, suffers from drug and alcohol abuse, and lacks adequate housing may first come to believe that he lacks a stake in society: society is an other and his interests are not bound up with it. Society's rules pertain to others and do not govern him. This lack of a belief in stakeholding, in turn, is what contributes most centrally to the risk of future criminal offending. The person who believes she has a stake in society and its future will be much less likely to find criminal activities suitably attractive all things considered.[5]

The promotion of stakeholding is perhaps the best route to being 'tough on the causes of crime' and reoffending. Stakeholding is achieved by enabling offenders and potential future offenders to view themselves as having a stake in society. For example, a criminal record may be a barrier to securing employment. One recommendation is to consider policies where the reporting of criminal convictions is temporary. Some crimes, such as the most serious violent crimes, may not be subject to such an exemption. However, minor crimes might not need to be noted on employment applications after a set period, or after offenders have been certified as reformed and no longer dangerous. Work may prove an important positive 'turning point' in promoting a constructive sense of stakeholding.[6]

Much more research is required to learn more concerning beliefs about stakeholding and how it contributes to crime reduction and rights promotion. It is nevertheless clear that a society where each believed he or she had a stake in society is a society that rejects crime and lacks need for punishment. One way to promote the restoration of rights is to reduce the need for punishment in the first place.

Responsibility as accountability

Punishment is about responsibility as accountability. Criminal justice concerns our rights and responsibility. Crime threatens our rights which punishment aims to restore. The restoration of rights is best achieved where stakeholders accept responsibility for engaging with one another to agree how the restoration of rights is best secured. One fundamental element is that offenders must accept responsibility for their crimes. An offender's acknowledgement of guilt is a prerequisite for any restorative conference.

The offender's responsibility for violating rights necessitating restoration is cashed out in terms of his accountability: the responsibility for crime requires his accountability to stakeholders who agree the content this will take as punishment. This requires the responsibility of stakeholders to participate in constructive engagement to determine how restoration is best achieved. The process requires the accountability of the offender who must honour the contractual terms agreed by stakeholders in order to avoid more punitive sanctions. There is a commitment in terms of the political community's acknowledgement of the importance of punitive restoration for promoting the restoration of rights. This process must aim to inspire confidence in its results first from stakeholders and then from the wider public. Finally, there is also a need to secure satisfactory transparency. This includes better access to legal information; legal information that is easier for non-lawyers to suitably comprehend; and promotion of educational opportunities for the young.[7] The law must not only be publicly available, it must be transparently accessible.

Building the stakeholder society

Punishment requires a just framework. Punishment must not only restore rights and promote stakeholding, but it must operate within a world worth our having a stake in. One important tool to promote the belief that citizens have a stake in society is to ensure that the society is a place where they would want to have a stake.[8] These issues highlight a wider context. We have considered various theories of punishment in isolation and how they meet the challenges presented by specific case studies. Theories of punishment also operate within wider contexts of justice. The idea of the stakeholder society is an outline of one such view about justice. A compelling theory of punishment must not only be linked with a satisfactory view about crime, but ultimately be situated within a view about political and legal justice more broadly.

This book has attempted to present and explain the wide diversity of arguments and counterarguments that make the philosophy of punishment an engaging and vibrant field of study. It is my hope that this book will have opened new doors of understanding and shed light where there may have been darkness in a comprehensive discussion of the leading ideas and figures working in the field. Moreover, I particularly hope that the views presented in this book will further your interest in punishment and its justification.

Punishment is a topic that never lacks debate. Nothing seems more fitting given the importance of the issues at stake. If you care about justice, then you should care about punishment. This book is an attempt to explain why.

Notes

1 See Research Councils UK (RCUK), *Big Ideas for the Future: UK Research That Will Have a Profound Effect on Our Future* (2010): 83 (http://www.rcuk.ac.uk/ Publications/reports/Pages/BigIdeas.aspx).

Introduction

1 US Bureau of Justice Statistics, http://www.usdoj.gov/bjs/.
2 Joan Petersilia, *When Prisoners Come Home: Parole and Prisoner Reentry* (Oxford: Oxford University Press, 2003): 10.
3 See Steven N. Durlauf and Daniel S. Nagin, 'Imprisonment and Crime: Can Both Be Reduced?', *Criminology and Public Policy* 10 (2011): 13.
4 Michael Cavadino and James Dignan, *The Penal System: An Introduction,* 3rd ed. (Thousand Oaks: Sage, 2002): 9.
5 It is important to note briefly that I will regularly refer to 'we'. I will understand 'we' to be the general readership. See Thom Brooks, 'Punishment', *Oxford Bibliographies Online* (2011).
6 My list of four elements comprising the definition of 'punishment' is related to Herbert Hart's definition, although the two differ in several important respects. These differences will be noted in the following discussion. (See H. L. A. Hart, *Punishment and Responsibility: Essays in the Philosophy of Law* [Oxford: Oxford University Press, 1968]: 4–5).
7 This is one difference between the examples. I do not claim that there are no other significant differences.
8 It is important to note that not all crimes are 'acts': crimes may also constitute a failure to act within specific contexts, such as criminalized omissions.
9 For a recent example, see Leo Zaibert, *Punishment and Retribution* (Aldershot: Ashgate, 2006).
10 See Cesare Beccaria, *Of Crimes and Punishments* (Indianapolis: Hackett, 1986): 53: 'only the law determines the cases in which a man deserves punishment'.
11 I should note an important clarification. I will speak interchangeably of punishment's 'definition' and 'justification'. I will do this because punishment is unjustified where the definitional parts are not fully present. This is the case no matter which of the leading theories of punishment discussed in both Part 1 and Part 2 of this book we endorse. I take this general understanding of 'justification' to be minimal, and it should not be confused with a punishment's general justifying aim.
12 See Andrew Ashworth, *Sentencing and Criminal Justice,* 5th ed. (Cambridge: Cambridge University Press, 2010): 74–6; Corey Brettschneider, 'The Rights of

the Guilty: Punishment and Political Legitimacy', *Political Theory* 35 (2007): 175–99; and Jonathan Wolff, *Ethics and Public Policy: A Philosophical Inquiry* (Abingdon: Routledge, 2011): 126.

13 J. D. Mabbott, 'Freewill and Punishment' in H. D. Lewis (ed.), *Contemporary British Philosophy, 3rd series* (London: George Allen and Unwin, 1956): 299.

14 See Joel Feinberg, 'The Expressive Function of Punishment' in *Doing and Deserving: Essays in the Theory of Responsibility* (Princeton: Princeton University Press, 1970): 95–8.

15 On expressivist theories of punishment, see chapter 6.

16 I am not alone in making this argument. See David Boonin, *The Problem of Punishment* (Cambridge: Cambridge University Press, 2008): 118.

17 See Ronald Blackburn, *The Psychology of Criminal Conduct: Theory, Research, and Practice* (New York: Wiley, 1993): 14.

18 This approach takes seriously the view that a theory of punishment must address the crimes we want to punish, and a theory that cannot speak to these crimes is incomplete at best. Some readers may find this approach instantly attractive, but it is worth reflecting in future chapters how different theories of punishment are able to address the crimes we want to punish. This is *not* a matter of justifying existing practices unreflectively. If there are activities we believe should be criminalized, then a theory of punishment should speak to how we might best justify the punishment of these crimes. The justification of punishment then rests to some degree on the justification of criminal law. Those who argue that we should only punish those crimes that are consistent with their theory of punishment put the cart before the horse.

19 This definition of punishment is broad enough to capture most 'abolitionists'. These theorists argue against punishment by supporting various alternatives to imprisonment. These alternatives are addressed in chapters 3 and 4.

20 We have noted earlier the importance of the justification of law for the justification of punishment: it is difficult to see how we would be justified in punishing someone for an unjustified law. This raises important questions about authority and legality that I will bracket here. For rich discussion of these topics, see Leslie Green, *The Authority of the State* (Oxford: Oxford University Press, 1989); Joseph Raz, *The Authority of Law: Essays on Law and Morality* (Oxford: Clarendon, 1983); and Scott J. Shapiro, *Legality* (Cambridge, Mass.: Belknap/ Harvard University Press, 2011).

21 Plato says that '[i]njuring people is no different from wrongdoing', but this mistakes the view that all losses are equal in justification. It is the justification that merits punishment that makes it different from simply wrongdoing. Punishment need not be understood as an institution where two wrongs make a right. See Plato, 'Crito', in *Complete Works*, ed. John M. Cooper (Indianapolis: Hackett, 1997): 49d.

22 The loss associated with punishment may occasionally be permanent, such as with the death penalty or life imprisonment.

23 See Hart, *Punishment and Responsibility*, 4.

24 See R. A. Duff and Stuart P. Green, 'Introduction: The Special Part and Its Problems' in R. A. Duff and Stuart P. Green (eds) *Defining Crimes: Essays on the Special Part of the Criminal Law* (Oxford: Oxford University Press, 2005): 1–20. While legal moralism and the harm principle represent the main rival approaches, I do not wish to suggest that they represent the only important approaches to thinking about criminalization. Such a broader analysis would take considerably more space and would easily make a long book in itself.

25 See Ronald L. Gainer, 'Federal Criminal Code Reform: Past and Future', *Buffalo Criminal Law Review* 2 (1998): 66–7.

26 Legal moralism is strongly linked with the natural law tradition. On natural law, see Brian H. Bix, 'Natural Law: The Modern Tradition' in Jules Coleman, Scott Shapiro, and Kenneth Einar Himma (eds), *The Oxford Handbook of Jurisprudence and Philosophy of Law* (Oxford: Oxford University Press, 2002): 61–103.

27 R. A. Duff, 'Towards a Theory of Criminal Law?', *Proceedings of the Aristotelian Society: Supplementary Volume* LXXXIV (2010): 1–28 at 10. See also R. A. Duff, *Trials and Punishments* (Cambridge: Cambridge University Press, 1986): 94 ('My argument fits within the Natural Law tradition insofar as it posits a necessary connection between law and certain moral concepts, and between legal and moral obligation').

28 See Hart, *Punishment and Responsibility*, 171: 'it is sociologically very naïve to think that there is even in England a single homogeneous social morality whose mouthpiece the judge can be in fixing sentence, and in admitting one thing and rejecting another as a mitigating or aggravating factor. Our society, whether we like it or not, is morally a plural society'.

29 See Andrew Ashworth, 'Ignorance of the Criminal Law, and Duties to Avoid It', *Modern Law Review* 74 (2011): 4.

30 The fact that legal moralists *might* argue for this position is not to say that legal moralists *do* argue or even that legal moralists *should* argue for criminalizing abortion.

31 Douglas Husak, '*Malum Prohibitum* and Retribution' in R. A. Duff and Stuart P. Green (eds), *Defining Crimes*, 66n8.

32 For example, see Sally Cunningham, *Driving Offences: Law, Policy, and Practice* (Aldershot: Ashgate, 2008). See also Tom Vanderbilt, *Traffic* (London: Penguin, 2009).

33 Blackburn, *The Psychology of Criminal Conduct*, 39.

34 The US oil crisis gave rise to reduced speed limits on many highway networks. Nor is this an isolated example. See Graham Keeley, 'Brakes and an Oil Change as Nation Forced into Slow Lane', *The Times* (London) (8 March 2011): 29.

35 A. P. Simester, G. R. Sullivan, J. R. Spencer, and Graham Virgo, *Simester and Sullivan's Criminal Law: Theory and Doctrine, 4th ed.* (Oxford: Hart, 2010): 3.

36 Boonin, *The Problem of Punishment*, 116. He argues that punishment is not morally justified.

37 The claim is not that the process and product are *always* morally distinct and different, but that they *may* be distinct and different.

38 The *naturalist fallacy* understood here refers to the natural law tradition, or what we might call the *naturalist* tradition. This tradition is a wide camp with a variety of differences. However, a general shared position is that there is a necessary connection between law and morality. The fallacy is that this connection cannot be necessary where not all violations of law are immoral, as we have seen above. The naturalist fallacy is naturalist insofar as it is a problem of natural law theories, including the theories of most legal moralists. The fallacy is compatible with the separability thesis: that law and morality are separable. For example, Matthew H. Kramer, *In Defense of Legal Positivism: Law without Trimmings* (Oxford: Oxford University Press, 1999).

39 John Stuart Mill, *On Liberty*, ed. Elizabeth Rapaport (Indianapolis: Hackett, [1859] 1978): 9.

40 Larry Alexander and Kimberley Kessler Ferzan, *Crime and Culpability: A Theory of Criminal Law* (Cambridge: Cambridge University Press, 2009): 3.

41 The autonomy principle shares broad similarities with the republican view of freedom. See John Braithwaite and Philip Pettit, *Not Just Deserts: A Republican Theory of Criminal Justice* (Oxford: Clarendon, 1990): 69–71. See also Philip

Pettit, *A Theory of Freedom: From Psychology to the Politics of Agency* (Cambridge: Polity, 1990). On autonomy and punishment, see Alan Brudner, *Punishment and Freedom: A Liberal Theory of Penal Justice* (Oxford: Oxford University Press, 2009).

1 Retributivism

1 On retributivism, see Mark D. White (ed.), *Retributivism: Essays on Theory and Policy* (Oxford: Oxford University Press, 2011).
2 See Derek Parfit, *On What Matters*, vol. 2 (Oxford: Oxford University Press, 2011): 316.
3 I will discuss victim-centred theories of punishment in chapter 4.
4 Thus, vengeance is not even a theory of punishment (in addition to not being a form of retribution). While vengeance may be a response to a crime, it is a purely private means of addressing a public wrong independent of legal authority.
5 Michael S. Moore, 'Justifying Retribution', *Israel Law Review* 27 (1993): 15–49.
6 See Christopher Bennett, 'The Varieties of Retributive Experience', *Philosophical Quarterly* 52 (2002): 159, 161.
7 Immanuel Kant, *The Metaphysics of Morals*, ed. and trans. Mary Gregor (Cambridge: Cambridge University Press, 1996): 105 [6:332].
8 Igor Primoratz, *Justifying Legal Punishment* (Atlantic Highlands: Humanities Press, 1989): 108–10.
9 Chin Liew Ten notes that 'there is no complete agreement about what sorts of theories are retributive except that all such theories try to establish an essential link between punishment and moral wrongdoing'. See C. L. Ten, *Crime, Guilt, and Punishment* (Oxford: Clarendon, 1987): 38.
10 Kant, *The Metaphysics of Morals*, 106 [6:333].
11 We shall see that many of retributivism's difficulties relate to the failure of most retributivist theories to account for the naturalistic fallacy: we punish crimes as crimes and not all crimes are instances of immorality.
12 Alan Brudner calls these retributivist theories species of 'moral retributivism' to be distinguished from his 'legal retributivism'. I will discuss legal retributivism in chapter 7. See Thom Brooks, 'Punishment: Political, Not Moral', *New Criminal Law Review* 14 (2011): 427–38 and Brudner, *Punishment and Freedom*.
13 This issue was raised originally in this book's introduction. I expand the discussion here.
14 Suppose there is a motorist with a broken speedometer. He believes he is driving 75 mph, but is actually driving 55 mph. Larry Alexander argues that 'in the absence of a good reason for driving unsafely, he is reckless with respect to lives, bodies, and properties' despite the fact that he is actually driving at 'a safe speed'. I believe this is a mistake. Speed limits are not always set exclusively with a view to public safety. For example, many speed limits on federal highways were reduced to 55 mph in the early 1970s because this would have the effect of lower public consumption of oil during an oil shortage crisis. Moreover, the belief that I may cause real risk to others where, in fact, no genuine risk either threatened or even possible is present, may be worrying in other regards but it is not punishable. See Larry Alexander, 'Crime and Culpability', *Journal of Contemporary Legal Issues* (1994): 29.
15 See Brettschneider, 'The Rights of the Guilty', 176: 'In a retributive account of punishment … the state merely serves as a means to enforce the punishment required by natural law'.
16 For example, see Ashworth, 'Ignorance of the Criminal Law', 25: 'there are still people who find a nagging attraction in the *malum in se* concept.

[My] argument ... was that there are very few *mala in se*, because in a culturally diverse country there is a range of different views about right and wrong'.

17 See R. A. Duff, *Punishment, Communication, and Community* (Oxford: Oxford University Press, 2001): 65–6.

18 Immanuel Kant, *Critique of Pure Reason*, trans. N. K. Smith (London: Macmillan, 1963): 475n [A552/B580].

19 Aggravating and mitigating factors will differ by jurisdiction. The factors noted are common to many legal systems, but far from exhaustive. See Ashworth, *Sentencing and Criminal Justice*, 156–94.

20 See Bennett, 'The Varieties of Retributive Experience', 145–63.

21 There are other important issues relating to whether we can be responsible for who we are that are worth brief mention. See Galen Strawson, 'The Impossibility of Moral Responsibility', *Philosophical Studies* 75 (1994): 5–24.

22 There are also further questions concerning retributivism and ignorance of the law. For example, there is a potential difficulty accounting for persons who through no personal fault lack broadly shared moral sentiments. Is *moral* ignorance an important factor to consider? On ignorance of the law and punishment more generally, see Ashworth, 'Ignorance of the Criminal Law', 1–26.

23 See Jeffrie G. Murphy, 'Marxism and Retribution', *Philosophy and Public Affairs* 2 (1973): 217–43.

24 Hart, *Punishment and Responsibility*, 9.

25 Zaibert, *Punishment and Retribution*, 195.

26 Romans 2:5–6, 8, 12–15.

27 Kant, *The Metaphysics of Morals*, 106 [6:333].

28 See James Q. Wilson, 'A Plea against Retributivism', *Buffalo Criminal Law Review* 7 (2003): 85–107.

29 See Thom Brooks, 'Retributivist Arguments against Capital Punishment', *Journal of Social Philosophy* 35 (2004): 188–97 and Thom Brooks, 'Retribution and Capital Punishment' in Mark D. White (ed.), *Retributivism: Essays on Theory and Practice* (Oxford: Oxford University Press, 2011): 232–45.

30 See Douglas Husak, 'Why Punish the Deserving?', *Nous* 26 (1992): 447–64.

31 There is also the problem of false confessions: one study found that perhaps as many as 20 per cent of cases may be affected. See Dennis Campbell and Mark Townsend, 'Police Warned about Dangers of False Confessions', *The Observer* (9 October 2011): 14.

32 G. W. F. Hegel, *Elements of the Philosophy of Right*, ed. A. W. Wood, trans. H. B. Nisbet (Cambridge: Cambridge University Press, 1991): 128 [§101 Remark].

33 This phrase is from C. S. Peirce. See Charles Saunders Peirce, 'Vague' in J. M. Baldwin (ed.), *Dictionary of Philosophy and Psychology* (New York: Macmillan, 1902): 748. For more on vagueness as a philosophical problem, see Timothy Williamson, *Vagueness* (London: Routledge, 1994).

34 John Cottingham, 'Varieties of Retribution', *Philosophical Quarterly* 29 (1979): 238.

35 On Hegel's theory of punishment see Thom Brooks, 'Corlett on Kant, Hegel, and Retribution', *Punishment* 76 (2001): 562–80; Thom Brooks, 'Is Hegel a Retributivist?', *Bulletin of the Hegel Society of Great Britain* 49/50 (2004): 113–26; and Thom Brooks, *Hegel's Political Philosophy: A Systematic Reading of the Philosophy of Right* (Edinburgh: Edinburgh University Press, 2007): 39–51.

36 Hegel, *Elements of the Philosophy of Right*, 127 [§101].

37 Ibid. 124 [§99].

38 See Michael Davis, 'How to Make the Punishment Fit the Crime', *Ethics* 93 (1983): 736–42.

39 Jeffrey H. Reiman, 'Justice, Civilization, and the Death Penalty: Answering van den Haag', *Philosophy and Public Affairs* 14 (1985): 129.

40 Susan Easton and Christine Piper, *Sentencing and Punishment: The Quest for Justice* (Oxford: Oxford University Press, 2005): 49.

2 Deterrence

1 David Hume, *A Treatise of Human Nature,* 2nd ed., ed. L. A. Selby-Bigge (Oxford: Oxford University Press, 1978): 410.
2 See Mill, *On Liberty*, 10.
3 Plato, 'Gorgias', in *Complete Works*, 525b-c.
4 Ted Honderich, *Punishment: The Supposed Justifications* (Harmondsworth: Penguin, 1969): 59.
5 This important distinction could be further understood as a macro-level approach to deterrence (macrodeterrence) and a micro-level approach to deterrence (microdeterrence). I believe that our understanding of deterrence and deterrent strategies is aided when considering this subject through this distinction.
6 J. S. Mill, 'On Punishment' in *Collected Works of John Stuart Mill*, vol. 21, ed. John M. Robson (Toronto: University of Toronto Press, [1834] 1984): 78.
7 The classic exposition of the incapacitation theory of punishment is William Paley's *Principles of Penal Law* in 1771.
8 The objection includes the qualification of 'virtually' (as in 'virtually everyone') as there would be a need for some persons to administer prisons housing everyone else. Imprisoning everyone is impossible even in a hypothetical case, but this counterexample remains an important argument against incapacitation.
9 Punishment is not always incapacitation. This is because we understand punishment to take more potential forms than imprisonment, but include community sentences, fines, and other possibilities. This is a break from some academic discussions of 'punishment' that have understood 'punishment' as 'imprisonment', especially since Feinberg's distinction between fines and punishment as noted in chapter 1. However, our more inclusive understanding of punishment as a response to crime (and not only responses involving imprisonment) is much closer to how punishment is understood in debates over criminal justice policy by policymakers.
10 This fact about the geography of crime may further problematize the possibility of deterrence. We should not only look to reductions in crime rates amongst the public (e.g. the standard scenario), but also to effects within prison walls. If deterrence is about crime reduction and crime takes place in public and prison, then we must adopt a wider perspective of approaches to crime reduction than often held.
11 Hegel, *Elements of the Philosophy of Right*, §99 Addition.
12 Beccaria, *Of Crimes and Punishments*, 51. Similarly, Green argues that 'will, not force' explains just political obligation although he ultimately rejects deterrence theories. See T. H. Green, *Lectures on the Principles of Political Obligation* (London: Longmans, 1941): sect. 113–36.
13 Plato, 'Gorgias', in *Complete Works*, 472e.
14 J. G. Fichte, *Foundations of Natural Right*, ed. Frederick Neuhouser (Cambridge: Cambridge University Press, 2000): 232.
15 See Bentham, *An Introduction to the Principles of Morals and Legislation*, 93–4.
16 Beccaria, *Of Crimes and Punishments*, 46 (emphasis added).
17 We will examine negative retributivism in further detail in chapter 5.
18 The argument here summarizes Anthony Ellis, 'A Deterrence Theory of Punishment', *Philosophical Quarterly* 53 (2003): 338–51.
19 See Zachary Hoskins, 'Deterrent Punishment and Respect for Persons', *Ohio State Journal of Criminal Law* 8 (2011): 373–4.
20 Ellis, 'A Deterrence Theory of Punishment', 345.

21 See Hegel, *Elements of the Philosophy of Right*, preface.
22 See Anthony Doob and Cheryl Webster, 'Sentence Severity and Crime: Accepting the Null Hypothesis' in Michael Tonry (ed.), *Crime and Justice: A Review of Research*, vol. 30 (Chicago: University of Chicago Press, 2003): 143–95. Some have claimed there is a deterrence effect via incapacitation (or 'incapacitation effect') whereby crime rates have risen in specific cases closely following criminals leaving prison. However, they have not argued that the solution to this problem is to give all criminals life sentences to reduce crime; instead, the argument is that imprisoning most criminally minded persons will reduce crime rates. See Durlauf and Nagin, 'Imprisonment and Crime', 30 and Steven D. Levitt and Stephen J. Dubner, *Freakonomics: A Rogue Economist Explores the Hidden Side of Everything* (New York: Harper Perennial, 2009): 119–29.
23 See Ministry of Justice data at http://open.justice.gov.uk/home/.
24 Patrick A. Langan and David J. Levin, *Recidivism of Prisoners Released in 1994* (Washington, DC: Bureau of Justice Statistics, 2002): 2.
25 For example, see G. Matthew Snodgrass, Arjan A. J. Blokland, Amelia Haviland, Paul Nieubeerta, and Daniel S. Nagin, 'Does the Time Cause the Crime? An Examination of the Relationship between Time Served and Reoffending in the Netherlands', *Criminology* 49 (2011): 1149–94.
26 Patrick Carter, *Managing Offenders, Reducing Crime: A New Approach* (London: Prime Minister's Strategy Unit, 2003): 15.
27 Carter, *Managing Offenders, Reducing Crime*, 10. The situation is no less true in the United States. See ibid. 15 and Editorial, 'The Crime of Punishment', *New York Times* (6 December 2010): A26.
28 See Easton and Piper, *Sentencing and Punishment*, 113.
29 See Durlauf and Nagin, 'Imprisonment and Crime', 28.
30 See *Brown* v. *Plata*, 563 U.S. (2011).
31 See Durlauf and Nagin, 'Imprisonment and Crime', 14, 21–3 and Michael Tonry, 'Less Imprisonment is No Doubt a Good Thing: More Policing is Not', *Criminology & Public Policy* 10 (2011): 138, 140–1.
32 Tonry, 'Less Imprisonment is No Doubt a Good Thing', 143 (quoting Kenneth Clarke).
33 See Ministry of Justice, *2011 Compendium of Re-Offending Statistics and Analysis* (London: Her Majesty's Stationery Office, 2011): 3–4. Reoffending rates do not generally differ between men and women. See Ministry of Justice, *Adult Re-Convictions: Results from the 2009 Cohort (England and Wales)* (London: Her Majesty's Stationery Office, 2011): 14.
34 For example, Levitt and Dubner argue that the US murder rate fell largely as a result of the legalization of abortion: 'the pool of potential criminals had dramatically shrunk'. See Levitt and Dubner, *Freakonomics*, 4. For other factors, see David Lazar (ed.), *DNA and the Criminal Justice System: The Technology of Justice* (Cambridge: MIT Press, 2004) and Barry Sheck, Peter Neufeld, and Jim Dwyer, *Actual Innocence: When Justice Goes Wrong and How to Make It Right* (New York: American Library, 2003).
35 See Cassia C. Spohn, *How Do Judges Decide? The Search for Fairness and Justice in Punishment* (Thousand Oaks: Sage, 2002): 285.
36 Sarah Britto, '"Diffuse Anxiety": The Role of Economic Insecurity in Predicting Fear of Crime', *Journal of Crime and Justice* (2011) (DOI:10.1080/0735648X.2011.631399).
37 Levitt and Dubner, *Freakonomics*, 109.
38 See R. Liedka, A. Piehl, and B. Useem, 'The Crime-Control Effect of Incarceration: Does Scale Matter?', *Criminology and Public Policy* 5 (2006): 245–75 and T. Marvell and C. Moody, 'Prison Population and Crime Reduction', *Journal of Quantitative Criminology* 10 (1994): 109–39.

39 J. G. Fichte, *Foundations of Natural Right*, 228.
40 I am grateful to Brian O'Connor for suggesting this idea to me.
41 Richard L. Lippke, *Rethinking Imprisonment* (Oxford: Oxford University Press, 2007): 41.
42 James Q. Wilson, *Thinking About Crime,* 2nd ed. (New York: Vintage Books, 1985): 121.
43 See Ashworth, 'Ignorance of the Criminal Law', 1–26.
44 For example, see Mandeep K. Dhami and David R. Mandel, 'Crime as Risk Taking', *Psychology, Crime and Law* (2011): 1–15. Thaler and Sunstein argue that only 'Econs', a fictional understanding of people as *homo economicus* and not people like you or me, make such rational choice calculations. Behavioural models must rely upon new models for predicting policy effects. See Richard Thaler and Cass Sunstein, *Nudge: Improving Decisions about Health, Wealth, and Happiness* (London: Penguin, 2008).
45 See Thomas A. Loughran, Raymond Paternoster, Alex R. Piquero, and Greg Pogarsky, 'On Ambiguity in Perception of Risk: Implications for Criminal Decision Making and Deterrence', *Criminology* 49 (2011): 1029–61.
46 Davis, 'How to Make the Punishment Fit the Crime', 735.
47 There is also 'the fallacy of the warden's survey research': the warden observes the many undeterred criminals at his prison and concludes that deterrence does not work. This is a fallacy because the warden reaches this conclusion without any consideration of the possible supermajority outside his prison that were deterred. See Albert Dzur and Alan Wertheimer, 'Forgiveness and Public Deliberation: The Practice of Restorative Justice', *Criminal Justice Ethics* 21 (2002): 15. The problem is not that we cannot know how many people have been deterred, but only how crime rates have changed over time.
48 This is not surprising, in part, because there can be much confusion. Take capital punishment for murder in the United States. The crime of murder is not unitary, but differs: the crime of murder where the victim is a private citizen is separate from the crime of murder where the victim is the US President. Each is criminalized by different jurisdictions and may have different tariffs. For example, murder is normally part of state statutes. While most states have legalized capital punishment, a significant minority have not. Whether or not the murder of another private citizen may warrant the possibility of execution will differ from state to state. Furthermore, the crime of murder of the US President does not fall under any state law, but under federal law and federal law permits the possibility of execution. A person found guilty of the murder of the US President in a state that did not accept capital punishment for murder might still be executed for his crime in that state. This is because he would be guilty of a federal crime even though the act took place in an abolitionist state. This illustration highlights that even the punishment of murder is not straightforwardly clear given the complex relationship between state and federal laws in the United States.
49 The punishment for arson differs across states. For one example, see http://firemarshal.state.md.us/crimes.htm. The punishment of arson in the UK is found in the Criminal Damage Act (1971). I leave it to the reader to discover the sanction for arson in his or her jurisdiction. This exercise further underscores the difficulty of penal threats having any clear deterrent effect where knowledge about possible sanctions is confusing or difficult to obtain for even the most serious crimes.
50 See Alan Travis, 'Governors Urge Fast Release of 2,500 Prisoners', *The Guardian* (12 October 2010): 8.
51 Mill, *On Liberty*, 95.
52 See Hoskins, 'Deterrent Punishment and Respect for Persons', 374–5.

53 For example, see Martha C. Nussbaum, '"Whether from Reason or Prejudice": Taking Money for Bodily Services', *Journal of Legal Studies* 27 (1998): 693–724.

54 Theorists who argue that deterrence does not address people as moral agents cite a passage from Hegel as supporting evidence. Hegel says (of Paul Johann Anselm Ritter von Feuerbach's theory of deterrence) that '[t]o justify punishment in this way is like raising one's stick at a dog; it means treating a human being like a dog instead of respecting his honour and freedom'. While Hegel did reject deterrence as a primary ground of punishment, he does not oppose deterrence within a unified theory of punishment. See Hegel, *Elements of the Philosophy of Right*, §99 Addition and Thom Brooks, 'Hegel and the Unified Theory of Punishment' in *Hegel's Philosophy of Right* (Oxford: Blackwell, 2012): 103–23.

55 The claim that 'there can be no justified punishment for an unjustified law' does not run afoul of the naturalistic fallacy. This is because what is central is the establishment of justification rather than the establishment of (moral) justice.

56 Beccaria, *Of Crimes and Punishments*, 42.

57 Jeremy Bentham, *The Works of Jeremy Bentham,* vol. 1: *Principles of Penal Law* (New York: Russell & Russell, 1961): 398.

58 Beccaria, *Of Crimes and Punishments*, 74.

3 Rehabilitation

1 For one use of this phraseology, see Barbara Hudson, *Penal Policy and Social Justice* (London: Macmillan, 1993).

2 For example, about 95 per cent of all prisoners in the United States will eventually be released from prison. See Petersilia, *When Prisoners Come Home*, 3.

3 One important exception is Richard Lippke. He argues that retribution is about responsibility. Criminals are punished in relation to their punishable desert. Where imprisonment damages an offender's moral capacities, he becomes less able to accept full responsibility for any reoffending. A retributivist theory of punishment must take seriously some element of reform in sentencing to avoid important problems like this. See Lippke, *Rethinking Imprisonment.*

4 Barnum-Roberts argues that we can apologize without regret. This is, in part, because a reformed criminal might not regret his crime because his punishment led to his reform and personal improvement. I believe there is something missing here. While a reformed criminal may have benefitted through post-crime reform, surely this person would regret his responsibility for criminal activity nonetheless. Suppose the criminal is a murderer. Perhaps the murderer is better off now post-reform than he was at the time of the murder. He should still recognize that he should not have murdered anyone in the first place. After all, the avoidance of murder is not a supererogatory duty under normal conditions. Many of us would be uneasy about a murderer who lacked regret for his crime to some degree. See Brooke Natalie Barnum-Roberts, 'Apologizing Without Regret', *Ratio* 24 (2011): 17–27.

5 See Iain Crow, *The Treatment and Rehabilitation of Offenders* (London: Sage, 2001): 7–9.

6 See UK Drug Policy Commission, *Reducing Drug Use, Reducing Reoffending: Are Programmes for Problem Drug-Using Offenders in the UK Supported by the Evidence?* (London: UK Drug Policy Commission, 2008): 7.

7 See ibid. 11.

8 See N. Singleton, H. Melzer, and R. Gatward, *Psychiatric Morbidity among Prisoners in England and Wales* (London: Office for National Statistics, 1998).

9 See Sainsbury Centre, *Diversion: A Better Way for Criminal Justice* (London: Sainsbury Centre Mental Health, 2009).

10 See D. Pratt, M. Piper, L. Appleby, R. Webb, and J. Shaw, 'Suicide in Recently Released Prisoners: A Population-Based Cohort Study', *The Lancet* 368 (2006): 119–23.

11 Briege Nugent and Nancy Loucks, 'The Arts and Prisoners: Experiences of Creative Rehabilitation', *Howard Journal of Criminal Justice* 50 (2011): 367.

12 See J. Blacker, A. Watson, and A. R. Beech, 'A Combined Drama-Based and CBT Approach to Working with Self-Reported Anger Aggression', *Criminal Behaviour and Mental Health* 18 (2008): 129–37.

13 For example, see Gerry Johnstone, 'The Psychiatric Approach to Crime: A Sociological Analysis', *Economy and Society* 17 (1988): 317–73.

14 Bertrand Russell, *What I Believe* (London: Kegan Paul, 1925): 62.

15 See Kevin McGrath, 'Ready for the Real World of Work' in Sadiq Khan (ed.), *Punishment and Reform: How Our Justice System Can Help Cut Crime* (London: Fabian Society, 2011): 73.

16 Some jurisdictions permit employers to ask prospective job candidates whether they have been convicted of a past felony. This may assist the deterrent power of punishment: potential criminals may decide against criminal activity to avoid such an obstacle to finding new employment. However, it may be worth reflecting on permitting employers to ask prospective job candidates about any past convictions, but only for a specific period of time with an exception made for the most serious crimes. Or ensure that any spent convictions need not be reported to prospective employers for most crimes. The reason is that it is important that offenders have achievable future benefits from rehabilitation.

17 See Tess Lanning, Ian Loader, and Rick Muir, *Redesigning Justice: Reducing Crime Through Justice Reinvestment* (London: Institute for Public Policy Research, 2011): 11.

18 See Social Exclusion Unit, *Reducing Re-Offending by Ex-Prisoners* (London: Social Exclusion Unit, 2002).

19 See Petersilia, *When Prisoners Come Home*, 6.

20 Honderich, *Punishment*, 90.

21 Jean Hampton, 'The Moral Education Theory of Punishment', *Philosophy and Public Affairs* 13 (1984): 212.

22 Hampton, 'The Moral Education Theory of Punishment', 212, 222.

23 See ibid. 214, 218, 233.

24 See ibid. 217.

25 Ibid. 209.

26 Ibid. 212.

27 Ibid. 212.

28 Mabbott, 'Freewill and Punishment', 297.

29 See Hampton, 'The Moral Education Theory of Punishment', 213: 'it is incorrect to regard simple deterrence as the aim of punishment; rather, to state it succinctly, the view maintains that punishment is justified as a way to prevent wrongdoing insofar as it can teach both wrongdoers and the public at large the moral reasons for choosing not to perform an offense'.

30 Carter, *Managing Offenders, Reducing Crime*, 16. Some of the best results have been in Northern Ireland. Part of the reason for this is greater targeted resources. See S. McMulland and D. Ruddy, *Adult Reconviction in Northern Ireland 2001: Research and Statistical Bulletin 3/2005* (Belfast: Northern Ireland Office, 2005).

31 Yvette Hartfree, Chris Dearden, and Elspeth Pound, *High Hopes: Supporting Ex-Prisoners in Their Lives after Prison* (Department of Work and Pensions Research Report No. 509) (London: Her Majesty's Stationery Office, 2008): 87.

32 See Hartfree et al., *High Hopes*, 4, 50, 89.
33 See ibid. 8.
34 See Department of Communities and Local Government, 'Troubled Families' (http://www.communities.gov.uk/communities/troubledfamilies/).
35 Jean-Jacques Rousseau, *The Social Contract and Other Later Political Writings*, ed. Victor Gourevitch (Cambridge: Cambridge University Press, 1997): 65 [Book 2, chapter 5]. On Rousseau's legal philosophy, see Thom Brooks (ed.), *Rousseau and Law* (Aldershot: Ashgate, 2005).
36 See Crow, *The Treatment and Rehabilitation of Offenders*, 131.
37 John Dewey and James H. Tufts, *Ethics* (New York: H. Holt and Co., 1938): 470.
38 J. Chapman and J. Smith, *The Purple Book* (London: Biteback, 2011): 228.

4 Restorative justice

1 This book understands punishment as a response to crime. Our consideration does not extend to cases of international law where there are important overlaps, but potentially significant differences. Our consideration does not consider discussions of how restorative justice might be used *in conjunction* with another theory of punishment. For example, some have advocated the use of restorative conferences for rapists and their victims as a constructive dialogue that may bring benefits to each where appropriate, but *not* to reduce penal tariffs or offer an alternative theory about sentencing. On Truth and Reconciliation Commissions, see Paul Gready, *The Era of Transitional Justice: The Aftermath of the Truth and Reconciliation Commission of South Africa and Beyond* (Abingdon: Routledge, 2010). On restorative justice as post-punishment, see Susan Miller, *After the Crime: The Power of Restorative Justice: Dialogues between Victims and Violent Offenders* (New York: New York University Press, 2011).
2 See Adam Liptak, '1 in 100 U.S. Adults Behind Bars', *New York Times* (28 February 2008) (http://www.nytimes.com/2008/02/28/us/28cnd-prison.html) and UK Parliament, 'Should We Build More Prisons?' (http://www.parliament.uk/business/publications/research/key-issues-for-the-new-parliament/security-and-liberty/the-prison-population/).
3 See Thom Brooks (ed.), *The Right to a Fair Trial* (Aldershot: Ashgate, 2009).
4 See Meredith Rossner, 'Emotions and Interaction Ritual: A Micro Analysis of Restorative Justice', *British Journal of Criminology* 51 (2011): 96. See also Sadiq Khan, 'Avoiding a Life of Crime: How the Youth Justice System Can Work for Young People' (http://www.sadiqkhan.co.uk/index.php/speeches/1330-speech-avoiding-a-life-of-crime-how-the-youth-justice-system-can-work-for-young-people).
5 There are several different kinds of restorative conferences and each has a different composition. These conferences include victim–offender mediation, family group conferences, and community conferencing. While there are important differences among them, this chapter will focus on the standard case of a restorative conference that includes offenders, victims, and community representatives with support officers.
6 T. F. Marshall, *Restorative Justice: An Overview* (London: Home Office, 1999): 5.
7 The idea of the *stakeholder society* is simple and complex. It is born from the claim that we should aspire to a 'stakeholder economy', proposed by British Prime Minister Tony Blair: the idea is that the economy works best where we all share some stake in its performance. Likewise, the stakeholder society is the idea that society works best where all share some stake in the society. My use of the stakeholder society is based upon concepts such as recognitional debt and political reconciliation, which are distinct from the uses of this term by

Ackerman and Alstott. See Bruce Ackerman and Anne Alstott, *The Stakeholder Society* (New Haven: Yale University Press, 2000).

8 See Jakob von Holderstein Holtermann, 'Outlining the Shadow of the Axe: On Restorative Justice and the Use of Trial and Punishment', *Criminal Law and Philosophy* 3 (2009): 198.

9 For example, see Restorative Justice Council website, available at http://www.restorativejustice.org.uk/.

10 See John Braithwaite, *Restorative Justice and Responsible Regulation* (Oxford: Oxford University Press, 2002): 167.

11 For example, see John Braithwaite, 'Setting Standards for Restorative Justice', *British Journal of Criminology* 42 (2002): 569.

12 For example, imprisonment in the UK is estimated to cost about £39,600 per year per offender. The full cost of a typical restorative conference is estimated to cost as much as £1,200. Marshall estimates these costs as between £150 to £500. Either way, the savings difference is substantial. See Marshall, *Restorative Justice*, 19.

13 See Andrew Ashworth, 'Sentencing' in Mike Maguire, Rod Morgan, and Robert Reiner (eds), *The Oxford Handbook of Criminology* (Oxford: Oxford University Press, 1994): 822.

14 See Braithwaite, *Restorative Justice and Responsive Regulation*, 35.

15 I believe this criticism is compelling and I will argue in chapter 7 that a unified theory of punishment may offer us such an account.

16 Braithwaite, *Restorative Justice and Responsive Regulation*, 35.

17 I will discuss restorative justice as a theory of punishment (and not as an incomplete theory) to consider the approach in its best light, although I don't believe proponents will find my arguments controversial.

18 John Gardner, 'Crime: In Proportion and in Perspective' in Andrew Ashworth and Martin Wasik (eds), *Fundamentals of Sentencing Theory: Essays in Honour of Andrew von Hirsch* (Oxford: Clarendon, 1998): 31.

19 See Thom Brooks, 'The Right to Trial by Jury', *Journal of Applied Philosophy* 21 (2004): 197–212.

20 See Michael J. Sandel, 'Should Victims Have a Say in Sentencing?' in Michael J. Sandel, *Public Philosophy: Essays on Morality in Politics* (Cambridge, Mass.: Harvard University Press, 2005): 107.

21 Nils Christie, 'Conflicts as Property' in Andrew von Hirsch and Andrew Ashworth (eds), *Principled Sentencing: Readings on Theory and Policy* (Oxford: Hart, 1998): 314.

22 Home Office, *Justice for All* (London: Her Majesty's Stationery Office, 2002): para. 0.3.

23 This claim is distinct from a second view which I do not accept, namely, that deontological approaches are uninterested in public confidence. There is more than a subtle difference between claiming they may not be, and are not, interested. The latter view is implausible. There may be many reasons that retributivists may plausibly offer in favour of taking some stock of public confidence. One such possibility might be that a just legal system must not only promote justice, but be seen to promote justice. Some retributivists may be interested in issues of public confidence. However, it is possible that not all retributivists will take significant account of public confidence in some cases.

24 See Andrew Ashworth, 'Responsibilities, Rights and Restorative Justice', *British Journal of Criminology* 42 (2002): 582.

25 See Home Office, *Justice for All*, 92.

26 For example, unpaid work (or 'community pay back') in this context is between 40 to 300 hours in the United Kingdom. Drug and alcohol treatment is set between 6 and 36 months and requires the offender's consent.

27 See Hartfree et al., *High Hopes*, 2, 15–38.
28 In the United Kingdom, about half of offenders sentenced to a community order were subject to only one requirement; 35 per cent two requirements; 12 per cent three requirements; and 3 per cent four or more requirements. Unpaid work was the most widely used requirement.
29 See Peter Raynor and Maurice Vanstone, *Understanding Community Penalties: Probation, Policy, and Social Change* (Buckingham: Open University Press, 2002): 121.
30 See Chapman and Smith, 'Cutting Crime and Building Confidence', 226.
31 See Ashworth, *Sentencing and Criminal Justice*, 223.
32 See Raynor and Vanstone, *Understanding Community Penalties*, 52.
33 See Lanning et al., *Redesigning Justice*.
34 See the Howard League for Penal Reform, 'Community Sentences Cut Crime – Factsheet' (http://www.howardleague.org/fileadmin/howard_league/user/pdf/Community_sentences_factsheet.pdf).
35 See Thom Brooks (ed.), *Shame Punishment* (Aldershot: Ashgate, 2013).
36 See Dan M. Kahan and Eric A. Posner, 'Shaming White-Collar Criminals: A Proposal for Reform of the Federal Sentencing Guidelines', *Journal of Law and Economics* 42 (1999): 365–91.
37 See John Braithwaite, 'Criminological Theory and Organizational Crime', *Justice Quarterly* 6 (1989): 341.
38 Martha C. Nussbaum, *Hiding from Humanity: Disgust, Shame and the Law* (Princeton: Princeton University Press, 2004): 206–7.
39 See R. G. Collingwood, 'Punishment and Forgiveness' in *Essays in Political Philosophy*, ed. David Boucher (Oxford: Clarendon, 1989): 131: 'The pain of punishment is simply the pain of self-condemnation'.
40 See Nussbaum, *Hiding from Humanity*, 376n99.
41 Andrew von Hirsch, *Censure and Sanctions* (Oxford: Oxford University Press, 1994): 82.
42 See Nussbaum, *Hiding from Humanity*, 337.
43 *U.S.* v. *Koon,* 34 F.3d. 1416, 1454 (9th Cir. 1994). See Dan M. Kahan, 'What Do Alternative Sanctions Mean?', *University of Chicago Law Review* 63 (1996): 591–653.
44 See Thom Brooks, 'Shame on You, Shame on Me? Nussbaum on Shame Punishment', *Journal of Applied Philosophy* 25 (2008): 322–34.
45 See *U.S.* v. *Gementera,* 379 F.3d. 596, 604 (2004) and Brooks, 'Shame on You, Shame on Me?', 329–32. Readers unconvinced by the arguments for shame punishments may be interested to know that Gementera's shaming failed and he was soon arrested for stealing mail once more. He was imprisoned.
46 Braithwaite, *Restorative Justice and Responsive Regulation*, 74.
47 Ashworth, *Sentencing and Criminal Justice*, 94. See Braithwaite, 'Setting Standards for Restorative Justice', 563–77.
48 See Seyla Benhabib, *The Claims of Culture: Equality and Diversity in the Global Era* (Princeton: Princeton University Press, 2002).
49 Bhikhu Parekh, *A New Politics of Identity: Political Principles for an Interdependent World* (Basingstoke: Palgrave Macmillan, 2008): 1, see 21–6.
50 See Parekh, *A New Politics of Identity*, 24.
51 Ashworth, 'Responsibilities, Rights, and Restorative Justice', 583.
52 Ian Edwards, 'The Place of Victims' Preferences in the Sentencing of "Their" Offenders', *Criminal Law Review* (2002): 700.
53 See John Braithwaite, 'Principles of Restorative Justice' in Andrew von Hirsch, Julian Roberts, Anthony E. Bottoms, Kent Roach, and Mara Schiff (eds), *Restorative Justice and Criminal Justice: Competing or Reconcilable Paradigms?* (Oxford: Hart, 2003): 2.

54 See Tali Gal and Shomrom Moyal, 'Juvenile Victims in Restorative Justice', *British Journal of Criminology* 51 (2011): 1014–34. On juvenile offending, see chapter 9.

55 For example, see William Dawes, Paul Harvey, Brian McIntosh, Fay Nunney, and Annabelle Phillips, *Attitudes to Guilty Plea Sentence Reductions* (London: Sentencing Council, 2011).

56 See Robert D. Putnam, *Bowling Alone: The Collapse and Revival of American Community* (New York: Simon and Schuster, 2000).

57 See Thom Brooks, 'A Critique of Pragmatism and Deliberative Democracy', *Transactions of the Charles S. Peirce Society* 45 (2009): 50–4.

58 See Kathleen Daly, 'Mind the Gap: Restorative Justice in Theory and Practice' in Andrew von Hirsch, Julian Roberts, Anthony E. Bottoms, Kent Roach, and Mara Schiff (eds), *Restorative Justice and Criminal Justice*, 219–36.

59 For example, see Christopher Bennett, 'Taking the Sincerity Out of Saying Sorry: Restorative Justice as Ritual', *Journal of Applied Philosophy* 23 (2006): 127–43.

60 See Annalise Acorn, *Compulsory Compassion: A Critique of Restorative Justice* (Vancouver: University of British Columbia Press, 2004).

61 See von Hirsch, *Censure and Sanctions*, 83–4.

62 John Braithwaite, 'Thinking Harder About Democratising Social Control' in J. Alder and J. Wundersitz (eds), *Family Conferencing and Juvenile Justice: The Way Forward or Misplaced Optimism* (Canberra: Australian Institute of Criminology, 1994): 205.

63 See Braithwaite, *Restorative Justice and Responsive Regulation*, 155.

64 We will consider the idea of punitive restoration much further in chapter 7.

65 See Restorative Justice Council, 'Ministry of Justice Evaluation of Restorative Justice' (http://www.restorativejustice.org.uk/resource/ministry_of_justice_evaluation_of_restorative_justice/).

66 See Hartfree et al., *High Hopes*, 87.

67 UK Drug Policy Commission, *Reducing Drug Use, Reducing Reoffending*, 14.

68 See Albert W. Dzur and Susan M. Olson, 'The Value of Community Participation in Restorative Justice', *Journal of Social Philosophy* 35 (2004): 95.

69 Andrew Ashworth, 'Responsibilities, Rights and Restorative Justice', 582.

70 Braithwaite, *Restorative Justice and Responsive Regulation*, 46.

71 John Braithwaite, 'Principles of Restorative Justice' in von Hirsch et al., *Restorative Justice and Criminal Justice*, 4.

72 See Michael Benson, Leanne Fiftal Alarid, Velmer Burton, and Francis Cullen, 'Reintegration or Stigmatization? Offenders' Expectations of Community Re-entry', *Journal of Criminal Justice* 39 (2011): 385–93.

5 Rawls, Hart, and the mixed theory

1 See John Rawls, *A Theory of Justice* (Cambridge: Harvard University Press, 1971) and *A Theory of Justice*, rev. ed. (Oxford: Oxford University Press, 1999).

2 For further illustration, see George Sher, *Desert* (Princeton: Princeton University Press, 1987): 13.

3 Several outstanding commentaries on Rawls's political philosophy that offer little, if any, explicit commentary on his views on punishment include leading work such as Samuel Freeman, *Rawls* (Abingdon: Routledge, 2007); Sebastiano Maffettone, *Rawls: An Introduction* (Cambridge: Polity, 2010); and Paul Weithman, *Why Political Liberalism? On John Rawls's Political Turn* (Oxford: Oxford University Press, 2010).

4 See John Rawls, 'Two Concepts of Rules', *Philosophical Review* LXIV (1955): 3–32, reprinted in John Rawls, *Collected Papers*, ed. Samuel Freeman (Cambridge, Mass.: Harvard University Press, 1999): 20–46. References will be to the article. My discussion will be limited to this essay because I believe it offers a major contribution to the subject and it is perhaps the only place where Rawls explicitly addresses punishment.

5 See Rawls, 'Two Concepts of Rules', 3.

6 See ibid. 5.

7 Ibid. 4.

8 Ibid. 5.

9 Ibid. 5–6.

10 My argument is that Rawls offers a novel understanding of how to construct a mixed theory of punishment; I am not arguing that Rawls is the first to offer a mixed theory. There are earlier such accounts found in perhaps surprising places. For example, John Locke argues that punishment should be distributed only to the deserving, but may aim at the repentance of offenders or the deterrence of others. See John Locke, *The Second Treatise* in *Two Treatises of Government*, ed. Peter Laslett (Cambridge: Cambridge University Press, 1988): 272 [Book II, chap. 1, sect. 8, lines 15–25].

11 Rawls, 'Two Concepts of Rules', 7.

12 See ibid. 7.

13 See ibid. 7–8. Rawls calls the punishment of the innocent 'telishment'. See ibid. 11.

14 Michael Sandel argues that Rawls's views on punishment may create new problems for his theory of justice. See Michael J. Sandel, *Liberalism and the Limits of Justice*, 2nd ed. (Cambridge: Cambridge University Press, 1998): 89–90.

15 My criticism is influenced by the work of Rick Lippke on this subject. See Richard L. Lippke, 'Mixed Theories of Punishment and Mixed Offenders: Some Unresolved Tensions', in *Southern Journal of Philosophy* XLIV (2006): 273–95. See also Lloyd L. Weinrib, 'Desert, Punishment, and Criminal Responsibility', *Law and Contemporary Society* 49 (1986): 47–80.

16 See Hart, *Punishment and Responsibility*. For a highly illuminating explanation and analysis of Hart's views on punishment, see John Gardner, introduction to H. L. A. Hart, *Punishment and Responsibility: Essays in the Philosophy of Law*, 2nd ed. (Oxford: Oxford University Press, 2008): xiii–liii.

17 See Hart, *Punishment and Responsibility*, 1.

18 Ibid. 2.

19 See ibid. 3.

20 Ibid. 72.

21 Ibid. 3.

22 See ibid. 5.

23 Ibid. 12.

24 See ibid. 39.

25 See ibid. 231–2.

26 See ibid. 233–6.

27 Ibid. 235–6.

28 See ibid. 236.

29 Husak, 'Why Punish the Deserving?', 453.

30 Duff, *Punishment, Communication, and Community*, 19–20. See Mark A. Michael, 'Utilitarianism and Retributivism: What's the Difference?', *American Philosophical Quarterly* 29 (1992): 173–82.

31 On rule consequentialism, see Brad Hooker, *Ideal Code, Real World* (Oxford: Oxford University Press, 2000).

32 I doubt these criticisms may convince all negative retributivists. This is not because I lack confidence in the strength of these arguments, but rather because a flexible mixed view has something perhaps inexplicably and intuitively attractive about it. We often want to have our cake and eat it, too. The problem is that this panacea, our penal utopia, may lie out of reach. There are other ways to conceive hybrid theories of punishment that we will consider in the following chapters. I believe that the unified theory of punishment may better address the intuitive 'compellingness' of mixed theories without falling into their theoretical traps. The unified theory is considered below.

6 Expressivism

1 Zaibert, *Punishment and Retribution*, 45.
2 Cited in Stephen Shute, 'The Place of Public Opinion in Sentencing Law', *Criminal Law Review* (1998): 465.
3 M. Cavadino and J. Dignan, *The Penal System: An Introduction*, 3rd ed. (Thousand Oaks: Sage): 43.
4 James Fitzjames Stephen, *A History of the Criminal Law of England* (London: Macmillan, 1883): 81–2.
5 For example, see Feinberg, *Doing and Deserving*, 95–118.
6 Igor Primoratz, 'Punishment as Language', *Philosophy* 64 (1989): 187. See Feinberg, *Doing and Deserving*, 98: 'Punishment, in short, has a symbolic significance largely missing from other kinds of penalties'.
7 Feinberg, *Doing and Deserving*, 96.
8 See Lippke, *Rethinking Imprisonment*, 1.
9 Feinberg, *Doing and Deserving*, 102.
10 Note that this claim is consistent with what we have said in the general introduction: punishment is a response to crime. Governments may express disapproval officially and unofficially. Our focus is squarely on how best to understand punishment as a response to crime, not state coercion concerning very different circumstances.
11 I owe this example to Richard Mullender.
12 This is an illustrative example. I do not suggest here or elsewhere that all crime is reducible to acts. Crimes may take many other forms, including criminal omissions.
13 Feinberg, *Doing and Deserving*, 118.
14 The dialogue between the public and offender is not limited to punishment, but extends to the trial. The trial is understood as a form of passion play where the prosecution and defence are engaged in an expressive communication with each other. Not only must punishment communicate public denunciation to the offender, but this message is expressed during the course of his trial, too.
15 Duff, *Punishment, Communication, and Community*, 80. See John Tasioulas, 'Punishment and Repentance', *Philosophy* 81 (2006): 279–322.
16 Duff, *Punishment, Communication, and Community*, 87, see 122–3, 133.
17 R. A. Duff, 'Alternatives to Punishment – or Alternative Punishments?' in W. Cragg (ed.), *Retributivism and Its Critics* (Stuttgart: Franz Steiner Verlag, 1992): 49. Cited in Nathan Hanna, 'The Passions of Punishment', *Pacific Philosophical Quarterly* 90 (2009): 237. See Duff, *Trials and Punishments*, 196: 'punishment must make her suffer'. This view is shared by Feinberg. See Feinberg, *Doing and Deserving*, 67: 'It is an essential and intended element of punishment ... that the victim be made to suffer and of liability that he be made to pay: these things are not mere regrettable derivatives of the undertakings, but rather their [goals]'.
18 Duff, *Punishment, Communication, and Community*, 108.

19 See ibid. 119.
20 See Duff, *Trials and Punishments*, 246; Duff, 'Restoration and Retribution', in Andrew von Hirsch, Julian Roberts, Anthony E. Bottoms, Kent Roach, and Mara Schiff (eds), *Restorative Justice and Criminal Justice*, 53; and Duff, *Punishment, Communication, and Community*, xix, 30, 106, 121, 134.
21 Duff, *Punishment, Communication, and Community*, 95.
22 R. A. Duff, 'In Defence of One Type of Retribution: A Reply to Bagaric and Amarasekara', *Melbourne University Law Review* 24 (2000): 420. See Duff, *Trials and Punishments*, 145 ('It is of course no part of my task to justify our actual practices'); Duff, *Punishment, Communication, and Community*, 107, 201; and R. A. Duff, 'Restoration and Retribution' 55.
23 See Duff, 'Crime, Prohibition, and Punishment', *Journal of Applied Philosophy* 19 (2002): 101.
24 See Duff, *Punishment, Communication, and Community*, 90 and Jeffrie G. Murphy, *Getting Even: Forgiveness and Its Limits* (Oxford: Oxford University Press, 2003): 48.
25 See Duff, *Punishment, Communication, and Community*, 108.
26 See von Hirsch, *Censure and Sanctions*.
27 See Alan Strudler, 'The Power of Expressive Theories of Law', *Maryland Law Review* 60 (2001): 494.
28 I am grateful to Les Green for pushing me on this point.
29 See W. E. W. St G. Charlton, 'Rules and Punishments', *Think* (1966): 3. I am very grateful to Willie Charlton and Mary Midgley for pressing this argument.
30 John Gardner suggested this argument to me.
31 Feinberg, *Doing and Deserving*, 100.
32 For example, see Yung-Lien Lai, Jihong Solomon Zhao, and Dennis R. Longmire, 'Specific Crime–Fear Linkage: The Effect of Actual Burglary Incidents Reported to the Police on Residents' Fear of Burglary', *Journal of Crime and Justice* (2011) (DOI: http://dx/doi.org/10.1080/0735648X.2011.631408).
33 See Nussbaum, *Hiding from Humanity*, 14.
34 See ibid. 83.
35 See ibid. 73.
36 See Duff, *Punishment, Communication, and Community*, 121.
37 Hart, *Punishment and Responsibility*, 171.
38 See Charles W. Collier, 'Speech and Communication in Law and Philosophy', *Legal Theory* 12 (2006): 8–9. See also Matt Matravers, '"Who's Still Standing?" A Comment on Antony Duff's Preconditions of Criminal Liability', *Journal of Moral Philosophy* 3 (2006): 320–30.
39 For an illustration of how messages may fail to convey their intended meanings in the area of political campaigning, see Frank Luntz, *Words That Work: It's Not What You Say, It's What People Hear* (New York: HarperCollins, 2007).
40 Duff, *Punishment, Communication, and Community*, 47.
41 Duff, 'Answering for Crime', *Proceedings of the Aristotelian Society* CVI (2006): 98.
42 For example, see Kate Warner and Julia Davis, 'Using Jurors to Explore Public Attitudes to Sentencing', *British Journal of Criminology* 52 (2012): 93–112. See also Monica Williams, 'Beyond the Retributive Public: Governance and Public Opinion on Penal Policy', *Journal of Crime and Justice* 35 (2012): 93–113.
43 There is some reason to believe that greater public education about criminal justice will support greater public confidence in the system overall although more research is required. See Barry Mitchell and Julian V. Roberts, 'Sentencing for Murder: Exploring Public Knowledge and Public Opinion in England and Wales', *British Journal of Criminology* 52 (2012): 141–58.

44 For example, see Bennett, 'State Denunciation of Crime', *Journal of Moral Philosophy* 3 (2006): 288–304 and Tasioulas, 'Punishment and Repentance', 279–322.
45 Duff, *Trials and Punishments*, 94, see 54, 57, 76.
46 R. A. Duff, *Intention, Agency and Criminal Liability: Philosophy of Action and the Criminal Law* (Oxford: Basil Blackwell, 1990): 10.
47 Duff, *Trials and Punishments*, 76.
48 Duff, ibid. 94.
49 See Primoratz, 'Punishment as Language', 197: 'Criminal laws are similar to moral rules in that they also state standards of behaviour'.
50 Cited in R. A. Duff, *Answering for Crime: Responsibility and Liability in the Criminal Law* (Oxford: Hart, 2007): 89.
51 See Duff, *Punishment, Communication, and Community*, 58.
52 See ibid. 64: 'the law does not create these wrongs as wrongs'.
53 R. A. Duff, 'Answering for Crime', 90.
54 Ibid. 91. See ibid. 81; and R. A. Duff and Stuart P. Green, introduction to *Defining Crimes*, 9.
55 Duff, *Punishment, Communication, and Community*, 67.
56 See ibid. 87–8.
57 R. A. Duff, 'Crime, Prohibition, and Punishment', 100.
58 H. L. A. Hart, *Law, Liberty, and Morality* (Oxford: Oxford University Press, 1963): 1.
59 Feinberg, *Doing and Deserving*, 100.
60 See Christopher Bennett, 'State Denunciation of Crime', 288–304.
61 Duff, *Punishment, Communication, and Community*, 58.
62 H. L. A. Hart, *The Morality of the Criminal Law: Two Lectures* (London: Oxford University Press, 1965): 39.
63 John Rawls, *Political Liberalism* (New York: Columbia University Press, 1996): xviii.
64 Ibid. 10.
65 Shute, 'The Place of Public Opinion in Sentencing Law', 471.
66 Douglas Husak, 'Is the Criminal Law Important?', *Ohio State Journal of Criminal Law* 1 (2003): 267.
67 Ibid. 267. Nor is the example of traffic laws irrelevant. Some argue that 'the typical criminal of today is the motorist'. See Blackburn, *The Psychology of Criminal Conduct*, 39.
68 An important qualification may be helpful on this point. I am not arguing that there is over-criminalization – how many criminal laws are too many? – but rather that the criminal law has grown too large to be known by anyone, or at least by most.
69 See Duff, *Punishment, Communication, and Community*, 29.
70 See Duff, *Trials and Punishments*, 5: 'But I do not have a complete theory of punishment – a coherent explanation and justification of all the significant features of an actual or ideal penal system – to offer in their place; and I suspect that none may be possible'. See also Duff, *Punishment, Communication, and Community*, 82: 'a communicative conception of punishment thus provides [hard treatment punishments'] complete justification'.
71 See Duff, *Trials and Punishments*, 260.
72 See Christopher Bennett, 'The Varieties of Retributive Experience', 145–63; Richard L. Lippke, 'Imprisonable Offenses', *Journal of Moral Philosophy* 3 (2006): 268; and Lippke, *Rethinking Imprisonment*, 21 ('communicative versions of retributivism').
73 See Chad Flanders, 'Retribution and Reform', *Maryland Law Review* 70 (2010): 87. See Russell Christopher, 'Deterring Retributivism: The Injustice of "Just" Punishment', *Northwestern University Law Review* 96 (2002): 845; Michelle

Cotton, 'Back with a Vengeance: The Resilience of Retribution as an Articulated Purpose of Criminal Punishment', *American Criminal Law Review* 37 (2000): 1314; David Dolinko, 'Three Mistakes of Retributivism', *UCLA Law Review* 39 (1992): 1623; Mark Tebbit, *Philosophy of Law: An Introduction,* 2nd ed. (Abingdon: Routledge, 2005): 205; and James Q. Wilson, *Harsh Justice: Criminal Punishment and the Widening Divide Between America and Europe* (Oxford: Oxford University Press, 2003): 23–4.

74 See Duff, 'Crime, Prohibition, and Punishment', 106.

75 See Andrew von Hirsch, *Past or Future Crimes: Deservedness and Dangerousness in the Sentencing of Criminals* (Manchester: Manchester University Press, 1985): 10.

76 See Duff, *Punishment, Communication, and Community,* 25, 30.

77 Duff, *Trials and Punishments,* 70.

78 See Duff, *Punishment, Communication, and Community,* 30.

79 Feinberg, *Doing and Deserving,* 103.

80 See Duff, *Punishment, Communication, and Community,* 80.

81 See Rupert Cross and Andrew Ashworth, *The English Sentencing System,* 3rd ed. (London: Butterworth, 1981): 145.

82 Duff, *Punishment, Communication, and Community,* 115–16.

83 Duff, 'In Defence of One Type of Retributivism', 420. See Duff, *Punishment, Communication, and Community,* xvii, 30.

84 Cited in Primoratz, 'Punishment as Language', 191. See A. C. Ewing, *The Morality of Punishment* (London: Kegan Paul, Trench, Trubner and Co., 1929).

85 Bernard Williams, 'Moral Responsibility and Political Freedom', *Cambridge Law Journal* 56 (1997): 100.

86 Cottingham, 'Varieties of Retribution', 245.

87 Hart, *Law, Liberty, and Morality,* 66. See Hanna, 'The Passions of Punishment', 241.

88 Collingwood, *Essays in Political Philosophy,* 131.

89 Michael Tonry, 'Obsolescence and Immanence in Penal Theory and Policy' *Columbia Law Review* 105 (2005): 1266.

90 This might be counterproductive because punishment is an instrument to convey public disapproval to bring about repentance. If repentance were achieved and imprisonment continued, then the message expressed might become muddled and repentance thwarted.

91 Tonry, 'Obsolescence and Immanence in Penal Theory and Policy', 1266.

92 Duff, *Punishment, Communication, and Community,* 123–4 (emphasis added).

93 Ibid. 155.

94 Cavadino and Dignan, *The Penal System,* 43. See Nigel Walker and C. Marsh, 'Do Sentences Affect Public Disapproval?', *British Journal of Criminology* 24 (1984): 27–48.

95 See Sian Moley, 'Public Perceptions' in Chris Kershaw, Sian Nicholas, and Alison Walker (eds), *Home Office Statistical Bulletin: Crime in England and Wales 2007/ 08* (London: Her Majesty's Stationery Office, 2008): 119.

96 See ibid. 128.

97 See ibid. 130.

98 Hart, *Punishment and Responsibility,* 172.

7 Unified theory

1 My thanks to Fabian Freyenhagen for first recommending to me that this view of punishment is perhaps best understood as a 'unified' theory of punishment.

2 See the American Law Institute, *Model Penal Code* (Philadelphia: American Law Institute, 1962). See also the Sentencing Council, 'Guidelines to Download', http://sentencingcouncil.judiciary.gov.uk/guidelines/guidelines-to-download.htm.

3 See American Law Institute, *Model Penal Code: Sentencing* § 1.02(2) (T.D. No. 1, 2007) (comment on 2a-b).

4 See Paul H. Robinson, *Distributive Principles of Criminal Law: Who Should Be Punished How Much?* (Oxford: Oxford University Press, 2008): 3–4.

5 The Sentencing Reform Act of 1984, 18 U.S.C. 3553 (a).

6 Few philosophers of punishment appear to appreciate how very different their positions are from how sentencing is determined in courtrooms. Perhaps radical reforms are necessary requiring substantive revisions of current practice. But there is relatively little, if any, recognition of the implications arising from their specific theories of punishment on the criminal law.

7 For example, see Robinson, *Distributive Principles of Criminal Law*, 1. See also ibid. chap. 11.

8 See ibid. 5.

9 There is perhaps little doubt that the Model Penal Code's justificatory framework is under-theorized and this has attracted deserved criticism. For example, its professed illustrations begin from the obvious point that sentencing can never say that any offender should receive 'precisely' a specific punishment, but move towards the view that sanctions are permissible where 'not undeserved'. Essentially, the Code offers multiple goals that should be considered when judges are determining proportionality within existing sentencing guidelines. Moreover, the Code does not presume its stated goals are 'applicable, or appropriate to pursue, in every individual case' without clear specific guidance on how we might make such judgements.

10 David Garland, *Punishment and Modern Society: A Study in Social Theory* (Oxford: Clarendon, 1990): 9.

11 See Samuel Johnson, 'Robert Chambers's Vinerian Lectures on the English Law' [1767], *The Major Works* (Harmondsworth: Penguin, 1984): 570–9 (punishment has a threefold end: to benefit the offender, the suffering party, and the general public).

12 G. W. F. Hegel, *Science of Logic*, trans. A. V. Miller (Amherst: Humanity Books, 1969): 465. On Hegel's theory of punishment, see Brooks, 'Is Hegel a Retributivist?', Brooks, *Hegel's Political Philosophy*, 39–51; and Brooks, 'Hegel and the Unified Theory of Punishment', 103–23.

13 See Hegel, *Science of Logic*, 465.

14 British Idealism flourished in the late nineteenth century and waned with the beginning of the First World War. British Idealists first popularized the work of Kant and Hegel for an Anglo-American audience. Idealists also attempted to offer new contributions that built on compelling insights uncovered in Kantian and Hegelian philosophies. On British Idealism more generally, see David Boucher (ed.), *The British Idealists* (Cambridge: Cambridge University Press, 1997); Thom Brooks, 'British Idealism', *Oxford Bibliographies Online* (2011); and W. J. Mander, *British Idealism: A History* (Oxford: Oxford University Press, 2011). On British Idealism and the unified theory of punishment, see Thom Brooks, 'T. H. Green's Theory of Punishment', *History of Political Thought* 24 (2003): 685–701; Thom Brooks, 'Punishment and British Idealism', in Jesper Ryberg and J. Angelo Corlett (eds), *Punishment and Ethics: New Perspectives* (Basingstoke: Palgrave Macmillan, 2010): 16–32; Thom Brooks, 'Is Bradley a Retributivist?', *History of Political Thought* 32 (2011): 83–95; and Thom Brooks, 'What Did the British Idealists Do for Us?' in Brooks (ed.), *New Waves in Ethics* (Basingstoke: Palgrave Macmillan, 2011): 28–47.

15 Green, *Lectures on the Principles of Political Obligation*, §178.

16 See James Seth, *A Study of Ethical Principles*, 3rd ed. (Edinburgh: William Blackwood and Sons, 1898): 312. Probably no other philosopher or work has

had a more profound effect on my thinking about the philosophy of punishment than this.

17 While there are many significant differences between individual British Idealists, many leading figures accepted a common position and it is this view that I offer. My main aim here is not to provide a scholarly analysis of British Idealists on legal philosophy, but instead to indicate how many of their leading figures contribute to a distinctive theory, the unified theory of punishment, and why this theory is worthy of our attention and further study. See Thom Brooks, 'Rethinking Punishment', *International Journal of Jurisprudence and Philosophy of Law* 1 (2007): 27–34.

18 The use of 'just' found here is shorthand for 'justified' (and not 'morally just'). The unified theory of punishment is not consistent with most versions of natural law nor legal moralism.

19 See Hume, *A Treatise of Human Nature*, 337 [3.2.6]: 'Society is absolutely necessary for the well-being of men; and [laws] are as necessary to the support of society'. See also Beccaria, *Of Crimes and Punishments*, 8.

20 See Johnson, *The Major Works*, 570: 'The first purpose of every political society is *internal peace*'.

21 My understanding of rights is broadly consistent with some versions of the capabilities approach, but note that the view of freedom used here may be consistent with several different theories of freedom. See Thom Brooks (ed.), *Justice and the Capabilities Approach* (Aldershot: Ashgate, 2012); Thom Brooks, 'Capabilities' in Hugh LaFollette (ed.), *International Encyclopedia of Ethics* (Oxford: Blackwell, 2012); Martha C. Nussbaum, *Women and Human Development: The Capabilities Approach* (Cambridge: Cambridge University Press, 2000); and Martha C. Nussbaum, *Creating Capabilities: The Human Development Approach* (Cambridge: Harvard University Press, 2011). This view of rights is also consistent with the view that dignity is the basis of rights. See Jeremy Waldron, 'How Law Protects Dignity', *Cambridge Law Journal* 71 (2012): 200–22, esp. 217–19. On rights more generally, see Wesley N. Hohfeld, *Fundamental Legal Conceptions* (New Haven: Yale University Press, 1964) and Leif Wenar, 'The Nature of Rights', *Philosophy and Public Affairs* 33 (2005): 223–53.

22 Rawls, *Political Liberalism*, 137.

23 For example, see Martha C. Nussbaum, *Liberty of Conscience: In Defense of America's Tradition of Religious Equality* (New York: Basic Books, 2008).

24 This has been a central idea in the legal philosophy of Ronald Dworkin. For example, see Ronald Dworkin, *Law's Empire* (Oxford: Hart, 1998).

25 James Seth, *Essays in Ethics and Religion with Other Papers*, ed. Andrew Seth Pringle-Pattison (Edinburgh: William Blackwood and Sons, 1926): 179.

26 My understanding of crime here includes the idea that crimes are criminal insofar as they violate or threaten to violate rights as substantial freedoms. Crimes may violate rights, but may also pose a threat to violate rights. See Hegel, *Elements of the Philosophy of Right*, §95: 'to infringe the existence of freedom in its concrete sense – i.e., to infringe right as right – is *crime*'.

27 Beccaria argues that the 'only true measurement of crimes is the harm done to the nation'. The unified theory of punishment rejects the idea that harm to the nation per se may demand punishment. Instead, we punish crimes as threats to violate our rights. See Beccaria, *Of Crimes and Punishments*, 16.

28 This view is presented forcefully by Seth, 'Individual and Social Ethics' in *Essays in Ethics and Religion*, 172. See also W. D. Ross, *The Right and the Good* (Oxford: Clarendon, 1930): 60.

29 See John D. Mabbott, 'Punishment', *Mind* 48 (1939): 152–67.

30 Mill, *On Liberty*, 77, see 93.

31 Mill, 'On Punishment', 79.

32 See Thom Brooks, 'Was Green a Utilitarian in Practice?' *Collingwood and British Idealism Studies* 14 (2008): 5–15.

33 Seth, *Essays in Ethics and Religion*, 179.

34 Green, *Lectures on the Principles of Political Obligation*, §§189, 204. See W. H. Fairbrother, *The Philosophy of Thomas Hill Green* (London: Methuen and Co., 1896): 151–2.

35 Green, *Lectures on the Principles of Political Obligations*, §177.

36 Ibid. §197.

37 For this distinction, see Brudner, *Punishment and Freedom*, 16.

38 Green, *Lectures on the Principles of Political Obligation*, §197.

39 Seth, *A Study of Ethical Principles*, 305. See H. J. W. Hetherington and J. H. Muirhead (eds), *Social Purpose: A Contribution to a Philosophy of Civic Society* (London: George Allen and Unwin, 1918): 129.

40 Seth, *Essays in Ethics and Religion*, 179.

41 See Seth, *Freedom as Ethical Postulate* (Edinburgh: William Blackwood and Sons, 1891): 337.

42 This distinction shares some similarities with Brudner's distinction between 'legal retributivism' and 'moral retributivism'. See Brudner, *Punishment and Freedom*. See also Thom Brooks, 'Punishment: Political, Not Moral', *New Criminal Law Review* 14 (2011): 427–38.

43 This understanding of restorative justice views restoration as a process that is post-sentencing and not a part of sentencing. Restorative justice is something we engage in after a punishment has been determined in light of some alternative theory of punishment. This view of restorative justice is not of restorative justice *as a theory of punishment*. My argument above is that restorative justice as a theory of punishment fails to acknowledge that our choice need not be either restoration or imprisonment. However, I would also argue that restorative justice understood as not a theory of punishment in the second sense is illuminating, but also too restrictive. Restorative justice can and should be a more ambitious theory of punishment than often argued. The unified theory is one attempt to show how a greater ambition as a view to punitive restoration is possible and compelling.

44 See James Seth, *Freedom as Ethical Postulate*, 336. Seth understands this as the 'private re-enactment of the social judgement' whereby 'the judgement of society upon the man must become the judgement of the man upon himself'.

45 See Seth, *A Study of Ethical Principles*, 314: 'The judgment of society upon the man must become the judgment of the man upon himself, if it is to be effective as an agent in his reformation'.

46 See Hegel, *Elements of the Philosophy of Right*, § Remark: Punishment is 'the restoration of right'.

47 The British Idealist Bernard Bosanquet, who was from the Newcastle upon Tyne area, argues similarly that 'deterrence and reformation are subordinate aspects'. Bernard Bosanquet, *Some Suggestions in Ethics* (London: Macmillan, 1918): 207.

48 One implication is that the question of how much we should punish is not divorced from the question of how we should punish. For example, see Lippke, *Rethinking Imprisonment*.

49 My identification of this problem is more sophisticated than the usual understanding of it. The usual understanding is that the Model Penal Code suffers from incoherence because the multiple goals *do* clash where this is thought inevitable for any hybrid theory of punishment. This objection is unsuccessful because the unified theory of punishment clearly shows that it is possible to conceive of a hybrid theory that may address multiple penal goals within a single, coherent account without such a clash. The new criticism of incoherence

in the Model Penal Code is that it lacks coherence because it does not provide a sufficiently satisfactory justificatory framework that may account for why *these* penal goals and how they are to fit together. So while the old objection ultimately misses its mark, it may be reconsidered from a different perspective which better addresses the problem at the core of the Model Penal Code.

50 See Garland, *Punishment and Modern Society*, 47.
51 See ibid. 58.
52 See Pierce O'Donnell, Michael J. Churgin, and Dennis E. Curtis, *Toward a Just and Effective Sentencing System* (New York: Praeger, 1977): 109.
53 See Robinson, *Distributive Principles of Criminal Law*, 236–7n414.
54 This view of 'negative retributivism' might also be understood as 'limiting retributivism'. See Robinson, *Distributive Principles of Criminal Law*, 240–2. Robinson proposes a view of empirical desert whereby punishment is distributed to those possessing blameworthiness as determined by 'the shared intuitions of justice of the community'. Punishment aspires to 'more effectively control crime' and set about ensuring crime reduction. Robinson admits that 'the greatest weakness of the proposal may be its failure to solve the problem of community blindness to injustice'. This is because he offers guidelines that direct us to reduce crime, but without a view about why we should reduce crime. He does not acknowledge that the justice of punishment is inextricably linked with the justice of the corresponding crime. If this link were recognized and accounted for, then this problem of blindness to injustice might be better overcome. See ibid. 248–9, 254.
55 Nor is the unified theory another name for restorative justice for reasons offered previously. The unified theory addresses more penal goals than this in a theory we might call *punitive restoration*.
56 For example, see Christopher Heath Wellman, 'The Rights Forfeiture Theory of Punishment', *Ethics* 122 (2012): 371–93.
57 Garland, *Punishment and Modern Society*, 17.
58 Ibid. 284.
59 Possible exceptions might include murder and treason.
60 See Aristotle, *Nicomachean Ethics*, in *The Complete Works,* vol. ii, ed. Jonathan Barnes (Princeton: Princeton University Press, 1984): 1730 [1094b22–23]: 'it is the mark of an educated [person] to look for precision in each class of things just so far as the nature of the subject admits'.
61 Hegel, *Elements of the Philosophy of Right*, §218 Remark.
62 Ibid. §218 Addition, Remark.
63 Alan Travis and Simon Rogers, 'Revealed: The Full Picture of Riot Sentences', *The Guardian* (19 August 2011): 1–2.
64 For example, see Beccaria, *Of Crimes and Punishments*, 18.
65 See Eric J. Widahl, Brett Garland, Scott E. Culhane, and William P. McCarty, 'Utilizing Behavioral Interventions to Improve Supervision Outcomes in Community-Based Corrections', *Criminal Justice and Behavior* 38 (2011): 386–405.
66 The idea of stakeholding has a history that includes British Prime Minister Tony Blair and the idea of the stakeholder economy. See Bruce Ackerman, 'Why Stakeholding?', *Politics and Society* 32 (2004): 41–60; Will Hutton, *The Stakeholding Society: Writings on Politics and Economics* (Cambridge: Polity, 1998); John Kaler, 'Morality and Strategy in Stakeholder Identification', *Journal of Business Ethics* 39 (2002): 91–9; John Kaler, 'Differentiating Stakeholder Theories', *Journal of Business Ethics* 46 (2003): 71–83; John Plender, *A Stake in the Future: The Stakeholding Solution* (London: Nicholas Brealey, 1997); Rajiv Prabhaker, 'Whatever Happened to Stakeholding?', *Public Administration* 82 (2004): 567–84; and Stuart White, 'The Citizen's Stake and Paternalism',

Politics and Society 32 (2004): 61–78. I have noted previously that my idea of the stakeholder society differs significantly from Ackerman and Alstott, *The Stakeholder Society*. A key difference is that past conceptions of stakeholding have focused almost exclusively on economic considerations, such as business ethics and corporate governance. The idea of the stakeholder society presented here is focused on political and legal justice.

67 On criminal profiling and forensic psychology, see Peter Ainsworth, *Offender Profiling and Crime Analysis* (Portland: Willan, 2001).

68 Hegel, *Elements of the Philosophy of Right*, §244, Addition (modified translation).

69 See ibid. §245. Recent research supports Hegel's position. See Paul K. Piff, Daniel M. Stancato, Stephane Cote, Rodolfo Mendoza-Denton, and Dacher Keltner, 'High Social Class Predicts Increased Unethical Behavior', *Proceedings of the National Academy of Sciences* 109 (2012): 4086–91.

70 See Green, 'Will, Not Force, is the Basis of the State' in *Lectures on the Principles of Political Obligation*, §§113–36.

71 For more on Hegel's proposed solutions to this problem, see Michael O. Hardimon, *Hegel's Social Philosophy: The Project of Reconciliation* (Cambridge: Cambridge University Press, 1994).

72 See Thom Brooks, 'Reciprocity as Mutual Recognition', *The Good Society* 21 (2012): 21–35.

73 Rawls, *Justice as Fairness*, 139. See Thom Brooks (ed.), *Rawls and Law* (Aldershot: Ashgate, 2012).

74 On legal realism, see William M. Fischer III, Morton J. Horwitz, and Thomas A. Reid (eds), *American Legal Realism* (Oxford: Oxford University Press, 1993) and Brian Leiter, *Naturalizing Jurisprudence: Essays on American Legal Realism and Naturalism in Legal Philosophy* (Oxford: Oxford University Press, 2007). The unified theory of punishment is consistent with legal realism, but not exclusively.

75 Citizens become more likely to engage in crime where they feel subjectively alienated from their community. For example, see Catherine E. Ross and John Mirowsky, 'Neighborhood Disorder, Subjective Alienation, and Distress', *Journal of Health and Social Behavior* 50 (2009): 49–64 and S. Saegert and G. Winkel, 'Crime, Social Capital, and Community Participation', *American Journal of Community Psychology* 34 (2004): 219–33.

76 For a recent example, see the Riots Communities and Victims Panel, *After the Riots: The Final Report of the Riots Communities and Victims Panel* (London: Riots Communities and Victims Panel, 2012): 6, 9, 21, 25, 31–2, 74, 80–1, 115, 126, 141.

77 See Robinson, *Distributive Principles of Criminal Law*, 260.

78 For example, see Edward Latessa, 'Why Work is Important, and How to Improve the Effectiveness of Correctional Reentry Programs that Target Employment', *Criminology and Public Policy* 11 (2012): 87–91 and Dora Schriro, 'Good Science, Good Sense: Making Meaningful Change Happen – A Practitioner's Guide', *Criminology and Public Policy* 11 (2012): 101–10.

79 Many argue for more integrated post-release programmes, but most offenders will not be imprisoned yet have a significant impact on crime. This requires greater attention to post-conviction and not only post-release. See Sophie R. Dickson, Devon L. Polaschek, and Allanah R. Casey, 'Can the Quality of High-Risk Violent Prisoners' Release Plans Predict Recidivism Following Intensive Rehabilitation? A Comparison with Risk Assessment Instruments', *Psychology, Crime, and Law* (2012) (DOI: 10.1080/1068316X.2011.640634) and Devon L. Polaschek, 'High-Intensity Rehabilitation for Violent Offenders in New Zealand: Reconviction Outcomes for High- and Medium-Risk Prisoners', *Journal of Interpersonal Violence* 26 (2011): 664–82.

80 See New York State Department of Corrections and Community Supervision, 'Who is Eligible for a Certificate of Relief?' (https://www.parole.ny.gov/certrelief. html). Interestingly, the Certificate of Relief and Certificate of Good Conduct are both designed *explicitly* with a view to 'the restoration of rights'. See New York State Department of Corrections and Community Supervision, 'Restoration of Rights' (https://www.parole.ny.gov/program_restoration.html).

81 Recognition as a stakeholder requires that persons believe themselves to have a stake in society. Poverty and deep inequality may present substantial obstacles for some to have this belief. See Richard Wilkinson and Kate Pickett, *The Spirit Level: Why Equality is Better for Everyone,* rev. ed. (London: Penguin, 2010).

82 For example, other theories of punishment, such as rehabilitation and restorative justice, may also accept the idea of a stakeholder society.

83 See Seth, *A Study of Ethical Principles,* 308–9.

84 It is worth reflecting on the implications that would follow if we accepted alternative penal theories. Each appears to run into significant problems addressing some substantive area of criminal law. For example, many retributivists run into problems with trying to account for strict liability or the criminalization of illegal but not immoral acts or omissions. One merit of the unified theory of punishment is that it avoids these problems while remaining committed to significant reforms of our political and legal institutions. The unified theory does not accept the world as we find it, but it does make best sense of it from a novel and critical perspective. We do not accept the world as we find it, but first bring an improved understanding to better grasp how our world may be better shaped. While they may be principled, theories that are substantially too divorced from practice may run the risk of becoming impractical and unrealistic for the price of conceptual purity.

8 Capital punishment

1 Leviticus 24:13–16; 1 Kings 21:10.

2 2 Kings 10:25.

3 Exodus 22:18; Leviticus 20:27.

4 Leviticus 20:2, 5.

5 Exodus 21:17, Leviticus 20:9.

6 Leviticus 20:10–13.

7 Genesis 38:24; Leviticus 21:9.

8 Leviticus 20:15–16.

9 See William Blackstone, *Commentaries on the Laws of England* (Oxford: Clarendon, 1775): Book IV, chapter 7.

10 Men comprise 98 per cent of all prisoners awaiting execution.

11 US Bureau of Statistics, *Capital Punishment, 2004* (NCJ 211349) (Washington, DC: US Department of Justice, 2005).

12 See Thom Brooks, 'Rethinking Remedial Responsibilities', *Ethics and Global Politics* 4 (2011): 199–200.

13 This qualification ('if we accept we may have a right to self-defence') may be intuitively obvious for some, but it is not so for all. Some pacifists might reject the idea that we have any right to harm others even in self-defence. Such views may not be compelling, but important to note. If we claim that we should never harm others under any circumstances all things considered, then such a view might forbid capital punishment in all cases. However, it might do so at the high cost of being counterintuitive and lacking compelling force for many, if not for most. For example, see Dalai Lama, *Ethics for a New Millennium* (New York: Riverhead, 2001).

14 See Linda G. Mills, *Insult to Injury* (Princeton: Princeton University Press, 2003).
15 It would be broadly welcome for restorative justice proponents to endeavour much more on making such a case. If restorative justice is to become a genuine alternative to existing theories of punishment, then it must strengthen the case for its application to more serious crimes, such as murder.
16 Hampton, 'The Moral Education Theory of Punishment', 223n22.
17 Eric Cullen and Tim Newell, *Murderers and Life Imprisonment: Containment, Treatment, Safety and Risk* (Winchester: Waterside Press, 1999).
18 See Hampton, 'The Moral Education Theory of Punishment', 223.
19 Green, *Lectures on the Principles of Political Obligation*, §206.
20 Consider bestiality. This was once criminalized and punished by capital punishment and the animal destroyed. In 2006, a council of elders in Sudan forced a local man to marry a goat after he was allegedly found having sex with it and pay a 15,000 Sudanese dinars dowry to the goat's owner. This is a unique case and circumstances. Nonetheless, it illustrates the point that permitted practices may change widely over time from demanding a punishment of execution to a requirement of marriage.
21 See Brian Barry, *Culture and Equality: An Egalitarian Critique of Multiculturalism* (Cambridge: Polity, 2001): 254.
22 See Parekh, *A New Politics of Identity*, 136: 'By claiming infallibility for their own interpretation, [literalists] imply that they know God's mind as well as God does Himself, and thus are guilty of an egregious blasphemy'.
23 Genesis 9:6.
24 See Genesis 4:8–16.
25 See Matthew 5:38–48.
26 See Thom Brooks, 'The Bible and Capital Punishment', *Philosophy and Theology* 22 (2010): 279–83.
27 There are several examples in the literature that highlight this diversity. For example, see Gardner C. Hanks, *Against the Death Penalty: Christian and Secular Arguments against Capital Punishment* (New York: Herald, 1997); Robert Postawko, 'Toward an Islamic Critique of Capital Punishment', *UCLA Journal of Islamic and Near Eastern Law* 1 (2002): 269–320; Michael L. Radelet, 'The Role of Organized Religions in Changing Death Penalty Debates', *William and Mary Bill of Rights Journal* 9 (2000): 201–14; and William A. Schabas, 'Islam and the Death Penalty', *William and Mary Bill of Rights Journal* 9 (2000): 223–36.
28 Kant, *The Metaphysics of Morals*, 105, 107 [6:332, 334].
29 See Brooks, 'Kant's Theory of Punishment'.
30 We might believe torturing someone to death more severe than a relatively painless execution. Note the qualification of 'satisfactory' in my statement: we may imagine many possible punishments that may be more severe, but what counts are only those punishments we might actually impose. Retributivists argue that the punishment must suit the crime. This presupposes that the chosen punishment is satisfactory. If we believed it inhumane or unsatisfactory to ever torture someone to death, then it would not be the case that the most severe punishment for murderers would be their being tortured to death because this punishment is impermissible.
31 Primoratz, *Justifying Legal Punishment*, 161.
32 John Stuart Mill, 'Speech in Favour of Capital Punishment' in Peter Singer (ed.), *Applied Ethics* (Oxford: Oxford University Press, 1986): 98.
33 Reiman, 'Justice, Civilization, and the Death Penalty', 131–3.
34 See David Baldus, George Woodworth, David Zuckerman, Neil Weiner, Alan Neil, and Barbara Brofitt, 'Racial Discrimination and the Death Penalty in the

Post-*Furman* Era: An Empirical and Legal Overview, with Recent Findings from Philadelphia', *Cornell Law Review* 83 (1998): 1638–1770.

35 *Furman* v. *Georgia*, 408 U.S. 238 (1972).

36 See Daniel McDermott, 'A Retributivist Argument against Capital Punishment', *Journal of Social Philosophy* 32 (2001): 317–33 and Stephen Nathanson, 'Does It Matter if the Death Penalty is Arbitrarily Administered?', *Philosophy and Public Affairs* 14 (1985): 149–64.

37 *U.S.* v. *Quinones*, 205 F. Supp. 2d. 256, 264 (2002).

38 See Brooks, 'Retributivist Arguments against Capital Punishment' and Brooks, 'Retribution and Capital Punishment'.

39 Note that this argument concerns our inability to offer reparations to the dead for our mistakes. We may be able to make reparations to their friends and family for our mistakes, but this is a different case. See Thom Brooks, 'A Two-Tiered Reparations Theory: A Reply to Wenar', *Journal of Social Philosophy* 39 (2008): 666–9. Note also the deliberate focus of framing this issue in terms of reparations and not only compensation.

40 One possible objection concerns life imprisonment. Suppose someone is sentenced to life imprisonment for a crime she did not commit. Her innocence is discovered after her death. Is her punishment unjust? We might argue it is unjust because we are unable to offer reparations because she died before our mistake became known. This is unconvincing. The appropriate timeframe we must work within is the course of a normal life. We cannot refuse to punish because it is possible that a person's innocence may be confirmed hundreds of years after all of us have died. We act within the course of a normal life. Provided the state does not promote premature deaths then the state may punish despite its mistake. Similarly, suppose an inmate dies suddenly in prison. It is later discovered he was innocent. This is also not a reason against the use of punishment provided his premature death is not a result of any action by the state. We may only work within the bounds of a normal life. The special problem of capital punishment is that it does not because the state inflicts premature deaths upon the condemned which may be inflicted in error. This is a very different case for this reason.

41 Jeffrey H. Reiman, 'The Justice of the Death Penalty in an Unjust World', in Kenneth C. Haas and James A. Inciardi (eds), *Challenging Capital Punishment: Legal and Social Science Approaches* (Thousand Oaks: Sage, 1988): 30.

42 One further objection is raised by the British politician David Davis. He argues that capital punishment should be reintroduced in the United Kingdom for murderers who have been convicted of two or more murders. Davis accepts that it is intolerable to condemn an innocent person and that there is always a risk of fallibility in death penalty cases. However, if someone is convicted of multiple murders, then we may have greater confidence that this person is guilty of at least one murder. We may be more confident that such persons do deserve capital punishment. Call this the Serial Murderer Case. It acknowledges the risk of mistake, but argues that such risks become miniscule if we raise the threshold for execution to two or more convictions for murder. I would argue that this objection also fails. Let us grant that we may have greater confidence in these cases. Greater confidence is not certainty and the risk of non-reparable mistakes involving the possible execution of innocent people remains. Retributivists should still reject capital punishment in these cases as well on the grounds of retributivist desert.

43 See Thom Brooks, 'Gilligan on Deterrence and the Death Penalty: Has Legal Punishment Failed Us?', *Ethics and Justice* 3/4 (2001/2002): 1–10.

44 See Isaac Ehrlich, 'The Deterrent Effect of Capital Punishment: A Question of Life and Death', *American Economic Review* 65 (1975): 397–417 and Isaac

Ehrlich, 'Deterrence: Evidence and Inference', *Yale Law Journal* 85 (1975): 209–27.

45 William J. Bowers and Glenn L. Pierce, 'Deterrence or Brutalization: What is the Effect of Executions?', *Crime and Delinquency* 26 (1980): 453–84.

46 See US Bureau of Statistics, *Capital Punishment, 2004*.

47 David A. Anderson, 'The Deterrence Hypothesis and Picking Pockets at the Pickpocket's Hanging', *American Law and Economic Review* 4 (2002): 295.

48 Primoratz, *Justifying Legal Punishment*, 155.

49 See Ernest van den Haag, 'On Deterrence and the Death Penalty', *Ethics* 78 (1968): 280–8.

50 The argument is analogous to Blaise Pascal's famous wager regarding religious belief. See Blaise Pascal, *Pensées* (Harmondsworth: Penguin, 1995).

51 Louis P. Pojman, 'For the Death Penalty' in Louis P. Pojman and Jeffrey H. Reiman (eds), *The Death Penalty: For and Against* (Lanham: Rowman and Littlefield, 1998): 40.

52 David A. Conway, 'Capital Punishment and Deterrence: Some Considerations in Dialogue Form', *Philosophy and Public Affairs* 3 (1974): 431–43.

53 Conway, 'Capital Punishment and Deterrence', 439.

54 See Cass R. Sunstein and Adrian Vermeule, 'Is Capital Punishment Morally Required? Acts, Omissions, and Life-Life Tradeoffs', *Stanford Law Review* 58 (2005): 703–50.

55 Mill, 'Speech in Favour of Capital Punishment', 99.

56 Bentham, *Principles of Penal Law*, 398.

57 On the idea of dignity, see Michael Rosen, *Dignity: Its History and Meaning* (Cambridge, Mass.: Harvard University Press, 2012).

58 See Dan M. Kahan, 'The Secret Ambition of Deterrence', *Harvard Law Review* 113 (1999): 437.

59 Ibid. 446.

60 The argument is that deterrence may be irrelevant for the reasons given. It is not my claim that crime reduction is irrelevant. We have noted previously that deterrence is a theory about crime reduction, but not all theories about crime reduction concern deterrence. See chapter 2.

61 Duff, *Punishment, Communication, and Community*, 155.

62 Ibid. 146.

63 Ibid. 153.

64 Ibid. 154.

65 Green, *Lectures on the Principles of Political Obligation*, 203 [§§204–5].

66 Ibid. 203 [§205]. See Brooks, 'T. H. Green's Theory of Punishment'.

67 This position does not deny that the reasons for why people have the capacity for rights is itself a matter of disagreement.

68 See Hegel, *Elements of the Philosophy of Right*, §218R, A.

69 Alan H. Goldman, 'Toward a New Theory of Punishment', *Law and Philosophy* 1 (1982): 72.

70 There is no such analysis yet that considers the unified theory on capital punishment. This is unsurprising given that the theory remains in its infancy and its future promise is not yet confirmed in this area.

71 Samuel R. Gross, 'Update: American Public Opinion on the Death Penalty – It's Getting Personal', *Cornell Law Review* 83 (1998): 1452.

9 Juvenile offenders

1 I shall refer interchangeably to 'juveniles' and 'youths'.

2 J. J. Tobias, *Crime and Industrial Society in the Nineteenth Century* (London: B. T. Batsford, 1967): 12.

3 Illinois Juvenile Court Act, 1899 Ill. Laws 132.

4 See Blackburn, *The Psychology of Criminal Conduct*, 10–11.

5 While adulthood is normally reached when someone becomes 18 years old, some jurisdictions may permit persons who are 16 or 17 to become adults and the rules may vary.

6 R. A. Duff, 'Punishing the Young' in R. A. Duff and Ido Weijers (eds), *Punishing Juveniles: Principle and Critique* (Oxford: Hart, 2002): 116.

7 Tamar Shapiro, 'What Is a Child?' *Ethics* 109 (1999): 715.

8 This chapter will later turn to the question of under which circumstances, if any, should youth offenders be tried and punished as adults.

9 There may be several such grounds, potentially including the defence of diminished responsibility (i.e. 'an abnormality of mental functioning'). See Coroners and Justice Act 2009, s. 52 and Simester et al., *Simester and Sullivan's Criminal Law*, 714–22.

10 See Easton and Piper, *Sentencing and Punishment*, 187.

11 This is sometimes referred to in terms of the defence of infancy. See Simester et al., *Simester and Sullivan's Criminal Law*, 722–4.

12 Please note the relevant qualifications. Juveniles *may* be held partially responsible, but there may be circumstances that justify their being held fully responsible. We will come to this issue shortly. Adults *may* be held fully responsible, but there may be circumstances where they are not.

13 See Children Act 1998.

14 Solicitor General cited in *Hansard*, Lords, 16 December 1997, col. 596.

15 The qualification of 'all things considered' is important. Of course, it may be possible that a youth may be found more criminally responsible than an adult where they are not similarly situated and the same crime performed under very different circumstances.

16 Quoted in Trevor Grove, *The Magistrate's Tale: A Frontline Report from a New JP* (London: Bloomsbury, 2002): 117.

17 See Hegel, *Elements of the Philosophy of Right*, §10 Addition: 'The child ... is only the potentiality of reason and freedom'.

18 For example, see Grove, *The Magistrate's Tale*, 118: 'But even Sharon had misgivings. Gruffly but with feeling she told us about the appalling circumstances most of "the boys" were going back to after their release. In the essays they wrote about what they'd do first when they got out, the priorities were invariably the same: a McDonalds hamburger, a spliff, a beer and sex, roughly in that order'.

19 US Bureau of Justice Statistics (http://www.ojp.usdoj.gov/bjs/). See Brian D. Johnson and Megan C. Kurlychek, 'Transferred Juveniles in the Era of Sentencing Guidelines: Examining Judicial Departures for Juvenile Offenders in Adult Criminal Court', *Criminology* 50 (2012): 1–40.

20 This perspective may also be accepted by restorative justice proponents that we will discuss later. Restoration aims at the restoration of what is damaged by crime. This must be tailored to the circumstances where juveniles may often be treated differently than adults similarly situated, but not always, such as in exceptional circumstances although there must be robust limitations in place.

21 This possible objection to deterrence theories is strongly relevant because juveniles are more likely than adults to engage in criminal behaviour. No deterrence theorist advances the position that juveniles should be punished more than adults under normal circumstances. However, this may clearly follow from the arguments. A potential reply is that the criminal law shouldn't offer multiple threats for the same crimes. On balance, there should not be one penal system for adults and another for juveniles because this may be counterproductive

to deterrence. Such a view would reject the idea that deterrence should be specific, not general, and tailored to particular individuals. The problem with this potential reply to the original objection is that it rejects the objection at a cost. It denies that deterrent punishment would justify greater punishment of juveniles than adults, but the cost is that it accepts that juveniles should normally be punished as if they were adults. If we wish to defend the view that the punishment of juveniles as adults should be limited to exceptional circumstances at best, if at all, then we should reject deterrence on the grounds that deterrence may lead to punishing juveniles more than adults in normal cases or punishing juveniles as adults in normal cases.

22 There is also the problem that older offenders are more likely to have past convictions that may lead to their being punished more for the same crimes than younger offenders. See Shawn Bushway and Anne Piehl, 'The Inextricable Link between Age and Criminal History in Sentencing', *Crime and Delinquency* 53 (2007): 156–83.

23 Ido Weijers and Anthony Duff, 'Introduction: Themes in Juvenile Justice' in *Punishing Juveniles*, 11.

24 On competence and adulthood, see Thom Brooks, 'Can We Justify Political Inequality?' *Archiv für Rechts und Sozialphilosophie* 89 (2003): 426–38 and Thom Brooks, 'Equality and Democracy: The Problem of Minimal Competency', *Ethical Perspectives* 14 (2007): 3–12.

25 I have said nothing about the negative retributivism of Rawls, Hart, and others. This is because the application of their theories – which we have explained are often incoherent at their core – will depend upon the particular mix found in a theory. This makes it somewhat difficult to state with any confidence how such theorists might grapple with the punishment of juvenile offenders.

26 Lippke, *Rethinking Imprisonment*, 92.

27 Home Office, *Justice for All*, 111.

28 See Margaret F. Severson, Kimberly Bruns, Christopher Veeh, and Jaehoon Lee, 'Prisoner Reentry Programming: Who Recidivates and When?', *Journal of Offender Rehabilitation* 50 (2011): 345.

29 See US Bureau of Justice Statistics, *Juvenile Victimization and Offending*, 1.

30 Ibid. 2.

31 See Michael R. Rand and Jayne E. Robinson, *Criminal Victimization in the United States, 2008 – Statistical Tables* (Washington, DC: Bureau of Justice Statistics, 2011): table 41.

32 See US Bureau of Justice Statistics, *Juvenile Victimization and Offending*, 7.

33 See Stephen Roe and Jane Ashe, 'Young People and Crime: Findings from the 2006 Offending, Crime and Justice Survey', *Home Office Statistical Bulletin* (London: Home Office, 2008): 15, 30 and US Bureau of Justice Statistics, *Juvenile Victimization and Offending*, 5.

34 See Dhami and Mandel, 'Crime as Risk Taking'.

35 Monica Barry, *Youth Offending in Transition: The Search for Social Recognition* (Abingdon: Routledge, 2006): 134.

36 See Eleonora Patacchini and Yves Zenou, 'Juvenile Delinquency and Conformism', *Journal of Law, Economics and Organization* 28 (2012): 1–31.

37 On the origins of stakeholding in business ethics, see Nigel de Bussy, 'Stakeholder Theory', in Wolfgang Donsbach (ed.), *The International Encyclopedia of Communication* (Oxford: Blackwell, 2008): 4815–17. See also Hutton, *The Stakeholder Society* and Will Hutton, *Them and Us: Changing Britain – Why We Need a Fair Society* (London: Little, Brown, 2010).

38 On the idea of a property-owning democracy, see Rawls, *Justice as Fairness*, 137–9. See also James Meade, *Efficiency, Equality, and the Ownership of Property* (London: George Allen and Unwin, 1964).

39 See Barry, *Youth Offending in Transition*, 26. While Barry does not explicitly endorse the idea of the stakeholder society, she does argue for the related idea of mutual recognition.

40 For example, see Ministry of Justice, *Adult Re-Convictions.*

41 See Easton and Piper, *Sentencing and Punishment*, 265.

42 One example is the UK's Youth Justice Board (http://www.justice.gov.uk/about/ yjb).

43 For example, one study of youth and restorative justice in Northern Ireland found reoffending rates of 37.7 per cent (restorative justice), 52.1 per cent (community sentences), and 70.7 per cent (custodial sentences). See Jessica Jacobson and Penelope Gibbs, *Making Amends: Restorative Youth Justice in Northern Ireland* (London: Prison Reform Trust, 2009).

44 See Gal and Moyal, 'Juvenile Victims in Restorative Justice', 1025–7.

45 See Rebecca S. Siegel, Annette M. La Greca, and Hannah M. Harrison, 'Peer Victimization and Social Anxiety in Adolescents: Prospective and Reciprocal Relationships', *Journal of Youth and Adolescence* 38 (2009): 1096–109.

46 These crime rates are not uncommon. Rates summarized have been drawn up with UK Home Office studies of self-reported crimes. The purpose of noting findings is purely indicative: the importance is to highlight various contours of criminal behaviour and not to promote any particular social science empirical study.

47 For example, see Traquina Emeka and Jon Sorensen, 'Female Juvenile Risk: Is There a Need for Gendered Assessment Instruments?', *Youth Violence and Juvenile Justice* 7 (2009): 313–30. On gender and essentialism, see Alison Stone, 'Essentialism and Anti-Essentialism in Feminist Philosophy', *Journal of Moral Philosophy* 1 (2004): 135–53 reprinted in Thom Brooks (ed.), *Ethics and Moral Philosophy* (Leiden: Brill, 2011): 385–407.

48 Barry, *Youth Offending in Transition*, 113.

49 It is relatively uncontroversial that stark differences exist between male and female offenders. It is controversial why this stark difference exists. One possible explanation is that young women are more likely to form pro-social attitudes earlier than young men. This might be partially explained by the idea that women are more likely to see themselves as having a stake in society although more must be said about why this might be the case. For example, see S. Bennett, D. P. Farrington, and L. R. Huesmann, 'Explaining Gender Differences in Crime and Violence: The Importance of Social Cognitive Skills', *Aggression and Violent Behavior* 10 (2005): 263–88. Such factors may not always play a positive constructive role. For an illuminating critique, see Elizabeth Caufmann, 'Understanding the Female Offender', *Future of Children* 18 (2008): 119–42.

50 For example, see Ashworth, *Sentencing and Criminal Justice*, 391.

51 See ibid. 392.

52 See Stephen Case and Kevin Haines, *Understanding Youth Offending: Risk Factor Research, Policy, and Practice* (Portland: Willan, 2009).

53 See Blackburn, *The Psychology of Criminal Conduct*, 160–80.

54 See ibid. 197.

55 See Patacchini and Zenou, 'Juvenile Delinquency and Conformism', 1–31.

56 See Emma Alleyne and Jane L. Wood, 'Gang-Related Crime: The Social, Psychological, and Behavioral Correlates', *Psychology, Crime, and Law* (2012) (DOI: 10.1080/1068316X.2012.658050).

57 See Barry, *Youth Offending in Transition*, 2, 161, 166. Se also ibid. 156–8.

58 See Green, *Lectures on the Principles of Political Obligation*, §209.

59 See Laura S. Abrams, Diane Terry, and Todd M. Franke, 'Community-Based Juvenile Reentry Services: The Effects of Service Dosage on Juvenile and Adult Recidivism', *Journal of Offender Rehabilitation* 50 (2011): 492–510.

60 See Independent Commission on Youth Crime and Antisocial Behaviour, *Time for a Fresh Start: The Report of the Independent Commission on Youth Crime and Antisocial Behaviour* (London: The Police Foundation, 2010).
61 BBC News, 'Young People Feel "Isolated" in Their Community', (27 October 2010) (http://www.bbc.co.uk/news/education-11629544).
62 See Barry, *Youth Offending in Transition*, 130.

10 Domestic abuse

1 'Domestic abuse' is known by many names, including 'domestic violence' and 'intimate partner abuse'. I will refer to these interchangeably with greater priority to 'domestic abuse' because it is most common and not because it is best all things considered.
2 See Michael P. Johnson and Kathleen J. Ferraro, 'Research on Domestic Violence in the 1990s: Making Distinctions', *Journal of Marriage and the Family* 62 (2000): 948–63 and Michael P. Johnson, 'Domestic Violence: It's Not About Gender – Or Is It?', *Journal of Marriage and the Family* 67 (2005): 1126–30.
3 One exception is California Penal Code s. 13700.
4 See Victor Tadros, 'The Distinctiveness of Domestic Abuse: A Freedom-Based Account' in R. A. Duff and Stuart P. Green (eds), *Defining Crimes*, 120.
5 See Shannon Catalano, *Intimate Partner Violence in the United States* (Washington, DC: US Department of Justice, 2007): 29–30.
6 See Rupert Chaplin, John Flatley, and Kevin Smith (eds), 'Crime in England and Wales 2009/10', *Home Office Statistical Bulletin* (London: Home Office, 2011): 36–7.
7 See Michelle Madden Dempsey, *Prosecuting Domestic Violence: A Philosophical Analysis* (Oxford: Oxford University Press, 2009): 109–12.
8 See Tadros, 'The Distinctiveness of Domestic Abuse', 122.
9 See Alaska's Definition of Domestic Violence AK ST 18.66.990(4)(E); Domestic Violence Crime and Victims Act 2004; Illinois Domestic Violence Act of 1986 750 ILCS 60/103(6); and New Jersey's Definition of Domestic Violence NJSA 2C: 25–19.
10 Special duties may connect family members, close friends, and perhaps many others including co-nationals. My argument is not that violence against co-nationals is domestic abuse because, in part, it is violence against persons to whom I owe special duties. I would distinguish between 'primary' special duties owed to family and perhaps close friends and 'secondary' special duties to others. Those who accept some account of special duties will recognize the greater weight that we may justify to those special duties owed to family than to compatriots; none will find secondary special duties more weighty than primary special duties. Domestic abuse is, in part, violence to those we owe primary special duties as I understand this distinction. On the idea of special duties, see David Miller, *On Nationality* (Oxford: Oxford University Press, 1995): 49–80. For a critique, see Robert E. Goodin, 'What is so Special about our Fellow Countrymen?', *Ethics* 98 (1988): 663–86. Both are reproduced in Thom Brooks (ed.), *The Global Justice Reader* (Oxford: Blackwell, 2008): 263–305.
11 See I. Bennett Capers, 'Home Is Where the Crime Is', *Michigan Law Review* 109 (2011): 979–91.
12 For example, Mills, *Insult to Injury*, 71: 'lesbians reported statistically significant higher levels of violence in all instances than women in heterosexual relationships'. See Robert L. Bowman and Holly M. Morgan, 'A Comparison of Rates of Verbal and Physical Abuse on Campus by Gender and Sexual Orientation', *College Students Journal* 32 (1998): 43–52 and Gwat-yong Lie and Sabrina

Gentlewarrier, 'Intimate Violence in Lesbian Relationships: Discussion of Survey Findings and Practice Implications', *Journal of Social Science Research* 15 (1991): 41–59.

13 For example, see Deborah Tuerkheimer, 'Renewing the Call to Criminalize Domestic Violence: An Assessment Three Years Later', *George Washington Law Review* 75 (2007): 613–26.

14 For example, see I. M. Johnson, 'Victims' Perceptions of Police Response to Domestic Violence Incidents', *Journal of Criminal Justice* 35 (2007): 498–510 and R. J. Kane, 'Patterns of Arrest in Domestic Violence Encounters: Identifying a Police Decision-Making Model', *Journal of Criminal Justice* 27 (1999): 65–79.

15 See Amanda Burgess-Proctor, 'Backfire: Lessons Learned When the Criminal Justice System Fails Help-Seeking Battered Women', *Journal of Crime and Justice* 35 (2012): 68–92.

16 See Eve Buzawa and Carl Buzawa, *Domestic Violence: The Criminal Justice Response*, 2nd ed. (Thousand Oaks: Sage, 1996): 11.

17 For example, see Refuge, 'Domestic Abuse: The Facts' (http://refuge.org.uk/get-help-now/what-is-domestic-violence/domestic-violence-the-facts/).

18 See Alpa Parmar and Alice Sampson, 'Evaluating Domestic Violence Initiatives', *British Journal of Criminology* 47 (2007): 678.

19 For example, see the Connecticut Coalition Against Domestic Violence (http://www.ctcadv.org/).

20 Mills, *Insult to Injury*, 6.

21 See Eve Buzawa and T. Austin, 'Determining Police Response to Domestic Violence Victims: The Role of Victim Preference', *American Behavioral Scientist* 36 (1993): 610–23; C. Hoyle and A. Sanders, 'Police Response to Domestic Violence: From Victim Choice to Victim Empowerment?', *British Journal of Criminology* 40 (2000): 14–36; and Johnson, 'Victims' Perceptions of Police Response to Domestic Violence Incidents'.

22 See Douglas K. Snyder and Nancy S. Scheer, 'Predicting Disposition Following Brief Residence at a Shelter for Battered Women', *American Journal of Community Psychology* 9 (1981): 559–65.

23 See Donald J. Rebovich, 'Prosecution Response to Domestic Violence: Results of a Survey of Large Jurisdictions' in Eve S. Buzawa and Carl G. Buzawa (eds), *Do Arrest and Restraining Orders Work?* (Thousand Oaks: Sage, 1996): 176–91.

24 See Mills, *Insult to Injury*, 25 and Linda G. Mills, 'Killing Her Softly: Intimate Abuse and the Violence of State Intervention', *Harvard Law Review* 113 (1999): 550–613.

25 See Mills, *Insult to Injury*, 101–18.

26 See Susan Landrum, 'The Ongoing Debate about Mediation in the Context of Domestic Violence: A Call for Empirical Studies of Mediation Effectiveness', *Cardozo Journal of Conflict Resolution* 12 (2011): 425–68.

27 For example, see Kerry Healey, Christine Smith, and Chris O'Sullivan, *Batterer Intervention: Program Approaches and Criminal Justice Strategies* (NCJ 195079) (Washington, DC: National Institute of Justice, 1998).

28 See Ashleigh Owens, 'Confronting the Challenges of Domestic Violence Sentencing Policy: A Review of the Increasing Global Use of Batterer Intervention Programs', *Fordham International Law Journal* 35 (2012): 576.

29 See Owens, 'Confronting the Challenges of Domestic Violence Sentencing Policy', 589–90.

30 See Lisa G. Lerman, 'Mediation of Wife Abuse Cases: The Adverse Impact of Informal Dispute Resolution on Women', *Harvard Women's Law Journal* 7 (1984): 57–113.

31 Rana Fuller, 'How to Effectively Advocate for Battered Women When Systems Fail', *William Mitchell Law Review* 33 (2007): 946.

32 The argument is not that retributivist punishment may run counter to the preferences of all victims. This is because many victims also prefer that their abusers are imprisoned. Note further that deterrence may require severe punishment against the preferences of some victims and families for some alternative.

33 See Parmar and Sampson, 'Evaluating Domestic Violence Initiatives'.

34 For example, see Green, *Lectures on the Principles of Political Obligation*, §243: 'But if an injured wife or husband is willing to condone a breach of his or her rights through adultery, it is generally best that it should be condoned'.

35 See David Hirschel, Eve Buzawa, April Pattavina, and Don Faggiani, 'Domestic Violence and Mandatory Arrest Laws: To What Extent Do They Influence Police Arrest Decisions?', *Journal of Criminal Law and Criminology* 98 (2007): 255–98.

36 See Hadar Dancig-Rosenberg and Dana Pugach, 'Pain, Love, and Voice: The Role of Domestic Violence Victims in Sentencing', *Michigan Journal of Gender and Law* 18 (2012): 423–83.

37 See discussion of *People* v. *Kelly*, 171 P.3d 548, 572 (Cal. 2007) and *People* v. *Zamudio*, 181 P.3d 105, 135–7 (Cal. 2008) in Rebecca Tushnet, 'Worth a Thousand Words: The Images of Copyright', *Harvard Law Review* 125 (2012): 696.

38 See Dan M. Kahan and Martha C. Nussbaum, 'Two Conceptions of Emotion in Criminal Law', *Columbia Law Review* 96 (1996): 269–374.

39 The argument is not that other stakeholders in justice should outweigh the primary victim individually or collectively, but instead that their voices should be heard where they have a stake in the outcome.

40 Katherine K. Baker, 'Gender and Emotion in Criminal Law', *Harvard Journal of Law and Gender* 28 (2005): 457–8.

11 Sexual crimes

1 For example, see the Sexual Offences Act 2003. Sex crimes also include meeting a child following sexual grooming, sexual abuse of vulnerable people with a mental disorder, voyeurism, and exposure. See Blackburn, *The Psychology of Criminal Conduct*, 280–308 and Crown Prosecution Service, 'Sexual Offences' (http://www.cps.gov.uk/news/fact_sheets/sexual_offences/).

2 See Sexual Offences Act 2003, s.1.

3 Unlawful penetration using an object is considered 'assault by penetration' and not rape in the UK.

4 See Simester et al., *Simester and Sullivan's Criminal Law*, 465–6.

5 See Ashworth, *Sentencing and Criminal Justice*, 134.

6 See Greenfeld, *Child Victimizers: Violent Offenders and their Victims* (NCJ 153258) (Washington DC: US Department of Justice): 3.

7 See ibid. 11.

8 See Michelle J. Anderson, 'From Chastity Requirement to Sexual License: Sexual Consent and a New Rape Shield Law', *George Washington Law Review* 70 (2002): 51–162.

9 See Sarah M. Harless, 'From the Bedroom to the Courtroom: The Impact of Domestic Violence Law on Marital Rape Victims', *Rutgers Law Journal* 35 (2003): 305–43 and Jill Elaine Hasday, 'Contest and Consent: A Legal History of Marital Rape', *California Law Review* 88 (2000): 1373–1505.

10 Richard Posner, *Sex and Reason* (Cambridge, Mass.: Harvard University Press, 1992): 388. See Joan McGregor, *Is It Rape? On Acquaintance Rape and Taking Women's Consent Seriously* (Aldershot: Ashgate, 2005): 115.

11 McGregor, *Is It Rape?*, 220.

12 Duff, *Trials and Punishments*, 212.

13 See Michelle Madden Dempsey and Jonathan Herring, 'Why Sexual Penetration Requires Justification', *Oxford Journal of Legal Studies* 27 (2007): 467–91.

14 See ibid. 476.

15 See McGregor, *Is It Rape?*, 104.

16 Ibid. 10.

17 See ibid. 210.

18 Duff, *Answering for Crime*, 247.

19 Note that the justification of this example rests on the view that autonomy might be respected in this case. If autonomy were not satisfactorily respected, then this may not be justified conduct.

20 For example, see *R v. Brown* [1993] 2 All ER 75. This decision has received much criticism. See Marianne Giles, '*R v Brown*: Consensual Harm and the Public Interest', *Modern Law Review* 57 (1994): 101–11.

21 Prior to the Sexual Offences Act, defendants had to possess an honest belief rather than a reasonable belief. See *Morgan* [1976] AC 182.

22 See Douglas N. Husak and George C. Thomas III, 'Rapes without Rapists: Consent and Reasonable Mistake', *Philosophical Issues* 11 (2001): 86–117.

23 See Catharine A. MacKinnon, *Women's Lives, Men's Laws* (Cambridge, Mass.: Belknap/Harvard University Press, 2005): 240.

24 See US Bureau of Justice Statistics, *Criminal Victimization in the United States*, Table 14. These victimization rates are for persons age 12 or older.

25 For example, see Ray Blanchard, 'The DSM Diagnostic Criteria for Pedophilia', *Archives of Sexual Behavior* 39 (2010): 304–16 and Kirpal Sahota and Paul Chesterman, 'Sexual Offending in the Context of Mental Illness', *Journal of Forensic Psychiatry* 9 (1998): 267–80.

26 For example, see Nancy C. Raymond, Eli Coleman, Fred Ohlerking, Gary A. Christenson, and Michael Miner, 'Psychiatric Comorbidity in Pedophilic Sex Offenders', *American Journal of Psychiatry* 156 (1999): 786–8.

27 See Greenfeld, *Child Victimizers*, iv.

28 See Annie Cossins, 'Restorative Justice and Child Sex Offences', *British Journal of Criminology* 48 (2008): 375.

29 Ashworth, 'Ignorance of the Criminal Law', 24.

30 See J. Bremner and A. Hillin, *Sexuality, Young People, and Care: Creating Positive Contexts for Training, Policy, and Development* (Lyme Regis: Russell House, 1994).

31 For example, see James Horley, 'Cognitions of Child Sexual Abusers', *Journal of Sex Research* 25 (1988): 542–5.

32 For example, see Constanze K. Gerhold, Kevin D. Browne, and Richard Beckett, 'Predicting Recidivism in Adolescent Sexual Offenders', *Aggression and Violent Behavior* 12 (2007): 427–38; Michael J. Vitacco, Michael Caldwell, Nancy L. Ryba, Alvin Malesky, and Samantha J. Kurus, 'Assessing Risks in Adolescent Sexual Offenders: Recommendations for Clinical Practice', *Behavioral Sciences and the Law* 27 (2009): 929–40; and Helen Wakeling, Anthony R. Beech, and Nick Freemantle, 'Investigating Treatment Change and Its Relationship to Recidivism in a Sample of 3773 Sex Offenders in the UK', *Psychology, Crime, and Law* (2011) (DOI: 10.1080/1068316X.2011.626413).

33 See McGregor, *Is It Rape?*, 4. See also Nina Lakhani, 'Unreported Rapes: The Silent Shame', *The Independent* (12 March 2012) (http://www.independent.co.uk/news/uk/crime/unreported-rapes-the-silent-shame-7561636.html).

34 Blackburn, *The Psychology of Criminal Conduct*, 285.

35 US Bureau of Justice Statistics, *Criminal Victimization in the United States, 2008 – Statistical Tables* (Washington, DC: US Department of Justice, 2010): Table 1.

36 See John Flately, Chris Kershaw, Kevin Smith, Rupert Chaplin, and Debbie Moon (eds), *Crime in England and Wales 2009/10: Findings From the British Crime Survey and Police Recorded Crime* (London: Home Office, 2010).
37 Greenfeld, *Child Victimizers*, vi.
38 For example, see Langan and Levin, *Recidivism of Prisoners Released*, 9–10.
39 See Langan, Schmitt, and Durose, *Recidivism of Sex Offenders Released from Prison*, 1.
40 Roger Hood, Stephen Shute, Martina Feilzer, and Aidan Wilcox, 'Sex Offenders Emerging from Long-Term Imprisonment', *British Journal of Criminology* 42 (2002): 371. See Don Grubin, *Sex Offending against Children: Understanding the Risk* (Police Research Series Paper, No. 99) (London: Home Office, 1998) and D. Thornton and R. Travers, 'A Longitudinal Study of the Criminal Behaviour of Convicted Sex Offenders', *Proceedings of the Prison Service Psychology Conference* (London: Her Majesty's Prison Service, 1991): 13–22.
41 See Langan, Schmitt, and Durose, *Recidivism of Sex Offenders Released from Prison*, 1. About 43 per cent of sex offenders and 68 per cent of non-sex offenders were rearrested for any crime.
42 See Ministry of Justice, *Adult Re-Convictions*, 15–16.
43 For example, see Carissa Byrne Hessick, 'Disentangling Child Pornography from Child Sex Abuse', *Washington University Law Review* 88 (2011): 853–902.
44 See Paul Guerino and Allen J. Beck, *Sexual Victimization Reported by Adult Correctional Authorities, 2007–2008* (NCJ 231172) (Washington, DC: US Department of Justice, 2011) and Jeannie Suk, 'Redistributing Rape', *American Criminal Law Review* 48 (2011): 111–19.
45 See *Coker v. Georgia*, 433 U.S. 584 (1977).
46 See *Kennedy v. Louisiana*, 554 U.S. 407 (2008).
47 See Davis, 'Setting Penalties'.
48 David Archard, 'The Wrong of Rape', *Philosophical Quarterly* 57 (2007): 382.
49 Davis, 'Setting Penalties', 71. See Julie Carpentier, Benoit Leclerc, and Jean Proulx, 'Juvenile Sexual Offenders: Correlates of Onset, Variety, and Desistance of Criminal Behavior', *Criminal Justice and Behavior* 38 (2011): 854–73 (finding that 'most adolescent sexual offenders who persist in a criminal career commit a variety of offenses and do not specialize in sexual crimes') and Julie Carpentier and Jean Proulx, 'Correlates of Recidivism among Adolescents Who Have Sexually Offended', *Sexual Abuse* 23 (2011): 434–55. For a critical examination, see Craig T. Palmer, 'Twelve Reasons Why Rape Is Not Sexually Motivated: A Skeptical Examination', *Journal of Sex Research* 25 (1988): 512–30.
50 For example, see Megan's Law in the US and Sarah's Law in the UK.
51 For example, see Alissa R. Ackerman, Jill S. Levenson, and Andrew J. Harris, 'How Many Sex Offenders Really Live among Us? Adjusted Counts and Population Rates in Five US States', *Journal of Crime and Justice* (2012) (DOI:10.1080/0735648X.2012.666407); Rachel Bandy, 'Measuring the Impact of Sex Offender Notification on Community Adoption of Protective Behaviors', *Criminology and Public Policy* 10 (2011): 237–63; Robert Hayes, Michael Barnett, Danny H. Sullivan, Olav Nielssen, Matthew Large, and Clarence Brown, 'Justifications and Rationalizations for the Civil Commitment of Sex Offenders', *Psychiatry, Psychology, and Law* 16 (2009): 141–9; Chrysanthi Leon, 'The Contexts and Politics of Evidence-Based Sex Offender Policy', *Criminology and Public Policy* 10 (2011): 421–30; and Karen J. Terry, 'What is Smart Sex Offender Policy?', *Criminology and Public Policy* 10 (2011): 275–82.
52 For example, see K. Fitch, *Megan's Law: Does It Protect Children?* (London: National Society for the Prevention of Cruelty to Children, 2006).

53 See Brian Stout, Hazel Kemshall, and Jason Wood, 'Building Stakeholder Support for a Sex Offender Public Disclosure Scheme: Learning from the English Pilots', *Howard Journal of Criminal Justice* 50 (2011): 406–18.
54 See B. Gallagher, 'The Extent and Nature of Known Cases of Institutional Child Sexual Abuse', *British Journal of Social Work* 30 (2000): 795–817.
55 See Matthew Colton, Susan Roberts, and Maurice Vanstone, 'Learning Lessons from Men Who Have Sexually Abused Children', *Howard Journal of Criminal Justice* 51 (2012): 79–93. See also B. Leclerc, J. Proulx, and A. McKibben, 'Modus Operandi of Sexual Abusers Working or Doing Voluntary Work with Children and Adolescents', *Journal of Sexual Aggression* 11 (2005): 187–95 and J. Sullivan and A. Beech, 'Professional Perpetrators: Sex Abusers Who Use Their Employment to Target and Sexually Abuse Children with Whom They Work', *Child Abuse Review* 11 (2002): 153–67.
56 Another potential problem concerns children who are convicted of sexual offences while underage and the requirement to be included on sex offender registers for the rest of their lives. See Laura Janes, 'Children Convicted of Sexual Offences: Do Lifelong Labels Really Help?', *Howard Journal of Criminal Justice* 50 (2011): 137–52.
57 See Vitacco et al., 'Assessing Risks in Adolescent Sexual Offenders', 937.
58 See Martin Drapeau, Annett Körner, Luc Granger, Louis Brunet, and Franz Caspar, 'A Plan Analysis of Pedophile Sexual Abusers' Motivations for Treatment: A Qualitative Pilot Study', *International Journal of Offender Therapy and Comparative Criminology* 49 (2005): 308–24.
59 R. Karl Hanson, 'Will They Do It Again? Predicting Sex-Offense Recidivism', *Current Directions in Psychological Science* 9 (2000): 108. See R. Karl Hanson and A. J. R. Harris, 'Where Should We Intervene? Dynamic Predictors of Sex Offense Recidivism', *Criminal Justice and Behavior* 27 (2000): 6–35.
60 See R. Karl Hanson, R. A. Steffy, and R. Gauthier, 'Long-Term Recidivism of Child Molesters', *Journal of Consulting and Clinical Psychology* 61 (1993): 119–36.
61 See US Bureau of Justice Statistics, *Criminal Victimization in the United States*, Table 34.
62 See Amy J. L. Baker, Mel Schneiderman, and Rob Parker, 'A Survey of Problematic Sexualized Behaviors of Children in the New York City Child Welfare System: Estimates of Problem, Impact on Services, and Need for Training', *Journal of Child Sexual Abuse* 10 (2001): 67–80 and McGregor, *Is It Rape?*, 54.
63 See Archard, 'The Wrong of Rape', 393.
64 See Cossins, 'Restorative Justice and Child Sex Offences', 360.
65 See Barbara Hudson, 'Restorative Justice and Gendered Violence – Diversion or Effective Justice?' *British Journal of Criminology* 42 (2002): 629.
66 For example, see Clare McGlynn, 'Feminism, Rape and the Search for Justice', *Oxford Journal of Legal Studies* 31 (2011): 825–42.
67 See McGlynn, ibid. 838.

Conclusion

1 Strictly speaking, fewer crimes performed may not always demonstrate fewer rights have been violated. It would seem intuitively compelling that success in crime reduction would consist in less rights violation overall.
2 One potential objection is that immediate help is impossible. This is because we must permit sufficient time for cases to be prepared before a trial commences. However, consider that the overwhelming majority of cases end in various forms of plea bargaining where trials are avoided. So while it may be impermissible to

engage immediately with all persons arrested, it is possible to perhaps engage intensively with the overwhelming majority.

3 For example, see George W. Joe, Kevin Knight, D. Dwayne Simpson, Patrick Flynn, Janis T. Morey, Norma G. Bartholomew, Michele Staton Tindall, William M. Burdon, Elizabeth A. Hall, Steve S. Martin, and Daniel J. O'Connell, 'An Evaluation of Six Brief Interventions That Target Drug-Related Problems in Correctional Populations', *Journal of Offender Rehabilitation* 51 (2012): 9–33.

4 Brief imprisonment is often linked to high rates of recidivism. The problem is that offenders may lack access to offender management programmes and supervision by probation services. If more support were available, then more satisfactory recidivism rates might be achieved. See Ministry of Justice, *2011 Compendium of Re-Offending Statistics and Analysis*, 4.

5 It is important to highlight that this is a normative argument about our self-identity in relation to others. While empirical evidence is suggestive that this account has further support, more research must be conducted. One hope for this study is that the idea of stakeholding for criminal justice policy will receive greater attention and further study.

6 See John H. Laub and Robert J. Sampson, *Shared Beginnings, Divergent Lives: Delinquent Boys to Age 70* (Cambridge, Mass.: Harvard University Press, 2003).

7 See Ashworth, 'Ignorance of the Criminal Law', 21.

8 Hegel argues that an important goal for individuals is to achieve political reconciliation and see their social world as a place where they are at home. The idea of stakeholding goes further and claims that the world must also be a place where we would want to be at home. See Brooks, *Hegel's Political Philosophy* and Hardimon, *Hegel's Social Philosophy*.

Bibliography

Abrams, Laura S., Diane Terry, and Todd M. Franke (2011). 'Community-Based Juvenile Reentry Services: The Effects of Service Dosage on Juvenile and Adult Recidivism', *Journal of Offender Rehabilitation* 50: 492–510.

Ackerman, Alissa R., Jill S. Levenson, and Andrew J. Harris (2012). 'How Many Sex Offenders Really Live among Us? Adjusted Counts and Population Rates in Five US States', *Journal of Crime and Justice*. DOI: 10.1080/0735648X.2012. 666407.

Ackerman, Bruce (2004). 'Why Stakeholding?', *Politics and Society* 32: 41–60.

Ackerman, Bruce and Anne Alstott (2000). *The Stakeholder Society.* New Haven: Yale University Press.

Acorn, Annalise (2004). *Compulsory Compassion: A Critique of Restorative Justice.* Vancouver: University of British Columbia Press.

Ainsworth, Peter (2001). *Offender Profiling and Crime Analysis.* Portland: Willan.

Alexander, Larry (1994). 'Crime and Culpability', *Journal of Contemporary Legal Issues*: 1–30.

Alexander, Larry and Kimberley Kessler Ferzan (2009). *Crime and Culpability: A Theory of Criminal Law.* Cambridge: Cambridge University Press.

Alleyne, Emma and Jane L. Wood (2012). 'Gang-Related Crime: The Social, Psychological and Behavioral Correlates', *Psychology, Crime and Law*. DOI: 10.1080/ 1068316X.2012.658050.

American Law Institute (1962). *Model Penal Code.* Philadelphia: American Law Institute.

Anderson, David A. (2002). 'The Deterrence Hypothesis and Picking Pockets at the Pickpocket's Hanging', *American Law and Economic Review* 4: 295–313.

Anderson, Michelle J. (2002). 'From Chastity Requirement to Sexual License: Sexual Consent and a New Rape Shield Law', *George Washington Law Review* 70: 51–162.

Archard, David (2007). 'The Wrong of Rape', *Philosophical Quarterly* 57: 374–93.

Aristotle (1984). *The Complete Works, 2 vols*, ed. Jonathan Barnes. Princeton: Princeton University Press.

Ashworth, Andrew (1993). 'Some Doubt about Restorative Justice', *Criminal Law Forum* 4: 277–99.

—— (1994). 'Sentencing' in Mike Maguire, Rod Morgan, and Robert Reiner (eds), *The Oxford Handbook of Criminology.* Oxford: Clarendon, pp. 819–60.

—— (2002). 'Responsibilities, Rights and Restorative Justice', *British Journal of Criminology* 42: 578–95.

—— (2010). *Sentencing and Criminal Justice, 5th ed.* Cambridge: Cambridge University Press.

—— (2010). 'Ignorance of the Criminal Law, and Duties to Avoid It', *Modern Law Review* 74: 1–26.

Baker, Amy J. L., Mel Schneiderman, and Rob Parker (2001). 'A Survey of Problematic Sexualized Behaviors of Children in the New York City Child Welfare System: Estimates of Problem, Impact on Services, and Need for Training', *Journal of Child Sexual Abuse* 10: 67–80.

Baker, Katherine K. (2005). 'Gender and Emotion in Criminal Law', *Harvard Journal of Law and Gender* 28: 447–66.

Baldus, David C., George Woodworth, David Zuckerman, Neil Alan Weiner, and Barbara Broffitt (1998). 'Racial Discrimination and the Death Penalty in the Post-*Furman* Era: An Empirical and Legal Overview, with Recent Findings from Philadelphia', *Cornell Law Review* 83: 1638–1770.

Bandy, Rachel (2011). 'Measuring the Impact of Sex Offender Notification on Community Adoption of Protective Behaviors', *Criminology and Public Policy* 10: 237–63.

Barnum-Roberts, Brooke Natalie (2011). 'Apologizing Without Regret', *Ratio* 24: 17–27.

Barry, Brian (2001). *Culture and Equality: An Egalitarian Critique of Multiculturalism*. Cambridge: Polity.

Barry, Monica (2006). *Youth Offending in Transition: The Search for Social Recognition*. Abingdon: Routledge.

Beccaria, Cesare (1986). *On Crimes and Punishments*, trans. David Young. Indianapolis: Hackett.

Benhabib, Seyla (2002). *The Claims of Culture: Equality and Diversity in the Global Era*. Princeton: Princeton University Press.

Bennett, Christopher (2002). 'The Varieties of Retributive Experience', *Philosophical Quarterly* 52: 145–63.

—— (2006). 'State Denunciation of Crime', *Journal of Moral Philosophy* 3: 288–304.

—— (2006). 'Taking the Sincerity Out of Saying Sorry: Restorative Justice as Ritual', *Journal of Applied Philosophy* 23: 127–43.

Bennett, S., D. P. Farrington, and L. R. Huesmann (2005). 'Explaining Gender Differences in Crime and Violence: The Importance of Social Cognitive Skills', *Aggression and Violent Behavior* 10: 263–88.

Benson, Michael, Leanne Fiftal Alarid, Velmer Burton, and Francis Cullen (2011). 'Reintegration or Stigmatization? Offenders' Expectatations of Community Re-entry', *Journal of Criminal Justice* 39: 385–93.

Bentham, Jeremy (1961). *The Works of Jeremy Bentham, vol. 1: Principles of Penal Law*. New York: Russell and Russell.

Bix, Brian H. (2002). 'Natural Law: The Modern Tradition' in Jules Coleman, Scott Shapiro, and Kenneth Einar Himma (eds), *The Oxford Handbook of Jurisprudence and Philosophy of Law*. Oxford: Oxford University Press, pp. 61–103.

Blackburn, Ronald (1993). *The Psychology of Criminal Conduct: Theory, Research and Practice*. New York: Wiley.

Blacker, J., A. Watson, and A. R. Beech (2008). 'A Combined Drama-Based and CBT Approach to Working with Self-Reported Anger Aggression', *Criminal Behaviour and Mental Health* 18: 129–37.

Blackstone, William (1775). *Commentaries on the Laws of England*. Oxford: Clarendon.

Blanchard, Ray (2010). 'The DSM Diagnostic Criteria for Pedophilia', *Archives of Sexual Behavior* 39: 304–16.

Boonin, David (2008). *The Problem of Punishment*. Cambridge: Cambridge University Press.

Bosanquet, Bernard (1918). *Some Suggestions in Ethics*. London: Macmillan.

Boucher, David (ed.) (1997). *The British Idealists*. Cambridge: Cambridge University Press.

Bowers, William J. and Glenn L. Pierce (1980). 'Deterrence or Brutalization: What is the Effect of Executions?', *Crime and Delinquency* 26: 453–84.

Bowman, Robert L. and Holly M. Morgan (1998). 'A Comparison of Rates of Verbal and Physical Abuse on Campus by Gender and Sexual Orientation', *College Students Journal* 32: 43–52.

Braithwaite, John (1989). 'Criminological Theory and Organizational Crime', *Justice Quarterly* 6: 333–58.

—— (1994). 'Thinking Harder About Democratising Social Control' in J. Alder and J. Wundersitz (eds), *Family Conferencing and Juvenile Justice: The Way Forward or Misplaced Optimism*. Canberra: Australian Institute of Criminology, pp. 199–216.

—— (2002). *Restorative Justice and Responsible Regulation*. Oxford: Oxford University Press.

—— (2002). 'Setting Standards for Restorative Justice', *British Journal of Criminology* 42: 563–77.

—— (2003). 'Principles of Restorative Justice' in Andrew von Hirsch, Julian Roberts, Anthony E. Bottoms, Kent Roach, and Mara Schiff (eds), *Restorative Justice and Criminal Justice: Competing or Reconcilable Paradigms?* Oxford: Hart, pp. 1–20.

Braithwaite, John and Philip Pettit (1990). *Not Just Deserts: A Republican Theory of Criminal Justice*. Oxford: Clarendon.

Bremner, J. and A. Hillin (1994). *Sexuality, Young People and Care: Creating Positive Contexts for Training, Policy and Development*. Lyme Regis: Russell House.

Brettschneider, Corey (2007). 'The Rights of the Guilty: Punishment and Political Legitimacy', *Political Theory* 35: 175–99.

Britto, Sarah (2011). '"Diffuse Anxiety": The Role of Economic Insecurity in Predicting Fear of Crime', *Journal of Crime and Justice*. DOI: 10.1080/0735648X.2011.631399.

Brooks, Thom (2001). 'Corlett on Kant, Hegel, and Retribution', *Philosophy* 76: 562–80.

—— (2001/2002). 'Gilligan on Deterrence and the Death Penalty: Has Legal Punishment Failed Us?', *Ethics and Justice* 3/4: 1–10.

—— (2003). 'T. H. Green's Theory of Punishment', *History of Political Thought* 24: 685–701.

—— (2003). 'Can We Justify Political Inequality?, *Archiv für Rechts und Sozialphilosophie* 89: 426–38.

—— (2004). 'Retributivist Arguments against Capital Punishment', *Journal of Social Philosophy* 35: 188–97.

—— (2004). 'Is Hegel a Retributivist?', *Bulletin of the Hegel Society of Great Britain* 49/50: 113–26.

—— (2004). 'The Right to Trial by Jury', *Journal of Applied Philosophy* 21: 197–212.

—— (ed.) (2005). *Rousseau and Law*. Aldershot: Ashgate.

—— (2007). *Hegel's Political Philosophy: A Systematic Reading of the Philosophy of Right*. Edinburgh: Edinburgh University Press.

—— (2007). 'Equality and Democracy: The Problem of Minimal Competency', *Ethical Perspectives* 14: 3–12.

—— (2007). 'Rethinking Punishment', *International Journal of Jurisprudence and Philosophy of Law* 1: 27–34.

—— (ed.) (2008). *The Global Justice Reader*. Oxford: Blackwell.

—— (2008). 'Was Green a Utilitarian in Practice?', *Collingwood and British Idealism Studies* 14: 5–15.

—— (2008). 'Shame on You, Shame on Me? Nussbaum on Shame Punishment', *Journal of Applied Philosophy* 25: 322–34.

—— (2008). 'A Two-Tiered Reparations Theory: A Reply to Wenar', *Journal of Social Philosophy* 39: 666–9.

—— (ed.) (2009). *The Right to a Fair Trial*. Aldershot: Ashgate.

—— (2009). 'A Critique of Pragmatism and Deliberative Democracy', *Transactions of the Charles S. Peirce Society* 45: 50–4.

—— (2010). 'Punishment and British Idealism' in Jesper Ryberg and J. Angelo Corlett (eds), *Punishment and Ethics: New Perspectives*. Basingstoke: Palgrave Macmillan, pp. 16–32.

—— (2010). 'The Bible and Capital Punishment', *Philosophy and Theology* 22: 279–83.

—— (2011). 'Retribution and Capital Punishment' in Mark D. White (ed.), *Retributivism: Essays on Theory and Policy*. Oxford: Oxford University Press, pp. 232–45.

—— (2011). 'Punishment: Political, Not Moral', *New Criminal Law Review* 14: 427–38.

—— (2011). 'Is Bradley a Retributivist?', *History of Political Thought* 32: 83–95.

—— (2011). 'Rethinking Remedial Responsibilities', *Ethics and Global Politics* 4: 195–202.

—— (2011). 'What Did the British Idealists Do for Us?' in (ed.), *New Waves in Ethics*. Basingstoke: Palgrave Macmillan, pp. 28–47.

—— (ed.) (2011). *Ethics and Moral Philosophy*. Leiden: Brill.

—— (2011). 'British Idealism', *Oxford Bibliographies Online*.

—— (2011). 'Punishment', *Oxford Bibliographies Online*.

—— (2012). 'Hegel and the Unified Theory of Punishment' in (ed.), *Hegel's Philosophy of Right: Ethics, Politics, and Law*. Oxford: Blackwell, pp. 103–23.

—— (ed.) (2012). *Justice and the Capabilities Approach*. Aldershot: Ashgate.

—— (ed.) (2012). *Rawls and Law*. Aldershot: Ashgate.

—— (2012). 'Reciprocity as Mutual Recognition', *The Good Society* 21: 21–35.

—— (ed.) (2013). *Shame Punishment*. Aldershot: Ashgate.

—— (2013). 'Capabilities' in Hugh LaFollette (ed.), *International Encyclopedia of Ethics*. Oxford: Blackwell.

Brudner, Alan (2009). *Punishment and Freedom: A Liberal Theory of Penal Justice*. Oxford: Oxford University Press.

Bureau of Justice Statistics (2010). *Criminal Victimization in the United States, 2008 – Statistical Tables*. Washington, DC: US Department of Justice.

Burgess-Proctor, Amanda (2012). 'Backfire: Lessons Learned When the Criminal Justice System Fails Help-Seeking Battered Women', *Journal of Crime and Justice* 35: 68–92.

Bushway, Shawn and Anne Piehl (2007). 'The Inextricable Link between Age and Criminal History in Sentencing', *Crime and Delinquency* 53: 156–83.

Buzawa, Eve and T. Austin (1993). 'Determining Police Response to Domestic Violence Victims: The Role of Victim Preference', *American Behavioral Scientist* 36: 610–23.

Buzawa, Eve and Carl Buzawa (1996). *Domestic Violence: The Criminal Justice Response, 2nd ed.* Thousand Oaks: Sage.

Capers, I. Bennett (2011). 'Home Is Where the Crime Is', *Michigan Law Review* 109: 979–91.

Carpentier, Julie, Benoit Leclerc, and Jean Proulx (2011). 'Juvenile Sexual Offenders: Correlates of Onset, Variety, and Desistance of Criminal Behavior', *Criminal Justice and Behavior* 38: 854–73.

Carpentier, Julie and Jean Proulx (2011). 'Correlates of Recidivism among Adolescents Who Have Sexually Offended', *Sexual Abuse* 23: 434–55.

Carter, Patrick (2003). *Managing Offenders, Reducing Crime: A New Approach.* London: Prime Minister's Strategy Unit.

Case, Stephen and Kevin Haines (2009). *Understanding Youth Offending: Risk Factor Research, Policy and Practice.* Portland: Willan.

Catalano, Shannan (2007). *Intimate Partner Violence in the United States.* Washington, DC: US Department of Justice, 2007.

Caufmann, Elizabeth (2008). 'Understanding the Female Offender', *Future of Children* 18: 119–42.

Cavadino, Michael and James Dignan (2002). *The Penal System: An Introduction, 3rd ed.* Thousand Oaks: Sage.

Chaplin, Rupert, John Flatley, and Kevin Smith (eds) (July 2011). 'Crime in England and Wales 2009/10', *Home Office Statistical Bulletin.* London: Home Office.

Chapman, Jenny and Jacqui Smith (2011). *The Purple Book: A Progressive Future for Labour.* London: Biteback, pp. 215–30.

Charlton, W. E. W. St G. (1966). 'Rules and Punishments', *Think*: 3–14.

Christie, Nils (1998). 'Conflicts as Property' in Andrew von Hirsch and Andrew Ashworth (eds), *Principled Sentencing: Readings on Theory and Policy.* Oxford: Hart, pp. 312–16.

Christopher, Russell (2002). 'Deterring Retributivism: The Injustice of "Just" Punishment', *Northwestern University Law Review* 96: 845–976.

Collier, Charles W. (2006). 'Speech and Communication in Law and Philosophy', *Legal Theory* 12: 1–17.

Collingwood, R. G. (1989). *Essays in Political Philosophy*, ed. David Boucher. Oxford: Clarendon.

Colton, Matthew, Susan Roberts, and Maurice Vanstone (2012). 'Learning Lessons from Men Who Have Sexually Abused Children', *Howard Journal of Criminal Justice* 51: 79–93.

Conway, David A. (1974). 'Capital Punishment and Deterrence: Some Considerations in Dialogue Form', *Philosophy and Public Affairs* 3: 431–43.

Cossins, Annie (2008). 'Restorative Justice and Child Sex Offences', *British Journal of Criminology* 48: 359–78.

Cottingham, John (1979). 'Varieties of Retribution', *Philosophical Quarterly* 29: 238–46.

Cotton, Michelle (2000). 'Back with a Vengeance: The Resilience of Retribution as an Articulated Purpose of Criminal Punishment', *American Criminal Law Review* 37: 1313–62.

Cross, Rupert and Andrew Ashworth (1981). *The English Sentencing System, 3rd ed.* London: Butterworth.

Crow, Iain (2001). *The Treatment and Rehabilitation of Offenders.* London: Sage.

Cullen, Eric and Tim Newell (1999). *Murderers and Life Imprisonment: Containment, Treatment, Safety and Risk.* Winchester: Waterside Press.

Cunningham, Sally (2008). *Driving Offences: Law, Policy and Practice.* Aldershot: Ashgate.

Dalai Lama (1999). *Ethics for a New Millennium.* New York: Riverhead.

Daly, Kathleen (2003). 'Mind the Gap: Restorative Justice in Theory and Practice' in Andrew von Hirsch, Julian Roberts, Anthony E. Bottoms, Kent Roach, and Mara Schiff (eds), *Restorative Justice and Criminal Justice: Competing or Reconcilable Paradigms?* Oxford: Hart, pp. 219–36.

Dancig-Rosenberg, Hadar and Dana Pugach (2012). 'Pain, Love, and Voice: The Role of Domestic Violence Victims in Sentencing', *Michigan Journal of Gender and Law* 18: 423–83.

Davis, Michael (1983). 'How to Make the Punishment Fit the Crime', *Ethics* 93: 726–52.

—— (1984). 'Setting Penalties: What Does Rape Deserve?', *Law and Philosophy* 3: 61–110.

Dawes, William, Paul Harvey, Brian McIntosh, Fay Nunney, and Annabelle Phillips (2011). *Attitudes to Guilty Plea Sentence Reductions.* London: Sentencing Council.

de Bussy, Nigel (2008). 'Stakeholder Theory' in Wolfgang Donsbach (ed.), *The International Encyclopedia of Communication.* Oxford: Blackwell, pp. 4815–17.

Dempsey, Michelle Madden (2009). *Prosecuting Domestic Violence: A Philosophical Analysis.* Oxford: Oxford University Press.

Dempsey, Michelle Madden and Jonathan Herring (2007). 'Why Sexual Penetration Requires Justification', *Oxford Journal of Legal Studies* 27: 467–91.

Dewey, John and James H. Tufts (1938). *Ethics.* New York: H. Holt and Co.

Dhami, Mandeep K. and David R. Mandel (2011). 'Crime as Risk Taking', *Psychology, Crime and Law* (2011): 1–15.

Dickson, Sophie R., Devon L. Polaschek, and Allanah R. Casey (2012). 'Can the Quality of High-Risk Violent Prisoners' Release Plans Predict Recidivism Following Intensive Rehabilitation? A Comparison with Risk Assessment Instruments', *Psychology, Crime and Law.* DOI: 10.1080/1068316X.2011.640634.

Dobash, Russell P. and R. Emerson Dobash (2004). 'Women's Violence to Men in Intimate Relationships', *British Journal of Criminology* 44: 324–44.

Dolinko, David (1992). 'Three Mistakes of Retributivism', *UCLA Law Review* 39: 1623–57.

Doob, Anthony and Cheryl Webster (2003). 'Sentence Severity and Crime: Accepting the Null Hypothesis' in Michael Tonry (ed.), *Crime and Justice: A Review of Research*, vol. 30. Chicago: University of Chicago Press, pp. 143–95.

Drapeau, Martin, Annett Körner, Luc Granger, Louis Brunet, and Franz Caspar (2005). 'A Plan Analysis of Pedophile Sexual Abusers' Motivations for Treatment: A Qualitative Pilot Study', *International Journal of Offender Therapy and Comparative Criminology* 49: 308–24.

Duff, R. A. (1986). *Trials and Punishments.* Cambridge: Cambridge University Press.

—— (1990). *Intention, Agency and Criminal Liability: Philosophy of Action and the Criminal Law.* Oxford: Basil Blackwell.

—— (1992). 'Alternatives to Punishment – or Alternative Punishments?' in W. Cragg (ed.), *Retributivism and Its Critics*. Stuttgart: Franz Steiner Verlag, pp. 43–68.

—— (2000). 'In Defence of One Type of Retribution: A Reply to Bagaric and Amarasekara', *Melbourne University Law Review* 24: 411–26.

—— (2001). *Punishment, Communication, and Community*. Oxford: Oxford University Press.

—— (2002). 'Crime, Prohibition, and Punishment', *Journal of Applied Philosophy* 19: 97–108.

—— (2002). 'Punishing the Young' in R. A. Duff and Ido Weijers (eds), *Punishing Juveniles: Principle and Critique*. Oxford: Hart, pp. 115–34.

—— (2003). 'Restoration and Retribution' in Andrew von Hirsch, Julian Roberts, Anthony E. Bottoms, Kent Roach, and Mara Schiff (eds), *Restorative Justice and Criminal Justice: Competing or Reconcilable Paradigms?* Oxford: Hart, pp. 43–59.

—— (2006). 'Answering for Crime', *Proceedings of the Aristotelian Society* CVI: 87–113.

—— (2007). *Answering for Crime: Responsibility and Liability in the Criminal Law*. Oxford: Hart.

—— (2010). 'Towards a Theory of Criminal Law?', *Proceedings of the Aristotelian Society: Supplementary Volume* LXXXIV (2010): 1–28.

Duff, R. A. and Stuart P. Green (2005). 'Introduction: The Special Part and Its Problems' in R. A. Duff and Stuart P. Green (eds), *Defining Crimes: Essays on the Special Part of the Criminal Law*. Oxford: Oxford University Press, pp. 1–20.

Durlauf, Steven N. and Daniel S. Nagin (2011). 'Imprisonment and Crime: Can Both Be Reduced?', *Criminology and Public Policy* 10: 13–54.

Dworkin, Ronald (1998). *Law's Empire*. Oxford: Hart.

Dzur, Albert W. and Alan Wertheimer (2002). 'Forgiveness and Public Deliberation: The Practice of Restorative Justice', *Criminal Justice Ethics* 21: 3–20.

Dzur, Albert W. and Susan M. Olson (2004). 'The Value of Community Participation in Restorative Justice', *Journal of Social Philosophy* 35: 91–107.

Easton, Susan and Christine Piper (2005). *Sentencing and Punishment: The Quest for Justice*. Oxford: Oxford University Press.

Edwards, Ian (2002). 'The Place of Victims' Preferences in the Sentencing of "Their" Offenders', *Criminal Law Review*: 689–702.

Ehrlich, Issac (1975). 'The Deterrent Effect of Capital Punishment: A Question of Life and Death', *American Economic Review* 65: 397–417.

—— (1975). 'Deterrence: Evidence and Inference', *Yale Law Journal* 85: 209–27.

Ellis, Anthony (2003). 'A Deterrence Theory of Punishment', *Philosophical Quarterly* 53: 337–51.

Emeka, Traquina and Jon Sorensen (2009). 'Female Juvenile Risk: Is There a Need for Gendered Assessment Instruments?', *Youth Violence and Juvenile Justice* 7: 313–30.

Ewing, A. C. (1929). *The Morality of Punishment*. London: Kegan Paul, Trench, Trubner and Co.

Fairbrother, W. H. (1896). *The Philosophy of Thomas Hill Green*. London: Methuen and Co.

Feinberg, Joel (1970). *Doing and Deserving: Essays in the Theory of Responsibility*. Princeton: Princeton University Press.

Fichte, J. G. (2000). *Foundations of Natural Right*, ed. Frederick Neuhouser. Cambridge: Cambridge University Press.

Fisher, William M., Morton J. Horwitz, and Thomas A. Reid (eds) (1993). *American Legal Realism*. Oxford: Oxford University Press.

Fitch, K. (2006). *Megan's Law: Does It Protect Children?* London: National Society for the Prevention of Cruelty to Children.

Flanders, Chad (2010). 'Retribution and Reform', *Maryland Law Review* 70: 87–140.

Flately, John, Chris Kershaw, Kevin Smith, Rupert Chaplin, and Debbie Moon (eds) (2010). *Crime in England and Wales 2009/10: Findings From the British Crime Survey and Police Recorded Crime*. London: Home Office.

Freeman, Samuel (2007). *Rawls*. Abingdon: Routledge.

Fuller, Rana (2007). 'How to Effectively Advocate for Battered Women When Systems Fail', *William Mitchell Law Review* 33 (2007): 939–69.

Gainer, Ronald L. (1998). 'Federal Criminal Code Reform: Past and Future', *Buffalo Criminal Law Review* 2: 66–7.

Gal, Tali and Shomrom Moyal (2011). 'Juvenile Victims in Restorative Justice', *British Journal of Criminology* 51: 1014–34.

Gallagher, B. (2000). 'The Extent and Nature of Known Cases of Institutional Child Sexual Abuse', *British Journal of Social Work* 30: 795–817.

Gardner, John (1998). 'Crime: In Proportion and in Perspective' in Andrew Ashworth and Martin Wasik (eds), *Fundamentals of Sentencing Theory: Essays in Honour of Andrew von Hirsch*. Oxford: Clarendon, pp. 31–52.

—— (2008). Introduction to H. L. A. Hart, *Punishment and Responsibility: Essays in the Philosophy of Law*, 2nd ed. Oxford: Oxford University Press, pp. xiii–liii.

Garland, David (1990). *Punishment and Modern Society: A Study in Social Theory*. Oxford: Clarendon.

Gerhold, Constanze K., Kevin D. Browne, and Richard Beckett (2007). 'Predicting Recidivism in Adolescent Sexual Offenders', *Aggression and Violent Behavior* 12: 427–38.

Giles, Marianne (1994). '*R v Brown*: Consensual Harm and the Public Interest', *Modern Law Review* 57: 101–11.

Goodin, Robert E. (1988). 'What Is So Special about our Fellow Countrymen?', *Ethics* 98: 663–86.

Gready, Paul (2010). *The Era of Transitional Justice: The Aftermath of the Truth and Reconciliation Commission of South Africa and Beyond*. Abingdon: Routledge.

Green, Leslie (1989). *The Authority of the State*. Oxford: Oxford University Press.

Green, Thomas Hill (1941). *Lectures on the Principles of Political Obligation*. London: Longmans.

Greenfeld, Lawrence A. (1996). *Child Victimizers: Violent Offenders and Their Victims* (NCJ 153258). Washington, DC: US Department of Justice.

—— (1997). *Sex Offenses and Offenders: An Analysis of Data on Rape and Sexual Assault* (NCJ 163392). Washington, DC: US Department of Justice.

Gross, Samuel R. (1998). 'Update: American Public Opinion on the Death Penalty – It's Getting Personal', *Cornell Law Review* 83: 1448–75.

Grove, Trevor (2002). *The Magistrate's Tale: A Frontline Report from a New JP*. London: Bloomsbury.

Grubin, Don (1998). *Sex Offending against Children: Understanding the Risk* (Police Research Series Paper, No. 99). London: Home Office.

Guerino, Paul and Allen J. Beck (2011). *Sexual Victimization Reported by Adult Correctional Authorities, 2007–2008* (NCJ 231172). Washington, DC: US Department of Justice.

Hampton, Jean (1984). 'The Moral Education Theory of Punishment', *Philosophy and Public Affairs* 13: 208–38.

Hanks, Gardner C. (1997). *Against the Death Penalty: Christian and Secular Arguments against Capital Punishment*. New York: Herald.

Hanna, Nathan (2009). 'The Passions of Punishment', *Pacific Philosophical Quarterly* 90: 232–50.

Hanson, R. Karl (2000). 'Will They Do It Again? Predicting Sex-Offense Recidivism', *Current Directions in Psychological Science* 9: 106–9.

Hanson, R. Karl and A. J. R. Harris (2000). 'Where Should We Intervene? Dynamic Predictors of Sex Offense Recidivism', *Criminal Justice and Behavior* 27: 6–35.

Hanson, R. Karl, R. A. Steffy, and R. Gauthier (1993). 'Long-Term Recidivism of Child Molesters', *Journal of Consulting and Clinical Psychology* 61: 119–36.

Hardimon, Michael O. (1994). *Hegel's Social Philosophy: The Project of Reconciliation*. Cambridge: Cambridge University Press.

Harless, Sarah M. (2003). 'From the Bedroom to the Courtroom: The Impact of Domestic Violence Law on Marital Rape Victims', *Rutgers Law Journal* 35: 305–43.

Hart, H. L. A. (1963). *Law, Liberty, and Morality*. Oxford: Oxford University Press.

—— (1965). *The Morality of the Criminal Law: Two Lectures*. London: Oxford University Press.

—— (1968). *Punishment and Responsibility: Essays in the Philosophy of Law*. Oxford: Clarendon.

Hartfree, Yvette, Chris Dearden, and Elspeth Pound (2008). *High Hopes: Supporting Ex-Prisoners in Their Lives after Prison*. Department of Work and Pensions Research Report No. 509. London: Her Majesty's Stationery Office.

Hasday, Jill Elaine (2000). 'Contest and Consent: A Legal History of Marital Rape', *California Law Review* 88: 1373–1505.

Hayes, Robert, Michael Barnett, Danny H. Sullivan, Olav Nielssen, Matthew Large, and Clarence Brown (2009). 'Justifications and Rationalizations for the Civil Commitment of Sex Offenders', *Psychiatry, Psychology and Law* 16: 141–9.

Healey, Kerry, Christine Smith, and Chris O'Sullivan (1998). *Batterer Intervention: Program Approaches and Criminal Justice Strategies* (NCJ 195079). Washington, DC: National Institute of Justice.

Hegel, G. W. F. (1969). *Science of Logic*, trans. A. V. Miller. Amherst: Humanity Books.

—— (1991) *Elements of the Philosophy of Right*, ed. A. W. Wood, trans. H. B. Nisbet. Cambridge: Cambridge University Press.

Hessick, Carissa Byrne (2011). 'Disentangling Child Pornography from Child Sex Abuse', *Washington University Law Review* 88: 853–902.

Hetherington, H. J. W. and J. H. Muirhead (1918). *Social Purpose: A Contribution to a Philosophy of Civic Society*. London: George Allen and Unwin.

Hirschel, David, Eve Buzawa, April Pattavina, and Don Faggiani (2007). 'Domestic Violence and Mandatory Arrest Laws: To What Extent Do They Influence Police Arrest Decisions?', *Journal of Criminal Law and Criminology* 98: 255–98.

Hohfeld, Wesley N. (1964). *Fundamental Legal Conceptions*. New Haven: Yale University Press.

Home Office (2002). *Justice for All*. London: Home Office.

Honderich, Ted (1969). *Punishment: The Supposed Justifications*. Harmondsworth: Penguin.

Hood, Roger, Stephen Shute, Martina Feilzer, and Aidan Wilcox (2002). 'Sex Offenders Emerging from Long-Term Imprisonment', *British Journal of Criminology* 42: 371–94.

Hooker, Brad (2000). *Ideal Code, Real World*. Oxford: Oxford University Press.

Horley, James (1988). 'Cognitions of Child Sexual Abusers', *Journal of Sex Research* 25: 542–5.

Hoskins, Zachary (2011). 'Deterrent Punishment and Respect for Persons', *Ohio State Journal of Criminal Law* 8: 369–84.

Hoyle, C. and A. Sanders (2000). 'Police Response to Domestic Violence: From Victim Choice to Victim Empowerment?', *British Journal of Criminology* 40: 14–36.

Hudson, Barbara (1993). *Penal Policy and Social Justice*. London: Macmillan.

—— (2002). 'Restorative Justice and Gendered Violence – Diversion or Effective Justice?', *British Journal of Criminology* 42: 616–34.

Hume, David (1978). *A Treatise of Human Nature, 2nd ed.*, ed. L. A. Selby-Bigge. Oxford: Oxford University Press.

Husak, Douglas N. (1992). 'Why Punish the Deserving?', *Nous* 26: 447–64.

—— (2003). 'Is the Criminal Law Important?', *Ohio State Journal of Criminal Law* 1: 261–71.

—— (2005). '*Malum Prohibitum* and Retribution' in R. A. Duff and Stuart P. Green (eds), *Defining Crimes: Essays on the Special Part of the Criminal Law*. Oxford: Oxford University Press, pp. 65–90.

Husak, Douglas N. and George C. Thomas III (2001). 'Rapes Without Rapists: Consent and Reasonable Mistake', *Philosophical Issues* 11: 86–117.

Hutton, Will (1998). *The Stakeholding Society: Writings on Politics and Economics*. Cambridge: Polity.

—— (2010). *Them and Us: Changing Britain – Why We Need a Fair Society*. London: Little, Brown.

Independent Commission on Youth Crime and Antisocial Behaviour (2010). *Time for a Fresh Start: The Report of the Independent Commission on Youth Crime and Antisocial Behaviour*. London: The Police Foundation.

Jackson, John D. (2003). 'Justice for All: Putting Victims at the Heart of Criminal Justice?', *Journal of Law and Society* 30: 309–26.

Jacobson, Jessica and Penelope Gibbs (2009). *Making Amends: Restorative Youth Justice in Northern Ireland*. London: Prison Reform Trust.

Janes, Laura (2011). 'Children Convicted of Sexual Offences: Do Lifelong Labels Really Help?', *Howard Journal of Criminal Justice* 50: 137–52.

Joe, George W., Kevin Knight, D. Dwayne Simpson, Patrick Flynn, Janis T. Morey, Norma G. Bartholomew, Michele Staton Tindall, William M. Burdon, Elizabeth A. Hall, Steve S. Martin, and Daniel J. O'Connell (2012). 'An Evaluation of Six Brief Interventions That Target Drug-Related Problems in Correctional Populations', *Journal of Offender Rehabilitation* 51: 9–33.

Johnson, Brian D. and Megan C. Kurlychek (2012). 'Transferred Juveniles in the Era of Sentencing Guidelines: Examining Judicial Departures for Juvenile Offenders in Adult Criminal Court', *Criminology* 50: 1–40.

Johnson, I. M. (2007). 'Victims' Perceptions of Police Response to Domestic Violence Incidents', *Journal of Criminal Justice* 35: 498–510.

Johnson, Michael P. (2005). 'Domestic Violence: It's Not About Gender – Or is It?', *Journal of Marriage and the Family* 67: 1126–30.

Johnson, Michael P. and Kathleen J. Ferraro (2000). 'Research on Domestic Violence in the 1990s: Making Distinctions', *Journal of Marriage and the Family* 62: 948–63.

Johnson, Samuel (1984). *The Major Works*. Harmondsworth: Penguin.

Johnstone, Gerry (1988). 'The Psychiatric Approach to Crime: A Sociological Analysis', *Economy and Society* 17: 317–73.

Kahan, Dan M. (1996). 'What Do Alternative Sanctions Mean?', *University of Chicago Law Review* 63: 591–653.

—— (1999). 'The Secret Ambition of Deterrence', *Harvard Law Review* 113: 413–500.

Kahan, Dan M. and Martha C. Nussbaum (1996). 'Two Conceptions of Emotion in Criminal Law', *Columbia Law Review* 96: 269–374.

Kahan, Dan M. and Eric A. Posner (1999). 'Shaming White-Collar Criminals: A Proposal for Reform of the Federal Sentencing Guidelines', *Journal of Law and Economics* 42: 365–91.

Kaler, John (2002). 'Morality and Strategy in Stakeholder Identification', *Journal of Business Ethics* 39: 91–9.

—— (2003). 'Differentiating Stakeholder Theories', *Journal of Business Ethics* 46: 71–83.

Kane, R. J. (1999). 'Patterns of Arrest in Domestic Violence Encounters: Identifying a Police Decision-Making Model', *Journal of Criminal Justice* 27: 65–79.

Kant, Immanuel (1963). *Critique of Pure Reason*, trans. N. K. Smith. London: Macmillan.

—— (1996). *The Metaphysics of Morals*, trans. Mary Gregor. Cambridge: Cambridge University Press.

Kershaw, Chris, Sian Nicholas, and Alison Walker (eds) (July 2008). 'Crime in England and Wales 2007/08', *Home Office Statistical Bulletin*. London: Home Office.

Ketcham, Ralph (ed.) (1986). *The Anti-Federalist Papers and the Constitutional Convention Debates*. Harmondsworth: Penguin.

Khan, Sadiq (ed.) (2011). *Punishment and Reform: How Our Justice System Can Help Cut Crime*. London: Fabian Society.

Kramer, Matthew H. (1999). *In Defense of Legal Positivism: Law without Trimmings*. Oxford: Oxford University Press.

Lai, Yung-Lien, Jihong Solomon Zhao, and Dennis R. Longmire (2011). 'Specific Crime-Fear Linkage: The Effect of Actual Burglary Incidents Reported to the Police on Residents' Fear of Burglary', *Journal of Crime and Justice* (DOI: 10.1080/0735648X.2011.631408).

Landrum, Susan (2011). 'The Ongoing Debate about Mediation in the Context of Domestic Violence: A Call for Empirical Studies of Mediation Effectiveness', *Cardozo Journal of Conflict Resolution* 12: 425–68.

Langan, Patrick A. and David J. Levin (2002). *Recidivism of Prisoners Released in 1994*. Washington, DC: Bureau of Justice Statistics.

Langan, Patrick A., Erica L. Schmitt, and Matthew R. Durose (2003). *Recidivism of Sex Offenders Released from Prison in 1994* (NCJ 198281). Washington, DC: US Department of Justice.

Lanning, Tess, Ian Loader, and Rick Muir (2011). *Redesigning Justice: Reducing Crime Through Justice Reinvestment*. London: IPPR.

Latessa, Edward (2012). 'Why Work is Important, and How to Improve the Effectiveness of Correctional Reentry Programs that Target Employment', *Criminology and Public Policy* 11: 87–91.

Laub, John H. and Robert J. Sampson (2003). *Shared Beginnings, Divergent Lives; Delinquent Boys to Age 70*. Cambridge, Mass.: Harvard University Press.

Lazar, David (ed.) (2004). *DNA and the Criminal Justice System: The Technology of Justice*. Cambridge, Mass.: MIT Press.

Leclerc, B., J. Proulx, and A. McKibben (2005). 'Modus Operandi of Sexual Abusers Working or Doing Voluntary Work with Children and Adolescents', *Journal of Sexual Aggression* 11: 187–95.

Leiter, Brian (2007). *Naturalizing Jurisprudence: Essays on American Legal Realism and Naturalism in Legal Philosophy*. Oxford: Oxford University Press.

Leon, Chrysanthi (2011). 'The Contexts and Politics of Evidence-Based Sex Offender Policy', *Criminology and Public Policy* 10: 421–30.

Lerman, Lisa G. (1984). 'Mediation of Wife Abuse Cases: The Adverse Impact of Informal Dispute Resolution on Women', *Harvard Women's Law Journal* 7: 57–113.

Levitt, Steven D. and Stephen J. Dubner (2009). *Freakonomics: A Rogue Economist Explores the Hidden Side of Everything*. New York: HarperPerennial.

Lie, Gwat-yong and Sabrina Gentlewarrier (1991). 'Intimate Violence in Lesbian Relationships: Discussion of Survey Findings and Practice Implications', *Journal of Social Science Research* 15: 41–59.

Liedka, R. A. Piehl, and B. Useem (2006). 'The Crime-Control Effects of Incarceration: Does Scale Matter?', *Criminology and Public Policy* 5: 245–75.

Lippke, Richard L. (2006). 'Imprisonable Offenses', *Journal of Moral Philosophy* 3: 265–87.

—— (2006). 'Mixed Theories of Punishment and Mixed Offenders: Some Unresolved Tensions', *Southern Journal of Philosophy* XLIV: 273–95.

—— (2007). *Rethinking Imprisonment*. Oxford: Oxford University Press.

Locke, John (1988). *Two Treatises of Government*, ed. Peter Laslett. Cambridge: Cambridge University Press.

Loughran, Thomas A., Raymond Paternoster, Alex R. Piquero, and Greg Pogarsky (2011). 'On Ambiguity in Perception of Risk: Implications for Criminal Decision-Making and Deterrence', *Criminology* 49: 1029–61.

Luntz, Frank (2007). *Words That Work: It's Not What You Say, It's What People Hear*. New York: HarperCollins.

Mabbott, John D. (1939). 'Punishment', *Mind* 48: 152–67.

—— (1956). 'Freewill and Punishment' in H. D. Lewis (ed.), *Contemporary British Philosophy, 3rd series*. London: George Allen and Unwin, pp. 289–309.

MacKinnon, Catharine A. (2005). *Women's Lives, Men's Laws*. Cambridge, Mass.: Belknap/Harvard University Press.

Maffettone, Sebastiano (2010). *Rawls: An Introduction*. Cambridge: Polity.

Mander, W. J. (2011). *British Idealism: A History*. Oxford: Oxford University Press.

Marshall, T. F. (1999). *Restorative Justice: An Overview*. London: Home Office.

Marvell, T. and C. Moody (1994). 'Prison Population and Crime Reduction', *Journal of Quantitative Criminology* 10: 109–39.

Matravers, Matt (2006). '"Who's Still Standing?" A Comment on Antony Duff's Preconditions of Criminal Liability', *Journal of Moral Philosophy* 3: 320–30.

McDermott, Daniel (2001). 'A Retributivist Argument against Capital Punishment', *Journal of Social Philosophy* 32: 317–33.

McGlynn, Clare (2011). 'Feminism, Rape and the Search for Justice', *Oxford Journal of Legal Studies* 31: 825–42.

McGrath, Kevin (2011). 'Ready for the Real World of Work' in Sadiq Khan (ed.), *Punishment and Reform: How Our Justice System Can Help Cut Crime*. London: Fabian Society, pp. 71–6.

McGregor, Joan (2005). *Is It Rape? On Acquaintance Rape and Taking Women's Consent Seriously*. Aldershot: Ashgate.

McMulland, S. and D. Ruddy (2005). *Adult Reconviction in Northern Ireland 2001: Research and Statistical Bulletin 3/2005*. Belfast: Northern Ireland Office.

Meade, James (1964). *Efficiency, Equality, and the Ownership of Property*. London: George Allen and Unwin.

Michael, Mark A. (1992). 'Utilitarianism and Retributivism: What's the Difference?', *American Philosophical Quarterly* 29: 173–82.

Mill, John Stuart (1978). *On Liberty*, ed. Elizabeth Rapaport. Indianapolis: Hackett.

—— (1984). 'On Punishment' in *Collected Works of John Stuart Mill, Vol. XXI*, ed. John M. Robson. Toronto: University of Toronto Press, pp. 77–9.

—— (1986). 'Speech in Favour of Capital Punishment' in Peter Singer (ed.), *Applied Ethics*. Oxford: Oxford University Press, pp. 97–104.

Miller, David (1995). *On Nationality*. Oxford: Oxford University Press.

Miller, Susan (2011). *After the Crime: The Power of Restorative Justice Dialogues between Victims and Violent Offenders*. New York: New York University Press.

Mills, Linda G. (1999). 'Killing Her Softly: Intimate Abuse and the Violence of State Intervention', *Harvard Law Review* 113: 550–613.

—— (2003). *Insult to Injury*. Princeton: Princeton University Press.

Ministry of Justice (2011). *2011 Compendium of Re-Offending Statistics and Analysis*. London: Her Majesty's Stationery Office.

—— (2011). *Adult Re-Convictions: Results from the 2009 Cohort (England and Wales)*. London: Her Majesty's Stationery Office.

Mitchell, Barry and Julian V. Roberts (2012). 'Sentencing for Murder: Exploring Public Knowledge and Public Opinion in England and Wales', *British Journal of Criminology* 52: 141–58.

Moley, Sian (2008). 'Public Perceptions' in Chris Kershaw, Sian Nicholas, and Alison Walker (eds), *Home Office Statistical Bulletin: Crime in England and Wales 2007/08*. London: Her Majesty's Stationery Office, pp. 117–42.

Moore, Michael S. (1993). 'Justifying Retributivism', *Israel Law Review* 27: 15–49.

Murphy, Jeffrie G. (1973). 'Marxism and Retribution', *Philosophy and Public Affairs* 2: 217–43.

—— (2003). *Getting Even: Forgiveness and Its Limits*. Oxford: Oxford University Press.

Nathanson, Stephen (1985). 'Does It Matter If the Death Penalty is Arbitrarily Administered?', *Philosophy and Public Affairs* 14: 149–64.

New York Times (6 December 2010). 'The Crime of Punishment', Editorial, A26.

Nugent, Briege and Nancy Loucks (2011). 'The Arts and Prisoners: Experiences of Creative Rehabilitation', *Howard Journal of Criminal Justice* 50: 356–70.

Nussbaum, Martha C. (1998). '"Whether from Reason or Prejudice": Taking Money for Bodily Services', *Journal of Legal Studies* 27: 693–724.

—— (2000). *Women and Human Development: The Capabilities Approach.* Cambridge: Cambridge University Press.

—— (2004). *Hiding from Humanity: Disgust, Shame and the Law.* Princeton: Princeton University Press.

—— (2008). *Liberty of Conscience: In Defense of America's Tradition of Religious Equality.* New York: Basic Books.

—— (2011). *Creating Capabilities: The Human Development Approach.* Cambridge, Mass.: Harvard University Press.

O'Donnell, Pierce, Michael J. Churgin and Dennis E. Curtis (1977). *Toward a Just and Effective Sentencing System.* New York: Praeger.

Owens, Ashleigh (2012). 'Confronting the Challenges of Domestic Violence Sentencing Policy: A Review of the Increasingly Global Use of Batterer Intervention Programs', *Fordham International Law Journal* 35: 565–610.

Paley, William (1771). *Principles of Penal Law.* London.

Palmer, Craig T. (1988). 'Twelve Reasons Why Rape is Not Sexually Motivated: A Skeptical Examination', *Journal of Sex Research* 25: 512–30.

Parekh, Bhikhu (2008). *A New Politics of Identity: Political Principles for an Interdependent World.* Basingstoke: Palgrave Macmillan.

Parfit, Derek (2011). *On What Matters*, 2 vols. Oxford: Oxford University Press.

Parmar, Alpa and Alice Sampson (2007). 'Evaluating Domestic Violence Initiatives', *British Journal of Criminology* 47: 671–91.

Pascal, Blaise (1995). *Pensées.* Harmondsworth: Penguin.

Patacchini, Eleonora and Yves Zenou (2012). 'Juvenile Delinquency and Conformism', *Journal of Law, Economics and Organization* 28: 1–31.

Peirce, Charles Saunders (1902). 'Vague' in J. M. Baldwin (ed.), *Dictionary of Philosophy and Psychology.* New York: Macmillan, p. 748.

Petersilia, Joan (2003). *When Prisoners Come Home: Parole and Prisoner Reentry.* Oxford: Oxford University Press.

Pettit, Philip (1990). *A Theory of Freedom: From Psychology to the Politics of Agency.* Cambridge: Polity.

Piff, Paul K., Daniel M. Stancato, Stephane Cote, Rodolfo Mendoza-Denton, and Dacher Keltner (2012). 'High Social Class Predicts Increased Unethical Behavior', *Proceedings of the National Academy of Sciences* 109: 4086–91.

Plato (1997). *Complete Works*, ed. John M. Cooper. Indianapolis: Hackett.

Plender, John (1997). *A Stake in the Future: The Stakeholding Solution.* London: Nicholas Brealey.

Pojman, Louis P. (1998). 'For the Death Penalty' in Louis P. Pojman and Jeffrey H. Reiman (eds), *The Death Penalty: For and Against.* Lanham: Rowman and Littlefield, pp. 1–66.

Polaschek, Devon L. (2011). 'High-Intensity Rehabilitation for Violent Offenders in New Zealand: Reconviction Outcomes for High- and Medium-Risk Prisoners', *Journal of Interpersonal Violence* 26: 664–82.

Posner, Richard (1992). *Sex and Reason.* Cambridge, Mass.: Harvard University Press.

Postawko, Robert (2002). 'Toward an Islamic Critique of Capital Punishment', *UCLA Journal of Islamic and Near Eastern Law* 1: 269–320.

Prabhaker, Rajiv (2004). 'Whatever Happened to Stakeholding?', *Public Administration* 82: 567–84.

Pratt, D., M. Piper, L. Appleby, R. Webb, and J. Shaw (2006). 'Suicide in Recently Released Prisoners: A Population-Based Cohort Study', *The Lancet* 368: 119–23.

Primoratz, Igor (1989). *Justifying Legal Punishment*. Atlantic Highlands: Humanities Press.

—— (1989). 'Punishment as Language', *Philosophy* 64: 187–205.

Putnam, Robert D. (2000). *Bowling Alone: The Collapse and Revival of American Community*. New York: Simon and Schuster.

Radelet, Michael L. (2000). 'The Role of Organized Religions in Changing Death Penalty Debates', *William and Mary Bill of Rights Journal* 9: 201–14

Rand, Michael R. and Jayne E. Robinson (2011). *Criminal Victimization in the United States, 2008 – Statistical Tables*. Washington, DC: Bureau of Justice Statistics.

Rashdall, Hastings (1891). 'The Theory of Punishment', *International Journal of Ethics* 2: 20–31.

—— (1907). *The Theory of Good and Evil: A Treatise on Moral Philosophy, vol. I*. Oxford: Clarendon.

Rawls, John (1955). 'Two Concepts of Rules', *Philosophical Review* LXIV: 3–32.

—— (1971). *A Theory of Justice*. Cambridge, Mass.: Harvard University Press.

—— (1996). *Political Liberalism*. New York: Columbia University Press.

—— (1999). *A Theory of Justice, rev. ed.* Oxford: Oxford University Press.

—— (1999). *Collected Papers*, ed. Samuel Freeman. Cambridge, Mass.: Harvard University Press.

—— (2001). *Justice as Fairness*, ed. Erin Kelly. Cambridge, Mass.: Harvard University Press.

Raymond, Nancy C., Eli Coleman, Fred Ohlerking, Gary A. Christenson, and Michael Miner (1999). 'Psychiatric Comorbidity in Pedophilic Sex Offenders', *American Journal of Psychiatry* 156: 786–8.

Raynor, Peter and Maurice Vanstone (2002). *Understanding Community Penalties: Probation, Policy, and Social Change*. Buckingham: Open University Press.

Raz, Joseph (1983). *The Authority of Law: Essays on Law and Morality*. Oxford: Clarendon.

Rebovich, Donald J. (1996). 'Prosecution Response to Domestic Violence: Results of a Survey of Large Jurisdictions' in Eve S. Buzawa and Carl G. Buzawa (eds), *Do Arrest and Restraining Orders Work?* Thousand Oaks: Sage, pp. 176–91.

Reiman, Jeffrey H. (1985). 'Justice, Civilization, and the Death Penalty: Answering van den Haag', *Philosophy and Public Affairs* 14: 115–48.

—— (1988). 'The Justice of the Death Penalty in an Unjust World' in Kenneth C. Haas and James A. Inciardi (eds), *Challenging Capital Punishment: Legal and Social Science Approaches*. Thousand Oaks: Sage, pp. 29–48.

Riots Communities and Victims Panel (2012). *After the Riots: The Final Report of the Riots Communities and Victims Panel*. London: Riots Communities and Victims Panel.

Robinson, Paul H. (2008). *Distributive Principles of Criminal Law: Who Should Be Punished How Much?* Oxford: Oxford University Press.

Roe, Stephen and Jane Ashe (15 July 2008). 'Young People and Crime: Findings from the 2006 Offending, Crime and Justice Survey', *Home Office Statistical Bulletin*. London: Home Office.

Rosen, Michael (2012). *Dignity: Its History and Meaning*. Cambridge, Mass.: Harvard University Press.

Ross, Catherine E. and John Mirowsky (2009). 'Neighborhood Disorder, Subjective Alienation, and Distress', *Journal of Health and Social Behavior* 50: 49–64.

Ross, W. D. (1930). *The Right and the Good.* Oxford: Clarendon.

Rossner, Meredith (2011). 'Emotions and Interaction Ritual: A Micro Analysis of Restorative Justice', *British Journal of Criminology* 51: 95–119.

Rousseau, Jean-Jacques (1997). *The Social Contract and Other Later Political Writings,* ed. Victor Gourevitch. Cambridge: Cambridge University Press.

Russell, Bertrand (1925). *What I Believe.* London: Kegan Paul.

Saegert, S. and G. Winkel (2004). 'Crime, Social Capital, and Community Participation', *American Journal of Community Psychology* 34: 219–33.

Sahota, Kirpal and Paul Chesterman (1998). 'Sexual Offending in the Context of Mental Illness', *Journal of Forensic Psychiatry* 9: 267–80.

Sainsbury Centre (2009). *Diversion: A Better Way for Criminal Justice.* London: Sainsbury Centre Mental Health.

Sandel, Michael J. (1998). *Liberalism and the Limits of Justice,* 2nd ed. Cambridge: Cambridge University Press.

—— (2005). 'Should Victims Have a Say in Sentencing?' in Michael J. Sandel, *Public Philosophy: Essays on Morality in Politics.* Cambridge, Mass.: Harvard University Press, pp. 105–8.

Schabas, William A. (2000). 'Islam and the Death Penalty', *William and Mary Bill of Rights Journal* 9: 223–36.

Schriro, Dora (2012). 'Good Science, Good Sense: Making Meaningful Change Happen – A Practitioner's Guide', *Criminology and Public Policy* 11: 101–10.

Seth, James (1891). *Freedom as Ethical Postulate.* Edinburgh: William Blackwood and Sons.

—— (1898). *A Study of Ethical Principles,* 3rd ed. Edinburgh: William Blackwood and Sons.

—— (1926). *Essays in Ethics and Religion with Other Papers,* ed. Andrew Seth Pringle-Pattison. Edinburgh: William Blackwood and Sons.

Severson, Margaret F., Kimberly Bruns, Christopher Veeh, and Jaehoon Lee (2011). 'Prisoner Reentry Programming: Who Recidivates and When?', *Journal of Offender Rehabilitation* 50: 327–48.

Shapiro, Scott J. (2011). *Legality.* Cambridge, Mass.: Belknap/Harvard University Press.

Shapiro, Tamar (1999). 'What is a Child?', *Ethics* 109: 715–38.

Sheck, Barry, Peter Neufeld, and Jim Dwyer (2003). *Actual Innocence: When Justice Goes Wrong and How to Make It Right.* New York: American Library.

Sher, George (1987). *Desert.* Princeton: Princeton University Press.

Shute, Stephen (1998). 'The Place of Public Opinion in Sentencing Law', *Criminal Law Review*: 465–77.

Siegel, Rebecca S., Annette M. La Greca, and Hannah M. Harrison (2009). 'Peer Victimization and Social Anxiety in Adolescents: Prospective and Reciprocal Relationships', *Journal of Youth and Adolescence* 38: 1096–109.

Simester, A. P., G. R. Sullivan, J. R. Spencer, and Graham Virgo (2010). *Simester and Sullivan's Criminal Law: Theory and Doctrine, 4th ed.* Oxford: Hart.

Singleton, N., H. Melzer, and R. Gatward (1998). *Psychiatric Morbidity among Prisoners in England and Wales.* London: Office for National Statistics.

Snodgrass, G. Matthew, Arjan A. J. Blokland, Amelia Haviland, Paul Nieubeerta, and Daniel S. Nagin (2011). 'Does the Time Cause the Crime? An Examination of the Relationship between Time Served and Reoffending in the Netherlands', *Criminology* 49: 1149–94.

Snyder, Douglas K. and Nancy S. Scheer (1981). 'Predicting Disposition Following Brief Residence at a Shelter for Battered Women', *American Journal of Community Psychology* 9: 559–65.

Social Exclusion Unit (2002). *Reducing Re-Offending by Ex-Prisoners*. London: Social Exclusion Unit.

Spohn, Cassia C. (2002). *How Do Judges Decide? The Search for Fairness and Justice in Punishment*. Thousand Oaks: Sage.

Stephen, James Fitzjames (1883). *A History of the Criminal Law of England*. London: Macmillan.

Stone, Alison (2004). 'Essentialism and Anti-Essentialism in Feminist Philosophy', *Journal of Moral Philosophy* 1: 135–53.

Stout, Brian, Hazel Kemshall, and Jason Wood (2011). 'Building Stakeholder Support for a Sex Offender Public Disclosure Scheme: Learning from the English Pilots', *Howard Journal of Criminal Justice* 50: 406–18.

Strawson, Galen (1994). 'The Impossibility of Moral Responsibility', *Philosophical Studies* 75: 5–24.

Strudler, Alan (2001). 'The Power of Expressive Theories of Law', *Maryland Law Review* 60: 492–505.

Suk, Jeannie (2011). 'Redistributing Rape', *American Criminal Law Review* 48: 111–19.

Sullivan, J., and A. Beech (2002). 'Professional Perpetrators: Sex Abusers Who Use Their Employment to Target and Sexually Abuse Children with Whom They Work', *Child Abuse Review* 11: 153–67.

Sunstein, Cass R. and Adrian Vermeule (2005). 'Is Capital Punishment Morally Required? Acts, Omissions, and Life-Life Tradeoffs', *Stanford Law Review* 58: 703–50.

Tadros, Victor (2005). 'The Distinctiveness of Domestic Abuse: A Freedom-Based Account' in R. A. Duff and Stuart P. Green (eds), *Defining Crimes: Essays on the Special Part of the Criminal Law*. Oxford: Oxford University Press, pp. 119–42.

Tasioulas, John (2006). 'Punishment and Repentance', *Philosophy* 81: 279–322.

Tebbit, Mark (2005). *Philosophy of Law: An Introduction, 2nd ed.* Abingdon: Routledge.

Ten, C. L. (1987). *Crime, Guilt, and Punishment*. Oxford: Clarendon.

Terry, Karen J. (2011). 'What is Smart Sex Offender Policy?', *Criminology and Public Policy* 10: 275–82.

Thaler, Richard and Cass Sunstein (2008). *Nudge: Improving Decisions about Health, Wealth, and Happiness*. London: Penguin.

Thornton, D. and R. Travers (1991). 'A Longitudinal Study of the Criminal Behaviour of Convicted Sex Offenders', *Proceedings of the Prison Service Psychology Conference*. London: Her Majesty's Prison Service, pp. 13–22.

Tobias, J. J. (1967). *Crime and Industrial Society in the Nineteenth Century*. London: B. T. Batsford.

Tonry, Michael (2005). 'Obsolescence and Immanence in Penal Theory and Policy', *Columbia Law Review* 105: 1233–75.

—— (2011). 'Less Imprisonment Is No Doubt a Good Thing: More Policing Is Not', *Criminology and Public Policy* 10: 137–52.

Travis, Alan and Simon Rogers (19 August 2011). 'Revealed: The Full Picture of Riot Sentences', *The Guardian*: 1–2.

Tuerkheimer, Deborah (2007). 'Renewing the Call to Criminalize Domestic Violence: An Assessment Three Years Later', *George Washington Law Review* 75: 613–26.

Tushnet, Rebecca (2012). 'Worth a Thousand Words: The Images of Copyright', *Harvard Law Review* 125: 683–759.

UK Drug Policy Commission (2008). *Reducing Drug Use, Reducing Reoffending: Are Programmes for Problem Drug-Using Offenders in the UK Supported by the Evidence?* London: UK Drug Policy Commission.

US Bureau of Statistics (2005). *Juvenile Victimization and Offending, 1993 – 2003*. Washington, DC: US Department of Justice (NCJ 209468). Available online at http://www.usdoj.gov.bjs/.

—— (2005). *Capital Punishment, 2004* (NCJ 211349). Washington, DC: US Department of Justice.

van den Haag, Ernest (1968). 'On Deterrence and the Death Penalty', *Ethics* 78: 280–8.

—— (1985). 'Refuting Reiman and Nathanson', *Philosophy and Public Affairs* 14: 165–76.

Vanderbilt, Tom (2009). *Traffic*. London: Penguin.

Vitacco, Michael J., Michael Caldwell, Nancy L. Ryba, Alvin Malesky, and Samantha J. Kurus (2009). 'Assessing Risks in Adolescent Sexual Offenders: Recommendations for Clinical Practice', *Behavioral Sciences and the Law* 27: 929–40.

von Hirsch, Andrew (1985). *Past or Future Crimes: Deservedness and Dangerousness in the Sentencing of Criminals*. Manchester: Manchester University Press.

—— (1994). *Censure and Sanctions*. Oxford: Oxford University Press.

von Holderstein Holtermann, Jakob (2009). 'Outlining the Shadow of the Axe: On Restorative Justice and the Use of Trial and Punishment', *Criminal Law and Philosophy* 3: 187–207.

Wakeling, Helen, Anthony R. Beech, and Nick Freemantle (2011). 'Investigating Treatment Change and Its Relationship to Recidivism in a Sample of 3773 Sex Offenders in the UK', *Psychology, Crime and Law*. DOI: 10.1080/1068316X.2011. 626413.

Waldron, Jeremy (2012). 'How Law Protects Dignity', *Cambridge Law Journal* 71: 200–22.

Walker, Nigel and C. Marsh (1984). 'Do Sentences Affect Public Disapproval?', *British Journal of Criminology* 24 (1984): 27–48.

Warner, Kate and Julia Davis (2012). 'Using Jurors to Explore Public Attitudes to Sentencing', *British Journal of Criminology* 52: 93–112.

Weijers, Ido and Antony Duff (2002). 'Introduction: Themes in Juvenile Justice' in R. A. Duff and Ido Weijers (eds), *Punishing Juveniles: Principle and Critique*. Oxford: Hart, pp. 1–19.

Weinrib, Lloyd L. (1986). 'Desert, Punishment, and Criminal Responsibility', *Law and Contemporary Society* 49: 47–80.

Weithman, Paul (2010). *Why Political Liberalism? On John Rawls's Political Turn*. Oxford: Oxford University Press.

Wellman, Christopher Heath (2012). 'The Rights Forfeiture Theory of Punishment', *Ethics* 122: 371–93.

Wenar, Leif (2005). 'The Nature of Rights', *Philosophy and Public Affairs* 33: 223–53.

White, Mark D. (ed.) (2011). *Retributivism: Essays on Theory and Policy.* Oxford: Oxford University Press.

White, Stuart (2004). 'The Citizen's Stake and Paternalism', *Politics and Society* 32: 61–78.

Widahl, Eric J., Brett Garland, Scott E. Culhane, and William P. McCarty (2011). 'Utilizing Behavioral Interventions to Improve Supervision Outcomes in Community-Based Corrections', *Criminal Justice and Behavior* 38: 386–405.

Wilkinson, Richard and Kate Pickett (2010). *The Spirit Level: Why Equality is Better for Everyone, rev. ed.* London: Penguin.

Williams, Bernard (1997). 'Moral Responsibility and Political Freedom', *Cambridge Law Journal* 56: 96–102.

Williams, Monica (2012). 'Beyond the Retributive Public: Governance and Public Opinion on Penal Policy', *Journal of Crime and Justice* 35: 93–113.

Williamson, Timothy (1994). *Vagueness.* London: Routledge.

Wilson, James Q. (1985). *Thinking about Crime, 2nd ed.* New York: Vintage Books.

—— (2003). *Harsh Justice: Criminal Punishment and the Widening Divide between America and Europe.* Oxford: Oxford University Press.

—— (2003). 'A Plea against Retributivism', *Buffalo Criminal Law Review* 7: 85–107.

Wolff, Jonathan (2011). *Ethics and Public Policy: A Philosophical Inquiry.* Abingdon: Routledge.

Zaibert, Leo (2006). *Punishment and Retribution.* Aldershot: Ashgate.

Online resources (all verified at time of publication)

BBC News 'Young People Feel "Isolated" in Their Community' (27 October 2010). Website: http://www.bbc.co.uk/news/education-11629544.

Connecticut Coalition Against Domestic Violence. Website: http://www.ctcadv.org/.

Crown Prosecution Service 'Sexual Offences'. Website: http://www.cps.gov.uk/news/fact_sheets/sexual_offences/.

Death Penalty Information Center. Website: http://www.deathpenaltyinfo.org/

Howard League for Penal Reform 'Community Sentences Cut Crime – Factsheet'. Website: http://www.howardleague.org/fileadmin/howard_league/user/pdf/Community_ sentences_factsheet.pdf.

Khan, Sadiq. 'Avoiding a Life of Crime: How the Youth Justice System Can Work for Young People'. Website: http://www.sadiqkhan.co.uk/index.php/speeches/1330-speech-avoiding-a-life-of-crime-how-the-youth-justice-system-can-work-for-young-people.

Lakhani, Nina (12 March 2012). 'Unreported Rapes: The Silent Shame', *The Independent.* Website: http://www.independent.co.uk/news/uk/crime/unreported-rapes-the-silent-shame-7561636.html.

Liptak, Adam (28 February 2008). '1 in 100 U.S. Adults Behind Bars', *New York Times.* Website: http://www.nytimes.com/2008/02/28/us/28cnd-prison.html.

New York State Department of Corrections and Community Supervision 'Who is Eligible for a Certificate of Relief?' Website: https://www.parole.ny.gov/certrelief.html.

—— 'Restoration of Rights'. Website: https://www.parole.ny.gov/program_restoration.html.

Refuge. 'Domestic Abuse: The Facts'. Website: http://refuge.org.uk/get-help-now/ what-is-domestic-violence/domestic-violence-the-facts/.

Restorative Justice Council. Wesbite: http://www.restorativejustice.org.uk/.

—— 'Ministry of Justice Evaluation of Restorative Justice'. Website: http://www. restorativejustice.org.uk/resource/ministry_of_justice_evaluation_of_restorative_ justice/.

Sentencing Council. 'Guidelines to Download'. Website: http://sentencingcouncil. judiciary.gov.uk/guidelines/guidelines-to-download.htm.

UK Department of Communities and Local Government. 'Troubled Families'. Website: http://www.communities.gov.uk/communities/troubledfamilies/.

UK Ministry of Justice. Website: http://open.justice.gov.uk/home/.

UK Parliament. 'Should We Build More Prisons?'. Website: http://www.parliament. uk/ business/publications/research/key-issues-for-the-new-parliament/security-and-liberty/ the-prison-population/.

US Bureau of Justice Statistics. Website: http://www.usdoj.gov/bjs/.

US State of Maryland. 'Crimes and Punishments: Arson and Burning'. Website: http://firemarshal.state.md.us/crimes.htm.

Youth Justice Board. Website: http://www.justice.gov.uk/yjb.

Index